INSIGHT GUIDES
FLORENCE

APA PUBLICATIONS **L**

Part of the Langenscheidt Publishing Group

2

☀ INSIGHT GUIDES

FLORENCE

Project Editor
Siân Lezard
Series Editor
Rachel Lawrence
Picture Editor
Steven Lawrence
Cartography Editor
Zoë Goodwin
Series Publishing Manager
Rachel Fox

Distribution

UK & Ireland
GeoCenter International Ltd
Meridian House, Churchill Way West,
Basingstoke, Hampshire, RG21 6YR
sales@geocenter.co.uk

United States
Langenscheidt Publishers, Inc.
36–36 33rd Street 4th Floor
Long Island City, NY 11106
orders@langenscheidt.com

Australia
Universal Publishers
1 Waterloo Road
Macquarie Park, NSW 2113
sales@universalpublishers.com.au

New Zealand
Hema Maps New Zealand Ltd (HNZ)
Unit 2, 10 Cryers Road
East Tamaki, Auckland 2013
sales.hema@clear.net.nz

Worldwide
Apa Publications GmbH & Co.
Verlag KG (Singapore branch)
7030 Ang Mo Kio Ave 5
#08-65 Northstar @ AMK
Singapore 569880
apasin@singnet.com.sg

Printing

CTPS-China

©2011 Apa Publications GmbH & Co.
Verlag KG (Singapore branch)
All Rights Reserved

First Edition 1989
Sixth Edition 2011

www.insightguides.com

ABOUT THIS BOOK

What makes an Insight Guide different? Since our first book pioneered the use of creative full-colour photography in travel guides in 1970, we have aimed to provide not only reliable information but also the key to a real understanding of a destination and its people.

Now, when the internet can supply inexhaustible (but not always reliable) facts, our books marry text and pictures to provide that more elusive quality: knowledge. To achieve this, they rely on the authority of locally based writers and photographers.

This book turns the spotlight on one of the most charming of museum cities. Packed full with inestimable artistic treasures, the real marvel of Florence is that as well as being a monument to past achievements it is also part of the modern world, with one foot in the 21st century and the other in the Renaissance. *Insight Guide: Florence* invites you to retrace its journey and covers the best of everything the city has to offer.

RIGHT: Pinocchio, a native Florentine.

CONTACTING THE EDITORS

We would appreciate it if readers would alert us to errors or outdated information by writing to:

**Insight Guides, P.O. Box 7910,
London SE1 1WE, England.
insight@apaguide.co.uk**

THE CONTRIBUTORS TO THIS BOOK

This new edition of *Insight Guide: Florence and Siena* was edited by **Siân Lezard**, building on an earlier edition by **Carine Tracanelli**. The book was comprehensively updated by our Italy specialist **Susie Boulton**, the author of over 20 guidebooks to the country; Susie acquired her abiding passion for all things Italian when she worked on an archaeological dig in Arezzo, and has been going back every year since then.

This edition builds on the excellent foundations laid down by many past contributors, including:

Natasha Foges, a travel writer and Florence enthusiast who used to live in Italy and returns as often as she can; **Adele Evans**, an Insight regular, who provided an expert overview of the vibrant shopping scene, and wrote *A Paradise of Exiles*; **Katie Parla**, who took time out from her work as a guide on private cultural walks to write the art and architecture chapter; **Angela Vannucci** who trekked the city streets to update our listings of hotels and restaurants. Thanks also go to **Rosie Westwood**, who worked on the Travel Tips section.

Other contributors include **Sarah Birke**, **Bruce Johnston**, who wrote the history chapter, **Christopher Catling**, **Lisa Gerrard-Sharp**, **Paul Holberton**, **Forrest Spears**, **David Clement-Davies**, **Tim Harper** and **Nicky Swallow**.

The majority of new photographs were by **Britta Jaschinski**, with other images from **Anna Mockford** and **Nick Bonnetti**, **Alessandra Santarelli** and **Jerry Dennis**. The book was designed by **Klaus Geisler**. Proofreading was by **Neil Titman** and the index was compiled by **Isobel McLean**.

THE GUIDE AT A GLANCE

The book is carefully structured both to convey an understanding of the city and its culture and to guide readers through its attractions and activities:

◆ The Best Of section at the front of the book helps you to prioritise. The first spread contains all the Top Sights, while Editor's Choice details unique experiences, the best buys or other recommendations.

◆ To understand Florence, you need to know something of its past. The city's history and culture are described in authoritative essays written by specialists in their fields who have lived in and documented the city for many years.

◆ The Places section details all the attractions worth seeing. The main places of interest are coordinated by number with the maps.

◆ A list of recommended restaurants, bars and cafés is printed at the end of each chapter.

◆ Photographs throughout the book are chosen not only to illustrate geography and buildings, but also to convey the moods of the city and the life of its people.

◆ The Travel Tips section includes all the practical information you will need, divided into five key sections: transport, accommodation, activities, shopping (including nightlife, events, tours and sports), and an A–Z of practical tips. Information may be located quickly by using the index on the back cover flap of the book.

◆ Two detailed street atlases are included at the back of the book, complete with a full index. On the second one, you will find all the restaurants and hotels plotted for your convenience.

PLACES & SIGHTS

Colour-coding at the top of every page makes it easy to find each area in the book. These are coordinated by specific area on the orientation map on pages 82–3.

A locator map pinpoints the specific area covered in each chapter. The page reference at the top indicates where to find a detailed map of the area highlighted in red.

Margin tips provide extra little snippets of information, whether it's a practical tip, a whimsical quote, a historical fact or advice on shopping and eating.

A four-colour map provides a bird's-eye view of the area covered in the chapter, with the main attractions co-ordinated by number with the main text.

PHOTO FEATURES

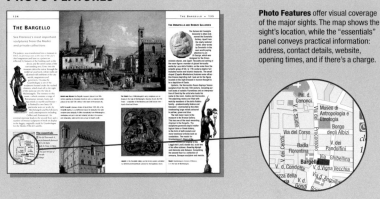

Photo Features offer visual coverage of the major sights. The map shows the sight's location, while the "essentials" panel conveys practical information: address, contact details, website, opening times, and if there's a charge.

RESTAURANT LISTINGS

Restaurant listings feature the best establishments within each area, giving the address, phone number, opening times and price category followed by a useful review. The grid reference refers to the atlas at the back of the book.

Teatro del Sale

Via dei Macci 111r

055-200 1492

Closed Sun and Mon.

€€ [p311, E1]

Run by the same people as Cibrèo, this is a unique three-meal-a-day restaurant and theatre all in one. Fabio Picchi

TRAVEL TIPS

Advice-packed Travel Tips provide all the practical knowledge you'll need before and during your trip: how to get there, getting around, where to stay and what to do. The A–Z section is a handy summary of practical information, arranged alphabetically.

Contents

Places

Restaurants & Bars

Travel Tips

TRANSPORT

ACCOMMODATION

SHOPPING

ACTIVITIES

A–Z of PRACTICAL INFORMATION
286

Maps

THE BEST OF FLORENCE: TOP SIGHTS

At a glance, everything you can't afford to miss in Florence, from the emblematic Duomo and Palazzo Vecchio to the world-class museums and the tranquil Boboli Garden

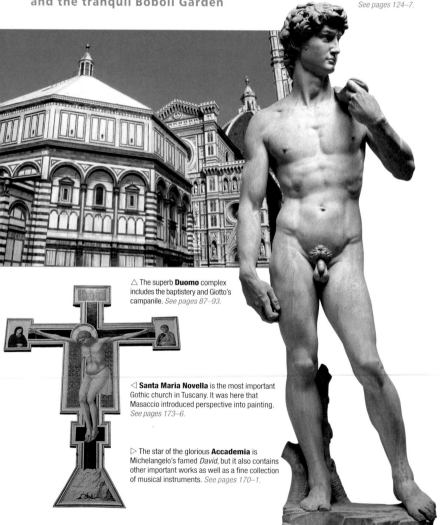

△ **Santa Croce**, perhaps the city's most glorious church, is full of art treasures. *See pages 124–7.*

△ The superb **Duomo** complex includes the baptistery and Giotto's campanile. *See pages 87–93.*

◁ **Santa Maria Novella** is the most important Gothic church in Tuscany. It was here that Masaccio introduced perspective into painting. *See pages 173–6.*

▷ The star of the glorious **Accademia** is Michelangelo's famed *David*, but it also contains other important works as well as a fine collection of musical instruments. *See pages 170–1.*

△ **San Lorenzo** church is home to the glorious **Cappelle Medicee**. *See pages 152–6.*

△ The **Uffizi** houses the world's greatest collection of Renaissance Italian painting. *See pages 114–19.*

△ The **Cappella Brancacci** is the site of Masaccio's sublime frescos. *See pages 190–1.*

◁ The beautiful medieval **Ponte Vecchio** still retains the small shops of its craftsmen. *See pages 108–9.*

▽ The **Giardino di Boboli** is amongst the finest public gardens in Italy, dotted with statuary and delightful fountains. *See pages 198–9.*

◁ The fortress-like **Palazzo Vecchio**, which dominates Piazza della Signoria, is the modern-day home of Florence's town hall. *See pages 104–7.*

THE BEST OF FLORENCE: EDITOR'S CHOICE

Unique attractions, best museums and gardens, top shops and restaurants, family outings and money-saving tips personally selected by our editor

FINEST CHURCHES

- **Ognissanti**
  This church is home to wonderful frescos by Ghirlandaio, Botticelli and Gaddi. *See pages 178–9.*
- **Orsanmichele**
  This converted medieval grain market is a showcase for Renaissance sculpture. *See pages 141–2.*
- **San Lorenzo**
  Contains many treasures, including the ornate Cappelle Medicee. *See pages 152–6.*
- **San Marco**
  As much an art gallery as a church, it has some of the finest works by Fra Angelico. *See pages 159–62.*
- **San Miniato**
  In a stunning position overloooking Florence from the hills, this exquisite Romanesque basilica has wonderful decoration. *See pages 204–6.*
- **Santa Croce**
  A beautifully decorated and spacious church, Santa Croce was the burial place of many famous Florentines. *See pages 124–7.*
- **Santa Maria del Carmine**
  One of the city's great treasures is here, the frescoed Cappella Brancacci. *See pages 190–1.*
- **Santa Maria del Fiore (the Duomo)**
  Florence's great cathedral, with a campanile by Giotto and crowned by Brunelleschi's superb cupola. *See pages 87–93.*
- **Santa Maria Novella**
  Behind the splendid facade is another treasure house of art, including Giotto's splendid *Crucifix*. *See pages 173–6.*

ABOVE: Brunelleschi's magnificent dome dominates the city's skyline.

LEFT: the hilltop church of San Miniato *(pictured at night)* has superb gilded frescos and offers breathtaking views of the city below.

BEST SHOPPING

- Via de' Tornabuoni
  Florence's most
  prestigious shopping
  street boasts its most
  famous designers,
  including Ferragamo,
  Gucci and Pucci. *See
  pages 56–7, 179–80
  and 275.*

- The Markets
  Florence's markets
  sell everything from
  leather goods to fruit
  and vegetables. Two
  of the best are the
  Mercato Nuovo and
  Mercato Centrale. *See
  pages 59,142–143
  and 149.*

- Giulio Giannini
  e Figlio
  Florence is famed for

marbled paper; this
is one of the finest
shops. *See page 276.*

- Antico Setificio
  Sells very high quality
  and locally made fab-
  rics, especially silks.
  See page 276.

BEST FOR VIEWS

- Bellosguardo
  Meaning literally
  "beautiful view", this
  spot above Oltrarno
  is in a wonderful loca-
  tion. *See page 191.*

- Fiesole
  The view from
  this hilltop suburb –
  site of the original
  Etruscan settlement –

gives a magnificent
panorama over
the entire city. *See
page 213.*

- Piazzale Michelangelo
  From this open
  square, the view over
  the city rooftops and
  the Arno is simply
  breathtaking.
  See page 206.

FLORENCE FOR FAMILIES

- Museo Archeologico
  The newly expanded
  Egyptian collection is
  full of mummies. *See
  pages 166–8.*

  - The Museo
    Galileo con-
    tains working
    experiments
    of Galileo. *See
    pages 110–11.*

    - The Museo
      di Antropo-
      logia e Etno-
      logia is
      packed full
      with curiosi-
      ties such as
      Peruvian
      mummies,
      Indian shadow
      puppets and
      Eskimo whaleskin
      anoraks. *See
      pages 122–3.*

      - La Specola
        (in the Museo
        di Zoologia)

exhibits realistic
anatomical waxworks
of body parts for chil-
dren with a gruesome
fascination for the
human body. *See pages
187–8.*

- The Giardino di Boboli
  and Le Cascine are
  Florence's two main
  parks where kids can
  run around. *See pages
  178 and 198–9.*

- One of the few chil-
  dren's playgrounds is
  in Piazza dell'Azeglio.
  See page 130.

- Children may also
  enjoy taking a ride on
  one of the horse-drawn
  carriages found in
  Piazza della Signoria.
  See page 99.

ABOVE: colourful Pucci.
ABOVE RIGHT: Florence is a
shoe-lover's paradise. **LEFT:**
kids love Pinocchio. **RIGHT:**
stunning Tuscan landscape.

MUSEUMS AND GALLERIES

- **Accademia**
  A wonderful collection, home to Michelangelo's *David*. *See pages 170–1.*
- **The Bargello**
  The city's greatest collection of sculpture. *See pages 134–5.*
- **Museo Archeologico**
  The city's archaeological museum has the finest collection of Etruscan artefacts to be found anywhere. *See pages 166–8.*
- **Museo dell'Opera del Duomo**
  Sculptural treasures from the cathedral. *See page 94.*
- **Museo di Zoologia "La Specola"**
  An unusual display of wax anatomical models – all very realistic and not a little gory. *See pages 187–8.*
- **Museo Horne**
  A charming villa with part of the collection of an English art historian. *See page 112.*
- **Museo Galileo**
  Florence has made great contributions to the advance of science, all documented in this

museum. *See pages 110–11.*
- **Natural History Museum**
  Spread over several sites, one of the best sections of this university-run institution is the Anthropological Museum with its many fascinating exhibits. *See pages 122–3 and 163.*
- **Palazzo Pitti**
  A huge Medici *palazzo* containing a number of museums and some extraordinary paintings. *See pages 194–7.*
- **Palazzo Vecchio**
  Florence's town hall is superbly decorated and has many treasures. *See pages 104–7.*
- **Uffizi**
  The world's greatest collection of Renaissance art. *See pages 114–19.*

ABOVE LEFT: *Angel Musician,* in the Uffizi.
ABOVE RIGHT: statue in the Giardino di Boboli.
RIGHT: Giambologna's *Rape of the Sabine Women.*

VILLAS, PARKS AND GARDENS

- **Giardino di Boboli**
  Exquisite formal gardens located just behind the Palazzo Pitti. *See pages 198–9.*

- **Giardino dei Semplici**
  Peaceful botanical gardens in the San Marco neighbourhood. *See pages 163-4.*
- **Villa di Castello**
  Beautiful Renaissance gardens with grottoes. *See page 217.*
- **Villa Demidoff and Parco di Pratolino**
  The gardens here contain extraordinary Mannerist sculpture as well as grottoes. *See page 217.*
- **Villa Poggio a Caiano**
  Thought by many to be the perfect Medici villa, with frescoed halls, a Greek facade and beautiful gardens. *See page 217.*
- **Villa Medici (Fiesole)**
  Delightful, with superb views. *See pages 215 and 216.*
- **Villa della Petraia**
  An elegant villa designed by Buontalenti set on a sloping hill and decorated with wonderful frescos. *See page 216.*

EATING OUT

- **Acqua al Due**
Book ahead for this very popular restaurant. *See page 132.*
- **Baldovino**
Run by a Scottish couple; wide-ranging menu using local produce. *See page 132.*
- **Buca Lapi**
Wonderful *bistecca alla fiorentina* served in the basement of the Palazzo Antinori. *See page 183.*
- **Caffè Italiano**
Excellent Tuscan food served up in a 14th-century *palazzo*. *See page 132.*

- **Cavolo Nero**
Elegant Mediterranean dishes. *See page 193.*
- **Cibrèo**
Very popular modern Tuscan food. *See page 132.*
- **Coco Lezzone**
Beautifully prepared traditional food. *See page 183.*
- **Enoteca Pinchiorri**
Thought by some to be the best restaurant in Europe. *See page 133.*
- **Filipepe**
A favourite of Florentines for its chic offbeat decor and creative

Mediterranean cuisine. *See page 207.*
- **Frescobaldi**
Classic Tuscan food and a fabulous wine list. *See page 113.*
- **La Giostra**
Acclaimed food, particularly the delicious *crostini. See page 133.*
- **Gustavino**
Creative dishes prepared in an open kitchen but no fuss. *See page 113.*
- **Oliviero**
Everything is fresh, from the pasta to the delicious desserts. *See page 113.*

- **La Pentola dell'Oro**
In this unique eatery, the recipes are inspired by the Renaissance. *See page 133.*
- **Pugi**
Possibly the best pizza in town. *See page 169.*
- **Trattoria Sostanza**
An authentic Tuscan dining experience, famous for its steaks. *See page 183.*

ABOVE: pizza, Florence-style.
LEFT: enjoying a romantic lunch alfresco.
BELOW: buses are a cheap way to get around.

MONEY-SAVING TIPS

Changing money You usually get a better rate of exchange at a bank than a bureau de change *(cambio)*, although *cambi* are useful out of banking hours. Be wary of those offering "No commission", as the exchange rate will almost certainly be higher. ATMs (cash machines) dotted round the city are, depending on your bank, one of the cheapest means of obtaining money.

Public transport Florence is compact enough to walk round, but if you want a cheap bus tour, take Nos 12 or 13 which make hour-long circuits of the city, or routes C1, C2 or D – small orange electric buses which can navigate the narrow streets. Bus tickets must be bought before boarding – from news-stands, tobacconists, some bars and the bus termini; you can buy a daily pass, or a ticket for *quattro corsi* (four trips) which work out slightly cheaper than single tickets.

Tipping This is not as common as in other European countries. Many restaurants include 10–15 percent for service in the bill. Elsewhere a tip of €3–6 is appreciated.

Telephoning Avoid high costs of calls abroad from mobiles or hotel rooms by purchasing a prepaid international phonecard. The cheapest time to call long-distance is between 10pm and 8am Monday to Saturday, and all day Sunday.

TO BE A FLORENTINE

Tourist Florence remains fabulous, but the city's inhabitants aren't immune from the familiar 21st-century problems: petty crime, urban decay, traffic chaos and high living costs

Mention the name Florence, and you are almost certain to conjure up images of the Renaissance, when the extraordinarily rich flowering of artistic and intellectual life under the enlightened rule of the Medici, coupled with the city's immense banking wealth, made it the most important centre in Europe.

Florence today is undoubtedly one of the finest open-air museums in the world, and the tourism which this fuels has itself become a major new source of wealth. Rarely, however, is it considered as a city in contemporary terms, except perhaps for its shopping. Yet even here, the fine handicrafts and stylish fashion accessories for which it is now almost equally famous are ultimately rooted in Florence's own early mercantile and creative traditions.

Yet struggling to break free of its historical straitjacket is another, more hidden Florence, which, when the surface is scratched, reveals

Pope Boniface summed up the enigma of the city when he described the world as composed of five elements; earth, air, fire and water... and the Florentines.

itself to be a sophisticated, tuned-in, complex and even slightly troubled modern city, and anything but one suffering from the passive nature of a resigned tourist capital.

PRECEDING PAGES: the facade of the Duomo; the Ponte Vecchio reflected in the Arno. **LEFT:** trendy Florentines. **RIGHT:** window-shopping on the Ponte Vecchio.

The three faces of Florence

As it happens, there are probably three Florences. The first is that of the old historic centre. While this continues to stand proud as a repository for everything that is the Renaissance, shopkeepers often treat it as an open-face mine to be shamelessly worked in order to reap the fruits of the mass tourism which flocks there.

However, many locals have by now discarded it as a viable place to live. Draconian traffic restrictions and rising prices have become a real deterrent, as well as the awareness that the centre is increasingly resembling a kind of Disneyland, although not everyone would agree with this view. Not surprisingly for a Renaissance city

with an impossibly small centre, modern buildings are confined to the suburbs. The ex-Fiat quarter of Novoli is home to the new university campus and the futuristic law courts building.

The second Florence is *la Firenze delle colline*, meaning the magical hills that ring, and in some cases help form the city. Despite the rampant urban development down below, these lofty upper reaches remain a loyal tribute to the Renaissance vision of *rus in urbe*, meaning the importing of a little bit of countryside into the city. Miraculously, delightful villages and hills such as Fiesole and Settignano, with their magnificent villas and lines of cypresses, their convents and castles, are still practically untouched.

The third Florence began in the 1860s when the city was redeveloped as the new, albeit temporary, capital of Italy. The old walls were mostly demolished to make way for the city's inner ring road of broad avenues, and new residential neighbourhoods were created away from the small centre. Today's urban sprawl, which is in effect a continuation of this development, features ambitious projects meant to renew areas of degradation and carrying internationally known architectural names. While they may seem exciting to some, auguring well for Flor-

ence as a city of the future, the projects also raise important questions about how they will affect what, in the past, has been one of the world's great aesthetic capitals.

The Florentines

Figures show that in demographic terms Florence is changing rapidly. At the turn of the 20th century, this was a residential city of prudent *rentiers*, merchants and minor craftsmen, and where as late as the post-war period there ruled a rigid class system made up of landed gentry, solid *borghesia* and poor *contadini*. Today, Florence is deeply middle-class, despite its left-wing council. The city operates a craft-and-services economy, with industry restricted to the outskirts.

Rampant commercialisation had been kept in check by a sophisticated if provincial culture, and an abiding belief in good education, the family and the good life, although it now seems to be gaining the upper hand. Figures, meanwhile, show that to maintain their old principles, denizens are now fast abandoning the

TOP LEFT: fashionable Florence. **TOP AND ABOVE:** Florentine belles. **TOP RIGHT:** view from Piazzale Michelangelo. **RIGHT:** the Vespa rules the streets.

metropolis for smaller centres. Taking their place in town now are the *extracommunitari*, or Third World immigrants.

As in the rest of Italy, immigration is a controversial topic. Tuscany is a centre-left stronghold, but even here, in the 2010 regional elections, the anti-immigration Northern League party saw its support increase fourfold since the previous regional elections in 2005. Some 10 percent of the city's population are now foreigners, and the employment needs of immigrants are a major political issue. Meanwhile the number of native Florentines, in line with Italy's famously negative birth rate, continues to drop – while the average age continues to rise. The over-65s now account for over a quarter of the population.

Old money, new commerce

To their credit, the Florentine aristocracy are no longer idle or absentee landlords, but are often dynamic entrepreneurs, yet who regard themselves meanwhile as the rightful keepers of their city's collective memory and as arbiters of taste. The local nobility continue to enjoy a key role in social and economic life, a detail that ensures that Florence, with its graceful manners extending across much of society, and its inherent Englishness –

heightened by the way so many key families also married into English blood – continues to belong to another world. Ordinary Florentines happily live alongside the aristocracy, but are rarely deferential towards them.

Some of the great families have had to reinvent themselves to survive. Others, like the Ferragamos – the fashion dynasty descended from Salvatore Ferragamo, the "shoemaker to the stars" – are relative upstarts with humble origins, yet who already live as if to the manor born.

The Frescobaldi family, marquises and one-time merchant bankers who were already determining Florence's fate in the 13th century, excel in the production and distribution of fine wines, much as they did when they supplied the court of Henry VIII. The difference is that now many of the 10 million bottles they produce end up on the tables of middle-class homes around the world.

The noble Pucci family, a byword of 1960s chic whose fashion house has been relaunched with the help of outside investors, still live in Palazzo Pucci.

Such a sense of continuity at home, let alone in the workplace, would be impossible for many families to conceive. However, it is anything but unusual in Florence.

Humble hang-outs

Florence has a wealth of creative and intellectual life at grass-roots level, where the so-called Case del Popolo ("Houses of the People") remain a vital institution. Bookshops also abound, as do places selling second-hand clothing, trendy hairdressers and alternative food stores.

Young Florentines, often from working-class backgrounds, regularly gather in the Case del Popolo, which provide the engine room, stage and escape valve for intellectual expression. Across Tuscany and Florence, the typical Casa del Popolo is a single structure, which provides a manifold venue today for everything from theatrical performances and those by *cantastorie*, to comedians, young bands, poets and artists, as well as a place to congregate and eat and drink together.

High-profile protests

The mood in such places ties in well with the leftist flavour that pervades the local administration of Florence, a city with a long anticlerical history but whose post-war political nature also has a strong Catholic element, and which has known political autonomy since it began its rise to prominence in the 12th century.

Hot topic of the Tramvia

After years of delay, Line 1 of the new Tramvia network was opened in 2010. This is the first of three interlinking tramlines connecting the centre with the airport and main railway station at Santa Maria Novella. Designed to alleviate congestion and pollution in the city

HOW SAFE IS FLORENCE?

Among the city's negative aspects is widespread petty and other crime, testimony to the fact that Florence is no longer just a pretty place, but at times now also a seething metropolis, with a darker side racked by inner-city problems of a kind that might have provided Dante with an ideal setting for the *Inferno* had he written it today. Bag-snatchers fly by on scooters in smart areas of town as they prey on tourists, although not exclusively, much as they do in Naples or Rome. Just as *calcio storico* – or colourful historic football – is played in Piazza Santa Croce, right in front of the church of the same name, so, too, is cocaine now flogged by pushers outside the church of Santo Spirito.

centre, the state-of-the-art tram system has sparked huge controversy, with thousands of protesters in the streets. The building works have caused major disruption in the city, and conservationists believe that the system will cause untold damage to the city's architectural treasures. Now that Line 1 is up and running, debate rages over the more controversial Line 2, to link Peretola (Florence Airport) with Piazza della Libertà. This would cut through the historic heart of the city, passing right by the cherished Duomo and baptistery. In 2009 Mayor Matteo Renzi announced the full pedestrianisation of the Piazza del Duomo, putting paid to any tramlines across the piazza. Officials are now exploring the possibility of running the tram rails below the city centre.

Where to live

There is now a real problem of historic shops in Florence being forced to close because of crippling rents, a reality which is also driving many citizens to live elsewhere. Nor is the city's great crafts tradition immune. Florence's delightful small neighbourhoods such as Sant' Ambrogio, with their vital cross-section of corner shops where gilders, book binders, printers and wrought-iron makers work, are the true essence of local life. But gentrification, along with higher prices, is now setting in.

> Florence regularly tops the league of Italian cities with the biggest increase in property prices.

Some locals complain that as a result of all this, Florence is losing some of its distinctive feel. Others warn that it is now entering a vicious circle already experienced by Venice, whereby locals are being priced out of their own city, as it turns into a factory for mass tourism, before inevitably ending up an empty husk.

But the Florence of today, while owing its fame and its tourism to its cultural feats of the past, is also a publishing, engineering,

FAR LEFT: eating *gelato* is a favourite pastime.
TOP LEFT: the religious community is very present.
ABOVE LEFT: bookbinders are threatened by the crippling city-centre rents. **ABOVE:** drinking alfresco.

New music

Considering its size, Florence appears to have a disproportionately vibrant nightlife. This ranges from a rich seam of underground music wafting out of tiny and often hidden clubs, to a variety of traditional and experimental theatre, and an array of venues offering a wide selection of classical music and productions of the performing arts.

The newspaper scene

However much it moves forward to resemble a progressive, modern city, Florence still struggles to shake off a lingering provincial side, as evidenced, for example, by the parochial coverage of the local media, led by the dull and conservative *La Nazione* newspaper.

Informed left-of-centre Florentines tend to read *La Repubblica*, which has a proper daily local-news insert. The more left-wing *L'Unità* has similar local coverage, something which the conservative *Corriere della Sera*, Italy's leading daily newspaper, is planning to introduce. The English-language community, meanwhile, is now served by *The Florentine*, a weekly magazine with information on what's on, together with lively, informed articles of local interest.

pharmaceutical and furniture-making centre, where the overall urban workforce numbers the highest proportion of commuters in Italy.

Its important leather trade is reliant on the hundreds of tanneries found along the valley of the River Arno all the way down to Pisa, where they have created other seams of wealth, much in the way that the textile industry has done around Florence and Prato.

Winemaking is another key industry, as is that of fine Tuscan food in general, where the accent is now on excellence, as can be seen by the rows of bottles for sale in shops of expensive and even designer olive oil.

A prisoner of its past

Part of the city's difficulty in fitting into the sophisticated new shoes that it would sometimes like to wear may be due to the way it has remained a prisoner of its original concept – namely, of a medieval-Renaissance city, and now, a museum one. Often Florence seems to have lost its chance of becoming a national mover and shaker after briefly serving as Italy's capital in the late 19th century. Often, the sensation of being stuck in time is

According to the national research institute ISTAT, Florentines read newspapers more than most Italians, and are better-informed about politics.

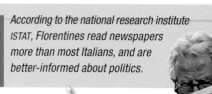

reinforced by the way foreign and Italian visitors, as well as Florentines, appear reluctant to consider the city in anything other than the most traditional terms.

Similarly, a design by the Japanese architect Arata Isozaki to build a towering, minimalist loggia in perspex, steel and stone to serve as a new exit for the Uffizi art gallery, has bitterly divided the city, with critics dismissing it as a "bus shelter" and even branding it the "Monster of Florence" – the name of a serial killer who once struck terror into the city. The stalemate over the project has left the city hall in an embarrassing quandary, since Isozaki's design won a competition that it had sponsored.

A modern mayor

Florence's new rising star is Matteo Renzi, a young politician who many believe can rejuvenate the city's flagging politics – and possibly Italy's too. Bucking the trend of grey-haired politicians, the progressive and energetic Renzi became president of the Florentine province at 29, and mayor of Florence in 2009 at 34. His approach is hands-on (he visits a school a week) and his 100-point action plan includes cutting red tape, investing in eco-friendly transport and reducing smog. The number of city councillors has been reduced to 10, split equally between males and females, green policies have been introduced and the Tramvia Line 1 completed. Soon after election Renzi announced the unexpected news that Piazza Duomo in the heart of the city would be banned to vehicles of any description, horses and carriages included. "Not even the mayor's car will pass through the Piazza, nor will that of the bishop," he said. The decision will substantially reduce the carbon monoxide and fine particulate that was suffocating the city centre – and sullying the Duomo. It seems the only Florentines not celebrating the decision are the taxi drivers, who have had to relocate.

Renzi also has plans for Florentines to have free access to all city museums one day a month, to open churches and museums at night, and to create "the finest jogging route in the world". Very much the modern man, Renzi is accelerating the spread of high-speed internet and WiFi in the city and posts his news on Twitter and Facebook. ❑

FAR LEFT AND LEFT: taking some time out to reflect.
ABOVE: historic parade on the Ponte Vecchio.

THE MAKING OF FLORENCE

Ancient traders sowed the seeds of Florence's artistic flowering, but it was a wealthy banking dynasty that propelled the city to the international cultural renown it enjoys today. In recent times, the city's sky has been darkened by political corruption and the threat of flooding

Florence was originally a Roman settlement, and the classical flowering of the Renaissance owes much to Rome's civilisation. But the vitality of 15th-century Florentine art is indebted at least as much to a culture that predated Rome by centuries, that of Etruria. Rising above Florence to Fiesole, you come upon the remains of an ancient Etruscan town. The massive stone walls were laid in the late 7th century BC, long before the Latins arrived. Today, Fiesole is just a satellite of the city, and for the traveller the Renaissance obscures an earlier dawn.

Craftsmen and traders

The Etruscans first flourished around 800 BC in the coastal regions of Tuscany and Lazio. Building their cities on high plateaux for defence, but with access to the sea, they soon rivalled the Greeks and Phoenicians as traders. Their wealth was founded on the rich metal deposits of the

Throughout Tuscany, hilltop villages founded by the Etruscans, as well as their harbours, tombs and statuary, testify to a remarkable and often overlooked civilisation.

mainland and the island of Elba. With a genius for craftsmanship, they worked metals and exchanged them for luxury goods, and trading links soon extended as far as Mesopotamia, Syria, Cyprus and Egypt.

LEFT: Lorenzo de' Medici, from Gozzoli's *The Journey of the Magi*. **RIGHT:** Etruscan tomb painting in Tarquinia.

The Etruscans thrived as powerful traders for around 300 years. At their peak, their cities covered Italy from Campania to the Po valley. By forging links with the Greeks in the 8th century BC, they set up an outpost in Latium (Lazio). This small encampment was to become the city of Rome, and Rome would one day eclipse Etruria. Unlike the Romans, the Etruscans never established a centralised empire. Their settlements remained independent from one another, and although their 12 main cities formed a loose confederation, this was primarily for religious purposes. That religion was complex and magical. Vases and tombs are haunted by their gods and demons, such as the Lasa or winged

Most remnants of Etruscan civilisation come from tombs such as these: their myriad funerary urns, painted sarcophagi, and many household objects which accompanied the wealthy into the afterlife.

Though empty now, the tombs of Tarquinia, buried safe from the dust that blows hard across the region's wild landscape, are covered in remarkable frescos. The scenes of hunting, fishing, wrestling and feasting evoke a lively and luxurious people, fond of music and dancing, while erotic figures capture a sensuality and naturalism rare in any art.

A central element in these paintings is the wildlife. Dolphins, bulls and sea horses leap to life from the walls. In Tarquinia's terracotta horses and the famous bronze she-wolf – later to become the symbol of ancient Rome – the Etruscans displayed an extraordinary empathy with their natural environment and a supreme ability to record life in movement.

Tarquinia's frescos are the most complete. Elsewhere we have only tantalising scraps, "fragments of people at banquets, limbs that dance without dancers, birds that fly into nowhere", as D.H. Lawrence described them.

women, symbolic of death, and Tulchulcha, a demon of the underworld. The Etruscans' special preserve was augury, interpreting the will of the gods in the entrails of animals, forks of lightning and the flight of birds. The Romans later absorbed these beliefs and every legion of the army had an Etruscan soothsayer.

Tarquinia

The search for the spirit of Etruscan art begins on the hillsides of Lazio, in the underground necropolises or citadels of the dead that cluster round the hilltop city of Tarquinia.

Bronze masterpieces

In the Archaeological Museum's Room of Urns you often find yourself alone among sculptures of the dead and intricate marble friezes that rival the best Greece and Rome produced.

The prize exhibits, however, are two exquisite bronzes, the Arringatore and the Chimera. The Arringatore (or Orator) dates from the 1st century BC, by which time Etruria had already

The wounded Chimera is one of the most celebrated masterpieces of high Etruscan art.

THE GREAT ENIGMA

Why this civilisation should have proved so fragile is just one of the enigmas that surround the Etruscans. Though their alphabet has been deciphered as being similar to Greek Chaldean, much of their language remains incomprehensible to modern scholars; its links to any known language are unproven.

Similarly, their origins elude us. Herodotus believed they came from Lydia in Asia Minor, led by Tyrrhenos, son of Athis, to settle on the shores of the sea that still bears his name. Yet Dionysius of Halicarnassus says the Etruscans themselves claimed to be indigenous to Italy, and the lack of any evidence of warfare at the early archaeological sites might support this. These lingering mysteries have captured the imagination of a plethora of writers throughout the years: from the Emperor Claudius, who wrote a 20-volume history of the Etruscans, to Virgil, Livy and, later, D.H. Lawrence. All were fascinated by the art that these people produced: marble statues, colourful frescos, powerful bronzes, pottery of great delicacy – potent, erotic and, above all, humane.

been conquered by Rome. It portrays a member of the Metelli family, once powerful Etruscan aristocrats who had adopted a new name and achieved new status by winning Roman citizenship. At once dignified and disturbing, it captures the tension between new energies and a sense of melancholy for a culture destined to lose its own identity. It is a wonderful example of the Etruscans' realism and mastery of bronze.

Discovered near Arezzo in 1553, the Chimera was entrusted to the care of Cellini, who restored the two left legs, marvelling at the skill of the original makers. The straining beast, part goat, lion and snake, bursts with a desperate energy as it struggles in mortal combat.

The Etruscan demise

Etruscan glories were fleeting. By the 5th century BC they were threatened by Gauls in the north and by local Italic tribes. The Romans, exploiting their vulnerability, rapidly overcame Etruria. The Etruscans survived for two centuries as Roman subjects, but their culture became diluted, and eventually they were absorbed into the fabric of a new society.

The date of the founding of Florence is generally agreed to be 59 BC, when it was established as a *colonia* for retired Roman soldiers, distinguished veterans of Caesar's campaigns.

FAR LEFT: head of a woman in an Etruscan necropolis near Orvieto. **TOP LEFT:** *The Founding of Florence*, by Vasari, 1565 (Salon dei Cinquecento, Palazzo Vecchio).

Roman rule

The retired Roman soldiers built the first city walls almost in a perfect square, with sides of about 400 metres (1,300ft) in length. The southwestern corner, not far from Ponte Santa Trinità, was the closest point the walls came to the Arno. The fact that the river embankment was not itself defended suggests that the Arno played little part in the economy of the Roman city, initially at least.

> The source of the Roman name, Florentia, remains a mystery. Perhaps it was named after the wild flowers of the Arno plain, or was an inspired prophecy, for florentia meant either "floriferous" or "flourishing".

Instead, the Roman settlers lived chiefly by farming the perimeter of the city. Out of this developed what was to become one of the principal industries, both in Roman times and in the centuries that were to follow – wool-dyeing.

Even in those early days, the city was setting itself apart in style and attitude. The Romans who settled Florence were dedicated to the Horatian and Virgilian ideal of *rus in urbe* – the countryside in the town. It is an ideal that has characterised Florence through the ages, for even now, while many Italians aspire to a chic city apartment, Florentines desire a country villa with a vineyard and olive grove.

Bandits tamed

The wealth and splendour of Florence from the 13th century onwards owed much to this same marriage of town and country, of nature and necessity. As the city prospered, she grew to resent the parasitical habits of landowners who descended from their hilltop fortresses to rob mule trains that passed through their domain. Armies were formed to counter the threat, while defeated landowners were forced to live in Florence to learn to read and write.

Forced to be civilised, they still built in the style of the countryside. Palaces – *palazzi*, the grandiose term that Florentines give to any townhouse of pretension, were built with fortress-like walls and towers, gaunt reminders of their rural prototypes. Yet the emphasis was on sunlight and warmth, bringing the glorious golden outdoors of Tuscany inside, past the columns and through the spacious arches and open windows.

THE FLORIN

In 1252 Florence minted modern Europe's first gold coin, the florin, which soon became a standard currency throughout the Continent. (Indeed, until the introduction of the euro, the Dutch florin still carried the name of the old Florentine coin.) The minting of the florin coincided with a spectacular growth in the city's wealth and population throughout the 1200s. By the end of the century the city walls were scarcely able to contain its 100,000 inhabitants. Florence was one of the five most populous cities in Europe, and one of the richest. Both banking and the wool trade were booming, and this opulence created new possibilities for art and culture.

The wool trade

In the 11th century, Florentine merchants began importing wool from Northern Europe and rare dye-stuffs from the Mediterranean and the East. They soon developed specialised weaving and dyeing techniques that made the wool trade the city's biggest source of income.

Soaring profits fuelled that other Florentine mainstay, banking. Financiers exploited the established trade routes, creating a network of lending houses. In 1252 a tiny gold coin was minted in the city that became the recognised unit of international currency, the florin.

Guelf versus Ghibelline

Emergent capitalism and the rapid expansion of the city served to fuel the long-standing conflict between two factions, the Guelfs and the Ghibellines. The whole Italian peninsula was embroiled in the struggle, but the prize – and therefore the vehemence of the feud – was all the greater in Florence.

ABOVE LEFT: *St Stephen* by Giotto (detail), 13th century (Museo Horne). **ABOVE:** the wool industry employed almost one-third of Florence's inhabitants by 1250.
ABOVE RIGHT: *Clement IV delivering arms to the leaders of the Guelf Party* by Vasari, 1565 (Palazzo Vecchio).

The Guelfs supported the Pope and the Ghibellines the Holy Roman Emperor in a battle for territory and temporal power. In Florence, the parties fought in the streets, attacking their enemies and retreating to their defended palaces.

The conflict saw no decisive victories, and new alliances were created every time an old one was defeated or its supporters sent into exile. In general, though, the new men were in the ascendant. The Florentine banking system reached its zenith in the late 13th century when the Guelf Party secured a monopoly over papal tax collection, and in 1293 the Ordinances of Justice barred the nobility from state office, concentrating power in the hands of the trade guilds.

Black versus white

But just as the *magnati,* aristocrats, survived as a powerful element in the city, so the Guelfs themselves began to split, as powerful families jostled for prominence. The origins of the new conflict – between the Blacks, the Neri, and the Whites, the Bianchi – lay outside Florence, in a feud between two branches of the Concellieri family in Pistoia. It was the excuse that the rival Florentine Cerchi and Donati families needed. They took up opposite sides in a quarrel that gained momentum and in 1302 led to the exile of Dante, among others, who were all expelled from the city in a mass purge of the Whites.

Golden age

During the 14th century, Florence was the richest city in Europe; the cathedral, the Palazzo Vecchio and Santa Croce were under construction, industry boomed, and Florentine artisans were skilled in metal-casting and terracotta, as well as the weaving and dyeing of cloth.

Moreover, whereas factionalism in other city states favoured the rise of *signori,* despots who exploited instability to impose their authority and establish hereditary dynasties, Florence for a long time did not succumb. Instead, it evolved its own style of broadly based government, with a council of members elected from the city's 21 guilds and executive officers chosen from the seven major guilds, appointed for a finite period to ensure that no individual could dominate.

Capitalism in crisis

New-found stability was continually put to the test and yet survived. In 1339, Edward III of England reneged on Florentine debts, precipitating a banking crisis. Three years later, the Black Death swept the city. It re-emerged seven times during the century, carrying off over half the population.

Internal revolts, such as the 1378 rebellion of the *ciompi,* the lowest-paid of

> *Ezzelino III da Romano (1192–1259) was one of the staunchest members of the Ghibelline Party in northern Italy, and always a faithful ally of the Holy Roman Emperor Frederick II.*

patrons, Florence's many religious foundations also began to compete in the sponsorship of artists. Patronage made many a Florentine artisan wealthy. Ghiberti, who trained as a goldsmith and was only 25 years old when he was awarded the commission for the baptistery doors, founded a workshop and foundry that employed countless craftsmen.

Florentine humanism

In this changing environment, intellectuals and artists had a chance to play a role in political life. Humanist scholars emerged from their absorption in classical texts to make new claims for Florence as the true inheritor of Roman virtues.

In 1375, Colluccio Salutati, the great classical scholar, became Florentine Chancellor, bringing to everyday politics all his immense learning, and swaying opinion by the power of his Ciceronian rhetoric. Other scholars followed him: Leonardo Bruni, Carlo Marsuppini, Poggio Bracciolini and Cosimo de' Medici.

the city's wool workers, who demanded the right to form a guild and be represented on the council, often resulted in the powerful merchant families closing ranks against "popular" elements. But each time this happened the leaders were sent into exile: the Alberti, then the Strozzi and finally the Medici.

Wars with foreign powers and neighbouring states also tended to unite factional leaders in a common cause: that of the defence and then the expansion of the Florentine republic. Between 1384 and 1406, Florence won victories over Arezzo, Lucca, Montepulciano and Pisa – the prize that gave the city direct access to the sea.

Style wars

Success helped to confirm that aggressive independence and sense of Florentine identity that played a shaping role in the cultural awakening of the Quattrocento. By the beginning of the 1400s the guilds, as well as individual patrons, had begun to find new ways of expressing the rivalry that was previously the cause of so much bloodshed, but was now to benefit, rather than threaten, the city. Patronage of the arts became the new source of prestige, a means of demonstrating wealth and power. As well as private

ENTHUSIASTIC HUMANIST

Cosimo was also a keen supporter of the movement we now call humanism – a name which, though it originated in the Renaissance, was not used in this sense until the 16th century. In the 15th century the nearest equivalent was "orator".

In its early stages, in Cosimo's time, the movement emphasised the instruction to be gained from studying the classical past. It was nourished by a great belief in the overriding power of the word: persuasion, knowledge and good sense, leavened by the grace of God, were enough to make the world the way it should be.

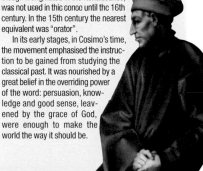

Dawn of the Medici dynasty

Cosimo proved too persuasive, too popular for his political opponents. Heir to the banking network established by his father, Giovanni, he supported the guilds against government attempts to expropriate their funds to finance its military operations. He suffered the fate of all who threatened to wrest or win power in Florence and was banished from the city in 1433. Exile lasted only a year, for, with the backing of Pope Eugenius IV, he returned in 1434 and acted as unofficial leader for the next 30 years. Thus began a period of unparalleled peace and stability, and the founding of what was to become the Medici dynasty.

Cosimo died in 1464, leaving Florence prosperous, peaceful and with just claim to the title of the "new Rome" – having given birth contemporaneously to humanism and the Renaissance. Upon him the *signoria* conferred the title once bestowed upon Cicero of Pater Patriae, Father of His Country. Cosimo's son, the sickly

Piero, inherited his father's gout and did not survive long. In 1469, Lorenzo was called upon to fill his grandfather's shoes.

> The Medici ruled Florence almost continuously from 1434 to 1737. There is scarcely a corner of the city which does not have some connection with them.

Lorenzo, poet and statesman

Lorenzo was no great patron of the pictorial arts. He owned few paintings and preferred the more princely pleasures of collecting antique gemstones, coins and vases (now in the Argenti Museum). He was an outstanding poet, writing satirical, often bawdy, sometimes romantic verse in his native tongue. Whereas in Cosimo's time it would have been unthinkable to read or write seriously except in Latin, Lorenzo promoted the study of Dante's work in the universities and encouraged respect for Boccaccio and Petrarch, also writers in the *volgare* (vernacular). This language would soon become the standard for all Italian literature.

FAR LEFT: Florence conquering Tuscany, by Vasari.
ABOVE LEFT: Lorenzo as Mercury, god of eloquence and conciliation, in Botticelli's *Primavera*. **ABOVE:** a 19th-century copy of a woodcut of Florence made in 1470.

Moreover, Lorenzo was, like Cosimo, a humanist, much taken with the new philosophy of neo-Platonism that his grandfather's protégé, Ficino, had begun to develop.

Although Lorenzo preferred literary pursuits to affairs of state, he won respect throughout Italy as he tried to heal old rifts and pacify warring city states. His aim was an alliance of states strong enough to defeat external threats, including the ambitions of the Holy Roman Emperor.

Papal dealings

Ironically, it was the Pope who proved to be Lorenzo's greatest enemy, for his own territorial ambitions depended on a divided Italy. It was Sixtus IV who took the papal bank account from the Medici bank, contributing to its near bankruptcy. Sixtus, too, was behind the Pazzi conspiracy of 1478 which aimed to murder Lorenzo and destroy the Medici. Sixtus even sent his allies, the Neapolitan army, to attack Florence, but Lorenzo so charmed the king of Naples that peace terms were rapidly agreed.

The news probably hastened Sixtus's death. Lorenzo took care to cultivate his successor, Innocent VIII, and succeeded in having his son, Giovanni de' Medici, created a cardinal, aged 13,

thus planting a Medici in the heart of the papal domain. Three weeks after Giovanni's consecration, in 1492, Lorenzo was dead. "The peace of Italy is at an end," declared Pope Innocent, who himself died two months later, and his prophecy proved correct. In 1494, the French king Charles VIII invaded Italy and marched to Florence. Piero de' Medici, Lorenzo's son, hoping to win the king's friendship, surrendered the city. Florentines slammed the doors of the Palazzo Vecchio in his face and that night the family fled.

Savonarola

Into the vacuum stepped Girolamo Savonarola, prior of San Marco (1491–8), who was convinced that Charles VIII was an agent of God, sent to punish Florentines for their obsession with pagan philosophies, secular books and profane art. He presided over the city for four ter-

ABOVE: *Adoration of the Magi*, *c.*1473 (Uffizi), showing Lorenzo de' Medici, Cosimo de' Medici (in front of the child), Piero de' Medici (red cape), Giovanni de' Medici (in white), Giuliano de' Medici (black cape), with a self-portrait of Botticelli (far right). **TOP RIGHT:** Girolamo Savonarola, an unbending ruler. **FAR RIGHT:** Pope Leo X flanked by cardinals, by Raphael, 1518 (Uffizi).

rible years, when to wear unbecoming dress was punishable by torture and when children were rewarded for reporting their parents' misdemeanours. Savonarola had fanatical supporters and equally determined opponents: opinion turned against him when he was excommunicated and the threat of papal interdict fell over the city. His lasting achievement was the new republican constitution adopted in 1494, and, even after he was executed in 1498, the republic continued to flourish under the leadership of Piero Soderini, assisted by Niccolò Machiavelli.

Return of the Medici

In 1512 the nascent republic suffered a heavy defeat at the hands of the Spanish, and the Medici forced their way back into the city, led by Cardinal Giovanni. The following year he was crowned Pope Leo X, and Florence celebrated for four days. Machiavelli, regarded as a threat by the Medici, was imprisoned and tortured, then allowed to retire from public life. He began working on *The Prince*, a justification of his own actions in office and a reflection on the qualities that make an effective leader.

Until now, this had not been the Medici style, but the family became determined to hold on to power with all the force at its disposal. Two Medici popes, Leo X and his cousin Clement VII, ruled Florence from Rome for the next 15 years through the agency of Alessandro de' Medici, believed to be the bastard son of Pope Clement.

A brave attempt to re-establish the republic in 1527, when Rome was sacked by imperial troops, was put down by combined imperial and papal forces in 1530. Alessandro was crowned duke of Florence and proved to be the first of generations of Medici dukes who, secure in their power, were corrupt, debauched and tyrannical. When he was murdered by his cousin Lorenzaccio, Florence was relieved of a great burden.

THE MEDICI LEGACY

We have generations of Medici to thank for the fabulous collections of art amassed by the family – and Cosimo's court painter Vasari to thank for the Uffizi building which houses so many of them.

Florence itself is indebted to the last of the Medici, Anna Maria Lodovica, for the fact that the great Medici art treasures are still to be admired in the city. On her death in 1743 her will stated that the family's vast wealth and hoards of art were to become the property of the future rulers of Tuscany – on condition that none of it should ever be moved outside Florence. Had it not been for her, the inestimable treasures of the Uffizi and the Bargello could well have been dispersed long ago.

Cosimo's achievements

He thus created an effective administration and brought political unity and security to the region. Ironically, after his death, Florence achieved something approaching the self-governing status that had so long eluded the city. Cosimo's descendants, who nominally ruled Florence for another six generations, proved so indolent, degenerate, drunken and debauched that they had little taste for affairs of state, which was left to the government machine created by Cosimo. Yet no one again challenged their right to rule, and when the last Medici, Anna Maria, died in 1743, there was genuine grief at the passing of a dynasty.

The twilight of the Medici era ushered in a relatively sedate period under the rule of the House of Lorraine. It also saw the flourishing of a relationship between Florence and its foreign visitors, which had begun the century before.

Before the 17th century, foreign visitors were mostly mercenaries or spies posing as diplomats. Gradually, a few adventurous eccentrics published their encounters with witty, if outlandish, Florentines. A century later, the attraction of an alien psyche, a perfect climate, the architecture, a low cost of living and undervalued works of art made Florence an essential stop on any European tour.

When the council met to elect a successor, it chose another Cosimo, son of the respected Giovanni delle Bande Nere and Maria Salviati, granddaughter of Lorenzo the Magnificent. Those who voted for him perhaps believed that he would accept constitutional limitations to his power. They were wrong – under his rule, they would enjoy less, not greater freedom.

Cosimo I set about destroying all opposition. First he defeated an army of republicans in exile and had the leaders publicly executed. Then he brought the cities of Tuscany to heel, attacking them with such brutality that Siena, for example, lost half its population. Unlike his ancestors, he was no enlightened patron of the arts. Such work as he did commission (the Palazzo Vecchio frescos) were for his own self-glorification or for practical purposes: the Uffizi was built to bring all the administrative functions, the guilds and the judiciary, under one roof and under his control.

During the Napoleonic Wars, travel to Florence was suspended. Following the Allied victory at Waterloo, the middle classes joined the throngs of aristocratic dilettanti and literati heading for Florence. Renaissance scholars, persecuted rebels, demure governesses and eloping couples incongruously filled the ranks *(see also pages 74–5).*

When Elizabeth Browning died, her last words were for Italy.

Italy's capital for a day

In 1865 Florence became the capital of the newly united Italy. Although its role would last only five years before Rome was made the permanent capital, Florence underwent profound and rapid change in this time. An ambitious plan of expansion and modernisation led to the demolition of the city walls, and their replacement with a ring of avenues punctuated with large piazzas in keeping with the French urban taste of the times.

Great collectors

At the start of the 20th century, the Anglo-Florentine community was as much a part of the fabric of the city as the Medici villas it inhabited. The collections assembled by people such as the parents of Harold Acton, grand man of letters, Arthur Acton and his American banking heiress wife Hortense Mitchell, the American art critic Bernard Berenson and the British architect Herbert Horne, remain a tribute to the enduring effect of the "Grand Tourists" on Florence.

FAR LEFT: street life on the Ponte Vecchio, 1892.
ABOVE LEFT: playing Le Chiavi, a Florentine game.
ABOVE: American Grand Tourist Allen Smith contemplating the Arno, by François-Xavier Fabre, 1797.

Mixed impressions

World War I chased away most of the foreign visitors and residents. D.H. Lawrence had a tourist's experience of the political aftermath of the war. He saw the shift from socialism to Fascism as different forms of "bullying". Under socialism "servants were rude, cabmen insulted one and demanded treble fare". Under Fascism, he reported that taxis had a lower price, but so did life; the socialist mayor of Fiesole

UNFINISHED HISTORY

On his death, Harold Acton left his superb Villa La Pietra, together with his art collection and 40,000 rare volumes, to New York University, and another property near the Arno to the British Institute. However, in an unexpected twist, his will has been challenged by the children of a late Florence innkeeper, Liana Beacci, claiming that she was Sir Harold's illegitimate sister from an affair which Arthur Acton had with his secretary, and so entitled to part of the estate. DNA testing has come out in her favour, but NYU is fighting the claims tooth and nail, and the case continues.

A City under Water

Shortly before dawn on 4 November 1966, after 48 centimetres (19 inches) of rain had fallen in 48 hours, the River Arno burst its banks. Thirty-five people were killed, 16,000 vehicles destroyed and hundreds of homes left uninhabitable as the muddy floodwaters rose to more than 6 metres (20ft) above street level. Heating oil was swept out of broken basement tanks.

The water crashed through the museums, galleries, churches and crafts shops. Thousands of works of art were damaged, some dating back to the 12th century – paintings, statues, frescos, tapestries and manuscripts, scientific instruments and ancient Etruscan pottery. The city had suffered from floods in the past – about one really serious inundation each century – but the only other event that caused as much devastation as the 1966 flood came during World War II.

Student volunteers flocked to Florence from around the world to help the army, which had sent in thousands of conscripts. They helped to wrap Japanese mulberry paper over paintings to keep the paint from buckling, and to scrape the slime off the base of Michelangelo's *David*. Many students gave up months to help with the restoration, to clean up the streets and pump out basements.

When word of the flood spread, millions of dollars of public and private money poured in from around the world. Art-restoration experts arriving from America and Europe agreed that it could take 20 years for all the damaged art objects – those not totally ruined – to be restored and for Florence to recover. They were half right. Florence has definitely recovered, but almost half a century on, the task of restoration is still not yet complete, although most major works that were damaged are back on display. The banks of the Arno have been re-dug and re-inforced, and valuable art objects have been moved to higher, safer places. Experts admit, however, that another major flood could occur, while administrators fail to agree on steps to prevent this.

The extensive damage to the Archaeological Museum, so inundated that curators resorted to digging techniques they had used to recover artefacts from long-buried civilisations, has now all but been repaired, but the reconstruction of ancient Etruscan tombs, once a popular feature of the museum gardens, has only recently been completed.

At the National Library, the institution hardest hit, students looking for rare reference books today may still expect to be told: "That book has not yet been restored from the flood." In total, 1½ million volumes were damaged, two-thirds beyond repair. But more than 500,000 modern books were saved, along with 40,000 rare or historic volumes. ❑

ABOVE: clearing up in Piazza della Repubblica.
RIGHT: debris from the flood outside Santa Croce.

was murdered in front of his family. In the 1920s and 1930s, the Grand Tour resumed, but for society figures and intellectuals rather than aristocrats. Aldous Huxley dubbed Florence "a second-rate provincial town with its repulsive Gothic architecture and its acres of Christmas card primitives", but E.M. Forster was besotted with the city's alien vivacity.

> Legend has it that all of the bridges would have been blown sky-high had it not been for Hitler's fond memories of the Ponte Vecchio.

World War II

World War II severely affected the city, especially in 1944 as the Germans, pursued by the advancing British forces, retreated. After a two-week pitched artillery battle between the Nazis on one side of the river and the Allies on the other, the retreating Germans abandoned Florence, blocking the Ponte Vecchio with rubble from demolished medieval buildings at either end and blowing up all the other bridges across the Arno. A few hours after the last German left, reconstruction of the bridges began.

The great flood of 1966

Despite post-war construction and the economic boom years that followed, Florence would wake to an even worse shock 22 years later as the banks of the River Arno burst with disastrous consequences, both on a human and a material level *(see opposite)*.

The damage of politics

With the Communist Party evolving a progressive, pro-regionalist stance, after World War II a "red belt" developed across central Italy, run by left-wing coalitions.

At a national level, however, by the early 1990s, more than 50 post-war "swing-door" governments had come and gone. To many observers, the source of this crisis lay in Italy's administration and dubious morality. Senior party leaders tended to die in office, governments suffered from opportunism, not lack of opportunity. *Partitocrazia* (party influence) supplanted democracy, extending from government to public corporations, infiltrating banking, the judiciary and media, and the public tacitly condoned this "old boys' network".

Clean hands

The early 1990s saw a series of political scandals involving bribes, and the result was the *Mani Pulite* ("Clean Hands") campaign under the fiery leadership of Antonio di Pietro, a former

ABOVE: girls on bicycles posing with two Fascist soldiers.
RIGHT: Mussolini and his WWII ally Hitler.

found to have enjoyed "friendly" and direct relations with the Mafia "up until 1980", but not later – meaning that due to statutory time limitations he could not now be prosecuted.

Mafia bombing

In the midst of the political upheaval, in May 1993 Florence suffered yet another blow, when a bomb behind the Uffizi gallery was set off by the Mafia. Five people were killed and priceless paintings and sculptures damaged, while a handful were destroyed. The fabric of the Uffizi's buildings was damaged, and several medieval buildings were virtually destroyed.

The Mafia's aim with the attack, and others in Milan and Rome, was to force the Italian state into submission, and agree to a deal of mutual convenience, as had been enjoyed with the Christian Democrats. The Sicilian Godfather, Salvatore "Toto" Riina, was sentenced to life for the Uffizi bombing, along with other crime bosses in 1998. However, those thought to have masterminded the attacks have never been caught.

The return of the corrupt

Meanwhile, while no area of Italy appeared to have been left untouched by corruption, in the end few if any *Tangentopoli* politicians served any real time in jail. Many, initially ostracised, were

magistrate who became Italy's most popular public figure when he spearheaded inquiries into public corruption.

A vast network was uncovered in which public contracts were awarded by politicians to businesses in return for bribes. Italian public life was convulsed by the scandal, dubbed *Tangentopoli* – literally, "Bribesville". Dozens of MPs and businessmen came under investigation. A number were preventively held in jail; some even took their lives. The Christian Democrat Party, which had dominated Italian politics since the war, collapsed. Two former prime ministers – the socialist leader Bettino Craxi and the Christian Democrat veteran and seven times former prime minister Giulio Andreotti – were investigated.

Craxi slipped through the net and died in self-imposed exile in Tunisia in January 2000, with international arrest warrants hanging over his head. Andreotti, who was instead charged with Mafia ties, was eventually let off after a mammoth trial lasting years. His acquittal was later held up on appeal by state prosecutors. However, in a long report published afterwards to show how they had reached their decision, appeal judges said that Andreotti had been

Silvio Berlusconi, a controversial premier.

later rehabilitated, while some of those originally embroiled have since returned to politics.

Silvio Berlusconi

Italy's most powerful media magnate, Silvio Berlusconi, is now in his third term of office. Depicting himself as the new face of Italy, he headed a short-lived, right-wing coalition in 1994. Despite corruption charges against him he was swept to power again in 2001. The premier and his sidekicks in the neo-Facist Alleanza Nazionale were booted out in the 2006 general election to make way for a two-year stint under a disparate coalition headed by Romano Prodi. Following Prodi's resignation and the failed attempts to set up an interim government, elections were called for in 2008 and Berlusconi was back in power.

In 2009 Italy's constitutional court annulled the law giving Berlusconi immunity from prosecution, jettisoning the laws he pushed through to shield himself and his cronies from legal proceedings. However, in 2010 he managed yet again to circumvent court hearings by passing a law allowing him and his ministers to avoid trials by arguing a "legitimate impediment", ie an official engagement. Trials can be suspended for up to 18 months, by which time the charges would expire under Italy's statue of limitations.

Corruption allegations, shady dealings and sex scandals have only slighted dented Berlusconi's popularity. He has won strong support through his hard line on illegal immigration, and has enormous influence through his media control. One way or another he controls some 90 percent of Italian television. The billionaire premier heads an empire that spans telecommunications to insurance, food and construction.

Despite Italy's runaway public debt, ageing infrastructure and organised crime, Berlusconi's centre-right coalition appears to be in a stronger position than ever. The anti-immigration Northern League, which holds key posts in Berlusconi's coalition, was a key winner in the Italian regional elections in 2010. The centre left held on to Tuscany, but Berlusconi's alliance won six of the 13 Italian regions where voting took place, having previously controlled only two. The success indicates a strong endorsement for Berlusconi's remaining three years in office. ❑

FAR LEFT: the Uffizi bombing aftermath. **ABOVE LEFT:** Matteo Renzi, mayor of Florence. **ABOVE:** central Italy's mayors protest in Florence over Berlusconi policies, 2010.

DECISIVE DATES

10th–8th centuries BC
Settlements on the site of Florence.

4th century BC
Fiesole is well established as a powerful Etruscan city with walls and temples.

351 BC
Etruria conquered by the Romans.

59 BC
Foundation of the Roman colony of Florentia, which grows rapidly at the expense of Fiesole.

3rd century AD
Christianity is brought to Florence by eastern merchants.

5th–6th centuries
The city is repeatedly sacked by Goths and Byzantines.

570
Lombards occupy Tuscany, ruling Florence from Lucca. Two centuries of peace, during which the baptistery was built.

774
Charlemagne defeats the Lombards and appoints a marquis to rule Tuscany, still based in Lucca.

1001
Death of Marquese Ugo, who made Florence the new capital of Tuscany. Florence has become a prosperous trading town.

11th century
Most of the city's churches are rebuilt.

1115
Countess Matilda dies, leaving her title to the Pope. Florence becomes a self-governing *comune* and conquers the surrounding countryside.

1125
Florence conquers Fiesole.

1173–5
The *comune* builds a new set of walls around the city.

1216
Start of civil strife between rival supporters of the Pope and of the Holy Roman Emperor over issues of temporal power fuelled by class warfare and family vendettas. The Papal Party prevails in Florence.

1252
Florence sees the minting of the first florin, which is to become the currency of European trade.

1260
Florentines suffer disastrous defeat by the Sienese at Montaperti. Florentine supporters of the Emperor dissuade the Sienese from razing the city.

1284
New town walls are erected.They will define the limits of Florence until 1865. Florence is one of Europe's richest cities.

1293
Strife between Guelf (Papal) and Ghibelline (Imperial) parties is now an outright class war. The merchant Guelfs pass an ordinance excluding aristocratic Ghibellines from public office.

1294
Construction of the cathedral begins.

1299
Palazzo Vecchio is begun.

1302
Dante is exiled. He exacts revenge by populating the Purgatory of his *Divine Comedy* with his enemies.

1315
Palazzo Vecchio is completed.

1338
Florence is at the height of its prosperity, despite continuing instability.

1339
Edward III of England defaults on massive debts incurred fighting the Hundred Years War. Two powerful banking families, the Bardi and Peruzzi, go bankrupt and the Florentine economy is in crisis.

1342
The Black Death sweeps through Tuscany. In 50 years it wipes out three out of five people in Florence.

1378
Revolt of the *ciompi*, the lowest-paid wool-industry workers, demanding guild representation and a say in government. Their demands are met, but the merchant families reinforce their oligarchy.

1400–1
Competition to design new doors for the baptistery is announced, marking the rise of Florence to both intellectual and artistic pre-eminence. Ghiberti wins the commission.

1406
Florence defeats Pisa, a victory that gave Florence direct access to the sea.

1432
Florence defeats Siena at the battle of San Romano.

1433
Cosimo de' Medici exiled from Florence but returns a year later to preside over 30 years of stability and artistic achievement.

1464
Death of Cosimo, hailed as Father of His Country.

1469
Lorenzo, grandson of Cosimo, takes charge of the city. He is an able leader.

1478
Pazzi conspiracy seeks to destroy the Medici dynasty but reinforces Lorenzo.

1492
Piero, Lorenzo's son, takes over.

1494
Charles VIII of France invades Italy and Piero surrenders Florence to him. In disgust, citizens expel Piero and, under the influence of Savonarola, declare Florence a republic with Christ as its ruler.

1498
Pope Alexander VI orders the trial of Savonarola for heresy and fomenting civil strife. He is burnt at the stake.

1504
Michelangelo completes his statue of *David*, symbol of republican Florence, which is placed in Piazza della Signoria.

1512
Florence is defeated by an invading Spanish army. The Medici take advantage of the city's weakness to re-establish control, led by Giovanni, son of Lorenzo the Magnificent and now Pope Leo X, and his cousin, Giuliano (the future Pope Clement VII).

1527
Clement VII tries to rule Florence from Rome but, when Rome is attacked by imperial troops, Florentines expel the Medici and return to a republican constitution.

1530
Pope Clement signs a peace treaty with Emperor Charles V and together they lay siege to Florence. Florence eventually falls.

1531
Alessandro de' Medici is made Duke of Florence.

1537
Alessandro is assassinated by his cousin, Lorenzaccio. Cosimo I is made Duke, defeats an army of republicans and begins a 37-year reign. Many artists, including Michelangelo, leave Florence, which declines as a centre of artistic excellence.

1555
Cosimo I starts to reunite Tuscany.

1564
Cosimo I unexpectedly resigns and his son, Francesco, is appointed regent.

1569
Cosimo I created Grand Duke of Tuscany by Pope Pius VI in belated recognition of his absolute control over the region.

1574
Cosimo I dies.

1610
Galileo is made court mathematician.

1631
Galileo is excommunicated.

1737
Gian Gastone dies without a male heir. The title passes, by treaty, to the Austrian imperial House of Lorraine.

1743
Anna Maria Lodovica, the last of the Medici, dies, bequeathing her property to the people of Florence.

1799
The French defeat Austria. Florence is ruled by Louis of Bourbon.

1815
Florence is again ruled by the House of Lorraine, but organisations set on securing independence gain popular support.

1848
In First Italian War of Independence Tuscany is the vanguard of the uprising.

1860
Tuscany votes to become part of the emerging United Kingdom of Italy.

1865
Florence is declared the capital of the newly united Italy.

1871
Rome in turn becomes the capital.

1887–1912
Tuscany remains economically buoyant, helped by textile production, and becomes a haven for foreign writers.

1919
Mussolini *(top right)* founds the Fascist Party.

1940
Italy enters World War II.

1944
Retreating Nazis destroy the bridges of Florence, leaving only the Ponte Vecchio.

1957–65
Florence transforms from an agricultural economy to a service- and culture-based economy.

1966
Florence devastated by floods. Many works of art destroyed.

1988
Florentines vote to ban all but residents' cars from the historic city centre.

1993
Bomb kills five and damages the Uffizi, destroying and harming artworks.

1998
Salvatore "Toto" Riina and other members of the Mafia given life sentences for planting the Uffizi bomb.

2001
Silvio Berlusconi becomes premier.

2006
The left coalition under Romano Prodi wins the general election. Italy win the World Cup but Fiorentina is fined for match-fixing.

2007
The Nuovi Uffizi project to expand the Uffizi gallery finally gets underway.

2008
Berlusconi returns to power for a third term.

2010
Opening of Line 1 of Florence's long awaited Tramvia. Berlusconi makes strong gains in regional elections but Tuscany remains a centre-left stronghold.

A TASTE OF FLORENCE

A traditional Florentine lunch is a seriously gastronomic event in which classic local dishes are accompanied by a vast proliferation of Tuscan wines

"I believe no more in black than in white, but I believe in boiled or roasted capon, and I also believe in butter and beer... but above all I have faith in good wine and deem that he who believes in it is saved." – Luigi Pulci

Whether Pulci is now being gently grilled on some infernal spit or playing his harp perched on an angelic soufflé, in life the 15th-century Florentine poet had a characteristically healthy appetite. In the city that sired the "mother of French cooking", Catherine de' Medici, the Renaissance heralded a new interest in food as an art.

Catherine was responsible for much of the renewed interest in the creation of original dishes during this period. Menus at Florentine banquets abounded with dishes such as pasta cooked in rose-water and flavoured with sugar, incredible candied fruit and almond confec-

Most Florentine food is healthy, hearty and draws on the raw wealth of the beautiful Tuscan countryside.

tionery, the famous hare stew called *lepre in dolce e forte* – made with candied lemon, lime and orange peel, cocoa, rosemary, garlic, vegetables and red wine – and many more.

The claim that Gallic cuisine dates from the marriage of Catherine to Henri II of France in

1535 is based on the similarity between characteristic French and Tuscan dishes: *canard à l'orange* is not unlike the Florentine *papero alla melarancia*; vol-au-vents are found in Florence under the name *turbanate di sfoglia*; *lepre in dolce e forte* is still called *dolce forte* in French – although Italian and French cooks are not in agreement about its origins.

Simple fare

And yet sobriety rather than sensuality was, and remains, an important element in the Florentine character. Despite their love of food, Florentines never really warmed to the complex recipes of the sauce-loving Medici. Popular Renaissance

---

PRECEDING PAGES: Pucci's shopfront. **LEFT:** Tuscans love their pizza. **RIGHT:** *ribollita* – classic Tuscan soup.

dishes were simple and robust, with plenty of vegetables and plainly grilled meats, eaten for utility as much as enjoyment; nourishing the soul and spirit as well as the body. Busy people in a thriving commercial environment, they had little time for over-sophistication.

> Florentines and Tuscans have been nicknamed the mangiafagioli, the great bean-eaters, because the pulse is used so much in local specialities.

This solid element persists to this day. Thick soups and bean stews (served in terracotta pots whatever the restaurant) and large steaks and heavy wines are typical of a meal in Florence.

Eating Italian-style

Italians love their food, and Florentines are no exception. Breakfast usually consists of just an espresso or cappuccino, drunk "on the hoof" in a local bar if not at home, perhaps with a *panino* (filled bread roll) if really hungry.

But a traditional Florentine lunch is a different story. This is a truly gastronomic event, to be shared with friends and family at leisure. A full-blown Italian meal will begin with an *antipasto* – a bit of salami, some roasted peppers. Then follows the first course, *il primo*, usually a pasta, risotto or soup. *Il secondo* is next, consisting of meat or fish and vegetables. Salad is always served *after* this, effectively cleansing the palate in preparation for *i formaggi* (cheese) and *i dolci* (dessert), the last often being fruit-based. Although there are still plenty of places where you can linger over a four-course midday meal, an increasing number of Florentines now grab lunch on the go and have dinner as their main meal.

Markets and vegetables

The most colourful introduction to the city's food is a morning spent amid the vegetable stalls of the Mercato Centrale, hidden among the colourful stalls of the San Lorenzo market, on Via dell' Ariento. Here, the fruit of the hills – courgettes, tomatoes, mushrooms, peppers, potatoes and aubergines – form a bright tapestry of potential

ABOVE: colourful array of seasonal produce at the San Lorenzo market. **TOP RIGHT:** a carnivore's delight. **FAR RIGHT:** tripe stand in Piazzetta del Bandino.

tastes. Florentines will happily eat any of these fried or brushed with Tuscany's purest *extra vergine* olive oil, and simply grilled until soft and melting.

But among these gaudy fruits, the undisputed aristocrats are the humble white beans or *fagioli*. Like the potato, the bean was introduced from the Americas by Florentine merchants, and it is now a staple of the city. In a soup or mixed with tuna fish, the little *fagioli* are a marvellously simple beginning to any Florentine meal.

Fresh Tuscan vegetables are rarely disappointing on their own, but together they make two of the city's great specialities, *ribollita* and *minestrone*. *Ribollita* means "reboiled" as in "recycled" – leftover vegetables are combined to create a dense soup. The naturally thrifty Florentine might put any spare vegetable in the pan to make this filling potage – though traditionally it should include white *cannellini* beans and *cavolo nero*, a type of black cabbage indigenous to Tuscany – which is thickened with stale bread. But Tuscan vegetables seem most at home in minestrone soup. Though they share a little of Italy's faith in pasta as the all-purpose dish, Florentines prefer their own rich and nutritious vegetable stews.

CHESTNUTS

In winter, the smell of roasted chestnuts *(castagne)* fills the air in Florence. *Castagne* are a Tuscan favourite, particularly in the mountain areas, where they are made into flour, pancakes, soups and sweet cakes. Keep an eye out at the Piazza Santo Spirito flea market for a small stand making fresh *necci*, delicious crêpes made with chestnut flour and served with ricotta cheese. The chestnut season peaks around mid-October, when chestnut – and steam train – lovers can travel on a restored 1920s steam train from Florence's Santa Maria Novella station to Marradi's Sagra delle Castagne, or Chestnut Festival, to partake in the celebrations.

A feast of meat

Florence may seem a vegetarian's idea of Eden, but the Florentine is undeniably a red-blooded carnivore. For a start and a starter try *crostini di fegato*, chicken liver pâté on fried bread, delicious with a young white wine. A feast to follow is *fritto misto*, mixed meats fried in batter, or the peasant dish *stracotto*, beef stewed for several hours and especially satisfying in winter.

But, above all, Florentines specialise in plain roasted meats: *arista* (roast pork), beef, lamb at Easter, and even wild boar in season. Tuscany's fertile pasture feeds some of the richest flavours in Italy, and Florentines refuse to clutter these tastes with over-adornment. Just as simple is their treatment of chicken and pheasant.

However, the master of meats – and as much a symbol of the city as the florin – is the famous *bistecca alla fiorentina* (steak Florentine). A huge, tender and succulent rib-steak from Tuscany's alabaster Chianina cattle, the *bistecca* is brushed with a drop of the purest virgin olive oil and charcoal-grilled over a scented wood fire of oak or olive branches, then seasoned with salt and pepper before being served, with the Florentine's characteristic lack of fuss. It is quite the most delicious meat in Italy.

In good restaurants, you will be able to see the meat raw before you order. If you can get a seat, the best *bistecca alla fiorentina* in the city is said to be served on the marble table tops of Sostanza (Via Porcellana) or at Buca Lapi. But beware, the price on the menu is per 100 grams (3½ ounces) of raw meat, and you are thought mean if you order less than a kilo to share between two people.

Another famous Florentine meat dish is *arista alla fiorentina* – pork loin highly seasoned with chopped rosemary and ground pepper. The origin of this dish goes back to the 15th century. At the Ecumenical Council of 1430 in Florence, the Greek bishops were served the dish at a banquet and pronounced it *aristos*, which in Greek means "very good". The name stuck and became a feature of Florentine cuisine.

At the cheaper end of the culinary spectrum and in their rational desire not to waste, Florentines have even made a speciality out of tripe. *Trippa alla fiorentina*, cooked with tomatoes and sprinkled with parmesan, is a favourite and inexpensive dish, though the tripe's slippery texture and intense garlic flavour make it an equivocal choice for the uninitiated.

Sweeteners

If Florentine food tends to be filling, full of flavour but unsophisticated, Florentine *dolci* (desserts) make up for any lack of imagination. In the bars, cake shops and *gelaterie* there is a constant carnival of colour. *Coppe varie*, bowls of mixed fruit and water ice, compete for attention with pastries and handmade sweets, huge slabs of nougat, chocolate "Florentines", *baci* – the angel's kiss – and, at carnival time, *schiacciata alla fiorentina*, a simple, light sponge cake.

GELATO

No visit to the city would be complete without a taste of its ice cream. You can see why Florentines claim to have invented *gelato*, for the city is awash with a rainbow of flavours. Always look for the sign Produzione Propria (home-made), and before you try anywhere else, make for Vivoli on the Via Isola delle Stinche. It remains unrivalled for both flavour and variety. Here you'll find *zuppa inglese*, which literally means "English soup" but is in fact trifle or trifle ice cream. Virtually a meal in itself, *gelato* is Florence's most delicious fine art.

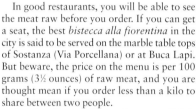

One pride of the city is the incredible *zuccotto*, a sponge-cake mould with a filling of almonds, hazelnuts, chocolate and cream. Once eaten, it is never forgotten. There is no general agreement, however, as to the origins of its name. Literally translated as "small pumpkin", *zuccotto*, being a dome-shaped speciality, is thought by some to refer affectionately to the Duomo – or perhaps to be a slightly irreverent allusion to the clergy. In the Tuscan dialect, a cardinal's skullcap is also called a *zuccotto*.

Eating out

Whether for business or for pleasure, and invariably for both, dining is an important event for the Florentine. Once a languid affair, lunch during the working week is increasingly treated as a lighter snack, as more businesses remain open through the lunch hour and the Florentines become more health-conscious. Caution is thrown to the winds, however, on a Sunday, when the midday meal is given great impor-

tance and may continue well into the afternoon. In the evening, Florentines usually eat at around 8.30pm. Lacking the Spaniards' nocturnal enthusiasm, the best restaurants close early.

> Because so many Florentines take their holidays in high summer – to avoid the city's heat and the tourists – many restaurants are closed throughout August.

Many wines

In the region where soil and sunlight nurture Italy's most famous wine, Chianti, Pulci was not alone in extolling the virtues of the blushful Hippocrene. "I believe", wrote Leonardo da Vinci, "that where there is good wine, there is great happiness for men." Happiness may be harder to find, even in Tuscany, but good wine isn't.

This is the kingdom of Sangiovese, the little grape that gives heart and strength to Tuscan classified reds, while innumerable other vines serve as royal subjects and even vie for the crown. Tuscany shares Italy's vast proliferation of vineyards and labels.

FAR LEFT: Florentines have a sweet tooth for nougat.
TOP LEFT: Italian staples: bread and cappuccino.
ABOVE: catching up with the news at an outdoor café.

Chianti

Chianti is grown in seven regions surrounding Florence and Siena. Perhaps Italy's most potent symbol, Chianti is not just one wine, but many. In its seven zones, the variety of climates, producers and vineyards is staggering, ensuring a huge breadth of quality and complexity.

The heartland of Chianti lies either side of the Chiantigiana road (SS222) connecting Florence and Siena, the "Via Sacra" (Sacred Road) of wine. This is the home of Chianti Classico, where the Chianti League was formed in the 13th century – a region that produces more consistently good wine than any other zone, except for the Rufina district. The latter, the most important wine-producing region near Florence, lies in the hills above the River Sieve. It produces some of the giants of Italian wine: Selvapiana, Castello di Nipozzano, Fatoria di Vetrie and the new heavyweight, Montesodi.

The region surrounding Florence itself, the Chianti Coli Fiorentina, is the source of many of those characteristic straw-covered bottles – known as *fiaschi* – that once filled the city. (Now considered by many producers to be too "rustic", they have largely been superseded by elegant, square-shouldered bottles.) Chianti Coli Fiorentina wines tend to be heavy and coarse.

White wines

Top brands to look for include Vino Nobile di Montepulciano, Brunello di Montalcino and Brolio – all red wines. Although reds are by far the best-known and, for the most part, superior wines in the region, whites are also out there. They are light, simple and rather pleasant – but generally could not be described as "great". Most are based on Trebbiano and Malvasia grapes.

The main exception is the dry, elegant, but quite full-bodied Vernaccia di San Gimignano, from the town that lies west of Siena. White wines of note are also made from the French grape variety Chardonnay. More and more producers have turned over one or more of their plots to this grape, and many have invested in *barriques* (oak barrels) from France in which to mature the wines. The end result is a great success.

OLIVE OIL

Tuscany's olive oil, long famous for its quality and excellent flavour and texture, is even accorded DOC status. Tuscans are passionate about olive oil, and it is an important cooking ingredient. Quality is measured by acid content, the finest oil being *extra vergine* with less than 1 percent acid content. A few excellent oils from Florence and the surrounding area are Extra Vergine di Scansano, Extra Vergine di Seggiano cru Querciole, Extra Vergine del Chianti, Extra Vergine di San Gimignano cru Montenidoli, and Extra Vergine Badia a Coltibuono.

The search for quality

The viticultural promiscuity of Tuscany makes standards hard to control, and quality does vary greatly. In line with EU regulations, "quality" wines are designated Denominazione di Origine Controllata (DOC), while DOCG guarantees the authenticity of certain favoured wines. Although considered by some to be the "lesser brethren" of the DOC wines, Tuscany has many remarkable *vini da tavola*, especially Sassicaia.

Individually named and often costly, these *vini da tavola* have become known as "super-Tuscans", and are often wines made solely with the Sangiovese grape – or Sangioveto, a superior clone. Sometimes they are a blend of Sangiovese and Cabernet Sauvignon. They are occasionally made solely with Cabernet.

To add even more confusion, a single name on a wine list will not necesarily signify a "super-Tuscan". Many estates have a particular vineyard whose wine, when kept separate, is always better than the rest. Each is labelled with its vineyard name as well as its official designation: Chi-anti or Chianti Classico. Tuscans are expected to know that Montesodi, for example, is a particular *cru* (single-vineyard wine) of Chianti Rufina from the Frescobaldi estate. So the one word is often all that is put on the list in a restaurant. In shops, where the label can be scrutinised before buying, life is easier.

Generally, but not always, Classico is better than non-Classico. On the better, more matured wines the label will state *Riserva*, which indicates the wine has been aged for at least three years. For easy drinking, the lively Chianti non-*riserva*, called simply *normale*, comes into its own.

Vin Santo

After you have enjoyed a Chianti and a Florentine steak, a delightful way to end the meal is to follow the ritual of nibbling *biscotti di Prato*, hard almond biscuits, dipped in a glass of dark gold Vin Santo ("Holy Wine"). This dessert wine is made from white Trebbiano and Malvasia grapes picked late into the harvest – at "the time of the saints" (near to All Saints' Day, 1 November). Most Vin Santo is sweet, but some is dry. Nearly all of it is rare and expensive. Indeed, Vin Santo seems to liquefy the Tuscan sunlight and unleash the complex tastes of the land. ❏

FAR LEFT: *salute!* **ABOVE LEFT:** red or white, the choice is yours. **ABOVE:** the *gallo nero* (black cockerel emblem of the Consorzio Chianti Classico) indicates a good Chianti.

SHOPPING FIRENZE

Florence is still recognised worldwide for quality and fine craftsmanship, and modern designer icons are plentiful, too

At the dawn of the 20th century a little-known artist in leather design called Gucci opened his first workshop supplying elegantly crafted saddlebags to the gentry. When Gucci opened its first store in Florence in 1921, few could have guessed that it would become the internationally successful glam-rock symbol that it is today. Others were to follow.

Salvatore Ferragamo settled in Florence in 1927 and went on to fashion shoes for the most beautiful women of the century. Still one of the most prestigious and internationally known luxury brands, the historical Florence flagship store in Palazzo Spini Feroni (Via de' Tornabuoni 14r) has employees so skilled that they can fit clients into shoes without even measuring them first. In the basement there is a fascinating Shoe Museum *(see page 180)*.

Dressing the well-heeled feet of Florentine families for decades, home-grown Tod's classic loafers and bags come in all shapes, sizes and colours. The store is located at Via de' Tornabuoni 103r.

Florentine designer Roberto Cavalli (Via de' Tornabuoni 83) is famous for his glamorous, sexy designs. His grandfather was an Impressionist painter whose works are on display at the Uffizi. He was the inventor of a revolutionary printing procedure for leather, stunned fashionistas with his bold style and animal prints, and has become synonymous with primeval and jungle sensuality.

ABOVE AND BELOW: many designers have diversified from purely leatherware and accessories to embrace entire fashion houses nowadays. The Florentine Pucci brand is pure retro, with swirly, sixties inspiration. Bold, brightly coloured psychedelic patterns are the hallmarks of Emilio Pucci, the eccentric, fun-loving founder who pronounced: "The aim of fashion is to produce happiness." Think Lucy in the sky with diamonds – real diamonds – in this distinctively popular designer house at Palazzo Pucci, Via de' Pucci 6e.

Botteg (Borgo d has every co leather item fro jackets, boots and to lipstick holders.

There are hundreds of shops scattered throughout the city devoted to sensory leather, like **Il Bisonte** (Via del Parione 31/33r).

Most designer shops in Florence are situated along three elegant streets: Via della Vigna Nuova, Via de' Tornabuoni and Via Roma.

Il Torchio (Via de' Bardi 17) makes marbled paper to a secret recipe in its workshop, and also sells leather and paper desk accessories.

ABOVE: vintage-clothes lovers should pop into Elio Ferraro (Via del Parione 47r) for vintage designer clothes, if only to browse: the prices here are not for the money-conscious.

Famous butter-soft Florentine leather had its beginnings in the historic square Piazza Santa Croce.

Florence is a bag and shoe heaven, so you'll be spoilt for choice. Some shops sell similar wares, so look around to compare prices.

a Fiorentina
ii Greci 5r)
etable
n bags,
shoes

OUT-OF-TOWN SHOPPING

The advantages of out-of-town shopping have caught on in Italy in general not only because of the obvious parking problems in Florence, but also because it eliminates the urban problem of illegal street sellers offering fake designer wear and, to a degree, petty crime against shoppers.

Florence's trump card is its proximity to the designer factory stores. About one hour's drive from the centre is Montevarchi, home to Prada's factory shop. Nearby, in Incisa, are Dolce e Gabbana and Fendi.

While The Mall shopping outlet may not be able to offer Prada, it is much bigger and closer to the city – around a 30-minute drive into the Tuscan hills – and has outlets for many designer names, such as Bottega Veneta, Emanuel Ungaro, Ermenegildo Zegna, Fendi, Giorgio Armani, Gucci, La Perla, Loro Piana, Marni, Pucci, Salvatore Ferragamo, Sergio Rossi, Stella McCartney, Tod's and Valentino. The Mall, Via Europa 8, Leccio Reggello (tel: 055-865 7775; www.outlet-firenze.it), open Mon–Sat 10am–7pm, Sun 3–7pm.

The Barberino di Mugello designer outlet, managed by the McArthurGlen mall complex group, has scores of shops offering all the top names in clothing, sportswear and accessories, with discounts from 30 percent to 70 percent. It is located 45 minutes from Florence and one hour from Bologna, close to the Bologna–Florence motorway (A1).

ABOVE: the covered market of San Lorenzo sells a wide range of foods, whilst the street market has clothes, shoes and leather goods galore, as well as jewellery. **BELOW AND RIGHT:** markets are a feature of Italian life, where real bargains can be had. Apart from the permanent open-air markets in the city, many neighbourhoods have a weekly market.

BEST BUYS IN THE MARKETS

Mercato Centrale, Piazza del Mercato, a 19th-century covered market selling Tuscan products.
Cascine, Pesco del Cascine, on the banks of the River Arno, selling just about everything (Tue 8am–1pm only).
Mercato delle Cure, Piazza delle Cure, an authentic Florentine market a little way out of town.
Mercato Nuovo, Via Por Santa Maria, also known as Mercato del Porcellino and the Straw Market, selling leather and souvenirs as well as Florentine straw, hand-embroidered work and flowers.
Mercato delle Plante, Via Pelliceria, selling flowers and plants under a portico near the post office.
Mercato delle Pulci, Piazza dei Ciompi, colourful flea market with some good bargains for objets d'art and smaller antiques.
Mercato di San Lorenzo, Piazza San Lorenzo, selling leather bags, belts, shoes and clothes. Probably the best leather and clothes bargains in town.
Mercato di Sant'Ambrogio, Piazza Ghiberti, for fruit and veg.
Mercato di Santo Spirito, Piazza Santo Spirito, sells almost everything and becomes a monthly flea market.

RIGHT: the ancient Dominican apothecary Officina Profumo Farmaceutica di Santa Maria Novella (Via della Scala 16) is one of the world's oldest pharmacies. The lotions and potions in this ornate 14th-century chapel are truly celestial and gorgeously scented.

ART AND ARCHITECTURE

More than any other Italian city, Florence is defined
by its artistic heritage, both blessed and burdened by
a civic identity bound up with the Renaissance,
and basking in its reflected glory

The earliest evidence of a substantial settlement at Florence comes from burial sites of the 10th to 8th centuries BC. This early Iron Age culture, known as Villanovan after a site in Emilia, produced burial urns typically comprising two conical vases joined together and often with a cap-like lid. Cemeteries imply villages, and settlements may have been fortified. Alongside the burial urns were weapons, combs, bronze clasps and spindles, indicating a strong sense of an afterlife.

Etruscan style

The succeeding Etruscan civilisation was established near Florence in Fiesole in around the 10th century BC. Rich archaeological finds in the area include monumental tombs, fine funeral objects and a large altar, all attesting to the sophistication and wealth of the Etruscans. One such work, the sarcophagus of Larthia Seianti

*While little Etruscan city architecture
survives, its legacy influenced Roman art,
temple design and city planning.*

(2nd century BC, Museo Archeologico), demonstrates some key elements of Etruscan aesthetics: a softly rendered human form, an interest in implying movement, and a slightly unnatural sense of proportion. The virtuosity of Etruscan

LEFT: portrait of a young man, probably a member of the Medici dynasty, by Botticelli (Uffizi). **RIGHT:** the Etruscan tomb of Larthia Seianti.

bronzework is epitomised by the Arezzo Chimera (*c.*400 BC, Museo Archeologico), with its stylised mane and tangible energy.

The Roman city of Florence – Florentia – was founded in 59 BC and planned according to a grid system, following an Etruscan tradition, a layout still apparent in the streets around Piazza della Repubblica. Florentia featured the monumental structures common to Roman cities: city walls, a forum, pagan temples, a semicircular theatre, public baths and a large amphitheatre, the last near to Santa Croce. Cemeteries were located outside city limits, ranging from monumental mausoleums to simple catacombs for the lower class.

Christianity arrives

In AD 250, San Miniato was martyred in Florence, indicating a Christian community in the city. Its first cathedral, the church of San Lorenzo, was consecrated in 393, a chapel was built at San Miniato al Monte, and Santa Reparata was established on the site of today's Duomo.

The Middle Ages

After the fall of the Roman Empire, Florence's importance diminished considerably and the city sank into obscurity. The early Middle Ages were troubled, and little art and architecture remains. Sant'Apollinare was founded around the middle of the 6th century.

In 774, Florence was established as a centre for ecclesiastical learning, which rekindled interest in architecture. New churches, like San Remigio,

The 13th-century mosaics in the dome of the baptistery display scenes from the Bible in shimmering glass and gold, with more realistic representations of humans.

were built to accommodate a growing Church community according to the basilica plan, a large rectangular hall comprising a tall central aisle called a nave flanked by two shorter aisles.

During the 11th century, Romanesque architecture emerged in Florence, blending established basilica models with vaulted structures, square belltowers, and heavy, round arches. Two fine examples were San Miniato al Monte and the Duomo baptistery, reconstructed *c.*1100.

The Gothic

In the years before 1200, Europe saw a fundamental change of thought, in which beauty began to be seen as a reflection and affirmation of God's creation rather than as a distraction from the contemplation of God. This new notion, rife with optimism, was expressed in the Gothic style of architecture. Ribs and pointed arches were employed to create billowing interior spaces, implying a sense of verticality and weightlessness, reaching upwards towards heaven but firmly anchored on the earth. Gothic architecture in Florence emphasised

spatial unity, light and harmony, and remained closely linked to Roman forms. Some examples are Santa Maria Novella (1246–1360), Santa Croce (1294–1442) and the new cathedral or Duomo (Santa Maria del Fiore), begun in 1294 by Arnolfo di Cambio, continued by Andrea Pisano and subsequently Francesco Talenti.

Thirteenth-century Florence was turbulent, and domestic and public architecture developed to reflect the city's hostile political rivalries. Many aristocrats built defensive tower houses such as the Torre della Castagna and Torre degli Alberti, both designed to symbolise the wealth and military strength of the residents. Even the Palazzo Vecchio, Florence's town hall begun in 1299, seems fortress-like with its rough, imposing facade, crenellated cornice and aggressively thrusting tower.

Gothic art was religious or funerary in nature. Altarpieces and votive offerings were created to glorify saints, frequently featuring enthroned figures displayed on Byzantine-inspired gold backgrounds and employing a hierarchical scale – Christ and the Virgin Mary are proportionally larger than other holy figures who, in turn, are larger than human donors. Other images were made to teach Bible stories and the lives of the saints to a largely illiterate public.

By the mid-13th century the style and aesthetics in art were beginning to change, sloughing off the gold-shrouded mysticism of Byzantine art, breaking away from the hierarchical rigidity of Gothic art, and approaching a new naturalism. Sculpture developed under the direction of such great masters as Nicola and Giovanni

Pisano. Nicola's carved pulpit for the baptistery at Pisa (1255–60) was a major point in the history of art. His composition introduced elements from Roman classical art, such as greater plasticity and more realistic drapery, inaugurating a revolution. His son Giovanni's pulpit at Pisa's cathedral (1302–11) continued Nicola's tradition of synthesising established styles with classical influences. One might say Giovanni goes even further by introducing an energy and vivacity to his compositions that was absent from his father's style.

Painting was developing, too. Cimabue's development of naturalism *(see box below)* greatly influenced his student

CIMABUE

Cimabue, also influenced by classical models, introduced naturalism, highly individualised figures, rudimentary perspective and simple modelling with light and shade. This new direction in art rejected the flatness and stiffness that typified medieval artwork, bringing compositions closer to realistic subjects and settings. Cimabue's *Santa Trinità Madonna* (1280, Uffizi), right (detail), portrays animated and individualised figures to suggest humanity.

ABOVE LEFT: San Miniato's facade has a five-bay marble veneer embellished with a mosaic in the 12th century.
ABOVE: arches inside the Palazzo Vecchio. **ABOVE RIGHT:** *The Annunciation* by Simone Martini, 1333 (Uffizi).

ralism, realism and perspective. In architecture, there was a strong penchant for emulating classical style and idealisation.

The 15th century began momentously with a grand artistic contest. In 1401 a competition to design a second set of bronze doors to be erected on the north side of the Duomo baptistery was announced. The trial pieces had to match the quadrilobed shape of Andrea Pisano's door panels produced 70 years earlier, and had to portray the Sacrifice of Abraham. The winning piece by Lorenzo Ghiberti (Museo dell'Opera del Duomo) features two groups of figures situated along a diagonal axis. In the main scene, set off to the right, Abraham energetically thrusts a knife towards Isaac kneeling on an altar. Over the course of the next 50 years, Ghiberti would make two sets of doors, the second called the "Gates of Paradise" by Michelangelo, for the Duomo's baptistery.

Giotto, who applied and extended what he had learnt to his works at the Basilica di San Francesco in Assisi, the Scrovegni Chapel in Padua and his commissions in Florentine churches. His frescos depict religious scenes with clarity and economy, and his figures display a wide range of emotions and gestures. By emphasising humanity, Giotto's works became more meaningful and accessible to the viewer. The lessons set forth during this era by Cimabue and Giotto were the foundations upon which the Florentine Renaissance would be laid in the next century.

The aesthetics and proportions of 15th-century architecture were laid out by the prolific and pensive Filippo Brunelleschi. His first major building was the Spedale degli Innocenti (Foundling Hospital) of 1418, a Florentine orphanage. There, he revived Roman architectural forms – entablatures, pilasters, Corinthian columns, porticoes and pedimented

The Renaissance

The Renaissance, which literally means rebirth, was the period spanning from the late 14th to early 16th centuries characterised by a renewed interest in the Classics and advancements in art, architecture, science and learning. The artistic style that developed during this era embodied humanist philosophies, drew on classical models and showed natu-

The delicacy of modelling, narrative coherence and believable illusionistic space that Ghiberti created granted him the prestigious commission, defeating the more innovative offering by Brunelleschi.

windows. He also employed simple geometry to achieve balance and serenity in his design. Brunelleschi applied rules of proportion to his designs at San Lorenzo (1419–80) and Santo Spirito (1444) as well.

Brunelleschi's greatest technical challenge was erecting the dome of the Duomo, a task that he began in 1426. He was the sole architect of the project, a departure from medieval traditions of corporate or shared responsibility. To create the surging vertical cone of the dome, he used two shells – an inner, corbelled, herringbone-brick swelling cone (that acted as its own scaffold) encased by a tiled dome supported on externally visible ribs. The whole was surmounted with a lantern reached by steps within the void between the two domes.

While his architectural works were profoundly influential, his greatest contribution to art was as the reputed inventor of one-point perspective, a geometric means of creating the convincing illusion of depth on a flat surface. Two-dimensional paintings and frescos could finally imply space beyond their frames.

Masaccio was the first painter to use one-point perspective, which he rigorously applied to the creation of illusionistic architecture. In his *Holy Trinity* (1426–7, Santa Maria Novella), a single vanishing point is used. This allows all of the composition's lines to converge, giving a sense of depth on a flat surface. Set against a Brunelleschi-type coffered vault, Christ rises on the Cross, supported by God and the dove symbolic of the Holy Ghost. At the base of the Cross are the Virgin Mary, St John the Evangelist and the two donors. Our eye level is that of the donors, and that of the vanishing point; we are meant to look up at the other figures and into the architecture, convinced of their depth and reality.

Masaccio was heavily influenced by Giotto and worked with Masolino, ultimately becoming one of the most influential artists of the 15th century. The Cappella Brancacci in Santa Maria del Carmine houses his most extensive frescos, supplemented by others by Masolino and Filippino Lippi. Masaccio's show scenes from the life of Saint Peter and of Adam and Eve. The

FAR LEFT: detail from the *Coronation of the Virgin* altarpiece by Giotto, *c.*1330 (Santa Croce). **ABOVE LEFT:** detail from Gentile da Fabriano's *Adoration of the Magi*, 1423 (Uffizi). **ABOVE:** Ghiberti's "Gates of Paradise" adorn the Duomo's baptistery.

a more relaxed approach. In his diptych portraits of the duke and duchess of Urbino (1472, Uffizi) the contrast of the duke's veristic portrait and the duchess's idealised one is tempered by the symmetry of the composition, its continuous landscape, and the coolness with which the duo survey their kingdom and one another. For Paolo Uccello, perspective was employed to subvert order and coherence. In his *Flood* in Santa Maria Novella's Chiostro Verde (1447), a dynamic foreshortened perspective conjures an uneasy and dramatic scene of chaos.

Sculpture

In the early years of the Renaissance, sculptural subjects were largely limited to religious figures, saints or noble portraits for tombs. Donatello's *St George* (1415–17) for the facade of Orsanmichele demonstrates Renaissance logic. He stands alone, isolated in his niche, protruding from its shallow depth. His determined gaze seems anxious and pessimistic. St George's solitude and uneasiness represents the Renaissance idea that man is fundamentally alone in the world and must battle for his place in it. Donatello's bronze *David* (c.1430, Bargello), one of the first large nude figures since antiquity and a classically driven representation of the human body, is static, a hero at rest. In his energetic *Cantoria* (1439), or singing gallery, in the Duomo, and his *Annunciation* (1435, Santa Croce), Donatello reveals his mastery of movement – proof that sculptors, too, were becoming more concerned with capturing the

Tribute Money (1425–7) most clearly demonstrates Masaccio's style, an intense preoccupation with realistic detail, perfect perspective, classically inspired clothing and poses, and a grasp of humanity. His works show real people, some shivering with cold, some ill, others matronly, all relating to one another, and none more emotional than the grief-stricken Adam and Eve expelled from Paradise.

Others were quick to pick up perspective and bring their own contributions to the Renaissance. Fra Angelico, an artist turned Dominican monk, employed perspective to give his paintings a serene order. His compositions were all of a religious nature, and are best exemplified by the frescos in the monastery of San Marco, where he painted figures embodying a sculptural tranquillity and simple grace. His *Annunciation* (1438–45) features a classically inspired perspective portico beneath which the holy scene unfolds. A softness and solemnity permeate the work, meant to inspire pious contemplation in the viewer.

To painters and mathematicians like Piero della Francesca, perspective's geometry evoked order and coherence. Della Francesca, however, rejected the rigid rules of perspective, using

ABOVE LEFT: detail from Filippino Lippi's *Virgin Appearing to St Bernard* (1486). **ABOVE:** a self-portrait by Lippi in the Brancacci Chapel. **ABOVE RIGHT:** detail from *The Annunciation*, by Fra Angelico (1438–45). **FAR RIGHT:** sculptures, Museo dell' Opera del Duomo.

immediate. This immediacy and plasticity is seen in Ghiberti's second set of doors for the Duomo baptistery (1425–52). He exploits perspective and architectural and landscape settings to show Old Testament subjects in a manner akin to contemporary painting.

Thus, by the mid-15th century, the Renaissance had a firm hold on Florentine art and architecture. Leon Battista Alberti, the quintessential "Renaissance man", brought an archaeological approach to his designs, reviving a pilastered temple-like form and using Roman references to architectural schemes of differing scales superimposed one upon the other. Alberti's facade to Santa Maria Novella elaborated Brunelleschi's feel for geometry. His patron there, Giovanni Rucellai, also commissioned him to build the Palazzo Rucellai (1446–51), a massive townhouse whose facade was embellished according to rules set forth by Vitruvius. Palzzo Rucellai and contemporary edifices like Michellozo's Palazzo Medici-

Riccardi (1444) and Brunelleschi's Palazzo Pitti (1458) were expressions of a new type of architecture, driven by money, power and artistic trends rather than piety or defence.

Patronage

Almost all Renaissance masterpieces were commissions from the city's most powerful families and merchant guilds. The most famous family to patronise the arts in Renaissance Florence was the Medici, and their subject matters were often allegorical. Gozzoli was commissioned to paint the *Nativity* and the *Adoration of the Magi* for the Medici Palace's private chapel. This subject was particularly resonant for these noble patrons, who saw it as an allegory of their own faith. The portraits of Lorenzo, Cosimo and Giuliano de' Medici

In 1431, Luca della Robbia carved a Cantoria for the Duomo, which features panels of music-making and dancing children of the utmost delicacy, their movements and gestures caught in mid-action.

appear in the procession that celebrates the humble birth of Christ. By participating in this holy scene the Medici were able to glorify their house, demonstrate their service to the Church and, above all, posit themselves as the Magi, ready to donate their wealth to the glory of the Catholic faith.

> The Epiphany became a common scene commissioned by noble families in Florence for its symbolic gravity.

The High Renaissance

Verrocchio's workshop was among the busiest and most versatile at the end of the 15th century. A goldsmith by training, he excelled as a painter, sculptor and draughtsman. Among his students were Botticelli, Ghirlandaio, Perugino and da Vinci. With such a stable of talent, his influence on the High Renaissance was inevitable. Leonardo da Vinci, Raphael and Michelangelo, together with Fra Bartolomeo and Andrea del Sarto, form a culmination to the Italian Renaissance in the years 1495 to 1520, a period

known as the High Renaissance. During the 1500s Florence was their centre of activity.

Leonardo, the eldest of these, was a multitalented humanist who was at once a scientist and an artist, concerned with discovering the nature of things and bringing an empirical approach to his creations. Trained in Verocchio's workshop, the pair worked together on *The Baptism of Christ* (1472–25, Uffizi). Building on the lessons of his master, da Vinci rendered drapery, landscapes and human forms in a naturalistic way that revealed their true nature. In his depiction of humans, he rejected the use of defined outlines, preferring to blur them, or relying on tonal shading. In consequence, the image appeared to breathe, as with the *Mona Lisa* (1503–6, Louvre) or the *Virgin and Child with St Anne* (1510, Louvre) painted for the Servite friars of Florence. He is credited with introducing a new painterly manner, with a love of invention – the mark, he said, of a great artist.

ABOVE: Botticelli's *Primavera* (c.1478), one of the most popular works in the Uffizi, is open to myriad interpretations which, to modern sensibilities, are secondary to the enchantment of spring. **RIGHT:** *The Journey of the Magi*, by Benozzo Gozzoli (c.1460).

Raphael arrived in Florence in 1504 at the age of 21 to take up his apprenticeship with Perugino, a painter known for his classicising tendencies. Raphael's *Marriage of the Virgin* (1504, Pinocateca di Brera, Milan) shows a style heavily steeped in that of his master. The image portrays an assured composition and extreme clarity of action, coupled with a serene sense of classicism, hallmarks of Raphael's early period. His *Madonna of the Grand Duke* (1505, Uffizi) was influenced by both Perugino and Leonardo's manner, while he developed his own lucid, controlled and balanced way of painting, epitomised in *The Madonna of the Goldfinch* (1507, Uffizi, *see painting on page 71*). With *The Entombment* (1507, Rome, *see painting on page 70*), Raphael initiated a more dynamic manner, with figures in straining action as they carry the dead Christ, a factor that would be continued in his works in Rome.

In 1508, he began painting scenes for Pope Julius II's apartments in the Vatican, a commission that would confirm him as one of Italy's most respected painters. Under Leo X he would continue the work while also carrying out private commissions. His *La Velata*, or Veiled Woman (1516, Palazzo Pitti), carefully manipulates light and shade to render the portrait of the seated, dignified woman, contrasting the colours and textures of her skin and clothing against a dark background. Raphael's new use of light is no better demonstrated than in his *Transfiguration* (1520, Vatican Pinacoteca). Figures writhe and contort in the

THE BEAUTY OF THE HUMAN FORM

The Renaissance preoccupation with Roman antiquity and, by extension, pagan mythology influenced Florentine artists, rekindling an interest in mythological subjects in sculpture and painting (echoed also in an interest in anatomy and proportions). The secularising tendencies of portraiture and mythology worried many who had seen the arts as essentially supporting the Christian Church. As a result, philosophers tried to reconcile Christianity with paganism. Accordingly, Botticelli's *Birth of Venus* (1482, Uffizi) was seen as reflecting baptism, for, just as Venus was miraculously born out of water, so we are spiritually reborn through the water of baptism.

But not everyone in Florence was convinced by this interpretation. The problem came to a head in 1494–8 when Florence became the epicentre of the anti-Renaissance art movement led by Dominican cleric Girolamo Savonarola of Ferrara. He called for widespread reforms and condemned the propagation of antiquity, calling for the burning of books and paintings he deemed immoral.

Savanarola was ultimately burnt as a heretic, but his teachings deeply affected artists, particularly Botticelli, whose works became dark and violent as a result of his spiritual crisis, as seen in his *Calumny of Apelles* (1494–5, Uffizi).

tension-ridden New Testament scenes, for-shadowing the Mannerist movement's preoc-cupation with colour contrast, hyperbole and disquieting subject matter.

Michelangelo had been trained as a painter in Florence under Ghirlandaio, whose work-shop, like Verrocchio's, was one of the busiest. Michelangelo also received training in sculp-ture with Bertoldo, a former pupil of Donatello. This took place at San Marco under the patron-age of the Medici, who introduced Michelan-gelo to leading Florentine thinkers. Considering himself as primarily a sculptor, Michelangelo was a painter, architect and poet, too. If he had one main artistic tenet it was that the human body, preferably male, preferably nude, was the perfect means by which to convey his vision. Thus the *David*, carved in 1504 as a symbol of the city of Florence, with its penetrating gaze and its Platonic idealised muscular body, con-veys an archetypal image of bodily power. He brought his experience as a sculptor to his approach to painting.

As a painter at this early period, Michelangelo began to experiment in the *Doni Tondo* (1503, Uffizi) with complex, twisting poses that resolve three dimensions into two. It was a theme he took up when in Rome, from 1508–12, while he was painting the Sistine Chapel ceiling; using per-spective, foreshort-ening and solid, heavily muscled forms, he cre-ated a space populated by

Michelangelo's Deposition, c.1550, is a pyramidal composition of three figures, which includes his self-portrait as Nicodemus, the hooded figure supporting the dead Christ, flanked by the Virgin and Mary Magdalene. Michelangelo was 80 years old when he carved this group, intended for his own funerary chapel.

seemingly three-dimensional figures. After the High Renaissance, Michelangelo continued to work but his style changed, abandoning the balance and coherence of the Renaissance in favour of the tension of Mannerism.

The achievements of Leonardo, Raphael and Michelangelo towards a more painterly style of figure composition with a strong sculptural sense and richness of colour (in part deriving from the growing acceptance of oil paint replacing tempera and fresco) led to a style known as the Grand Manner. Both Fra Bartolomeo and Andrea del Sarto demonstrate this. The former, a pupil of Ghirlandaio, developed a powerfully sculptural style that in tonality owed much to Leonardo, but with absolute clarity of outline, well exemplified by his *Marriage of St Catherine* (1512, Accademia). Andrea del Sarto, a student of Piero di Cosimo, evolved a manner that owed much to Fra Bartolomeo, strongly emphasising light and shade, but with a measured sense of gravitas well seen in *The Madonna of the Harpies* (1517, Uffizi).

Mannerism

Da Vinci died in 1519, Raphael and Pope Leo X in 1520. The Protestant Reformation was gathering pace and in 1527 Rome was sacked by the Holy Roman Emperor's troops; a critical

turning point had been reached, and artwork reflected the anxiety of the age and the end of a golden era. A rejection of the ideal and of the logical began around 1516 and led into the Mannerist period, whose chief initial exponents were Florentine. The new style was theatrical, tense, stylised and often went against established Renaissance proportions and architectural rules. This was a new direction for art, one that served to shock the spectator out of a sense of normality by emphasising idiosyncrasies.

Michelangelo's Medici Chapel in San Lorenzo (1520–34) employs architecture that broke many established rules: cornices, columns and windows were carved with strange proportions, rejecting the order and tradition of Renaissance architecture. The sculptural adornment, though never completed, comprised tombs of Lorenzo and Giuliano de' Medici opposite one another. Seated, they wear Roman armour and turn their heads to look at Michelangelo's statue of the *Madonna and Child*, who face the altar. Below the two Medici are sarcophagi upon which figures of Dusk and Dawn, Night and Day lie uneasily. A chilly intellectualism seems to override the humanity of the images.

ABOVE LEFT: Raphael's *Entombment*. **ABOVE:** a sketch in charcoal by Leonardo (Uffizi). **ABOVE RIGHT:** Raphael's *The Madonna of the Goldfinch* (Uffizi) reveals a lyrical sweetness in the soft modelling of the figures.

The Baroque

In 1545 the Council of Trent initiated the Catholic Church's Counter-Reformation, in which artists were exhorted to emphasise an emotional mysticism for religious subjects, which by 1600 had resulted in the theatrical Baroque style. Art and architecture were used as implements in celebrating Catholic tenets and papal authority. Its centre was Rome; Florence's antiquarian climate was at odds with the new style, and so there are relatively few examples of the style in the city.

Exceptions include the facade of San Gaetano (1645) by Gheraldo Silvani. The enlargement of the Palazzo Pitti by Parigi (1620–30s), though architecturally conservative, included enchanting frescos by Pietro da Cortona of Rome, notably that of *The Golden Age* (1641–46). Cortona's bucolic, gestural manner was echoed in Furini's impressive *Allegory on the Death of Lorenzo the Magnificent* (1639–42). In the 1680s, the Neapolitan Luca Giordano frescoed the Palazzo Medici-Riccardi with *Allegory of Navigation*, anticipating the lighter style of the next century.

Pontormo epitomises Mannerist tendencies in terms of spatial ambiguity and dichotomies of scale. This is often coupled with great contrasts in colour, as demonstrated in *The Deposition* (1528, Santa Felicità) or *The Martyrdom of St Maurice* (1530, Palazzo Pitti). Bronzino, the most noted Florentine Mannerist of the mid-century, had studied with Pontormo and developed a stylised coldness in his portraits. His *Eleonora of Toledo* (1545, Uffizi) is an aloof subject, devoid of emotion and strangely proportioned with a small head and elongated arms.

MANNERIST SCULPTURE

Sculptors picked up elements of Mannerism through an appreciation of Michelangelo, whose *Victory* (1525, Palazzo Vecchio) provided a pattern for Bandinelli's much-derided *Hercules and Cacus* (1543, Piazza della Signoria). More successful were Cellini's bronze *Perseus* (1545–54, Loggia del Lanzi), at once dynamic and elegant, and Danti's *Honour Triumphant over Falsehood* (1561, Bargello). This last displays elongated and perfectly rounded forms, typical of Mannerist painting and present in Ammannati's bronze figures on the *Fountain of Neptune* (1565–75, Piazza della Signoria, *right*).

Virtuosity and complexity of pose are an important factor in Mannerism, and possibly the most successful example of a complex grouping of figures is Giambologna's *Rape of the Sabine Women* (1581–3, Loggia dei Lanzi). Intended to be seen from all angles, it draws the viewer into the intensity of the composition with its multiple viewpoints. Giambologna's *Mercury* (1564–80, Bargello), by contrast, is an essay in balance. More sophisticated are his small bronze figurines that often have poses comprising both frontal and side views. His intention was that in turning them, the spectator was constantly impressed and surprised by the changing silhouette.

18th–21st centuries

Europe in the late 18th and 19th centuries was gripped by the idea of historicism contributing to the development of neoclassicism. The chief exponent was the Venetian Antonio Canova, who erected the Alfieri monument in Santa Croce. Also in Santa Croce is Lorenzo Bartolini's tomb for the Countess Czartorysky (1837–44), which, though rooted in the work of Desiderio and Bernardo Rossellino, embodies a stark realism that becomes rather softer in the remarkable cemetery sculptures of 1850–1930.

Between 1871–87, Florence's Emilio de Fabris, taking the original Romanesque fabric of the Duomo as a pattern, added a new geometric facade. Following Florence's temporary nomination as the capital of Italy after unification, architect Giuseppe Poggi undertook a major urban development project in which parts of the city were replanned, new areas were built with wide avenues, and the Piazzale Michelangelo was laid out.

Florence's classicist leanings led to only a few truly progressive structures, among them Pier Luigi Nervi's stadium of 1932, located in the northeast of town. Most impressive are those by Giovanni Michelucci. His Stazione Santa Maria Novella (1935) is perhaps the city's finest public structure. Uncompromisingly of its time, spacious and practical, it makes a fitting entry to the city that gave the world the coherence of the Renaissance.

The newest developments of note are out of the centre in the ex-Fiat region of Novoli: the new university campus and the futuristic-looking Palazzo di Giustizia (law courts). Currently under discussion is Norman Foster's innovative underground railway station for the high-speed rail link (the TAV), a 45,000-sq metre (484,300 -sq ft) glass-roofed station, descending 25 metres (82ft), and forming the core of a new railway system extending to Santa Maria Novella station. Partially built and highly controversial is the ultra-modern, seven-storey steel, stone and polycarbonate loggia for the Uffizi art gallery exit by Japanese architect Arata Isozaki. Built to relieve the current bottleneck exit, this has been slated by Sandro Bondi, Italy's Minister of Culture, and is currently on hold. ❏

FAR LEFT: Giambologna's *Rape of the Sabine Women*.
ABOVE LEFT: a Baroque ceiling in the Palazzo Pitti.
ABOVE: Santa Maria Novella railway station.

A PARADISE OF EXILES

The English poet Shelley famously called Florence "a paradise of exiles", an escape from persecution and poverty to art and sunshine

By the 1850s, escapees from mid-Victorian England made Florence *une ville anglaise*, according to the French Naturalist Goncourt brothers. In the morning, the English would go for a "constitutional" in the Cascine Park. They would then meet at Vieusseux library for a chat, and then it was time for *i muffins* at *i tirumni* (tearooms). Even the Italian language and society were forced into retreat as the English acquired shops, paintings and villas.

The exiled Lord Byron *(above)* was "dazzled, drunk with Beauty" in Santa Croce and immersed himself in sybaritic pleasures and an entrée into Tuscan society afforded by his Italian mistress. But he also became actively involved in the movement for Italian independence while most of his contemporaries simply ignored the native Florentines.

From the splendid Villa Palmieri, Henry James pondered ruefully on the fate of Florentine villas, not built "with such a solidity of structure and superfluity of stone, simply to afford an economical winter residence to English and American families". World War I chased away most of the foreign visitors and residents. D.H. Lawrence stayed on and witnessed the rise of Fascism; but it was in libertine Florence that Lawrence's best-known work, *Lady Chatterley's Lover*, was first published privately in 1928.

LEFT: Bernard Berenson, the American art critic and expert on Italian Renaissance art, lived in Italy from 1900.

LEFT: poet Elizabeth Barrett Browning never tired of praising Italy at the expense of England. "Our poor English want educating into gladness. They want refining not in the fire but in the sunshine."

BELOW: portrait of English aristocrat Miss Walsch with a horse and a miniature poodle at Villa di Montefonte, in the Poggio Imperiale area of Florence.

FILMS WITH VIEWS

Florence has starred in many films, perhaps most memorably in Merchant Ivory's adaptation of E.M. Forster's *A Room with a View* (1985). His social comedy is a witty observation of the English middle classes based on Forster's own Florentine experiences when staying at Pensione Simi. He found the company of his mother and other English guests suffocating, but soon discovered that Italy was beginning to "thaw" his northernness. Pouting Helena Bonham-Carter is the young heroine, Lucy Honeychurch, accompanied by Charlotte the poisonous chaperone, played by Maggie Smith. Both women had asked for rooms with a view and receive just the opposite. But Lucy's heart and vistas are awakened by her experiences in Florence.

Zeffirelli's gently comic coming-of-age story *Tea with Mussolini* (1999) has a galaxy of stars including Dame Judi Dench, Joan Plowright and Maggie Smith. This "story of civilised disobedience" in 1935 portrays a group of prim British expatriate women whose ritual of afternoon tea is interrupted by the rising tide of Fascism and invasion by Nazi forces. Florentine sunsets and sunrises over the Arno are lovingly captured on the silver screen with lingering shots of all the great icons.

In the same piazza, more gruesome fates await in Ridley Scott's *Hannibal* (2001), which displays Florence in all its Gothic glory. Appearing to be an expert on Dante, Anthony Hopkins's Hannibal gives lectures in the Palazzo Vecchio and commits his most blood-curdling crimes in both the Piazza della Signoria and Piazza della Repubblica.

Siena stars in the latest Bond movie, *Quantum of Solace*, with 007 being chased through the town while the Palio thunders around the Campo.

MAIN PICTURE: Helena Bonham-Carter is Lucy Honeychurch, a young Englishwoman who falls for the charms of disreputable George Emerson in James Ivory's adaptation of *A Room with a View* (1985). **TOP RIGHT:** In *Tea with Mussolini* (1999), Judi Dench plays the eccentric aspiring artist Arabella, who sets out to restore the famous St Fina Ghirlandaio frescos in a San Gimignano chapel. **ABOVE:** Anthony Hopkins is Dr Lecter in *Hannibal* (2001), the clever, cold and calculating cannibal on the loose in Florence.

ORIENTATION

The Places section details all the attractions worth
seeing, arranged by area. The areas are shown on a
colour-coordinated map on pages 82–3. Main sights
are cross-referenced by number to individual maps

Characterised by the huge domed cupola of the cathedral rising out of
the dense, rustic-coloured city nestled in the Tuscan hills, Florence is
overflowing with history, culture and artistic patrimony.

Florence's centre is so compact that every street seems to reveal new wonders – and it's very difficult to get lost here. At the centre of everything is
the magnificent, candy-striped Duomo, whose
bulk makes a useful, almost ever-present
guide; from here, the major districts are Santa
Croce to the east, San Marco to the north,
Santa Maria Novella to the west and the
Oltrarno over the river to the south. Most of
the major sights are concentrated near the
Duomo, within walking distance of each
other and north of the two main bridges,
Ponte Vecchio and Ponte Santa Trinità.

Not only is Florence home to a clutch of
world-class museums, most notably Palazzo Pitti and the Uffizi, but a dazzling
array of smaller museums and churches, crammed with precious artworks and
frescos. There is more priceless art per square metre here than in any other city
in the world. The city's staggering cultural wealth makes negotiating the illog-
ical opening hours a worthwhile, if frustrating, task for the least enthusiastic to
the most hardy of art-lovers. However, its lure goes far beyond the sum total of
galleries, churches and monuments: in order to experience more than the Florence of the Renaissance, visitors should take the time to appreciate the beauty
and ambience of the city by wandering through the many piazzas and backstreets, and along the banks of the Arno and into the surrounding countryside.
There is no better time for this than the early evening: as the bustle of the day
winds down, the city feels altogether more Italian, especially in the summer
when the weather is stifling and the streets packed with tourists.

As for the noise, the heat, the cheating stallholders, pickpockets and rude
waiters, surely every city worth its salt has these. The problem has been
much exaggerated by those who affect an ennui for the stop on the Grand
Tour that has, in their eyes, fallen from fashion. Florence is not so easily dismissed, nor will the discriminating visitor want to leap to easy conclusions
about such a complex and rewarding destination.   ❏

PRECEDING PAGES: the *calcio storico* festival in front of Santa Croce; zooming in on
Florence's historic centre. **LEFT:** Florentine rooftops from Brunelleschi's cupola.

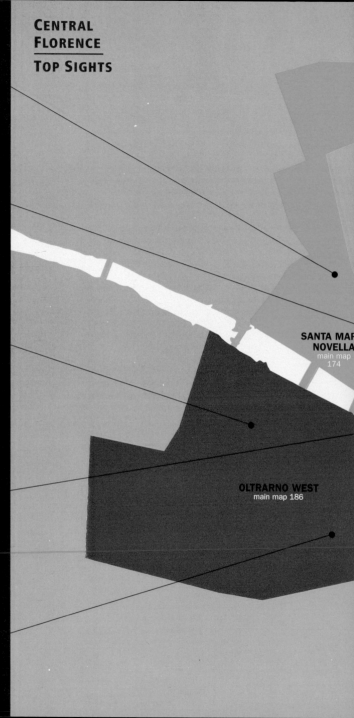

CENTRAL
FLORENCE
TOP SIGHTS

Santa Maria Novella
pages 173–6

Palazzo Vecchio
pages 104–7

Brancacci Chapel
pages 190–1

Ponte Vecchio
pages 108–9

Boboli Garden
pages 198–9

**SANTA MARIA
NOVELLA**
main map
174

OLTRARNO WEST
main map 186

SAN MARCO
main map 160

SAN LORENZO
main map 150

DUOMO
main map 88

PIAZZA DELLA REPUBLICA
main map 138

SANTA CROCE & THE NORTHEAST
main map 122

PIAZZA DELLA SIGNORIA
main map 100

OLTRARNO EAST
main map 186

Accademia
pages 170–1

San Lorenzo
pages 152–6

Duomo
pages 87–93

Santa Croce
pages 124–7

Uffizi
pages 114–19

Florence

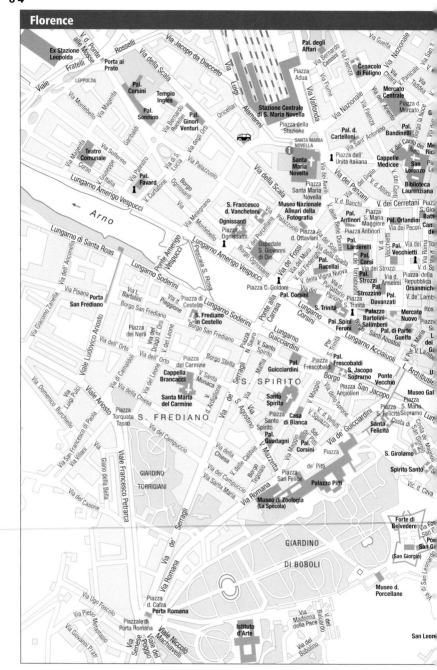

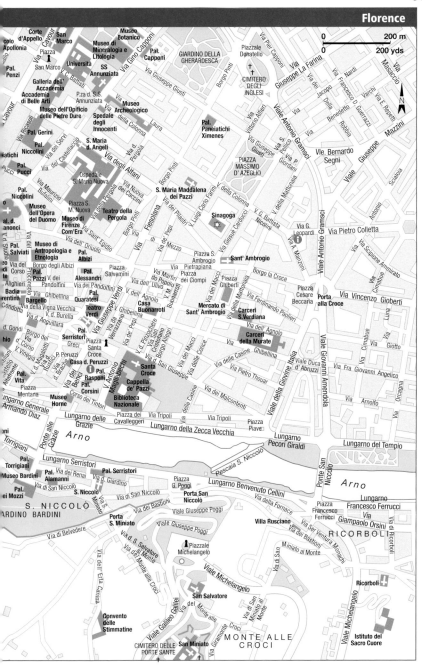

Recommended Restaurants, Bars, Cafés & Gelaterie on page 97

THE DUOMO

One of the largest cathedrals in the world stands at the heart of this impressive area of Florence, notable for its grandiose architecture as well as its art

raffic has been banned from the heart of the city, which allows the sheer scale of the magnificent Duomo (cathedral), clad in polychrome marble, to be fully appreciated. Next to the Duomo, whose steps are always full of tourists and locals, lie the baptistery and the campanile (belltower); all three are harmoniously constructed in the same striking white, green and pink stone.

The Piazza del Duomo and the Piazza di San Giovanni, in which the baptistery sits, are edged by expensive shops and cafés, and filled with street sellers flogging overpriced water, guidebooks, caricatures and tacky models of famous Florentine landmarks. The two main streets which head further into the city centre also lead off from here: Via dei Calzaiuoli and Via Roma.

Standing at the end of Via dei Pecori (behind the baptistery) gives a wonderful view and perspective for photographing the buildings; the illustrious facade of the Duomo is visible, sandwiched between the campanile to the right and the baptistery to the left. From here most of the scaffolding from the current work to construct a visitors' centre and a queuing system is hidden.

CATTEDRALE SANTA MARIA DEL FIORE ❶

✉ www.operaduomo.firenze.it
☎ 055-230 2885 🕒 Mon–Wed, Fri 10am–5pm, Thur 10am–3.30pm, Sat 10am–4.45pm, Sun 1.30–4.45pm, 1st Sat of month 10am–3.30pm
💶 charge for crypt and dome, cathedral free

Main attractions

CATTEDRALE SANTA MARIA
  DEL FIORE
BAPTISTERY
MUSEO DELL'OPERA DEL
  DUOMO
LOGGIA AND MUSEO DEL
  BIGALLO

LEFT: the ornately decorated facade of the cathedral and Giotto's graceful belltower.
RIGHT: a horse gets a well-earned break from carting tourists.

Cosimo I de' Medici decided to have the dome painted with a representation of the Last Judgement. *This enormous work was started in 1572 by Giorgio Vasari and Federico Zuccari and would take until 1579 to complete.*

RIGHT: one of Niccolò Barabino's 19th-century mosaics on the facade.

The Duomo (from Domus Dei, House of God) is a symbol of Florentine determination always to have the biggest and the best. It was once the largest in the world, and now ranks fifth in Europe. Being a state church, it was funded by a property tax on all citizens, and is a continuing financial burden on the city and state, requiring constant repair. It took almost 150 years to complete, from 1294 to 1436, though it was not until the late 19th century that the cathedral got its flamboyant neo-Gothic west facade.

The addition makes us appreciate Brunelleschi's genius all the more – his dome draws the eye upwards from the jumble below to admire the clean profile of the cathedral's crowning glory, 107 metres (351ft) above the ground.

As a tribute to the greatest architect and engineer of his day, no other building in Florence has been built as tall as the dome since its completion in 1436, when the cathedral was consecrated by Pope Eugenius IV.

Scarcely less tall, at 85 metres (278ft), is the **campanile** alongside, begun by Giotto shortly after he was appointed chief architect in 1331, and finished off after his death in 1337 by Andrea Pisano and then Talenti. Work was eventually completed in 1359. The climb to the top offers intimate views of the upper levels of the cathedral and the panoramic city views (8.30am–7.30pm; charge).

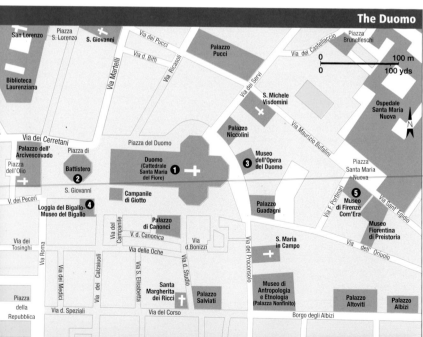

The Duomo

Recommended Restaurants, Bars, Cafés & Gelaterie on page 97

Stark simplicity

By contrast with the polychrome exterior, the cathedral interior is strikingly vast and stark, in keeping with the austere spiritual ideal of Florence during the early Renaissance. At the east end are Luca della Robbia's bronze doors to the new sacristy (1445–69) and the fine wooden inlaid cupboards that line the interior. Here, Lorenzo the Magnificent sought refuge in 1478 after the Pazzi conspirators, in a failed bid to seize power from the Medici, had tried to murder him during High Mass.

The highlight is the fresco on the underside of the dome, high above the altar, which depicts the *Last Judgement*. Painted in 1572–9 by Giorgio Vasari and Federico Zuccari, it was intended as the Florentine equivalent to the scenes Michelangelo painted in the Sistine Chapel in the Vatican, and is a truly spectacular sight.

In the north aisle, there is a famous painting of Florence's native son Dante standing outside the city walls, symbolic of his exile. It was commissioned in 1465 to celebrate the bicentenary of the poet's birth.

Close to it is the famous mural of 1436 depicting the English mercenary Sir John Hawkwood. It is often cited as an example of Florentine miserliness, for Hawkwood's services to the city were commemorated not by a real bronze statue but by Paolo Uccello's *trompe l'œil* mural. Uccello also painted the fresco clock on the west wall that tells the time according to *ora Italica*, which prevailed until the 1700s, whereby sunset marks the last hour of the day.

ABOVE: *Dante and the Divine Comedy*, by Domenico da Michelino, 1465.

BELOW: Brunelleschi's dome, a poetic symbol of Renaissance grace.

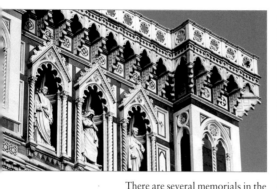

ABOVE: detail from the intricate facade of the Duomo.
BELOW: the Duomo complex is comprised from left to right of the baptistery, the cathedral and the belltower.

tures and the gift shop. The slab covering Brunelleschi's tomb bears an inscription comparing him to Icarus. The analogy, as it happens, is apt – for, like the flight of the mythical hero, the dome seems to defy gravity. A model helps interpret the tangle of remains, which include the fragments of successive churches on the site, dating back to the 8th century, as well as the walls and mosaic floors of late Roman buildings.

Brunelleschi's dome

Ⓒ Mon–Fri 8.30am–7pm, Sat 8.30am–6.20pm, last admission 5pm
ⓒ charge

The master plan for the cathedral had always envisaged a central dome (cupola), but no one knew how to erect one of the required height and span without prodigious expenditure on timber for scaffolding. Brunelleschi travelled to Rome to study the prototype of all domed structures – the Pantheon – after which he came up with his master plan: a solution based on classical Roman technology.

There are several memorials in the cathedral, but only one man – Filippo Brunelleschi – was granted the singular privilege of burial within its walls, belated recognition of his genius in resolving the problem of the dome. His grave slab can be seen by climbing down the steps located at the rear of the Duomo.

These steps lead to a jumble of stonework discovered in 1965, consisting of what remains of **Santa Reparata** (Mon–Fri 10am–5pm, Sat 10am–4.45pm; charge), the church that was demolished to make way for the Duomo, some Roman struc-

Recommended Restaurants, Bars, Cafés & Gelaterie on page 97

Poor Brunelleschi must sometimes have hated the Florentines. Sceptical financiers first made him build a model on the bank of the Arno to prove that his dome would stand up, and then appointed the cautious, interfering and incompetent Ghiberti, Brunelleschi's old rival in the competition for the baptistery doors, to supervise the overall construction.

A great problem-solver, Brunelleschi got rid of Ghiberti by simply walking out of the project, pretending to be ill. Without him, work ground to a halt, and he agreed to return only if he was put in sole charge.

Brunelleschi's aesthetic achievement is known to the whole world through countless travel posters. The dome has come to symbolise the city of Florence, an instantly recognisable landmark, rising above a sea of red terracotta roof tiles and seeming to soar as high as the surrounding mountains. To appreciate his engineering achievement it is necessary to climb up to the dome.

The staircase passes between two shells. The inner one is built of brick laid-herringbone fashion, providing a virtually self-supporting structure that could be built from above without support from below. This then provided a platform for the scaffolding to erect the outer shell.

The dome was completed in 1436, but the lantern, planned by Brunelleschi, was completed by Michelozzi Michelozzo in 1461, 15 years after the original architect's death. The final touch was the external gallery running round the base. This was begun in 1506 by Baccio d'Agnolo, but work stopped in 1515 with only one side finished, when Michelangelo, whose word was law, described it as a "cricket's cage", implying that the design was rustic and childish. Few visitors will agree with his judgement, which has left the base of the dome with no facing to disguise the raw stonework on seven of its sides.

THE BAPTISTERY ❷

✉ Piazza di San Giovanni 🕐 Mon–Sat 12.15–6.30pm, 1st Sat of month 8.30am–1.30pm, Sun 8.30am–2pm 💶 charge

After visiting the Duomo, the next port of call is the battistero (baptistery). In exile, Dante fondly referred to this building as his *"bel San Giovanni"* and described it as "ancient" – a word loaded with meaning. Florentines have always exaggerated its

If you're thinking of climbing up to the dome, it is best to do it early in the day, when you still have some stamina: there are 464 spiralling stairs to negotiate before reaching the top. But once there, the view of the city is fabulous.

LEFT: the facade of the Duomo is punctuated with niches containing delicately carved statues of saints and prophets.

An Engineering Marvel

In practical terms, the dome's octagonal shape is defined by eight marble ribs, matched by 16 ribs on the inside, with the structure strengthened by bands of stone and herringbone-patterned brickwork in the ancient Roman manner. Constructed without scaffolding, the cupola was built by means of a cantilevered system of bricks that could support itself as it ascended. As in imperial Roman buildings, the brickwork was placed in a framework of stone beams. Brunelleschi's other stroke of genius was to devise a system of an inner skeleton and outer dome in order to distribute the weight of the cupola evenly, with thick walls negating the need for further buttressing. The space between the two concentric shells made the structure supple and light, yet highly resistant.

If you look closely at the door frames on the baptistery's east doors, you'll see a self-portrait of the sculptor, Lorenzo Ghiberti: the third head up in the centre of the frame on the left. The similar-looking figure on the right is his father.

antiquity, asserting that it was originally the Temple of Mars, built by the Romans to commemorate victory over the Etruscan city of Fiesole. In the inter-communal rivalry of the Middle Ages, every Tuscan town claimed to be older than its neighbours, and the baptistery symbolised the Florentine pedigree, its link with the golden classical age.

All the evidence suggests that it was, in fact, built in the 6th or 7th century, albeit reusing Roman masonry. From the 12th century it was taken under the wing of the wool importers' guild, which itself claimed to be the first and most ancient trade association in the city.

The guild paid for the beautiful marble cladding of green geometric designs on a white background. This was widely admired and imitated throughout Tuscany, the prototype of many a church exterior, including that of Florence's own cathedral. The splendid interior was reworked between 1270 and 1300, when the dome received its ambitious cycle of mosaics – illustrating the entire biblical story from Creation to the Last Judgement – and the zodiac pavement around the font was laid.

Next, the guild turned to the entrances, determined to outdo the great bronze doors of Pisa cathedral. They did so, but not until several decades later. Andrea Pisano's doors, now in the south portal, were completed in 1336, and the 28 panels show scenes from the life of San Giovanni (St John), the patron saint of the city, as well as allegoric themes of the Virtues. They are outstanding examples of the best Gothic craftsmanship, but it was

RIGHT: a figurehead on the baptistery door.
BELOW: *Abraham and the Sacrifice of Isaac.*
BELOW RIGHT:
Lorenzo Ghiberti's self-portrait (top left) on his celebrated doors.

Recommended Restaurants, Bars, Cafés & Gelaterie on page 97

Ghiberti's north and east doors that really set Europe talking 60 years later.

Work stopped on the baptistery during the intervening period due to a series of disasters – including plague, appalling weather, crop failures and famine, as well as bankruptcies and further political turmoil in Florence.

Gates of Paradise

The year 1401 was a watershed date. In the winter of that year the wool importers' guild announced a competition to select a designer for the remaining doors, with the result that some of the greatest sculptors of the age competed against each other, having been invited to submit sample panels on the theme of the sacrifice of Isaac. Only those designs by Lorenzo Ghiberti and Filippo Brunelleschi have survived, and they are now on display in the Bargello (see page 135).

Ghiberti (c.1378–1455) was judged the winner in 1403 – though the year hardly matters since art historians, a little reluctant to award the title of Father of the Renaissance to any one artist, generally consider 1401, the year of the competition, as the starting point of the Renaissance.

Ghiberti's work demonstrates some of the features of the emerging Renaissance style, but it was Brunelleschi's submission that was truly radical, with the use of deep perspective, realism in the portrayal of the human body and allusions to classical sculpture (see also page 64).

Ghiberti finished the north doors, illustrating the life of Christ, in 1424, having worked on them for more than 20 years. The east doors, hailed by Michelangelo as worthy of being the "Gates of Paradise", took almost all of the rest of his life.

In their original state, with their 10 large panels illustrating the Old Testament, gilded and burnished to a resplendent gold, they must have fully justified Michelangelo's description. The original panels (replaced by resin reproductions) were removed for restoration after being damaged in the 1966 flood and can now be admired in the Museo dell'Opera del Duomo (see page 94).

ABOVE: a mosaic depicting angels from inside the baptistery.
BELOW: the Piazza del Duomo is bustling with tourists at all times.

The main room on the ground floor contains statues from the workshop of Arnolfo di Cambio.

MUSEO DELL'OPERA DEL DUOMO ❸

✉ Piazza del Duomo 9, www.opera duomo.firenze.it Ⓒ Mon–Sat 9am–7.30pm, Sun 9am–1.40pm Ⓒ charge

The cathedral museum occupies the old cathedral workshop, established in the 15th century to maintain the fabric and commission new works to adorn the building. It has carvings from the baptistery, Duomo and campanile, brought indoors for protection from pollution and weathering.

Leading off the courtyard are rooms full of weathered stone figures of saints and prophets from niches around the exterior of the Duomo, including several carved for the original facade. This was never completed, and the Gothic statues were removed in 1587. To bring them back together in this museum, the curators scoured storerooms, private collections and even Florentine gardens.

Penitence and joy

But these are all curiosities; the great art treasures lie upstairs. Dramatically positioned on the half-landing is Michelangelo's powerful *Pietà*. He began work on it around 1550, intending it to cover his own tomb. Having completed only the expressive body of Christ and the head of Nicodemus (a self-portrait), he broke it up, dissatisfied with the faulty marble and his own work. A pupil reconstructed it, finishing the figure of Mary Magdalene after the master's death.

The first room upstairs contains two delightful choir galleries *(cantorie)*, removed from the cathedral in the 17th century. On the left is Luca della Robbia's marble loft (1431–8); on the right, Donatello's work of 1433–9. Both portray boys and girls singing, dancing and playing music in joyful celebration. In contrast, Donatello's statue in wood of Mary Magdalene (*c*.1455), in a room off to the right, is a striking study of the former prostitute in old age, dishevelled, haggard and penitent.

The next room shows early 14th-century bas-reliefs from the base of the campanile, some designed by Giotto, but most carved by Andrea Pisano, who was responsible for the baptistery's south doors. They illustrate the Creation of Adam and Eve and the arts, sciences and industries by which humans have sought to understand and beautify the world since the barring of the Gates of Paradise. Though Gothic in style, they are Renaissance in spirit, a proud celebration of human knowledge and achievement.

A corridor displays pulleys, ropes and brick moulds from the construction of the cathedral's dome, as well as sketches and scale models made at various dates in an attempt to agree on a design for the facade.

Last but not least are the so-called "Gates of Paradise". These are the focal point of the courtyard, now glassed over, where Michelangelo carved *David*. The 10 bronze panels from the baptistery were recently restored and can be seen as a whole for the first time in over 30 years.

Recommended Restaurants, Bars, Cafés & Gelaterie *on page 97*

LOGGIA DEL BIGALLO ❹

On the corner of Via dei Calzaiuoli, the Loggia del Bigallo (1352–8) was built for the charitable Misericordia, which cared for abandoned children left in the loggia, or porch. The organisation still runs an ambulance service and has its headquarters in the square. It later joined forces with the Bigallo, another religious body.

Loggias, typical features of a piazza, were originally built to provide shelter from the sun or the rain, but many now harbour street markets. Although not a market itself, the Loggia del Bigallo – with some fine marble decor typical of the International Gothic style of the 14th century – houses a museum containing the various works of art accumulated over the years by both organisations associated with it.

The Museo del Bigallo

✉ Piazza di San Giovanni 1 📞 055-271 801 🕒 Thur–Mon 10am–2pm, 3–7pm 💶 charge

This museum is almost inconspicuous among the monumental grandeur of

In the 14th century, unwanted babies used to be left on the porch of the Loggia del Bigallo; if they were not claimed within three days, they would be sent to foster homes.

the other buildings in the square, but contains some exceptional artworks. Most famous of these is Bernardo Daddi's fresco of the *Madonna della Misericordia*, in which the earliest-known view of Florence is found (1342). Also worth viewing is Daddi's triptych with the *Madonna and Child and Fourteen Saints*, as well as other works by Domenico Ghirlandaio, Iacopo del Sellaio, Nardo di Cione and sculptor Alberto Arnoldi.

LEFT: cycling among the tourists. **BELOW:** detail from *The Annunciation*, depicting the angel Gabriel, from a stained-glass window by Fra Paolo di Mariotto da Gambassi (Museo dell'-Opera del Duomo).

The Museo di Firenze Com'Era is housed in a former convent with a graceful loggia surrounding three sides of a grassy courtyard.

BELOW:
spoilt for choice.

AROUND THE DUOMO

Via dell'Oriuolo leads off Piazza del Duomo, and down on the left the Via Folco Portinari gives a glimpse of the **Ospedale Santa Maria Nuova**, still one of the city's main hospitals. It was founded in 1286 by Folco Portinari, father of Beatrice, the subject of Dante's *Divine Comedy*. The portico (1612) is by Buontalenti.

Museo di Firenze Com'Era ⑤

✉ Via dell'Oriuolo 24 ☎ 055-261 6545 🕒 Apr–Oct Mon–Wed 9am– 2pm, Sat 9am–6.30pm, Nov–Mar Mon–Tue 9am–2pm, Sat 9am– 6.30pm 💲 charge

Further up the road, the museum of "Florence as It Was" contains maps and topographical paintings showing how little Florence has changed since the first view of the city was sketched in 1470. Most interesting is the *Pianta della Catena*: a huge plan of Renaissance Florence in tempera, which is a 19th-century copy of an original engraving. Anyone will enjoy spotting the many buildings that still exist.

It might so easily have been otherwise. Another room displays the 19th-century drawings of the city architect, Giuseppe Poggi, who planned to sweep away the "slums" of Florence and replace them with the large avenues then in vogue. The Piazza della Repubblica was built and the 14th-century walls demolished before international opposition halted the scheme. Most of Poggi's plans, which included a suspension bridge over the Arno, ended up as museum curiosities.

Most endearing of the city views are the lunettes illustrating the villas and gardens of the Medici, by the Flemish artist Giusto Utens (1599).

Museo Fiorentino di Preistoria

✉ Via Sant'Egidio 21, www.museo fiorentinopreistoria.it ☎ 055-295 159 🕒 Mon 2–5pm, Wed, Fri and Sat 9.30am–12.30pm, Tue and Thur 9.30am–4.30pm 💲 charge

North of Via dell' Oriuolo, in the library complex in Via Sant'Egidio, this museum narrates the earliest evidence of human settlement and activity in the Arno valley. ❑

BEST RESTAURANTS, BARS, CAFÉS AND *GELATERIE*

Restaurants

Prices for three-course
dinner per person with
a glass of wine:
€ = under €25
€€ = €25–40
€€€ = €40–60
€€€€ = more than €60

Alle Murate
Via del Proconsolo 16r
C 055-240 618 **D** D only;
closed Mon. **€€€€**
[p313, D2]
Now located in the
Palace of Judges and
Notaries, this high-class
restaurant also boasts
high-class atmosphere.
Part of the Caffè Italiano
group, this is one of
the new generation of
Florentine restaurants
dishing up nouvelle cuis-
ine. It offers a creative

twist on Tuscan food –
there is lots of fish and
tender Chianina steak.

Angels
Via del Proconsolo 29/31
C 055-239 8762 **D** D only;
L in summer. **€€€** [p313, D2]
Chic bar and restaurant
adjoined to the Grand
Hotel Cavour which
offers good-quality food
in an elegant ambience.
The pasta-based *aperi-
tivo* is filling, whilst the
restaurant serves up tra-
ditional Tuscan fare.

Coquinarius
Via delle Oche 15r **C** 055-
230 2153 **D** Closed D Sun.
€€ [p313, D2]
This tiny yet fashionable
restaurant is always full,
and you can eat here at

almost any time of day.
Try the lunch salads,
the carpaccios, platters
of cheese and cured
meats or the rightfully
famous pear and pecorino
ravioli. Save some space
for the exquisite home-
made desserts.

Nuvoli
Piazza dell'Olio 15
C 055-239 6616 **D** Mon–
Sat 8am–8pm. **€** [p312, C1]

Located just behind
the baptistery, this tiny
eatery serves up
Florentine specialities
daily. Create a sandwich
and sip a glass of wine
on the stools out front,
or head downstairs,
where you'll find rustic
seating and friendly
Tuscan waiters. A much-
needed inexpensive
option in an otherwise
overpriced area.

Bars, Cafés and Gelaterie

Oil Shoppe
Via Sant'Egidio 22r.
Tel: 055-200 1092.
Open Mon–Fri 11am–
6pm. [p313, E2]
Order a glass of wine
and pick your *panino*
bread, filling and sauce
from the delicatessen –
one good choice is the
pecorino garnished with
rocket and walnut
sauce. Get there early
in order to avoid the
long queues.

Grom
Via del Campanile 2.
Tel: 055-216 158.
Open daily. [p313, C2]
This chain of artisan
gelaterie started in
Turin and have quickly
become a favourite in
Florence. They use only
fresh and in-season
organic fruit, no colour-
ings. Mineral water is
used as a base for
sorbets, and high-
quality whole milk and

organic eggs for the
creams. Check out the
monthly flavours and
suggested pairings.
Also worth trying: the
almond granita.

Scudieri
Piazza San Giovanni
19r. Tel: 055-210 733.
Open B & L.
[p312, C1]
A fancy grand café by
the baptistery, perfect
for breakfast or a snack,
especially a chocolate-
based one.

Le Parigine
Via dei Servi, 41r.
Tel: 055-239 8470.
Open daily 11am–
11pm. [p313, D1]
Close to the Duomo,
this is a newly opened
retro-styled artisan
gelateria. A good place
to sit inside or out and
enjoy the range of
flavours, which change
according to the season.

Recommended Restaurants & Cafés on page 113

PIAZZA DELLA SIGNORIA

The dramas that have unfolded over the centuries in the city's main square, the Piazza della Signoria, would rival those of the finest theatre

I f the Duomo complex is the historic religious heart of Florence, then Piazza della Signoria is at its political core, with the Palazzo Vecchio as its civic showpiece.

PIAZZA DELLA SIGNORIA ❶

The main, L-shaped square in Florence evokes strong reactions. Florentines argue furiously about its future, and citizens of neighbouring towns are contemptuous of its lack of grace and architectural unity compared with, say, Siena's harmonious Campo. The buildings, now mainly occupied by banks and insurance companies, seem to belong to some cold northern climate rather than the city that gave birth to the colour and vitality of the Renaissance. However, the piazza – in addition to being virtually an alfresco museum of sculpture – makes an atmospheric setting for the cafés as well as the open-air ballet and concerts in the summer.

The piazza has suffered from the fact that no sooner had the Palazzo Vecchio and the nearby Uffizi gallery emerged from the scaffolding that had enshrouded them for a decade or more during an extensive restoration programme than a terrorist bomb caused major structural damage in May 1993. The majority of the art has now been restored and is back on display.

Ancient strife

Of course, the controversy surrounding the square's image is not entirely new; the piazza is littered with the symbols of competing ideologies. A plaque near the Neptune Fountain marks the spot where Savonarola was burnt at the stake as a heretic in 1498, whilst statues around the square are loaded with political allusions.

Main attractions
LOGGIA DEI LANZI
PALAZZO VECCHIO
THE UFFIZI
SANTO STEFANO AL PONTE
PONTE VECCHIO
MUSEO GALILEO
PIAZZA MENTANA
MUSEO HORNE

LEFT: looking through the Palazzo degli Uffizi to the Palazzo Vecchio. **RIGHT:** catching up with the news near the Piazza della Signoria.

RIGHT: Giambologna's
*Rape of the Sabine
Women* in the Loggia
dei Lanzi.

Politicians have addressed the un-
suspecting public from the front of
the Palazzo Vecchio since the 14th
century – originally from the raised
platform, the *ringheria* (which gave
rise to the term "to harangue"), until
it was demolished in 1812.

Piazza della Signoria was even born
out of strife. The land was owned by
the Uberti, supporters of the Ghibelline (Imperial) faction, losers to
the Guelf (Papal) Party in the struggles that tore Florence apart in the
13th century. The property of the
exiled Uberti was first left to crumble
as a sign of the family's defeat, but
then chosen as the site of a new
palace to house the city government.

A civic showpiece

The Palazzo Vecchio dominates the
square. Built on the site of the old
Roman theatre, its foundation stone
was laid in 1299 and the palace was
finished by 1315; later the great bell
(removed in 1530) was hung in the

tower to ring out danger warnings
and summon general assemblies.

The name of the building has
changed almost as often as power in
the city has changed hands. From the
Palazzo del Popolo – the People's
Palace – it became the Palazzo della
Signoria when the *signori*, the heads
of the leading families, took over the

reins of government. It continued so from 1434, the start of Cosimo de' Medici's unofficial leadership of the city, until the death of his grandson, Lorenzo the Magnificent, in 1492. The years 1494–1537 saw attempts, inspired by the teaching of Savonarola, to establish a republic; the Medici were expelled from the city, and an inscription was raised above the palace entrance (where it still remains) declaring Christ to be the only king of Florence.

In 1537, Cosimo I seized control of the city and three years later moved into the palace, now the Palazzo Ducale. In 1550, the Pitti Palace became the duke's new official residence, and from that time the building has been known as the Palazzo Vecchio, the Old Palace. It is now the town hall, so this is where the citizens of Florence come to arrange birth and death certificates, pay their fines and get married. It is not unusual to get caught up in a rice-throwing wedding party while viewing the inner courtyards.

A gallery of statues

Before you enter the Palazzo Vecchio, you should take the time to look at the statues outside. The graceful little three-arched **Loggia dei Lanzi** ❷, near the palace on the south side of the square, is named after Cosimo I's personal bodyguards, the lancers, whose barracks were located nearby. But it was constructed much earlier – completed in 1382 – to shelter dignitaries from the weather during public ceremonies.

Cosimo considered extending the tall, round arches all around the square, on Michelangelo's advice, to give the piazza a degree of architectural harmony, but the plan was abandoned because it was too costly. Instead, the loggia came to serve as an outdoor sculpture gallery, housing antique statues as well as new works.

The first statue was erected not as an aesthetically motivated decision but as an act of political defiance. Donatello's *Judith and Holofernes* was cast between 1456 and 1460 as a fountain for the courtyard of the Medici Palace. It was brought into the square by the citizens of the newly declared republic of Florence after the expulsion of the Medici in 1494. The symbolism was clear for everyone to read: the virtuous Judith executing the drunken tyrant Holofernes stood for the triumph of liberty over despotism. (The statue was transferred to the Sala dei Gigli inside the Palazzo Vecchio to protect it from the elements and pollution.)

In 1554, another bronze statue depicting a decapitation was erected in the loggia. Cellini's *Perseus* was commissioned by Cosimo I to celebrate his return to power and carried an implied threat – just as Perseus used the head of Medusa to turn his

Benvenuto Cellini's Perseus *in the Loggia dei Lanzi.*

BELOW: the Palazzo Vecchio towers above the piazza.

ABOVE: the ornate
frontispiece is adorned
with gold fleur-de-lys,
emblems of Florence.
BELOW: the copy
of *David* outside the
Palazzo Vecchio.

enemies to stone, so opponents could expect exile, or even worse.

Florentines once believed that images had the magical power to bring good or ill upon the city, and so it was not long before the wisdom of displaying *Judith and Holofernes* began to be questioned. It symbolised death and the defeat of a man by a woman, and so was moved to a less prominent site. However, the statues that remain are equally impressive, in particular Giambologna's *Rape*

of the Sabine Women and Cellini's bronze statue *(see page 101)*.

Enter David

The appearance of Michelangelo's ***David*** in its position outside the Palazzo Vecchio was a popular decision that transformed the square and gave it a new focal point. Even now, the pollution-streaked copy (the original stands in the Accademia, *see page 171*) has an arresting force and exudes ambiguity. David is both muscular and effeminate, between adolescence and maturity, relaxed but ready to fight, a glorious celebration of the naked human body, yet apparently distorted, with overlarge head and limbs.

Moreover, the political symbolism was open to numerous interpretations. Those who wished could see David's bravery before the giant Goliath as a metaphor for Florence, prepared to defend her liberty against all who threatened it; or they could read it more specifically and choose the Medici, the Pope, the Holy Roman Emperor, Siena or Pisa as the particular enemy.

Neptune Fountain

After the great success of David, more works were commissioned on the same monumental scale, but all were greeted with varying degrees of ridicule. Hercules was chosen as a subject because of the legend that the city of Florence was built on swamps drained by the mythical hero. But when the carving by Baccio Bandinelli (1493–1560) was unveiled in 1534, Benvenuto Cellini compared the exaggerated musculature to "an old sack full of melons".

Bartolomeo Ammannati's Neptune Fountain, an allegory of Cosimo I's scheme to make Florence a great naval power, was carved in 1563–75 and immediately nicknamed Il Biancone (or Big White One), with deliberately lewd connotations. Neptune, whose face resembles that of Cosimo, looks as uncomfortable as the artist must have felt on hearing his work dismissed in a popular street cry as a waste of a good piece of marble.

The pedestal in the middle is decorated with the mythical chained figures of Scylla and Charybdis.The bronze satyrs and nymphs splashing at Neptune's feet are livelier work, in a style typical of the Mannerist art of the period, with elongated necks and limbs. They are also decidedly salacious, and the artist, in a fit of piety

One famous resident of the Palazzo della Signoria – as the Palazzo Vecchio was once known – was Dante, who lived there for two months as a representative of the people.

later in life, condemned his own work as an incitement to licentious thoughts and deeds.

Near the fountain, standing on its own to the north of the Palazzo Vecchio, is Giambologna's equestrian statue of Cosimo I, commissioned by his son Ferdinando and unveiled in 1594. It is imposing but of indifferent artistic quality – the same could be said of Florence under Cosimo's reign, for though he left it powerful,

ABOVE LEFT: armless statues of Adam and Eve flank the entrance of the Palazzo Vecchio.
BELOW LEFT: Bartolomeo Ammannati's Mannerist Neptune Fountain.

The Politics of the Piazza

One of the most contentious recent debates in Florence centred on work in the Piazza della Signoria. Such is the exaggerated respect for Old Florence that the city took 13 years to decide that the piazza needed to be resurfaced. However, Francesco Nicosia, the archaeological supervisor for Tuscany, stepped in and argued that the repaving would cover the Roman baths and ancient buildings that lay beneath the square. He launched a campaign to excavate the piazza and create an underground museum. But the city government did not want another museum, especially one with entrances, exits, air ducts and pavement skylights that would disrupt the piazza. A compromise was reached: the archaeologists could dig, and document everything, but then they would have to cover it back up so the repaving could proceed. Nicosia agreed, but then found a whole town, including a Roman wool-dyeing plant, under the square. He vowed to continue his battle for a museum; city leaders were unmoved. In the end, the square has been repaved – with ugly modern paving stones – much to the relief of all who make a living from its pavement cafés, busking and carriage rides.

An early caricature? Look for this profile of a man to the right of Palazzo Vecchio's main entrance, just behind the statue of Hercules – it is attributed to Michelangelo.

art went into a serious decline. And nowhere is the decline that characterised Cosimo I's rule more evident than in the interior of the massive Palazzo Vecchio.

Palazzo Vecchio ❸

✉ Piazza della Signoria ☎ 055-276 8224 🕒 Fri–Wed 9am–7pm, Thur 9am–2pm 🅖 charge, combined ticket with Capella Brancacci available

The *palazzo* was completely remodelled when Cosimo moved into it in 1540, having quashed republicanism in Florence and established himself as hereditary duke. It is not all bad, of course; the Cortile (courtyard), designed by Michelozzo Michelozzi in 1453 as the main entrance, is delightful. The little fountain in the centre was designed by Vasari around 1555 – copying the putto and dolphin made for the Medici villa at Careggi by Verrocchio in 1470.

The stucco and frescos are also Vasari's work. On the walls are views of Austrian cities, painted to make Joanna of Austria feel at home when she married Francesco de' Medici

(Cosimo's son) in 1565. The ceiling is covered in "grotesque" figures – that is, in imitation of the ancient Roman paintings in the grotto of Nero's garden – a colourful tapestry of sphinxes, flowers, birds and playful satyrs.

This courtyard leads through to the main ticket office, where you might like to sign up for one of the "Secret Routes of the Palace" tours (Percorsi Segreti; daily at various times), which take in secret passages

RIGHT: Vasari's Putto Fountain in the *palazzo*'s courtyard.
BELOW: the inner courtyard.

and odd corners made for the rulers, such as the Treasury of Cosimo I and the staircase of the duke of Athens. These are usually off limits and only accessible by tour, along with the attic of the Salone dei Cinquecento and the study of Francesco I.

The state chambers start on the first floor with the Salone dei Cinquecento (Room of the Five Hundred). This was designed in 1495 by Cronaca for meetings of the ruling assembly – the Consiglio Maggiore – of the penultimate republic. It was the largest room of its time. The vast space, despite appalling acoustics, is now used occasionally as a concert hall.

Leonardo da Vinci and Michelangelo were both commissioned to paint the walls and ceilings of the Salone dei Cinquecento, but neither got much further than experimental sketches. It was left to Giorgio Vasari (court architect from 1555 until his death in 1574) to undertake the work, executed with great speed between 1563 and 1565. Nominally the paintings celebrate the foundation of Florence and the recent victories over its rivals, Pisa and Siena. The ubiquitous presence of Cosimo I in all the scenes, however, makes it simply a vast exercise in ducal propaganda.

It is not unusual for visitors to feel uneasy and wonder why Vasari stooped to such overt flattery. Michelangelo's *Victory* is equally disturbing. Brutally realistic, it depicts an old man forced to the ground by the superior strength of a muscular youth. It was carved for the tomb of Julius II in Rome, but Michelangelo's heirs presented it to Cosimo I to commemorate the 1559 victory over Siena. The artist intended it to represent the triumph of reason over ignorance, but in this context it seems part of a gross celebration of war. Even so, artists have frequently sought to imitate Michelangelo's twisted, tortured figures, and it was one of the works most admired by the later 16th-century Mannerists.

Light relief is provided by the *Hercules and Diomedes* of Vincenzo de' Rossi, a no-holds-barred tussle in which the inverted Diomedes takes revenge by squeezing Hercules' genitals in an agonising grip.

Off the main hall is the study, the Studiolo, of the reclusive Francesco I, built between 1570 and 1575. The beautiful cupboards were used to store his treasures and the equipment for his experiments in alchemy. His parents, Cosimo I and Eleonora di Toledo, are depicted on the wall frescos.

ABOVE: frieze of coats of arms on the *palazzo*'s facade. **BELOW:** a lion standing guard outside the Loggia dei Lanzi.

A tortoise with a sail on its shell, Cosimo I de' Medici's "seal", is reproduced more than 6,000 times in the Palazzo Vecchio. The museum organises great children's events, including a hunt for sail-bearing tortoises hidden in pictures and frescos throughout the palace.

RIGHT: Titian's *Flora* in the Uffizi. **BELOW:** busy Florentine.

Next in sequence comes the suite of rooms known as the Quartiere di Leone X, decorated in 1556–62 by Vasari and named after Giovanni de' Medici, son of Lorenzo the Magnificent, who was created a cardinal at the age of 13 and eventually became Pope Leo X.

Second floor

Above is the Quartiere degli Elementi, with allegories of the elements, including a watery scene reminiscent of the work of Botticelli, once again by Vasari. The corner room, the Terrazza di Saturno, provides fine views east to Santa Croce and south to San Miniato, while in another small room is Verrocchio's *Boy with Dolphin* taken from the courtyard.

The Quartiere di Eleonora di Toledo, the private rooms of the beautiful wife of Cosimo I, include the chapel. A masterpiece of Florentine Mannerism, it is adorned with stunning frescos by Bronzino (1540–5), a rare opportunity to study fresco work at close quarters. The sheer range and brilliance of the colour is striking – hues rarely seen in modern painting:

vivid pinks, luminescent blues and almost phosphorescent green.

Eleonora's bedroom is decorated with a frieze based on her initials, and has a lovely marble washbasin; another is painted with domestic scenes – spinning, weaving and the tasks that correspond to the classical idea of virtuous motherhood – the last with Florentine street scenes and festivities.

A corridor containing the serene death mask of Dante leads to the two most sumptuous rooms of the palace, the Sala d'Udienza and the Sala dei Gigli. Both have gilded and coffered ceilings, decorated with every conceivable form of ornament. The 16th-century intarsia doors between the two depict the poets Dante and Petrarch.

The Sala dei Gigli is named after the so-called lilies (irises, in reality) that cover the walls and are used as a symbol of the city. The frescos are by Ghirlandaio and the ceiling by the Maiano brothers. Donatello's original *Judith and Holofernes* is the highlight here, with panels explaining how the bronze was cast and, more recently, restored.

The Cancelleria, a small chamber off to the side (entered through the remains of a 13th-century window), was built in 1511 as an office for Niccolò Machiavelli during his term as government secretary. A portrait by

Santi di Tito depicts the youthful, smiling author of *The Prince*, looking nothing like the demonic figure he was branded when this study of politics and pragmatism was published.

Just off the Sala dei Gigli is another small room, the Sala del Mappamondo (more commonly known as La Guardaroba – the wardrobe), containing a large 16th-century globe showing the extent of the then known world. The room is lined with wooden cupboards adorned with a remarkable series of maps; the 53 panels were painted in 1563 by Ignazio Danti and in 1581 by Stefano Buonsignori.

Also inside the Palazzo Vecchio is the **Museo dei Ragazzi** (Children's Museum), which puts on a host of well-organised activities and events for children. There's a Renaissance-themed playroom for three- to seven-year-olds, and actor-led workshops and tours for older children.

THE UFFIZI ④

✉ Loggiato degli Uffizi 6, www.polo museale.firenze.it 📞 055-238 8651; for bookings 055-294 883 🕒 Tue–Sun 8.15am–6.50pm 💶 charge

The Piazza degli Uffizi sits in the centre of the U-shaped building which houses the gallery, lined with statues of Italian personalities such as Dante and occupied by artists and entertainers. A reading of Giorgio Vasari's *Lives of the Artists* (1550), or Browning's poems based on them, is a good preparation for an encounter with the greatest works of the Renaissance, housed in the Galleria degli Uffizi *(see pages 114–19)*. Vasari's anecdotes teach us not to be too adulatory, and to realise that many of the great artists were ordinary men, lustful, greedy and always willing to pander to the whims of their patrons.

When Vasari designed the Uffizi, he incorporated a continuous corridor that runs from the Palazzo Vecchio, via the Uffizi and the Ponte Vecchio, all the way to the Palazzo Pitti on the opposite bank of the

In 1580, the open loggia of the Uffizi administrative building was turned into rooms for the art collections of the Medici – effectively a galleria enclosed in glass. Today's expression "art gallery" is derived from it.

BELOW LEFT: detail from Botticelli's *Primavera,* one of the highlights of the Uffizi. **BELOW:** the Uffizi and Vasari Corridor seen from the Ponte Vecchio.

Arno. Along this elevated walkway, known as the Corridoio Vasariano, symbolic of their pre-eminent status, Cosimo I and his heirs could walk between their palace and the seat of government without being soiled by contact with people they ruled.

In 1737, Anna Maria Lodovica, the last of the Medici, bequeathed the entire collection of the museum and the corridor to the people of Florence.

The gallery is undergoing major restructuring to double the exhibition space and enable several hundred masterpieces, normally in store rooms, to see the light of day. Recent additions include a new wing, bookshop, multimedia information centre, top-floor café with terrace and a modern and highly controversial new gallery exit *(see page 114)*.

Leaving the Uffizi, walk back to the river and turn right towards the Ponte Vecchio. Another right turn brings you into Via Por Santa Maria. Modern buildings here indicate that the original medieval buildings were deliberately demolished in World War II to block the approaches to the bridge and hold up the advancing Allies. The first turning right off Via Por Santa Maria leads to **Santo Stefano al Ponte** ❺ (Piazza Santo Stefano; tel: 055-271 0732; Fri 4–7pm; free), founded in around AD 969 and with a fine Romanesque facade of 1233. Now used as a concert hall, it also has a small museum.

The narrow lanes east of this secluded piazza lead to buildings used as workshops for the goldsmiths and jewellers whose creations are sold in the quaint kiosks lining the historic Ponte Vecchio.

THE PONTE VECCHIO ❻

The oldest bridge of Florence, the Ponte Vecchio is as much a symbol of the city as the Duomo or Palazzo Vecchio. It dates, in its present form, from 1345, replacing an earlier wooden structure that was swept away in a flood.

ABOVE: admiring the statues lining the Uffizi's sculpture gallery.
BELOW: the museum's South Corridor, at dusk.

Recommended Restaurants & Cafés on page 113

Notably, it was the only bridge in the city to be spared being bombed during World War II; legend has it that this was because of Hitler's fond memories of it.

Workshops have always flanked the central carriageway, and in 1565 the Vasari Corridor, linking the Palazzo Pitti and the Palazzo Vecchio, was built high above the pavement along the eastern side.

In 1593, Ferdinando I, annoyed at the noisy and noxious trades that

were carried on beneath his feet as he travelled the length of the corridor, ordered the butchers, tanners and blacksmiths to be evicted. Indeed, they conveniently used to throw their waste into the river. The workshops were rebuilt and let to goldsmiths, and this traditional use has continued ever since, though no craftsmen work in the cramped but quaint premises any more. Ferdinando took the opportuinty to double the rent, and so the goldsmiths built extensions overhanging the river at the back of their shops, supported by timber brackets.

Today, it is not just the shop-owners on the Ponte Vecchio who earn their livelihood from the million-plus visitors that are drawn to the bridge every year. Hawkers, buskers and portrait painters, artists and souvenir vendors all contribute to the festive atmosphere that prevails on the bridge, especially after dark. There is no better place for people-watching or taking in the attractive river views.

Follow the river east along the Lungarno, taking in the view of the

Several of Florence's major artists were skilled in the art of the goldsmith, notably Benvenuto Cellini (1500–71), whose bust now sits proudly in the middle of the Ponte Vecchio.

LEFT: gold necklace for sale on the Ponte Vecchio. **BELOW:** the picturesque bridge.

opposite bank, to the Museo Galileo in Piazza de' Giudici.

MUSEO GALILEO ❼

✉ Piazza de' Giudici 1, www.imss.firenze.it
☎ 055-265 311
🕐 Mon, Wed–Sat 9.30am–6pm, Tue and Sat 9.30am–1pm, Sun 10am–6pm ⓒ charge

ABOVE RIGHT: alchemist's laboratory, Museo Galileo.
BELOW: old and modern telescopes inside Museo Galileo.

Attached to the Institute of the History of Science, this museum is housed in Palazzo Castellani, where recent restorations found evidence of an ancient castle. It is one of the most absorbing museums in Florence and a very welcome change after an over-indulgence in the arts. The exhibits show that Renaissance Florence was pre-eminent in Europe as a centre of scientific research as well as of painting and sculpture – indeed, the humanistic concept of the "universal man" did not recognise any dichotomy between the two.

Reaching for the stars

A great deal of encouragement was given to scientific research by Cosimo II, who, it is said, saw the similarity of his own name to the cosmos as auspicious, and so he announced a grand scheme to master the universe through knowledge. The best mathematicians, astronomers and cartographers were hired from all over Europe and the Middle East, and their beautifully engraved astrolabes and armillary spheres, showing the motion of the heavenly bodies, are well displayed in this museum.

Ironically, though, the most brilliant scientist of his age, and the one whose discoveries and methodology laid the foundations for modern science, suffered greatly as a consequence. Galileo was popular enough when he discovered the first four moons of Jupiter and named them after members of the Medici family. He was appointed court mathematician, and his experiments in mechanics and the laws of motion must have given great pleasure to the Medici court, even if their true significance might not have been understood. Beautiful mahogany-and-brass reconstructions of these experiments, like giant executive toys, are displayed in the museum and demonstrated from time to time by the attendants.

But Galileo fell foul of the authorities when, from his own observations, he supported the Copernican view that the sun, and not the earth, was at the centre of the cosmos. Refusing to retract a view that ran counter to the teachings of the Church, he was tried before the Inquisition in 1633, excommunicated and made a virtual prisoner in his own home until his death in 1642.

The year 2009 marked the 400th anniversary of Galileo's telescope, with astronomy-themed exhibitions and events held in Florence and Tuscany throughout the year. The former Museo di Storia della Scienza underwent a radical transformation and in 2010 reopened under the name of the Museo Galileo. The first floor showcases the outstanding scientific collection of the Medicis, with sections devoted to Galileo's only surviving instruments. Also on show are two recently rediscovered fingers of the famous scientist, which were removed from his body in 1737, when his remains where exhumed from a temporary grave to their final resting place in Florence's Santa Croce. The fingers, which were sold at auction in 2009 and authenticated

by the museum, joined a third digit which was already on display. The museum has moved into the modern age with state-of-the-art technology, information-system resources, portable audiovisual devices and a large multimedia area.

Equally intriguing are the rooms devoted to maps and globes, which demonstrate how rapidly the discoveries of the 15th and 16th centuries were revolutionising old ideas about the shape of the world.

The early 16th-century map by Fra Mauro still defines the world in religious and mythological terms, with Jerusalem at the centre and the margins inhabited by menacing monsters. Only 50 years later, in 1554, Lopo Homem was producing a recognisably accurate map of the world, which had to be extended, even as it was being drawn, to accommodate the newly surveyed west coast of the Americas and discoveries in the Pacific, such as New Guinea.

FURTHER EAST ALONG THE ARNO

From the Museo Galileo, diagonally opposite is Via dei Saponai, which

WHERE

Lungarno translates from Italian as "along the Arno". On both sides of the river in Florence, the streets are known as Lungarno This or Lungarno That.

BELOW:
tranquil balcony.

leads to **Piazza Mentana** ❽, the site of the Roman port. Via della Mosca follows the curve of this ancient harbour. At the point where it joins the Via dei Neri, cross to the junction with Via San Remigio to the building on the left that has two plaques high up on the wall. One records the level of the flood reached in 1333, and 0.5 metres (2ft) above it is the 1966 mark.

Via dei Neri leads to Via dei Benci and the Museo Horne.

Museo Horne ❾

✉ Via dei Benci 6, www.museohorne.it
☎ 055-244 661   🕒 Mon–Sat 9am–1pm   💲 charge

The best of the art collection assembled by the English art historian Herbert Percy Horne (1864–1916) is now in the Uffizi, and, although there are no great treasures here, the remaining art includes Benozzo Gozzoli's last work, *The Deposition*, Giotto's golden-backed *St Stephen*, as well as works by Luca Signorelli and others. On the second floor is a diptych thought to be by Barna di Siena; also on display is a book containing 18th-century sketches by Tiepolo.

Latterly Horne's home, the building was first owned by the Alberti family, who then passed it on to the Corsi family in the 15th century. The Corsi were involved in the city's thriving cloth trade; washing and dyeing of fabrics took place underground, the tradings on the ground floor and family life on the upper floors. The *palazzino* has a delightful courtyard, and on view within are all kinds of memorabilia – the remnants of a distinguished life. The kitchen, built on the top floor to stop cooking fumes passing through the whole house, retains its original form – a simple range, chimney and sink – and is used to display Horne's collection of ancient pots and utensils.

Walking further east leads to the impressive-looking **Biblioteca Nazionale** (National Library) in Piazza dei Cavalleggeri, and immediately south, the Ponte alle Grazie is a modern bridge which was built to replace the Ponte Rubiconte, first built in 1237 and destroyed in 1944. Upstream, to the east, the modern stone embankment of the Arno gives way to natural grassy banks, trees and reeds.   ❑

ABOVE: painting of a man lying on grass (15th-century Florentine School), Museo Horne.
BELOW: expressive fountain.

BEST RESTAURANTS AND CAFÉS

Restaurants

Prices for three-course dinner per person with a glass of wine:
€ = under €25
€€ = €25–40
€€€ = €40–60
€€€€ = more than €60

Antico Fattore
Via Lambertesca 1/3r
☎ 055-288 975 ☺ Closed Sun. €€ [p313, C3]
This traditional trattoria offers good meat and game dishes as well as the standard Tuscan and Florentine fare like *trippa* (tripe) and *ribollita* (vegetable and bread soup).

Buca dell'Orafo
Via de' Girolami 28r
☎ 055-213 619 ☺ L & D Tue–Sat. €€ [p312, C3]

A crowded little location which originated as a locals' hang-out but, to their chagrin, is now over-run with tourists. However, the simple peasant food – based on pasta and pulses – is filling and of good quality.

Frescobaldi
Via de' Magazzini 2/4r
☎ 055-284 724 ☺ L & D; closed all day Sun and Mon L. €€–€€€ [p313, D3]
Just off Piazza delle Signoria, this inviting restaurant and wine bar makes flavoursome Tuscan dishes to complement its huge range of local wines. Try the roast pig with a glass of Chianti from the cantina. Outside seating in the summer months.

Cafés

Caffè Italiano
Via della Condotta 56r.
Tel: 055-289 020.
Open Mon–Sat 8am–8pm, Sun 11am–8pm. [p313, C3]
An old-fashioned café decked out in wood offering a range of food and drink. Relax with a newspaper over a coffee or one of their speciality hot chocolates.

Gustavino
Via della Condotta 37r
☎ 055-239 9806 ☺ D only; closed Mon. €€€ [p313, C3]
This is a glossy modern restaurant whose open kitchen allows you to see your meal being prepared. The food is creative without being too elaborate or over-fussy, and is served beautifully on large white plates. Look out for the speciality wine-and-food evenings they run.

Oliviero
Via delle Terme 51r ☎ 055-240 618 ☺ D only; closed Sun. €€€ [p312, B3]
Historical restaurant which markets itself as being part of the *dolce vita fiorentina* (Florentine good life). The menu changes every couple of months, and everything is prepared

Rivoire
Piazza della Signoria 4r.
Tel: 055-214 412.
Closed Mon. [p313, C3]
Grand café located on the corner of the piazza famed for its chocolate products. Treat yourself to a coffee or *gelato* in the day or a cocktail in the early evening. Outside tables offer great views on the piazza.

freshly in house – from the pasta to the desserts.

Trattoria del Benvenuto
Via della Mosca 15r ☎ 055-214 833 ☺ Closed Wed and Sun. €–€€ [p313, D4]
This offers reasonably priced food in the centre. It is a basic trattoria, but still popular with locals and tourists alike for its welcoming atmosphere.

Vini e Vecchi Sapori
Via dei Magazzini 3r
☎ 055-293 045 ☺ L & D; closed all day Mon and Sun D. €–€€ [p313, D3]
Tiny, atmospheric trattoria off Piazza della Signoria, this remains a good bet for Tuscan food. The atmosphere manages to retain something of the Florentine, despite the number of tourists who flock to the place.

LEFT: chef showing off her skills at Gustavino.

THE UFFIZI

Welcome to the greatest collection of Renaissance art in the world

Florence's most famous gallery is in a U-shaped building whose former use as administrative buildings gave it its name, "The Offices". It now holds the highest concentration of Renaissance art in the world, including works by Botticelli, Leonardo, Michelangelo and Raphael. The majority of the collection originates from the Medici family, from the latter half of the 16th century.

The Nuovi Uffizi project (www.nuoviuffizi.it) to double the size of the gallery will continue for several years, so expect disruptions, including closures of certain rooms and paintings in places you don't expect them. The long queues make it worthwhile buying tickets in advance (tel: 055-294 883; costs €4) and in season this is almost essential, preferably a couple of months in advance. The most notable changes so far are the new rooms, restored after the 1993 bomb explosion, with works by Caravaggio and Caravaggesque painters, and the modern new exit at the back of the gallery conceived by the Japanese architect Arata Isozaki in 1998 and still incomplete. At the rear of the Uffizi and built in stone, steel and polycarbonate, this huge structure, likened by one art critic to "a seven-storey bed frame" has met with strong opposition, and the project is currently on ice.

ABOVE: Room 15 has Leonardo da Vinci's early paintings – including the *Annunciation* (1475) and the unfinished *Adoration of the Magi* (1482) – and also works by Perugino and Signorelli.

FAR RIGHT: Room 8 holds Filippo Lippi's sweet *Madonna and Child with Angels* (c.1455), based on the nun with whom he was in love. In this admired work, the realism of the landscape prefigures Leonardo, while the fine draughtsmanship, heightened by his sense of colour and movement, influenced his follower, Botticelli.

RIGHT: The Botticelli Rooms (10–14) are the most popular exhibit, containing the world's best collection of work by the artist. Here are the famous mythological paintings which fused ideas of *the spiritual and the secular: the Birth of Venus*, (c.1485) and *Primavera* (c.1480). The meaning of the latter remains a subject of fervent discussion, whilst Venus has overtones of the Virgin Mary

The essentials

✉ *Loggiato degli Uffizi 6, www.polomuseale.firenze.it*

☎ *055-238 8651*

🕐 *Tue–Sun 8.15am–6.50pm*

💶 *charge*

THE EASTERN CORRIDOR

The two corridors from which the 45 rooms lead off are filled with sculptures, whilst the strip connecting the sides allows magnificent views down the river and towards the Ponte Vecchio. Rooms 2–4 are dedicated to works from Siena and Florence during the Trecento and Quattrocento (14th and 15th centuries), exhibiting the decorative and icono-graphic pre-Renaissance style. Notable works are the interpretations of the Madonna by Giotto and Duccio, as well as that of Cimabue, Giotto's master.

Room 7 is dedicated to the early Renaissance and its founders and leading figures, who include Masaccio and Uccello and, later, Fra Angelico. The Filippo Lippi Room (8) holds the Franciscan monk's lovely *Madonna and Child with Angels*, as well as a number of other celebrated works, and is worth visiting for Piero della Francesca's portraits of the duke and duchess of Urbino *(pictured above)*. Room 9 holds works by the Pollaiuolo brothers, whose paintings show no distinctive style but are nonetheless decorative.

The Tribuna (Room 18, closed for restora-tion until 2011) is an octagonal room lit from above, with a mother-of-pearl-encrusted ceiling, designed by Buon-talenti. This room's structure, decor and holding was designed to allude to the four elements and used to exhibit the objects most highly prized by the Medici. It holds a collec-tion of portraits and sculpture, as well as Rosso Fiorentino's famous *Putto Che Suona*, or *Angel Musi-cian (pictured opposite)*. When the Tribuna reopens there will sadly be no access inside the room, though visitors can view the works of art from the doorways.

RIGHT: Rooms 5–6 form the International Gothic Rooms, whose paintings are characterised by realistic detail and rich colouring. Lorenzo Monaco's Crowning of Mary provides a good example of this by one of the main practitioners of the era.

ABOVE: the High Renaissance continues in Room 19, which exhibits Perugino and Signorelli's work. These Umbrian artists worked during the 15th and 16th centuries, and the latter's tondo (circular painting) *Holy Family* is reputed to have inspired Michelangelo's version. Room 20 is a break from Italian art, with work by Dürer (including his *Madonna and the Pear* pictured here) and Cranach. The last few rooms on the Eastern Corridor hold works from the 15th and 16th centuries: the Venetian school in Room 21, followed by Holbein and other Flemish and German Realists in Room 22 and more Italian work by Mantegna, the daringly influential painter, and Correggio in Room 23. Room 24 contains a collection of miniatures.

THE WESTERN CORRIDOR

The Western Corridor starts with the Michelangelo room and his vivid *Holy Family* tondo *(below)*. This prelude to Mannerism was produced for the wedding of Angelo Doni to Maddalena Strozzi, and the depth of the figures betrays Michelangelo's penchant for sculpture. Early works by Raphael – such as the glowing *Madonna of the Goldfinch* – and Andrea del Sarto's *Madonna of the Harpies* can be seen in the next room. The subsequent room (27) is the last to focus on Tuscan art before moving on to other regions of Italy.

LEFT: Room 28 displays work by Titian, including the erotic *Venus of Urbino (left)*. Rooms 29–30 focus on Emilia-Romagnan art and Mannerists Dosso Dossi and Parmigianino. Veronese's *Annunciation* is in Room 31, whilst Tintoretto's sensual *Leda and the Swan* hangs in Room 32. A few rooms are dedicated to minor works of the Cinquecento (16th century) before the Flemish art of Rubens and van Dyck (41). The Sala della Niobe (closed for restoration) holds sculpture, whilst Room 44 has works by Rembrandt.

THE UFFIZI ◆ 117

On the first floor are five rooms of paintings as well as the Verone sull'Arno – the bottom of the U-shaped corridor which looks over the River Arno and the Piazza degli Uffizi on the other side.

The Sala di Caravaggio holds three paintings by the troubled artist whose style is characterised by his Realism and use of light (see his *Sacrificing of Isaac*, right). His method inspired the works by other artists contained in the same room and the next three: the Sala di Bartolomeo Manfredi, the Sala di Gherardo delle Notti and the Sala dei Caravaggeschi.

The last room adjacent to the Verone is the Sala di Guido Reni, where three paintings by the classicist artist of the first half of the 17th century are displayed.

Gabinetto and Contini Bonacossi Collection

The Gabinetto, currently on the second floor (closed for restoration), holds a number of important and precious drawings – including works by Renaissance masters (such as Fra Bartolomeo's *Portrait of a Young Woman*, right), some of which are only viewable for academic study purposes. The reorganisation of the Uffizi should see the revamping of the collection. The Contini Bonacossi Collection (moved from its previous home in Palazzo Pitti) contains paintings, furniture, majolica and coats of arms.

Galleria degli Uffizi

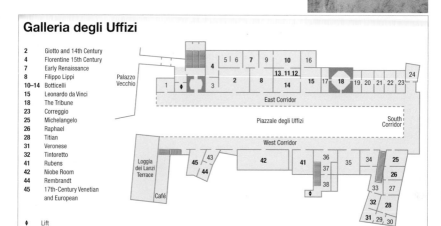

2	Giotto and 14th Century
4	Florentine 15th Century
7	Early Renaissance
8	Filippo Lippi
10–14	Botticelli
15	Leonardo da Vinci
18	The Tribune
23	Correggio
25	Michelangelo
26	Raphael
28	Titian
31	Veronese
32	Tintoretto
41	Rubens
42	Niobe Room
44	Rembrandt
45	17th-Century Venetian and European

✦ Lift

Palazzo Vecchio

East Corridor

Piazzale degli Uffizi

South Corridor

West Corridor

Loggia dei Lanzi Terrace

Café

THE VASARI CORRIDOR

This formerly private Renaissance corridor opened in 1973 to the public after 500 years of secrecy. It is currently closed for restoration but is likely to reopen for special visits of small groups organised by the Uffizi gallery (tel: 055-265 4321; go to www.polomuseale.firenze.it for information). As a substitute, the virtual visit available from any of the Palazzo Vecchio multimedia terminals provides a flavour of the experience, designed as a leisurely stroll along the corridor in the company of the architect, Giorgio Vasari.

Hailed as the first city walkway, a veritable Renaissance rooftop passage, the corridor runs from the Palazzo Vecchio and the Uffizi gallery to the Palazzo Pitti and Boboli Garden on the far side of the Arno. The corridor was built during the reign of Cosimo de' Medici (1519–74) to connect the seat of government, the Palazzo Vecchio, with the court and residence at the Pitti Palace. The aim was to enable the de facto city rulers to cross the city in safety, away from the prying eyes of lesser citizens, and to allow safe passage in times of flood or siege.

In 1565, Giorgio Vasari *(above)*, court architect and master of public works for the Medici, was summoned to build the new walkway from the Uffizi, or public offices, along the quayside to the Ponte Vecchio, and from there over the medieval bridge and gold workshops to the Pitti Palace.

A walk along the passage affords glimpses of the Duomo, tiled rooftops and medieval alleys. The first stretch is lined by 17th- and 18th-century works, while the walkway over the bridge has a great collection of self-portraits, which is still being added to by contemporary artists.

ABOVE AND BELOW: the Uffizi was created as the administrative nerve centre of the grand duchy, reinforcing the chain of command between the Palazzo Vecchio, the Medici power-base, and the court at the Pitti Palace. In 1560, Vasari was charged with the project, although it was only completed by Buontalenti 20 years later. Vasari opted for a U-shape plan enclosing a rectangular piazza, with the Uffizi later linked to the Loggia dei Lanzi by Buontalenti. Although not a particularly graceful palace, it is still a remarkable engineering feat, planted as it is on unstable, sandy ground. The building work involved truncating the Romanesque church of San Pier Scheraggio, which Vasari cunningly incorporated into the Uffizi; it now forms part of the exhibition space.

THE SOUTH CORRIDOR

The short but significant South Corridor has lovely views stretching from San Miniato to the Duomo and embracing the Palazzo Vecchio, the River Arno, Santo Spirito and countless ochre-coloured palaces stacked up on the slopes. On display are key works, including a *Sleeping Cupid*, a statue of a mythical *Roman She-Wolf*, and a graceful *Seated Nymph*, which dates from the 2nd century BC. The romantic *Cupid and Psyche* is a perennial favourite with visitors, while *Apollo* is an accomplished Hellenistic copy of an original by Praxiteles.

BELOW LEFT: the artists featured in the Vasari Corridor include Bernini, Bronzino, Canova, David, Raphael, Rembrandt, Rubens, Vasari and Velázquez. Among the highlights are Guido Reni's rakishly decadent *David with the Head of Goliath* (c.1605), above the staircase leading down to the Corridor, and Eugène Delacroix's penetrating *Self-Portrait* (c.1840), in the Ponte Vecchio walkway.

BELOW: the much-admired *Cupid and Psyche*.

Recommended Restaurants, Bars, Cafés & Gelaterie on pages 132–3

SANTA CROCE AND THE NORTHEAST

Stars of this section of the city, which still bustles with Florentines getting on with day-to-day chores, include the austere Bargello and the serene Santa Croce, another symbol of civic pride

The densely populated area on the north bank of the River Arno, east of the Palazzo Vecchio, was the workers' quarter of medieval Florence, its narrow alleys packed with the workshops of cloth-dyers and weavers. The human toll in the 1966 flood was greater here than anywhere in the city, and numerous wall plaques set 6 metres (20ft) up show the level that it reached at its peak *(see picture page 38)*. After the flood, many former residents were rehoused elsewhere, but it remains an area of workshops, early-morning markets, low-built houses and pre-Renaissance towers.

Piazza San Firenze ①, where seven streets meet, is busy with traffic – which everyone manages to ignore as they stop to chat or have a cup of coffee on the way to work. On the west side, a florist's shop occupies one of the most graceful courtyards in the city, that of **Palazzo Gondi ②**.

The provision of the stone benches running round the base of the palace, called *muriccioli*, for public use was once a condition of planning permission, but the ubiquitous pigeon has now ensured that few Florentines

choose to exercise their ancient right to sit in the shade of the palace walls and pass the time of day.

Opposite is the church of **San Firenze ③** (1772–5), now partly housing the Tribunale, the city law courts. To the left, **San Filippo Neri** still functions as a church. Built in the Baroque style, the church boasts an ornate interior; the ceiling depicts the *Apotheosis of San Filippo Neri*.

Heading north, on the left is the Badia Fiorentina; the entrance is on Via Dante Alighieri *(see page 140)*.

Main attractions

PIAZZA SAN FIRENZE
PALAZZO GONDI
SAN FIRENZE
BARGELLO
PALAZZO PAZZI
MUSEO DI ANTROPOLOGIA
  E ETNOLOGIA
SANTA CROCE
CASA BUONARROTI
SANT'AMBROGIO CHURCH
  AND MARKET
SINAGOGA E MUSEO DI ARTE
  E STORIA EBRAICA
SANTA MARIA MADDALENA
  DEI PAZZI

LEFT: Santa Croce church amidst the rooftops of the northeastern district, with the Tuscan hills in the background.
RIGHT: market scene.

The Bargello and Via del Proconsolo

Opposite the Badia is the rather grim-looking **Bargello** ❹ *(see pages 134–5)*, begun in 1255 as the city's first town hall but later used as a court and prison. Bernardo Baroncelli was among those hanged from its walls; he was put to death in 1478 for his part in the Pazzi conspiracy, an ill-judged attempt to wrest power from the hands of the Medici.

From the Bargello, the Via del Proconsolo runs north past the **Palazzo Pazzi** ❺, built between 1458 and 1469, before the anti-Medici conspiracy, and unusually handsome, with roses, moons and ball-flowers decorating the upper windows.

The next building on the right – No. 12 – across Borgo degli Albizi is the **Palazzo Nonfinito** (Unfinished Palace) – begun by Bernardo Buontalenti in 1593 but still incomplete when it became Italy's first anthropological museum in 1869.

The unfortunate fate of the notorious Bernardo Baroncelli was recorded for posterity by none other than Leonardo da Vinci, who sketched the body as it swung from a Bargello window; a clear warning to other anti-Medici conspirators.

Museo di Antropologia e Etnologia ❻

✉ Via del Proconsolo 12, www.msn. unifi.it ☎ 055-239 6449 © Mon, Tue, Thur, Fri and Sun 9am–1pm, Sat 9am–5pm © charge

This forms part of the Museum of Natural History – a complex of six

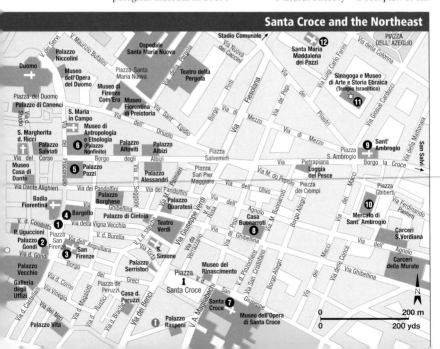

Santa Croce and the Northeast

Recommended Restaurants, Bars, Cafés & Gelaterie on pages 132–3

sites run by the University of Florence. This museum contains native art from the former Italian colonies in Africa, as well as objects collected by Captain James Cook on his last voyage to the Pacific in 1776–9.

There are fascinating exhibits from all over the world, from Peruvian mummies to Arctic clothing (made from whale and dolphin intestines), musical instruments as well as Polynesian wood carvings.

Backstreets and ice cream

Leading off Via del Proconsolo is Borgo degli Albizi, at the end of which lies Piazza San Pier Maggiore, a busy little square with the odd market stall below the ruined portico of the church that gave the square its name, and a couple of cheap restaurants and bars. Unfortunately it is also a hang-out for drug addicts and drunks, who congregate around the seedy Vicolo di San Piero. This area, and the narrow streets that lead south from it, are different in character from much of the city centre. The low houses and unadorned towers recall the medieval city that existed before wealthy merchants began building grandiose palaces.

Via Matteo Palmieri leads to Via Isola delle Stinche. Here you find the Palazzo di Cintoia, a solid medieval building with *sporti* – massive stone brackets which support the upper storeys, jettied out over the narrow street to increase the living space. The ground floor now houses a smart *osteria* and a pizzeria.

Further along the road, the **Gelateria Vivoli** (Via Isole delle Stinche 7; tel: 055-292 334; www.vivoli.it; Tue–Sat 7.30am–midnight, Sun 9.30am–midnight) is regarded as the home of the world's best ice cream – this is not their own claim, in fact, but that of numerous journalists, whose articles have spread the name and fame of the *gelateria* worldwide. Long queues in summer are commonplace, but these are worth enduring for the alcoholic

zabaglioni or rich chestnut ice cream – just two of the numerous tempting choices. It is a standing-only bar, so you might as well buy a tub and move on.

You can continue south to the Via Torta, where the pronounced curve of the street reflects the outline of the Roman amphitheatre (which was still standing when the medieval houses were built up against its walls), and into the **Piazza Santa Croce**.

In Piazza Santa Croce, you can sit and watch young Florentines play football with all the skill and control

FAR LEFT: the Gothic tower of the Bargello.
ABOVE: book stall in Piazza San Firenze.
BELOW: mouthwatering *gelato* from Vivoli.

Crowds of people used to gather on Piazza Santa Croce for festivals, games and entertainment. Today, tourists and street vendors crowd the square.

BELOW: *calcio storico* matches are not for the faint-hearted.

that will surely make some of them international stars one day. A form of football has been played here since the 16th century – a plaque on the frescoed **Palazzo dell'Antella** (No. 21), dated 1565, marks the centre line of the pitch. Today, Piazza Santa Croce remains the venue for the violent *calcio in costume* (or *calcio storico*) football game, played on the Feast of San Giovanni (24 June) and three other Sundays in late June or early July.

The square was also used for jousting tournaments between teams from each of the city's wards, and for public spectacles, animal fights and fireworks, mounted by the Medici grand dukes. During the Inquisition, heretics were burnt here, and paintings, mirrors, embroidered clothing and other finery were piled onto great "bonfires of vanity".

THE FLORENTINE PANTHEON

Santa Croce ❼

✉ Piazza Santa Croce, www.santa croce.firenze.it 📞 055-246 6105 🕒 complex: Mon–Sat 9.30am–5.30pm, Sun 1–5.30pm 💶 charge

Originally a Franciscan foundation, the church of Santa Croce was one of three – with the Duomo and Santa Maria Novella – that were built and funded by the *comune*, the city government, as public buildings and symbols of civic pride. The colour scheme of all three is identical, as are the crowds which flock to the steps both at night and during the day. It was one of the largest churches in the Christian world when built, and was used as a burial place for the great and the good of Florence.

Monuments

Monuments to Dante, Petrarch, Boccaccio, Michelangelo and other luminaries attracted 19th-century travellers in great numbers, who came as pilgrims to the shrines of the creators of Western civilisation. Foreigners paid for the unfortunate 1842 neo-Gothic facade and campanile and the lifeless statue of Dante in the square.

But this should not deter, for the interior of Santa Croce (enter on Largo Piero Bargellini) is a splendid example of true Gothic – huge and airy, with a richly painted ceiling and

Recommended Restaurants, Bars, Cafés & Gelaterie on pages 132–3

an uninterrupted view of the polygonal sanctuary, whose tall lancet windows are filled with extraordinary 14th-century stained glass.

A series of tombs in the aisles begins, on the right, with Giorgio Vasari's monument to Michelangelo – an irony here, for the artist who left Florence after refusing to work for the repressive Medici ended up buried beneath the tomb carved by the Medici's chief propagandist.

Next is a massive 19th-century cenotaph to Dante (who is buried in Ravenna), surmounted by an uncharacteristically crabby and introverted portrait of the poet, flanked by neoclassical female figures. Further on is a monument to Machiavelli (18th-century) and Donatello's partly gilded stone relief of the *Annunciation*.

Beyond lies one of the earliest and most influential funerary monuments of the Renaissance, the tomb of Leonardo Bruni – humanist, historian and eminent politician – by Rossellino (1446–7). It was widely imitated, but rarely so ineptly as in the neighbouring 19th-century tomb of the composer Rossini.

TIP

If you're in Florence in the run-up to Christmas, don't miss one of the city's most impressive *presepi* (Nativity scenes) inside Santa Croce, with live animals drawing the crowds.

In the floor nearby are niello-work tomb slabs covering the graves of Florentine worthies. Continuing right, into the south transept, the Capello Castellani is decorated with frescos by Agnolo Gaddi (*c.*1385), and contains the tomb of the Countess of Albany. She was the widow of Prince Charles Edward Stuart (Bonnie Prince Charlie) who fled to Italy after defeat at the Battle of Culloden in Scotland (1746) and settled in Florence under the spurious title of Count of Albany (Albion being the archaic name for Britain).

ABOVE LEFT: statue of Dante in Piazza Santa Croce.
BELOW: Santa Croce's neo-Gothic facade.

One of Santa Croce's beautiful stained-glass windows.

BELOW: detail from the *Coronation of the Virgin* altarpiece, by Giotto.
BELOW RIGHT: the altar in Santa Croce.

Giotto and his pupil

The Cappella Baroncelli contains frescos dating from 1332–8 and once thought to be by Giotto, but now attributed to his pupil Taddeo Gaddi, father of Agnolo. He was no slavish imitator of his teacher's work, but an innovator in his own right. The scene in which the angels announce the birth of Christ to the shepherds is one of the earliest attempts to paint a night scene in fresco.

A corridor to the right leads to the sacristy, with its gorgeous 16th-century inlaid wooden cupboards, and a souvenir shop whose walls are hung with photographs of the 1966 flood. At the end of the corridor a chapel, usually locked, contains the tomb where Galileo was buried until 1737. He was originally denied burial within the church because his contention that the sun, not the earth, was at the centre of the solar system earned him the condemnation of the Inquisition *(see box opposite)*. In 1737, however, he was moved to a place of honour in the north aisle.

Returning to the church, the frescos in the two chapels to the right of the high altar were done by Giotto. The Cappella Bardi, on the left (*c.*1315–20), shows the life of St Francis, and the Cappella Peruzzi, to the right (*c.*1326–30), depicts the lives of St John the Baptist and St John the Divine.

These fabulous frescos have been through the wars; they were whitewashed over in the early 18th century, rediscovered only in 1852 and finally restored in 1959. Although fragmentary, they are the best surviving work in Florence of the man who introduced a new clarity, energy and colour into the art of the fresco and influenced generations of artists to come.

In the north transept, Donatello's wooden *Crucifixion* in the second Cappella Bardi is said to be the one that his friend Brunelleschi dismissed as making Christ look like "a peasant, not a man". You may like to compare this with Brunelleschi's own attempt at the same subject if you visit Santa

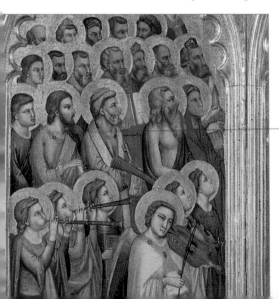

Recommended Restaurants, Bars, Cafés & Gelaterie on pages 132–3

Maria Novella church *(see page 175)*.

Further up the north aisle, near the west doors, is Galileo's tomb, erected in 1737 in belated recognition of his fundamental contributions to modern science; in the nave floor nearby is the tomb slab of his ancestor and namesake, a physician of some standing in 15th-century Florence.

Cloisters of serenity

The cloister walk is lined with 19th-century monuments, fascinating for their muddled combination of Christian and pagan classical subjects and only just the right side of mawkishness. It leads to the **Cappella de' Pazzi** (Pazzi Chapel), one of the purest works of the Renaissance, a serene composition of grey stone and white walls, of arches, domes, scallops and blank arcading, and featuring 12 terracotta tondi of the Apostles by Luca della Robbia.

Brunelleschi planned the chapel in 1430, but the work did not begin until 1443 and was completed after his death in 1446. It shows that even the inventor of Renaissance architecture sometimes faltered, for the fragmentary corner pilasters, squeezed into the angles, are an uncomfortable punctuation of the overall grand design.

The recently expanded **Museo dell'Opera di Santa Croce** (included in Santa Croce entrance fee) is housed in the monastic buildings across the

first cloister. The second cloister is arguably the loveliest in all Florence, enclosed by hemispherical arches on slender columns, with a medallion in each of the spandrels.

The refectory here contains detached frescos, removed from the church to expose earlier works, and Cimabue's *Crucifixion*. Although it was restored after having been virtually ruined in the 1966 flood, it is still in rather poor condition, and serves as a reminder both of the tragic consequences of that event and of just how much great art did, in fact, survive.

ABOVE: the tranquil cloister of Santa Croce.

Galileo: Man of Controversy

Although born in Pisa, Galileo Galilei had strong ties with Florence. His first contact came shortly after he left university, when he taught mathematics in the city. But the real connection came in the early 1600s, when he made a series of telescopes, through which he made many astronomical discoveries. Among them, he saw four small bodies orbiting Jupiter, which he shrewdly named "the Medicean stars". The fawning move worked: Galileo was soon appointed Mathematician and Philosopher to the Grand Duke of Tuscany. He also became a more outspoken proponent of the Copernican system, which theorised that everything revolved around the sun. This did not sit well with the Catholic Church, which condemned him and sent him into exile, first in Siena and then in his villa in Arcetri, just outside Florence. He remained there under house arrest until his death in 1642. In honour of the Tuscan scientists, the overhauled Science Museum reopened in 2010 as the Galileo Museum *(see pages 110–11).*

Luca della Robbia – whose work graces the Cappella dei Pazzi in Santa Croce, as well as many other buildings in Florence – perfected the art of glazed terracotta and kept the technique a secret, known only to his family, who thereby enriched themselves mightily.

ABOVE: local produce for sale at the Sant'Ambrogio market.
ABOVE RIGHT AND BELOW: typical sights in this offbeat district.

ARTISTS IN DIFFERENT GUISES

Casa Buonarroti ❽

✉ 70 Via Ghibellina, www.casa buonarroti.it ☎ 055-241 752
🕐 Wed–Mon 9.30am–2pm, 4pm during exhibitions ⓒ charge

North of Santa Croce, reached by walking up Via delle Pinzochere, the Casa Buonarroti is the house of the man we know better by his Christian name, Michelangelo. He never lived here, but bought the property as an investment, and his heirs turned it into a museum in 1858. It contains one outstanding sculpture – the *Madonna della Scala*, thought to be his earliest work, carved when he was only 15 years old. It is a remarkably humane and noble relief, in which the Virgin lifts her tunic to comfort the infant Christ with the softness of her breasts whilst Joseph labours in the background.

As for the rest of the museum, it is best enjoyed as a rare glimpse inside a 16th-century *palazzo*, frescoed and furnished in the style of the time. Most of the exhibits are of work once attributed to Michelangelo, or paintings and sculpture inspired by his work. They serve only to highlight the difference between a great artist and the deservedly unknown.

SANT'AMBROGIO AND THE NORTHEAST

Via Buonarroti leads north from Michelangelo's house to one of the most bustling areas of Florence, Sant'Ambrogio. Taking its name from the parish church, this is an area of narrow streets filled with dusty junk shops, local bars, grocer's shops and crumbling facades strung with dry-

ing laundry. It is also an area that is becoming increasingly trendy of late, so these same crumbling facades often hide upmarket apartments within.

Just east of the junction of Via Buonarroti and Via Pietrapiana, in Piazza dei Ciompi, is the **Loggia del Pesce**, which was designed by Vasari in 1568. The delicate arcade is decorated with roundels full of leaping fish and crustaceans, but it is no longer used as a fish market. It was moved here in the 19th century when the Mercato Vecchio was demolished to create the Piazza della Repubblica. By day, it is a market for junk and "near antiques". By night it is a rendezvous for prostitutes and their clients.

The nearby church of Sant'Ambrogio, at the southeastern end of Via dei Pilastri, is one of those small, unassuming parish churches that Florence has in abundance, full of fascinating detail, but eclipsed by bigger attractions.

Sant'Ambrogio ❾

✉ Piazza Sant'Ambrogio
☎ 055-240 104 🕒 daily 8am–noon, 4.30–7pm 🎫 free

Sant'Ambrogio was built on the site of a house where St Ambrose stayed whilst visiting the city in AD 393. Despite its 19th-century neo-Gothic facade, the fine church within is 10th-century in date and is full of interesting features. One is the splendid marble tabernacle in the sanctuary to the left of the high altar. This was designed in 1481 by Mino da Fiesole to house a miraculous communion chalice that was one day found to contain several drops of real blood rather than symbolic wine. Some delightful frescos by Cosimo Rosselli (painted in 1486) tell the story.

Back on the left side of the church lies the slab marking the grave of the great sculptor Verrochio (died 1488).

Located further to the south, in Piazza Ghiberti, is the **Mercato di Sant'Ambrogio** ❿ (Mon–Sat 7am– 2pm), the second-largest produce market in the city (the biggest is the Mercato Centrale). It is housed in a somewhat deteriorating cast-iron market hall constructed in 1873, and is a wonderfully lively place to do the shopping in the company of locals.

A bust adorning Casa Buonarroti, an intimate and charming museum.

BELOW: buildings are a bit more run-down in the northeastern parts of town.

Florence's synagogue towers above the surrounding rooftops.

RIGHT: strolling along one of the narrow medieval streets.
BELOW: the area is awash with colourful ice-cream parlours.

From the market, it is a short walk back to Piazza Sant'Ambrogio, up Via dei Pilastri and right up Via Luigi Carlo Farini, to the synagogue.

Sinagoga e Museo di Arte e Storia Ebraica

✉ Via Luigi Carlo Farini 4
☏ 055-245 252 🕒 Nov–Mar Sun–Thur 10am–3pm, Fri 10am–2pm, Apr–May, Sept–Oct Sun–Thur 10am–5pm, Fri 10am–2pm, June–Aug Sun–Thur 10am–6pm, Fri 10am–2pm (synagogue and museum) 💰 charge

The huge synagogue (Tempio Israel-itico), whose green, copper-covered dome is such a prominent feature of the Florentine skyline, was built in the Hispano-Moresque style between 1874 and 1882. Cosimo I founded Florence's ghetto for the city's Jewish community here in 1551; the original place of worship was demolished in the mid-19th century, and a new synagogue built in its place.

The oriental ambience continues inside, where golden light filters through the windows, lighting an interior made splendid by the red

and blue arabesques decorating the underside of the dome. There is a small museum here which documents the history of the Jews in Florence.

It is somewhat sobering to think that, had the 19th-century city planners had their way, a significant section of the city from here west to the Piazza della Repubblica would have been demolished and redeveloped as grand avenues. At the end of the road sits **Piazza dell'Azeglio** – one of the quieter recreational spaces in Florence. From this point, Via della Colonna leads to Borgo Pinti. A left turn back towards the centre of town at this point passes the entrance to the church of Santa Maria Maddalena dei Pazzi.

Santa Maria Maddalena dei Pazzi

✉ Borgo Pinti 58 ☏ 055-247 8420
🕒 daily 7.30am–noon, 2.30–4.30pm
💰 donation expected

The church is dedicated to the nun who was a descendant of the anti-Medici conspirators. She died in 1609 and was canonised in 1685, when the church was renamed in her honour. It was originally run by the Cistercian order, but the Carmelites took over in 1628. In 1926, Augustinian monks moved in, and remain to this day.

Recommended Restaurants, Bars, Cafés & Gelaterie on pages 132–3

The church originally dates from the 15th century and has a lovely quiet cloister of 1492 formed of square Tuscan columns with flat, rather than rounded, classical arches. The fresco of the *Crucifixion* in the chapter house – which is entered from the crypt – is one of Perugino's masterpieces, painted in 1493–6 (temporarily closed to the public). The figures kneeling in adoration of their Saviour are glimpsed, as if through a window, between a series of *trompe l'œil* arches.

The Cross of Christ is set in a delightful landscape of winding rivers and wooded hills, and the whole scene is lit by a limpid blue light. Perugino (*c*.1445–1523), whose real name was Pietro Vannucci, was a founder of the Umbrian school of artists.

Further out of town (2km/1¼ miles to the east), at Via San Salvi 16, is the 14th-century church of the former **monastery of San Salvi** (tel: 055-238 8603; Tue–Sun 8.15am–1.50pm). It houses one of the most famous of all Renaissance frescos, Andrea del Sarto's *Last Supper*.

Football stadium

Also a little out of town, to the northeast of Santa Maria Maddalena dei Pazzi, is the huge **Stadio Comunale** (also known as the Stadio Artemio Franchi), one of the city's few modern buildings of any architectural merit (with the exception of Michelucci's Santa Maria Novella station building), designed by Pier Luigi Nervi in 1932. It is the home of the city's football club, ACF Fiorentina.

Along the road leading to it, Viale dei Mille, is the **Sette Santi church** – a neo-Gothic, neo-Romanesque fusion which is attractive and original. ❑

ABOVE: Hebrew on the synagogue.
BELOW: Fiorentina celebrate.

BEST RESTAURANTS, BARS, CAFÉS AND *GELATERIE*

[p313, E2]

Restaurants

Prices for three-course dinner per person with a glass of wine:
€ = under €25
€€ = €25–40
€€€ = €40–60
€€€€ = more than €60

Acqua al Due
Via della Vigna Vecchia 40r
☎ 055-284 170
🕒 D only. **€€**
[p313, D3]
A real dining experience which requires booking ahead due to its popularity. If you have a big appetite, try the *assaggi di primi* (five pasta dishes as chosen by the chef) followed by the *assaggi di dolci* (a selection of the desserts of the day).

Antico Noè
Volta di San Piero 6r
☎ 055-234 0838
🕒 Closed Sun. **€** [p313, E2]
Tiny wine bar which offers authentic Tuscan food at cheap prices. The *tagliatelle ai porcini* (mushroom tagliatelle) is recommended.

Baldovino
Via di San Giuseppe 22r
☎ 055-241 773 🕒 L & D; closed Mon. **€€** [p311, E]
This popular trattoria offers a bit of everything: traditional Tuscan dishes, great pasta, pizzas and salads. Menus change monthly and much of the produce comes from restaurateur/hotelier David Gardner's farm in Greve in Chianti. Under

the same management, the Baldobar next door at 20r, open daily, serves tasty snacks, tapas and gourmet salads, along with a good selection of European wines.

La Botte
Via di San Giuseppe 18r
☎ 055-234 7220 🕒 L & D. **€–€€** [p311, E1]
Opened in 2010, this is the only bar in Florence to use enomatic technology to offer a wide selection of wines by the glass, half-glass or *in assaggio* – just a taste. Customers use a wine card and can choose from 64 varieties. Food is tapas-style with salamis, prosciutto and Tuscan street food – either in

whole or half-portions. The bar is run by David Gardner following the success of his trattoria Baldovino *(see above)*.

Caffè Italiano (Osteria)
Via Isola delle Stinche 11/13r ☎ 055-289 368
🕒 L & D; closed Mon. **€€€€** [p313, E3]
A smart restaurant set inside the 14th-century Salviati Palace, with a changing menu of high-quality Tuscan cuisine. Try the huge Florentine *bistecca* to share.

Caffè Italiano (Pizzeria)
Via Isola delle Stinche 11/13r
☎ 055-289 368 🕒 L & D; closed Mon. **€** [p313, E3]
The tastiest pizza in Florence, with entertainment from the chef often included. Only three varieties – *marinara*, *margherita* and *napoletana* – are offered, and it is worth visiting enough times to try them all. This place is highly recommended – though ask for a table in the back room for a more intimate atmosphere.

Cibrèo
Via del Verrocchio 8r
☎ 055-234 1100 🕒 Tue– Sat. **€€€€** [p309, E4]
Justly famous restaurant; elegant yet relaxed, one of the most popular with visitors and Florentines alike. The fare is Tuscan

with an innovative twist. Eat much the same food but for a cheaper price in the Cibrèino trattoria, which is entered from Piazza Ghiberti.

Enoteca Pinchiorri

Via Ghibellina 87 ⬛ 055-242 777 ⬙ Closed Sun and Mon; D only Tue and Wed. €€€€ [p313, E3]
A gourmet paradise and garlanded with awards; hailed by some as one of the best restaurants in Europe and scorned by others as pretentious. The only way to find out is by taking your credit card in hand and diving in. Tuscan food with a French influence and an outstanding wine list. Booking is essential.

Finesterrae

Via de' Pepi 3/5r ⬛ 055-263 8675 ⬙ D daily. €€–€€€ [p313, E3]
Mediterranean bar and restaurant with a choice selection of food from various cuisines. Start with tapas, followed by a Moroccan-style tagine or pasta dish. The ambience is relaxed and sultry, especially in the bar area.

La Giostra

Borgo Pinti 12r ⬛ 055-241 341 ⬙ L & D daily. €€€ [p313, E2]
This is a renowned restaurant run by a Habsburg prince. The crostini are delicious, as are the range of pasta dishes on offer.

LEFT: typical informal restaurant.

Godò

Piazza Edison 3/4r ⬛ 055-583 881 ⬙ B, L & D; closed Sun. €€–€€€ [off map]
A little out of town but on the bus route to Fiesole, this restaurant offers great meals throughout the day. The gnocchi al pomodoro (gnocchi in tomato sauce) are lovely, and the salads generous.

Moyo

Via de' Benci 23r ⬛ 055-247 9738 ⬙ daily 8.30am–late. €–€€ [p313, D4]
Lively café/restaurant with free WiFi access and generous aperitivo buffet. Popular with locals and American students from nearby language schools.

La Pentola dell'Oro

Via di Mezzo 24/26r
⬛ 055-241 821 ⬙ Closed Sun. €€ [p309, E4]
As well as being unique, this is one of the friendliest restaurants in the city. Chef Giuseppe Alessi is more than willing to explain the dishes; the recipes are inspired by medieval and Renaissance cookery.

Il Pizzaiuolo

Via dei Macci 113r ⬛ 055-241 171 ⬙ L & D; closed Sun. €–€€ [p311, E1]
The pizzas here are Neapolitan-style wonders, with lots on offer, including mixed antipasto.

Ruth's

Via Luigi Carlo Farini 2a
⬛ 055-248 0888 ⬙ L & D;

closed Fri D. € [p309, E4]
Next to the synagogue, this little Jewish restaurant is one of the few to cater for vegetarians, and offers a range of kosher and Middle Eastern-style dishes.

Targa

Lungarno Colombo 7
⬛ 055-677 377 ⬙ L & D; closed Sun. €€€ [p311, E2]
Formerly Caffè Concerto, this bistro has a delightful riverside setting, where the Tuscan food is given a creative edge.

Teatro del Sale

Via dei Macci 111r
⬛ 055-200 1492
⬙ Closed Sun and Mon. €€ [p311, E1]
Run by the same people as Cibrèo, this is a unique three-meal-a-day restaurant and theatre all in one. Fabio Picchi produces Tuscan dishes, buffet-style, on the theatre stage. Reservations are required for this novel experience. Fixed price for dinner plus a small fee for theatre membership.

Bars, Cafés and Gelaterie

Caffè Cibrèo

Via del Verrochio 5r. Tel: 055-234 5853. Open Tue–Sat 8am–2.30pm. [p309, E4]
Part of the Cibrèo emporium, this charming antique-style café serves creative light lunches and gorgeous desserts.

Caffè dei Benci

Via dei Benci 13r. Tel: 055-216 887. Open L. [p313, D4]
Small, relaxed café next to the eponymous osteria, where drinks and panini are served from the early morning to the late evening. Or pop to the restaurant next door for something more substantial.

Gelateria dei Neri

Via dei Neri 20/22r. Tel: 055-210 034. [p313, D4]
Wonderfully creamy ice cream in a range of

fruit and sweet flavours. In summer try the granitas and frappés.

Gelateria Vivoli

Isola delle Stinche 7. Tel: 055-292 334. [p313, E3]
Reputed to be the best gelateria in Florence. Try the amaretto and tiramisu flavours.

The Lion's Fountain

Borgo degli Albizi 34r. Tel: 055-234 4412. Open daily 6pm–2am. [p313, E2]
Overpriced but cheery Irish pub. Has a range of panini and bar snacks and TV for sporting events.

The William

Via A. Magliabechi 7/9/11r. Tel: 055-263 8357. [p313, E4]
An English pub just off Piazza Santa Croce that offers pub grub and a good range of beers.

THE BARGELLO

See Florence's most important sculptures from the Medici and private collections

The *palazzo* was transformed into a museum in 1865; its previous uses as the seat of the city's chief magistrate and later as a prison are reflected by features of the building such as the decor, and the street names of the surrounding area. Entry into the museum takes the visitor through the medieval courtyard, whose walls are adorned with emblems of the city wards, magistrates and governors. *Oceanus* by Giambologna is one of the sculptures housed under the vaulted cloisters, which lead off to the right of the staircase into the Sala di Michelangelo. The entrance to this room – which contains a range of Renaissance statues, busts and bas-reliefs in marble and bronze – is flanked by two lions. Of particular note are works by Michelangelo and his followers and contemporaries including Cellini and Ammannati. An external staircase leads to the second floor and a number of bronze sculptures of birds on display in the loggia, originally made by Giambologna for the Medici Villa di Castello.

ABOVE AND BELOW: the Bargello museum (above in an 18th-century painting by Giuseppe Zocchi) is set in a massive Gothic *palazzo* of the mid-13th century in the heart of the ancient city.

LEFT: Donatello's famous version of *David* (from 1430–40), in the Donatello Gallery, is a small bronze known for being the first nude sculpture since antiquity. It differs dramatically from Michelangelo's masterpiece not just in size and material, but also in its coyness and melancholy, which some view as truer to David's youth.

The essentials

✉ *Via del Proconsolo 4, www.polomuseale.firenze.it*
📞 *055-238 8606*
🕐 *daily 8.15am–1.50pm, closed 2nd and 4th Mon, 1st, 3rd and 5th Sun of the month*
💶 *charge*

THE DONATELLO AND BRONZE GALLERIES

The Salone del Consiglio Generale is often nick-named the Donatello Gallery. Apart from the newly restored *David*, other works by Donatello in the room worth paying attention to are *St George*, which was designed for the Orsan-michele church, and *Cupid*. The walls and ceiling of the room figure a number of glazed terracotta works by Luca della Robbia; on the same floor the eclectic group of 5th- to 17th-century objets d'art includes ivories and Islamic treasures. The small chapel (Capella Maddelena) features some attractive frescos depicting hell: look out for the figure located on the right dressed in maroon thought to be a depiction of Dante.

Upstairs, the Verrocchio Room displays Tuscan sculpture from the late 15th century, including portrait busts of notable Florentines and an interpretation of David by the artist who lends his name to the room, Andrea del Verrocchio. The adjoining rooms are filled with work by members of the della Robbia family – predominantly Andrea and Giovanni – dominated by the often overbearing large reliefs coloured in yellow, green and blue.

The last major room in the museum is the Bronze Gallery. This has one of the most rewarding displays in the Bargello. The sculptures generally depict mythological tales or Greek history, in the form of both models and more functional articles such as candelabra. The model for Giambologna's *Rape of the Sabine Women* (on display in the Loggia dei Lanzi) stands out, as do two of his other statues: *Kneeling Nymph* and *Hercules and Antaeus*. Completing the second floor is a collection of armoury, Baroque sculpture and medals.

TOP RIGHT: four of Michelangelo's early sculptures are on display in the Sala di Michelangelo: *Bacchus Drunk*, the Pitti Tondo – a depiction of the Madonna and Child shown here – *Apollo-David* and *Brutus*.

ABOVE: in the Donatello Gallery are the bronze panels submitted by Ghiberti and Brunelleschi *(above)* for the baptistery doors.

RIGHT: Giambologna's bronze of Mercury is in the Sala di Michelangelo.

Recommended Restaurants, Cafés & Gelaterie on page 147

PIAZZA DELLA REPUBBLICA

This part of Florence is one of stereotypical contrasts: although vestiges of the ancient city remain, these are mixed with 21st-century neon. Still, the area has its attractions

Framing the western exit dividing the covered walkway that runs along Piazza della Repubblica is a triumphal arch bearing a pompous inscription to the effect that "the ancient heart of the city was restored to new life from its former squalor in 1895".

With hindsight, the message has the hollow ring of irony. The plan to develop central Florence was conceived between 1865 and 1871, when the city was, briefly, the capital of Italy. The ancient and "squalid" buildings of the former ghetto – a reminder of feudal, divided Italy – were to be swept away and replaced by broad avenues, symbolic of the new age of the United Kingdom of Italy.

PIAZZA DELLA REPUBBLICA ❶

The site of the Roman forum, at the heart of Florence, was chosen as the appropriate place to begin this transformation. Down came the 14th-century Mercato Vecchio – then still the principal food market in the city – and along with it numerous cafés and taverns with names like Inferno and Purgatorio (names still preserved in the streets southwest of the square). These had been the haunt of artists

and writers who later adopted the new café in the square, the Giubbe Rosse *(see page 147)*.

At this point, enter the interfering foreigner, determined that medieval Florence should be preserved. Was it the cries of "halt" that went up all over Europe that saved the city or simply lack of money to see the scheme through?

In any event, demolition ceased, and the square, with its swish cafés, department stores and billboards, remains a modern intrusion into the

Main attractions
SANTA MARGHERITA DEI CERCHI
MUSEO CASA DI DANTE
BADIA FIORENTINA
ORSANMICHELE
MERCATO NUOVO
PALAZZO DI PARTE GUELFA
PALAZZO DAVANZATI
PALAZZO STROZZI

LEFT: arcades on the Piazza della Repubblica.
RIGHT: Gilli, Florence's oldest café, displays its tables outside on the piazza all year round.

ABOVE: Dante at work.

THE DANTE DISTRICT

By means of Via degli Speziali, which intersects the two main streets, and the lively Via del Corso, you reach the part of the city associated with the poet Dante.

The charming Beatrice

In the Corso is **Santa Margherita dei Ricci**, a small church which hosts music concerts in the evenings. A little further on, opposite the Palazzo Salviati (now a bank), an alley leads to the little 11th-century church of **Santa Margherita dei Cerchi ❷** (on the left), which contains a fine 13th-century altarpiece by Neri di Bicci.

This is where Dante is said to have married Gemma Donati and where, some years earlier, he regularly set eyes on nine-year-old Beatrice Portinari, a girl whose beauty he considered to be nothing short of divine. Infatuated, he experienced the most violent passions on the few occasions he was able to speak to her,

heart of the city; useful as a counterpoint to the rest of Florence for, as one turns away and heads for the narrow medieval streets, the sombre old buildings seem all the more endearing for their contrast to the 19th-century pomp.

while she, heavily chaperoned and destined to marry a rich banker, regarded him as a figure of fun. Three years after her marriage she died, so that she never read the *Divine Comedy*, in which Dante presented her as the embodiment of every perfection.

Museo Casa di Dante ❸

✉ Via Santa Margherita 1, www.museocasadidante.it ☎ 055-219 416 ⏰ daily 10am–6pm 🎫 charge

Nearly opposite Santa Margherita dei Cerchi, on the right, is the Casa di Dante, claimed as the poet's birthplace. The tower is 13th-century, the rest an attractive group of old houses restored during the 19th century and joined together to create a museum of material relating to the poet's work. In fact, there is virtually nothing in the way of original material there.

Politics and exile

A right turn leads into the tiny **Piazza San Martino**, with its 13th-century Torre della Castagna, one of the best-preserved of the towers that once filled central Florence, soaring to 60

metres (200ft) or more until the city government imposed a ban on structures that were more than 15 metres (50ft) in height. During the turbulent 13th and 14th centuries, the private armies of warring factions organised hit-and-run attacks on their enemies from towers such as these.

This particular tower also served, briefly in 1282, as the residence of the *priori*, as they awaited the completion of the Palazzo Vecchio, the new town hall. The *priori* consisted of six members of the leading guilds, the Arte Maggiore, elected to serve two-month terms on the city council.

Dante, a member of the Guild of Physicians and Apothecaries (books were then sold in apothecary shops), was elected to the priorate to serve between 15 June and 15 August 1300. In 1302, he was sentenced to two years' exile on a false charge of corruption during his term of office, part of a mass purge of supporters of the Holy Roman Emperor by supporters of the Pope. Dante chose never to return to Florence, preferring a life of solitary wandering, during which he wrote his best poetry.

This historic café in the Piazza della Repubblica is famous for its hot chocolate.

BELOW: Gilli's Belle Epoque interior.

*Niche statue of
St Mark by Donatello
outside Orsanmichele,
created for the Linen
Drapers' Guild, 1413.*

RIGHT: Orsanmichele
medallion. **BELOW
LEFT AND RIGHT:** many
shopping opportunities.

Opposite the tower is the tiny
Oratorio di Sant Martino (Piazza
San Martino; daily 10am–noon, 3–
5pm; free), decorated with fine frescos by followers of Ghirlandaio.

From here, Via Dante Alighieri
leads one way to the entrance to the
Badia Fiorentina.

Badia Fiorentina ❹

✉ Via del Proconsolo   ☎ 055-264
402   ⏰ Mon 2.30–6pm, Tue–Sat
6.30am–6pm   💰 donation expected

This church of a Benedictine abbey
was founded in AD 978 but much
altered in 1627–31. The interior is
uninspiring, but inside the door is a
delightful painting by Filippo Lippi,
(c.1485) showing St Bernard and
the Virgin: no ethereal vision, but a
warm-blooded woman accompanied
by angels whose faces are those of
the children of the Florentine streets.

The little-visited cloister, the
Chiostro degli Aranci (so named
because the monks grew orange trees
there), is reached through a door to
the right of the sanctuary and up a
flight of stairs (Mon 3–6pm). This

beautifully peaceful inner courtyard
is adorned with frescos depicting the
miracles of St Bernard by Rossellino
(c.1434–6); and there are attractive
views of the restored 14th-century
campanile, Romanesque below and
Gothic above.

The other direction, along Via dei
Tavolini, leads to Via dei Calzaiuoli.
This street, originally Roman, was the
principal thoroughfare of medieval
Florence, linking the Duomo and
Piazza della Signoria. Before being
pedestrianised, it was so busy that anyone who stopped to admire a building
was likely to be jostled off the pavement into the road, risking injury from
an impatient stream of traffic. Now it

Recommended Restaurants, Cafés & Gelaterie on page 147

is a bustling shopping street – packed during summer evenings and Sunday afternoon *passeggiate* (strolls) – where mime artists and other performers keep tourists entertained, and the warm nights bring out a range of tarot card readers, vendors and street life.

Halfway down towards Piazza della Signoria on the right is the two-storey church of Orsanmichele.

Orsanmichele ❺

✉ Via dell'Arte della Lana 📞 055-284 944 🕑 Tue–Sun 10am–5pm ◎ free

Orsanmichele was built in 1337 on the site of the garden *(hortus)* of the church of San Michele and originally served as an open-arcaded grain market. In 1380 the arcades were filled in and the ground floor converted to a church, while the upper storey was used as an emergency grain store to be drawn on in times of siege or famine.

The new aesthetics

A scheme to decorate the exterior was launched in 1339. Each of the major Florentine guilds was allocated a niche, which was to be filled with a statue of their respective patron saints. The Black Death intervened, so that the first statues were not commissioned until the early 15th century, and they illustrate well the contemporary emergence of the new Renaissance aesthetic.

Also decorating the exterior of the building are 15th-century enamelled terracotta medallions, bearing the heraldic devices *(stemme)* of the various Florentine guilds, by Luca della Robbia and his workshop.

Donatello's outstanding *St George*, which is hailed as the first truly Renaissance statue, is here represented by a bronze copy of the marble original, now to be found in the Bargello *(see page 135)*. Near to it, on the north side (in Via San Michele) you'll admire Nanni di Banco's great *Four Crowned Saints*, painted around 1415, with an interesting frieze below illustrating the

work of carpenters and masons, whose guild commissioned the work.

The west face is decorated with elaborate Gothic cartwheel tracery and faces the Palazzo dell'Arte della Lana, the Guildhall of the Wool Workers, as might be guessed from the numerous Lamb of God emblems that decorate the facade. This building provides access, by means of an overhead bridge, to the splendid Gothic vaulted grain store above the church. It also houses a small museum

ABOVE: section of Orcagna's tabernacle showing the *Death and Assumption of the Virgin*. **BELOW:** the Gothic west facade of Orsanmichele.

(Mon 10am–5pm only; charge), which holds mainly statuary from the church and is occasionally used for temporary exhibitions.

Inside the church

The odd arrangement of Orsanmichele's dark interior was dictated by the form of the building. In place of the usual nave flanked by aisles, the central arcade of the original open market divides the church into two parallel naves of equal size. The gloomy interior is somewhat enlivened by frescoed vaults and Gothic stained-glass windows.

The southernmost is dominated by Andrea Orcagna's huge tabernacle (1339–59), encrusted with coloured glass. In the centre, scarcely visible behind cherubs and votive offerings, is a *Madonna* by Bernardo Daddi, painted in 1347 to replace one that appeared miraculously on a pillar of the old grain market. The base of the tabernacle is decorated with scenes from the life of the Virgin.

Mercato Nuovo ❻

To reach the Mercato Nuovo (New Market; mid-Feb–mid-Nov daily 9am–7pm, mid-Nov–mid-Feb Tue–Sat 9am–5pm), take the Via de' Lamberti and turn left into the Via Calimala. A market has existed here since the 11th century, and the current arcade was built in 1547–51 for the sale of silk and gold.

ABOVE: a postbox line-up. **BELOW:** shopping for masks in the Mercato Nuovo.

Il Porcellino

To the south of the Mercato Nuovo, Il Porcellino attracts countless visitors who come to rub the snout of the bronze boar copied from the Roman one in the Uffizi, itself a copy of a Hellenic original. The statue you see today is yet another copy; its predecessor was carried off for restoration at the end of 1998. It is said that anyone who rubs the snout is certain to return to the city. Coins dropped in the trough below are distributed to city charities.

Later it gained the name "straw market" *(Mercato della Paglia)* from the woven-straw (raffia) goods sold there by peasants from the countryside. Various cheap and colourful raffia souvenirs are still sold, but, as elsewhere in Florence, leather goods and T-shirts now form the bulk of the market's offerings.

The southwestern exit of the market square, past a popular tripe vendor's stall, leads to the Piazza Santa Maria Sovraporta, completely surrounded by medieval buildings. On the right are two 14th-century palaces, and, on the left, the 13th-century battlemented buildings of the **Palazzo di Parte Guelfa** ❼ which houses a library. It was enlarged by Brunelleschi in the 15th century and given its external staircase by Vasari in the 16th.

This palace was the official residence of the political faction that ruled the city from the mid-13th to the mid-14th centuries, when Cosimo de' Medici's pragmatic leadership put an end to the Guelf/Ghibelline feud that had split Florence for the preceding 150 years.

Palazzo Davanzati ❽

✉ Via Porta Rossa 13, www.polo museale.firenze.it ☎ 055-238 8610 ◷ daily 8.15am–1.50pm; closed 1st, 3rd and 5th Mon, 2nd and 4th Sun of the month; the two upper floors, which have reopened after restoration, can be visited in a group only, by appointment; visits take place at 10am, 11am and noon ◉ charge

EAT

On the top floor of La Rinascente department store on Piazza della Repubblica is a pleasant café where genteel staff serve coffees and food throughout the day. The view over the cathedral and rooftops is spectacular.

LEFT: colourful flowers for sale under the arcades on Piazza della Repubblica.
BELOW: the busy Mercato Nuovo.

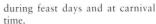

In style and decor, the lofty, galleried palace bridges the medieval and Renaissance eras, making Palazzo Davanzati the most authentic surviving example of a patrician dwelling from the period.

ABOVE: old Fiat 500s are sadly fast becoming a rare sight.
BELOW: the interior of the Palazzo Davanzati.

In the Via Porto Rossa, just round the corner from the Palazzo di Parte Guelfa, is the Palazzo Davanzati, home of a museum that gives a fascinating insight into life in medieval Florence. The palace is much more luxurious inside than would initially appear from the dour exterior; and it can be positively colourful on festive occasions, because the long iron poles on the facade were traditionally used to carry banners and flags during feast days and at carnival time.

Otherwise, the unremitting plainness of the facade, as with most 14th-century Florentine palaces, is relieved only by the typically Tuscan depressed window arches that thicken to a slight point at the apex, and by the coat of arms of the Davanzati family. This family acquired the property in 1578 and owned it until 1838, when the last of the line, perhaps suffering from centuries of inbreeding, committed suicide.

An antiquarian, Elia Volpi, bought the *palazzo* in 1904 and restored it sympathetically as a private museum. This was acquired in turn by the Italian state in 1951. Most Florentine palaces are still owned by the descendants of the first owners; this one, uniquely, is open to the public.

The vaulted entrance hall was designed mainly for protection, enabling the inner courtyard to be cut off from the street during times of trouble. Later, it was subdivided into three wool shops, much as contemporary aristocratic owners lease the ground floors of their palaces for use as shops, offices and galleries.

Domestic life revolved around the delightful inner courtyard, a peaceful retreat open to the sky but shaded from the sun by the high surrounding walls. A well in the corner by the entrance supplied water to all five floors – a rare luxury at a time when most households depended on the public fountains in nearby piazzas for their water supply.

From here, a graceful external staircase of banded white-and-grey stone rises on corbels and wall brackets to the upper floors.

Splendid interiors

In terms of decoration, the great Gothic halls on the second and third floors are the most unusual spaces.

The living quarters, with their gorgeous wall hangings, frescos and

Recommended Restaurants, Cafés & Gelaterie on page 147

painted ceilings, begin on the first floor. The Sala Madornale is above the entrance hall, and four holes in the floor enabled missiles to be dropped on would-be intruders.

The Sala dei Pappagalli (Room of the Parrots) is named after the bird motif that covers the walls, in rich reds and blues, imitating, in fresco, fabric wall hangings. The windows, now filled with leaded lights, were originally fitted with turpentine-soaked cloth to repel water and admit some light.

Off to the side of the little child's bedroom is one of several medieval bathrooms. In the main bedroom the sparseness of the furnishings is compensated for by the warmth and splendour of the wall paintings, a running frieze of trees and birds above armorial shields. The bedroom above is even more sumptuously decorated, with scenes from the French romance *La Châtelaine de Vergy*. Antique lace is displayed in a small side room.

The top floor was the domain of the women, the usual site of the kitchen so that smoke and cooking smells would not penetrate the living rooms. According to contemporary accounts of household management, far from leading a glamorous life, women were virtual slaves to the kitchen, and were found spinning and weaving when they were not preparing meals, rarely leaving the house except for church and festivals.

Even today, it is said that the daughters of the – apparently conservative – Florentine aristocracy are accompanied by a chaperone wherever they go. In some respects, it seems little has changed in the city since Dante first caught a fleeting glimpse of his beloved Beatrice and fed his fertile imagination for decades to come on a few equally brief encounters.

From Palazzo Davanzati, Via de' Sassetti leads into Piazza Strozzi via a left turn. Here you will find one of the last of the hundred or so great Florentine palaces built during the Renaissance, and certainly the largest.

ABOVE: students in Piazza della Repubblica.
BELOW: shopping is a popular pastime.

Palazzo Strozzi ⦿

✉ Piazza Strozzi, www.palazzo
strozzi.org 📞 055-264 5155
🕐 daily 9am–8pm, Thur until 11pm
💲 charge for exhibitions

Filippo Strozzi watched its construction from the family's house, itself of palatial dimensions, which stands on the opposite side of the piazza.

Bankrupt ambition

This grandiose building is a testament to the overweening pride of the powerful merchant and banker. He dared build a bigger palace than the Medici's Palazzo Medici-Riccardi.

The construction of the *palazzo* began in 1489; it was still not complete 47 years later, in 1536, when Strozzi died leaving his heirs bankrupt. The massive classical cornice was added as an afterthought towards the end of the construction when Roman-style architecture came into fashion. Original Renaissance torchholders and lamp brackets, carried on winged sphinxes, adorn the corners and facade. The interior, by contrast, has been ruined by the addition of a huge modern fire escape, installed

"temporarily" when the building began to be used as an exhibition hall.

By then, most of the arches of the Renaissance courtyard had been filled in with 19th-century windows to create office space for the various institutions that now occupy the upper floors. A small museum on the left displays the original model made by Giuliano da Sangallo, one of several architects who worked on the palace, and has exhibits explaining its construction.

Today Palazzo Strozzi is Florence's largest exhibition space and hosts popular art shows. These are held on its Piano Nobile (first floor), but there is public access at all times to the palace's courtyard, with its café and a small permanent exhibition on the building and the Strozzi family.

On the right of the courtyard is the **Gabinetto Vieusseux** (Mon, Wed and Fri 9am–1.30pm, Tue and Thur 9am–6pm), a public library with an excellent collection of books on the city and its art. Commonly known as Libreria Vieusseux, it is a favourite meeting place of scholars, literati and art historians of every nationality.

Around this area, to the west of Piazza della Repubblica, lies Via de' Sassetti and Anselmi, large and impressive-looking streets where all the banks are located, as well as some very expensive shops *(see also pages 274–7)*. ❏

The Gabinetto Vieusseux, commonly known as the Libreria Vieusseux, once welcomed virtually every visiting writer, from Thackeray and Ruskin to Stendhal, Zola and Tolstoy. Remarkably, Dostoevsky finished The Idiot *against a backdrop of chatter from the library's expatriate community and went on to plan* The Brothers Karamazov *here.*

RIGHT: designer bag.
BELOW: this area is popular with young, trendy Florentines.

BEST RESTAURANTS, CAFÉS AND *GELATERIE*

Restaurants

Prices for three-course dinner per person with a glass of wine:
€ = under €25
€€ = €25–40
€€€ = €40–60
€€€€ = more than €60

Cantinetta dei Verrazzano
Via dei Tavolini 18r ☎ 055-268 590 ☻ Mon–Sat 8am–9pm, July–Aug 8am–4pm. € [p313, C2]
This is part bakery, part *enoteca*. The bakery has special flavoured breads, pastries and tiny pizzas. Or sit in the enoteca for a glass of Chianti and some pecorino cheese with balsamic vinegar, or an assortment of foccaccia with prosciutto.

Giubbe Rosse
Piazza della Repubblica 13/14 ☎ 055-212 280 ☻ B, L & D daily. €€–€€€ [p312, C2]

Florence's famous literary café is still a haunt of writers and actors. *Panini* and a buffet for lunch with an upmarket dinner menu.

L'Incontro (The Savoy)
Piazza della Repubblica 7 ☎ 055-273 5891 ☻ L & D daily. €€€€ [p313, C2]
The Savoy's bar and restaurant is an elegant setting in which to enjoy Tuscan cuisine from a select menu. Not cheap, but the food is delicious and the service excellent.

Il Paiolo
Via del Corso 42r ☎ 055-215 019 ☻ Closed Sun and Mon L. €€ [p313, C2]
Cosy restaurant which serves up good-quality Italian food at lunch and dinner. Fresh fish and home-made desserts.

BELOW: Festival del Gelato.

Cafés and Gelaterie

Caffè della Posta
Via Pellicceria 24r. Tel: 055-214 773. Open L daily. [p312, C2] This simple café offers outdoor seating and light lunches.

Chiaroscuro
Via del Corso 36r. Tel: 055-214 227. Open Mon–Sat 8am–9.30pm, Sun 3–8.30pm. [p313, D2] Coffee from all over the world, flavoured hot chocolates, cocktails, a buffet lunch and one of the best *aperitivi* in Florence.

Festival del Gelato
Via del Corso 75r. Tel: 055-239 4386. Closed Mon. [p313, C2] Don't let the neon lighting and tourists put you off. Every flavour possible features here.

Gilli
Piazza della Repubblica 3. Tel: 055-213 896. Open daily 8am–midnight. [p312, C2] Claims to be Florence's oldest café, with a lavish interior.

Paszkowski
Piazza della Repubblica 31/35r. Tel: 055-210 236. Closed Mon. [p312, C2] This grand café may be overpriced but it's great for lunch and after-dinner drinks accompanied by live music.

Perchè No?
Via de' Tavolini 19r. Tel: 055-239 8969. [p313, C2] One of the oldest ice-cream parlours in town and a pioneer of the *semifreddo* – a mousse-like *gelato*.

Recommended Restaurants, Bars, Cafés & Gelaterie on page 157

SAN LORENZO

The powerful Medici family left its mark
all over the city – and all over Tuscany.
But nowhere is their ancestry more evident
than in this area north of the Duomo

Cosimo I, duke of Florence and later Grand Duke of Tuscany, consolidated his grip on the newly created Principality of Florence by moving out of the ancestral palace and into the Palazzo Vecchio in 1540. In doing so, he left behind an area of the city that had been home to the Medici for generations, the place from which an earlier Medici dynasty had been content to rule.

Nevertheless, the family connection with the parish remained so strong that every Medici of any consequence would always return, albeit in a coffin, for burial in the family chapel, attached to the church of San Lorenzo.

Under Cosimo de' Medici (later called Cosimo il Vecchio, the elder), Piero the Gouty and Lorenzo the Magnificent, this area was the centre of power from 1434–92. It is now neither beautiful nor especially imposing. The Medici Palace has become simply the familiar backdrop to the everyday life of the city, the nearby streets littered with the debris of the **Mercato Centrale ❶**, the central market, a huge indoor food market (Mon–Sat 7am–2pm), while the church of San Lorenzo itself is obscured by the canvas awnings of the leather, souvenir and cheap clothes stalls of the **San Lorenzo market** (daily 9am–7pm, Tue–Sun in winter).

But then again, perhaps the district has always been like this – busy, noisy, a jumble of the almost splendid and the almost squalid, home to some of the richest and poorest people. Above all, in the time of the early Medici, it must have looked like one great construction site, with masons, carpenters and tile-makers busy on the dome of the nearby cathedral and Cosimo himself one of the busiest builders.

Main attractions
MERCATO CENTRALE
PALAZZO MEDICI-RICCARDI
SAN LORENZO
BIBLIOTECA LAURENZIANA
CAPPELLE MEDICEE
CENACOLO DI FULIGNO

LEFT: a splendid fresco covers the interior of San Lorenzo's dome. **RIGHT:** scarves for sale in the market.

San Lorenzo's lively market – in the network of streets around the church of San Lorenzo – is a great place to shop for souvenirs, particularly leather goods and clothes. Head to the covered Mercato Centrale, with its tempting array of fresh produce, to pick up a picnic.

VIA CAMILLO CAVOUR

ABOVE RIGHT: colourful fruit-and-vegetable stall in the Mercato Centrale. **BELOW:** San Lorenzo stallholder.

At No. 1 on the busy street running between San Marco and the Duomo – Via Camillo Cavour – is the **Florence Tourist Office** (Via C. Cavour 1; tel: 055-23320; www.firenzeturismo.it; Mon–Sat 8.30am–6.30pm, Sun 8.30am–1pm). This is a useful place to pick up maps, and information on

Florence's museums and events. The office also gives you a break from studying art and architecture before moving on to the Palazzo Medici further down the road.

Cosimo de' Medici has been described as a man with a passion for building, convinced that what he built would, like the monuments of ancient Rome, last for 1,000 years or more and immortalise his name; and to a large extent this has proved to be true. He commissioned scores of buildings, not just in Florence but as far away as Paris and Jerusalem – cities in which the Medici name was associated with the banking empire founded by his father, Giovanni.

Ironically, and perhaps inevitably, he did not always see the finished product. His own palace, now the Palazzo Medici-Riccardi – incorporating the name of its later owners – was begun in 1444 but was still not complete when he took up residence there, in 1459, just five years before his death.

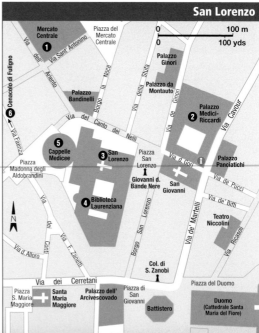

San Lorenzo

Palazzo Medici-Riccardi ❷

✉ Via Cavour 1, www.palazzo-medici.it
📞 055-276 0340 🕐 Thur–Tue
9am–7pm 💲 charge

The colossal *palazzo*, built by Cosimo Il Vecchio and described by Pope Pious II as "fit for a king", was the prototype for Florentine palace architecture. If it looks austere, that was entirely deliberate. Cosimo carefully cultivated the image of a man of few pretensions, a man concerned with matters of the mind rather than with material finery. He rejected the first plans, drawn up by Brunelleschi, as they were too ostentatious, and instead chose Michelozzo, his favourite architect, to design something simpler.

Today, it looks more elaborate than it originally was, because the simple arches of the ground floor, once an open loggia, were given their classical, pedimented windows by Michelangelo in the 16th century. The only real concession to ornament are the Gothic-style windows of the upper floors – recalling those of the 13th-century Palazzo Vecchio – and the much simplified classical cornice.

Inside the palace

Inside, the main courtyard purposely evokes the monastic cloister, for Cosimo was a religious man who took retreats in the specially reserved cell of the Dominican priory, San Marco, his own foundation. Antique Roman inscriptions and friezes set into the walls recall that he was also a keen classical scholar, who hired agents to scour Europe and the Near East for ancient manuscripts.

A small garden beyond the courtyard harks back to the medieval, but, like so much of the palace, it looks sparser because it now lacks the antique sculptures and art treasures – including Donatello's *Judith and Holofernes* – that went to the Uffizi and Palazzo Pitti when the Medici family moved out.

Only one room, the Medici Chapel – also known as the Cappella dei Magi – retains its 15th-century appearance; it is reached by stairs leading off a corner of the courtyard. Many of the rest – which are now used for temporary exhibitions – were altered after the Riccardi family bought the palace in 1659, and again, more recently,

The Riccardi marquises, who bought the palace in 1659, were the wealthiest family in Florence until the early 18th century.

BELOW LEFT: street life near San Lorenzo.
BELOW: fresh local produce.

when they were converted into the offices of the Town Prefecture.

The chapel frescos were commissioned by Piero, Cosimo's sickly eldest son (known as the Gouty) and were painted by Benozzo Gozzoli in 1459.

Entrance to the chapel is limited to groups of eight visitors every seven minutes. To avoid queues, call a day in advance to make a reservation.

Piero's liking for rich colours, in contrast to the simple taste of his father, is well reflected in the gorgeous scenes of Benozzo Gozzoli's *Journey of the Magi* (1459, *see painting on page 69*), with their retinue passing through an idealised vision of the Tuscan landscape. Many contemporary personalities of the time are depicted in the scene, including, of course, members of the Medici family, identified by ostrich-feather emblems: among them are Lorenzo the Magnificent on the white horse, his father Piero di Cosimo behind him wearing the red beret, and the latter's brother Giovanni. Look, too, for Gozzoli's self-portrait; his name is written around the rim of his cap. The frescos were restored in 1992, and their colours and gold leaf are now extraordinarily vivid.

SAN LORENZO

The Palazzo Medici-Riccardi backs onto Piazza San Lorenzo, where the equestrian statue of Giovanni delle Bande Nere by Bandinelli (1540) looks out of place amid the bustle of the modern street market. Above the sea of canvas awnings rises the dome of San Lorenzo, unmistakably the work of Brunelleschi, cousin to his cathedral dome, and partnered by the smaller cupola of Michelangelo.

San Lorenzo ❸

✉ Piazza San Lorenzo 📞 055-264 5184 🕐 Mon–Sat 10am–5.30pm, Sun 1.30–5.30pm 💰 charge

The church's facade is rough and unfinished (Michelangelo's design, which can be seen in the Casa Buonarroti, was never built), but the interior is outstanding, a gracious composition of the aptly named grey stone *pietra serena* and white walls. It is one of the earliest and most harmonious of all Renaissance churches, representing a break with French Gothic and a return to an older, classical style.

ABOVE souvenir T-shirts for sale.
BELOW: Brunelleschi's dome, San Lorenzo.

Giovanni, father of Cosimo de' Medici, commissioned Brunelleschi to design San Lorenzo in 1419, but the vicissitudes of the Medici banking empire meant that progress was halting, and neither Giovanni nor Brunelleschi lived to see it complete. Thereafter, successive members of the Medici family continued to embellish it, commissioning the greatest artists of their age to add frescos, paintings and – ultimately – their mausoleum. The two great tank-like bronze pulpits in the nave include reliefs by Donatello (*c.*1460) – the crowded and realistic *Deposition* and *Resurrection* scenes – which are among his last and most mature works. They were completed by his pupils after he died.

Beneath Brunelleschi's great soaring dome, in front of the high altar, a massive inlaid marble slab covers the grave of Cosimo de' Medici, buried here in great pomp – despite his characteristic request for a simple funeral – in 1464, after which he was posthumously awarded the title Pater Patriae – Father of His Country.

On the left, off the north transept, the Old Sacristy, which was designed by Brunelleschi, contains the monuments of Cosimo's parents and two grandchildren; frescos on the altar dome painted in 1442 depict the night sky and the positions of the signs of the zodiac as they were on 4 July 1439 *(see margin right)*.

Nearby, the Bronzino fresco of the *Martyrdom of St Lawrence* (1565–9) is a masterful study of the human form in a multitude of contorted gestures, bending to stoke the fire beneath the martyr's gridiron, pumping the bellows and altogether, in their nudity, forming an ironic counterpoint to the notice in the church entrance requesting that all visitors "rigorously avoid the wearing of indecent clothes such as miniskirts and shorts".

The *cantoria* (choir gallery), opposite the left pulpit, copying the style

of Donatello, is no great work, but is one of the few to have survived in its original position. Next to it is another rarity, a modern painting by Pietro Annigoni (1910–88) – along with a work showing Joseph and Christ in a carpenter's workshop against the hills of Tuscany and a blood-red sky, symbolic of Christ's sacrifice, by sculptor Marino Marini of Pistoia, who trained in Florence (he spent much of his working life in Milan).

The quiet cloister to the north of the church (take the entrance to the left

The dome over the altar is painted with the passage of the sun through the stars and constellations as they were on 4 July 1439. This was a date of great importance in the history of Florence, for it was on this day that a document was signed in the cathedral designed to unite the Roman Catholic and the Eastern Orthodox churches. It was not to be: no sooner had the Eastern delegates returned to Constantinople than they abandoned the agreement.

ABOVE LEFT: a holy water stoup in San Lorenzo. **BELOW:** the church's nave.

of the church facade), with its box-lined lawns and pomegranate bushes, gives access by the stairwell in the corner to the Biblioteca Laurenziana.

Biblioteca Laurenziana ④

📞 055-211 590 🕒 during exhibitions only, Mon–Sat 9.30am–1.30pm
🅒 charge (includes entrance to church)

The library was designed by Michelangelo between 1524 and 1534. The vestibule is almost totally occupied by Ammannati's extraordinary monumental staircase which leads up to the library itself. It is a dramatic and sophisticated design, which shows Michelangelo trying to cram too many elements into a tiny space, brilliantly inventive but needing a room many times bigger for the ideas to be fully worked out.

By contrast, the interior of the rectangular library is deliberately simple and serene, a scholar's retreat with no visual distractions, lined with lectern-like reading benches. It houses an important collection of classical manuscripts – some of them beautifully illustrated – which was

> *Every block of stone has a statue inside it and it is the task of the sculptor to discover it.*
>
> Michelangelo

begun by Cosimo de' Medici, including the famous 5th-century Virgil Codex and the 8th-century Codex Amiatinus from the monastery at Jarrow in England.

Cappelle Medicee ⑤

✉ Piazza Madonna degli Aldobrandini, www.polomuseale.firenze.it 📞 055-238 8602 🕒 daily 8.15am–1.50pm, closed 1st, 3rd and 5th Mon of the month 🅒 charge

RIGHT: catching up on the news.
BELOW: San Lorenzo's quiet cloister.

Recommended Restaurants, Bars, Cafés & Gelaterie on page 157

In the cold, dark mausoleum to the rear of San Lorenzo lie the graves of Medici family members who once ruled great swathes of Europe, having married into the major ruling dynasties of Naples, France and Spain. You enter the mausoleum via the crypt, where simple floor slabs commemorate the lesser members of the family, including cardinals and archbishops.

Stairs lead upwards from here to the opulent Cappella dei Principi (Chapel of the Princes, currently undergoing some restoration work), so ambitious in its use of costly marbles and semi-precious stones that, from its beginning in 1604, it took nearly 300 years to complete.

The roof of the cupola contains impressive frescos, whilst each of the four great sarcophagi, big enough to contain a score or more burials, is surmounted by a crown, a monument to imperial pretensions and a symbol of nouveau riche wealth and power.

Two niches contain bronze statues of the deceased dukes Cosimo II and Ferdinando I. The other three, Cosimos II and III and Francesco I, were planned but never executed. The only details that delight are the 16 colourful intarsia coats of arms, one for each of the principal towns in Tuscany.

A passage off to the left leads to Michelangelo's New Sacristy and his masterful tombs of an earlier generation of the family. On the right, the reclining figures of *Night* and *Day* adorn the monument to Giuliano, son of Lorenzo the Magnificent, and, on the left, the figures of *Dawn* and *Dusk* sit below the meditative statue of Lorenzo, grandson of the Magnificent. Neither member of the Medici family played any significant role in the city, and only the sculpture – which, some claim, is Michelangelo's greatest work – has kept alive their names.

One of the few Medici worthy of a monument by Michelangelo, Lorenzo the Magnificent himself – the popular and talented poet, philosopher, politician and patron of the great artists of his day – is buried here in near-anonymity in a double tomb with his brother Giuliano. Above the tomb is Michelangelo's *Madonna and Child*, intended as part of an unfinished monument to Lorenzo.

In 1516, Pope Leo X commissioned Michelangelo to design the facade for San Lorenzo. Michelangelo visited Carrara to select marble for the work, but the Pope then changed his mind and asked the artist to turn his attention to the Sagrestia Nuova instead.

BELOW: eating alfresco on Piazza del Mercato Centrale.

Michelangelo the rebel

Despite the quality of the work he did for them, Michelangelo never really enjoyed working for the Medici. The New Sacristy was commissioned by Popes Leo X and Clement VII, both Medicis. It was his first commission.

But he resented how they were subverting the old republican political institutions which Cosimo and Lorenzo had guided so adroitly. This is reflected in the sombre mood of the sculpture and the incompleteness of the sacristy – he only worked on it sporadically in 1520 and again in 1530–3. In between these dates he was an active opponent of the Medici.

ABOVE: a Medici chapel ceiling panel.
BELOW RIGHT: Michelangelo's *Night*.

The Medici were expelled from the city in 1527, but they returned to take Florence by force, backed by the army of the Holy Roman Emperor. Michelangelo supervised the construction of fortifications and established a battery of cannons in the campanile, enabling the city, briefly, to withstand the siege.

In 1530, however, the city fell to the imperial army – the *Night* sculpture is said to be associated with Michelangelo's shock at the city's loss of freedom – and he went into hiding in this very sacristy. The walls of the small room to the left of the altar are covered in pencil sketches thought to have been drawn at that time. These are not normally shown to the public, but some of Michelangelo's drawings for column bases are visible on the walls either side of the altar.

Northwest of San Lorenzo, at Via Faenza 42, is the **Cenacolo di Fuligno** ➏ (tel: 055-286 982; Tue, Thur and Sat 9am–noon; donation expected), which contains Perugino's well-preserved frescoed version of the *Last Supper* in the refectory. ❑

A Lot of Tripe

If you want to "eat as the locals do" in Florence, then the tripe stands around San Lorenzo's Mercato Centrale (and elsewhere) will provide you with a perfect opportunity to do so – *if* you're game. Known as *tripperie*, these small mobile stalls sell not only tripe but just about every other part of the cow that is edible and left over after the butcher has cut up the best bits. The offal is served up either in a little dish with a plastic fork or on a *panino* or roll, to customers ranging from dust-coated builders and local shopkeepers to high-heeled secretaries and suited businessmen. Manna from heaven to the initiated, unspeakable horror to anyone else, the choice of goodies on offer varies, but you can usually find most of the following. *Trippa alla fiorentina* is traditionally stewed tripe with tomatoes and garlic, served hot with parmesan; it is also served cold as a salad. *Lampredotto* are pigs' intestines, and are usually eaten in a roll after having been simmered in a rich vegetable stock; *nervetti* are the leg tendons, again cooked in stock, while *budelline* are intestines cooked in a rich sauce. All this is normally washed down with a glass of rough-and-ready wine, often served in a plastic cup; there are no frills on tripe stands. The *tripperie* are usually open all day, from about 9am to 7pm.

BEST RESTAURANTS, BARS, CAFÉS AND *GELATERIE*

Restaurants

Prices for three-course dinner per person with a glass of wine:
€ = under €25
€€ = €25–40
€€€ = €40–60
€€€€ = more than €60

Giannino in San Lorenzo
Borgo San Lorenzo 35/37r
☏ 055-212 206 ☺ L & D daily. €€€ [p313, C1]
One of the better restaurants in this area, offering traditional food such as *bistecca alla fiorentina* and *ribollita* and a selection of wines. Themed evenings too.

LOBS
Via Faenza 75/77 ☏ 055-212 748 ☺ L & D daily. €€€ [p308, B3]
One of the best fish restaurants in Florence, LOBS offers a range of seafood including swordfish, prawns, octopus and lobster, which should be ordered in advance.

Nerbone
Piazza del Mercato Central (inside the market) ☏ 055-219 949 ☺ L Mon–Sat. € [p308, C3]
One of the most popular lunch spots of the area, Nerbone serves up local dishes featuring seasonal ingredients and a daily menu. The *bollito* sandwich, with boiled meat, is a favourite. No credit cards.

Osteria dell'Agnolo
Borgo San Lorenzo 24r
☏ 055-211 326 ☺ L & D daily. €€ [p313, C1]
Home-made pasta and a range of pizzas, *calzoni* and desserts make this *osteria* a good, solid, albeit touristy, option near the market.

Trattoria Mario
Via Rosina 2r ☏ 055-218 550 ☺ L only; closed Sun. € [p308, C3]
Hidden away behind market stalls, this tiny trattoria boasts a lively atmosphere and is popular with the local stallholders. Try the typical *trippa alla fiorentina* or the *ribollita*. No credit cards.

Trattoria ZàZà
Piazza del Mercato Centrale 26r ☏ 055-215 411 ☺ L & D daily. €€–€€€ [p308, C3]
Set in the piazza behind the market, this popular trattoria offers a range of pasta, meat- and fish-based dishes.

Bars, Cafés and Gelaterie

Casa del Vino
Via dell'Ariento 16r. Tel: 055-215 609. Open Mon–Sat 9.30am–4.30pm, closed Aug and Sat in summer. [p308, C3]
One of the oldest wine bars in Florence, and a favourite haunt of stallholders from the Mercato Centrale.

Nannini
Borgo San Lorenzo 7r. Tel: 055-212 680.
Open daily 7.30am–7.30pm. [p313, C1]
A good place to stop off for a drink or ice cream or to try some traditional *panforte*.

Sieni
Via Sant'Antonio 54r. Tel: 055-213 830. Open L daily. [p308, C3]
This quiet café next to the market is famous for its traditional pastries, but you can also order a light bite to eat.

BELOW: Trattoria ZàZà serves up traditional Tuscan fare in a charming rustic setting.

SAN MARCO

As well as the art treasures in the church of San Marco, this part of the city is home to one of Florence's most famous works – Michelangelo's *David* – held in the Accademia, the world's first school of art

The area north of the cathedral, now occupied by the buildings of Florence's university, was once very much an extension of the Medici domain. **Piazza San Marco**, where students now gather between lectures, is named after the convent and cloisters on the north side of the square, whose construction was financed by Cosimo de' Medici. Unfortunately the square is ruined by the buses coming and going from the stops on both sides.

An older convent on the site was in ruins when Dominican friars from Fiesole took it over in 1436, and the following year, at Cosimo's request, the architect Michelozzo began to rebuild it.

SAN MARCO CHURCH ❶

✉ Piazza San Marco 📞 055-287 628
🕒 Mon–Sat 8.30am–noon, 4–6pm, Sun 4–5.30pm 🎫 free

The church of San Marco was remodelled subsequently and is decorative, but of more interest are the peaceful cloisters and monastic buildings that make up the fascinating Museo di San Marco.

Museo di San Marco

✉ www.polomuseale.firenze.it 📞 055-238 8608, booking: 055-294 883
🕒 Mon–Fri 8.15am–1.50pm, Sat–Sun 8.15am–4.50pm, closed 1st, 3rd and 5th Sun of the month, 2nd and 4th Mon of the month 🎫 charge

The museum showcases outstanding paintings and frescos by Fra Angelico, who spent much of his life within the walls of this peaceful monastery.

Main attractions

SAN MARCO CHURCH
CASINO MEDICEO
THE UNIVERSITÀ
GIARDINO DEI SEMPLICI
GALLERIA DELL'ACCADEMIA
PIAZZA AND CHURCH OF
  SANTISSIMA ANNUNZIATA
SPEDALE DEGLI INNOCENTI
MUSEO ARCHEOLOGICO
CIMITERO DEGLI INGLESI

LEFT: art students learning about the old Renaissance masters.
RIGHT: fresco adorning the walls of the Spedale degli Innocenti.

Bronze statue of General Manfredo Fanti in front of San Marco church.

Henry James said of Fra Angelico that all his paintings convey a passionate pious tenderness, and that "immured in his quiet convent, he never received an intelligible impression of evil". That may be true of most of his work, but he did not lack the imagination to conceive the horrors of eternal punishment. In the Ospizio dei Pellegrini (Pilgrims' Hospice), the first room on the right of the cedar-filled cloister, the lively *Last Judgement* is one of the most intriguing of the many altarpieces he painted.

The blessed gather in a lovely garden below the walls of the Heavenly City, but the damned are being disembowelled and fed into the mouth of hell, there to undergo a series of tortures appropriate to their sins: the gluttons are forced to eat snakes and toads, the gold of the misers is melted and poured down their throats.

Gentler by far is one of his most accomplished works, the *Tabernacle of the Linaiuoli*, commissioned in

BELOW: Fra Angelico's *Crucifixion*.

1443 by the Flax-Workers' Guild, depicting the Madonna enthroned and surrounded by saints. Across the courtyard in the Sala del Capitolo (Chapter House) is Fra Angelico's great *Crucifixion* (c.1442). Vasari reports that the artist wept whenever he painted this subject. The angry red sky, throwing into high relief the pallid flesh of Christ and the two thieves, invites comparisons with Van Gogh's work.

In the Refettorio Piccolo (Small Refectory), at the foot of the dormitory stairs (follow signs for the Bookshop), the *Last Supper* is one of two painted by Domenico Ghirlandaio (the other can be admired in the convent next to the church of Ognissanti). A small cat occupies the focal position at the bottom of the fresco, adding to the extraordinary naturalism, in which each Apostle is individually characterised, and the tableware and garden scene reveal much about 15th-century style and taste.

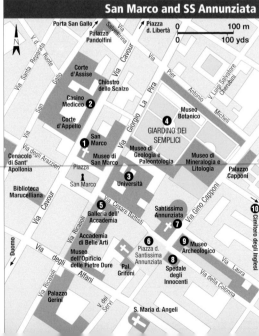

San Marco and SS Annunziata

Monastic opulence

The Dormitorio is the high point of the museum, consisting of 44 monastic cells under a great open roof. Fra Angelico's *Annunciation* greets visitors at the top of the stairs, as fresh as the morning when the angel arrived to greet the young Virgin with the good news. It reflects the particular reverence the Dominicans had for the Mother of God. Beyond, each cell contains a small fresco, intended as an aid to contemplation, stripped to its essential religious significance, unlike the gorgeous and crowded paintings commissioned by the guilds and rich patrons.

Cells 1 to 10, on the left of the left corridor, are probably the work of Fra Angelico, the rest by his assistants. Cell 7, the *Mocking of Christ*, is typical of his mystical, almost surrealistic style, where, against a black background representing the darkness of night, disembodied hands beat Christ about the head, and others count out the 30 pieces of silver, the price paid to Judas for his betrayal.

Savonarola believed in the futility of earthly deeds and passions and saw only the afterlife as important, so, fittingly, Cells 12 to 14 contain his hair shirt, as well as a copy of a contemporary painting of his execution, an event which caused a riot in the city. Having been struck a mortal blow by the executioner, Savonarola's body was raised on a pile of faggots and set on fire. Suddenly, the flames and smoke cleared and the dead Savonarola was seen to raise his hand in blessing. Terrified Florentines fought to escape from the square; many died in the stampede.

The other wing of the Dormitory leads past the Biblioteca (library), designed by Michelozzo in 1441, a graceful hall built to house the illuminated manuscripts donated by Cosimo de' Medici to create Europe's first public library. The cells that Cosimo reserved for his own retreats (38 and 39) are at the end of the corridor. The wall of Cell 39 is decorated with

ABOVE: the *Last Supper* by Ghirlandaio.
BELOW: San Marco faithful.

*Casino Medico
literally means "the
Medici's little house"
which, considering
its size, is quite an
inappropriate name.
However, at the time
is was built (1574),
it was situated at the
edge of the city, and
was considered a
rural retreat.*

ABOVE RIGHT: old-fashioned dairy shop.
BELOW: University office building.

the Three Kings and their retinue visiting the Nativity, in a scene painted by a young Benozzo Gozzoli.

AROUND SAN MARCO

Back in Piazza San Marco, Via Cavour, in the northwestern corner, leads past the **Casino Medico** ❷ (at No. 57), an imposing house ornamented with rams' heads and scallops. The garden (hidden behind a high wall) once contained Cosimo's collection of antique sculpture (now in the Uffizi), which Michelangelo studied ardently as an adolescent. The *palazzo* now houses Florence's Corte d'Appello, or Court of Appeal.

Further up the street, at No. 69, is the elegant **Chiostro dello Scalzo** (tel: 055-238 8604; Mon, Thur and Sat 8.15am–1.50pm; free), with frescos by Andrea del Sarto of scenes from the life of John the Baptist.

At the end of the road, **Piazza della Libertà** is an imposing square which is now a giant roundabout. Before reaching this, a left turn on Via Salvestrina leads to Via San Gallo, where **Palazzo Pandolfini** is on the corner at No. 74. This country villa, designed by Raphael in 1520, is one of his few architectural works to have survived. The entrance provides views of the peaceful gardens, and the facade is decorated with playful dolphins, a pun on the name of the owner, Bishop Pandolfini. Nearby is the impressive colonnaded ex-Hospital di Bonifacio, now the Questura, or

Recommended Restaurants, Cafés & Gelaterie on page 169

police station. To the north lies Porta San Gallo, the ancient gate that defended the old road to Bologna, which marks the northernmost point of the walled city.

To the south, Via San Gallo leads to Via XXVII Aprile and the **Cenacolo di Sant'Apollonia** at No. 1 (tel: 055-238 8607; daily 8.15am–1.50pm, closed the 2nd and 4th Mon, 1st, 3rd and 5th Sun of month; free). As the dining room of the 14th-century convent of Sant'Apollonia, it was, like most monastic refectories, decorated with a fresco of the Last Supper. But this one is a newly restored masterpiece of early Renaissance art, painted by Andrea del Castagno around 1450. Note how Judas, separated from the other disciples, has the facial features of a mythical satyr – or, some would say, of the devil himself.

The Università ❸

On the northeastern side of Piazza San Marco are the buildings now occupied by the administrative offices of the Università – originally built as stables for the horses and wild animals kept by Duke Cosimo I. The University comprises several small museums at Via Giórgio La Pira 4; the collections housed here were mostly started by the Medici family. A cumulative ticket offering entrance to all of the University's museums is worth investing in if you're visiting more than one.

There is a fabulous array of fossils in the **Museo di Geologia e Paleontologia** (tel: 055-275 7536; Mon, Tue, Thur, Fri and Sun 9am–1pm, Sat 9am–5pm; charge). The **Museo di Mineralogia e Litologia** (tel: 055-275 7537; Mon, Tue, Thur, Fri and Sun 9am–1pm, Sat 9am–5pm; charge) has a collection of exotic rocks, including a 68kg (151lb) topaz and 12 enormous Brazilian quartzes. Also on display are glass models of famous gems.

Giardino dei Semplici ❹

✉ Via Micheli 3 ☎ 055-275 7402
🕑 Apr–mid-Oct Thur–Mon 10am–7pm, off season Sat–Mon 10am–5pm
© charge

Attached to the University's Natural History Museum, this delightful botanical garden was begun by Duke Cosimo in 1545 and is one of the world's oldest botanical gardens. Medicinal herbs were grown and studied here: Semplici refers to the "simples", ingredients used by medieval apothecaries in the preparation

Look up when walking through the streets around the San Marco district: interesting architectural details abound.

LEFT: in the Giardino dei Semplici.
BELOW: preparing for a lecture in Piazza San Marco.

Michelangelo's David stands proudly at the heart of the Galleria dell'Accademia.

of medicine. Today, tropical plants and Tuscan flora have been added to the collection.

On the southeastern side of Piazza San Marco is one of the oldest loggias in Florence (built in 1384). It leads to the **Galleria dell'Accademia** ❺ *(see pages 170–1)*.

From the Accademia, Via Ricasoli leads south to its junction with Via degli Alfani and the Conservatorio. Midway down Via degli Alfani at No. 78, the **Museo dell'Opificio delle Pietre Dure** (tel: 055-294 883; Mon–Wed, Fri–Sat 8.15am–2pm, Thur 8.15am–7pm; charge, combined ticket available with the Galleria dell'Accademia) has a small museum devoted to

the Florentine art of decorating furniture with inlaid semi-precious stone *(pietra dura)*. It also houses an important restoration centre.

A left turn into Via dei Servi takes you to one of the loveliest squares in Florence, **Piazza della Santissima Annunziata** ❻, surrounded on three sides by a colonnade, and recently restored to traffic-free status. In the middle is an impressive bronze statue of Ferdinando I mounted on a horse by Giambologna and his pupil Pietro Tacca. The latter's elaborate bronze fountains flanking the equestrian statue have been recently restored.

The fair held in the piazza on the feast of the Annunciation (25 March) fills it with festive stalls selling home-made biscuits and sweets, and another delightful festival in the first week of September – La Festa della Rificolona – sees children gather in the square at dusk with candlelit lanterns to commemorate the birth of the Virgin.

To the north is the church of Santissima Annunziata.

RIGHT: one of Luca della Robbia's terracotta roundels for the Spedale degli Innocenti.
BELOW: a studious monk reading on the steps of Santissima Annunziata.

Santissima Annunziata ❼

✉ Piazza della Santissima Annunziata
☎ 055-266 181 ☉ daily 8am–12.30pm, 4.30–6.30pm ☉ free

Built in 1516–25, Santissima Annunziata (The Most Holy Annunciation) is still a living church and has not become a tourist haunt. It is a place of worship that is far more typical of the rest of Italy than it is of Florence.

Compared to the rational interiors of so many of the city's churches, this one is heavily ornamented. Devout Florentines come in and out all day to pray before the candlelit baldachin that is so cluttered with votive offerings that the object of their veneration is almost hidden; it is an image of the Virgin, said to have been painted by Fra Bartolomeo. Devout worshippers believe that the friar fell asleep, exhausted by his attempts to

Recommended Restaurants, Cafés & Gelaterie on page 169

capture the spiritual beauty of the Virgin, and he awoke to find that the image had been completed for him, by angelic hands. It is from that legend that the church got its name.

The seven-bay portico of the church deliberately echoes the design of the Spedale degli Innocenti *(see below)*. It is interesting for its frescos, several of which were painted by Andrea del Sarto. Though damaged, his *Visitation of the Magi* is still a rich and colourful scene, in which the three kings are accompanied by an entourage of giraffes, camels and splendidly dressed courtiers.

A door from the left aisle leads to the Chiostro dei Morti (Cloister of the Dead), which contains more of his frescos and the burial vaults of many leading 16th- and 17th-century artists, including Cellini.

On the east side of the square is Florence's Renaissance orphanage.

Spedale degli Innocenti ⓼

✉ Piazza Santissima Annunziata 12
☎ 055-203 7308 ⓒ daily 10am–7pm ⓒ charge

A revolving door in the wall of the Spedale degli Innocenti was designed as a depository of unwanted newborns, often those of domestic servants, to be collected by the nuns on the other side.

The world's first orphanage opened in 1445, as the enlightened Republic of Florence took radical measures to put an end to the habit of abandoning babies. Part hospital, part orphanage, the Ospedale has acted as a refuge for children ever since and is home to a Unicef Research Centre.

The colonnade, which Brunelleschi began in 1419, was the first of

ABOVE LEFT: a good way of getting around town. **BELOW:** fountain in Piazza della Santissima Annunziata.

the city's classical loggias and the inspiration behind all the others. The portico is decorated with Andrea della Robbia's famous blue-and-white tondi of swaddled babies.

The museum collection

The museum within is not much visited and is a quiet, cool retreat in summer. It occupies the upper rooms of the cloister, from which there are views onto the green courtyard and Brunelleschi's slender Ionic columns. Above, the spandrels are decorated with sgraffito – drawings of infants and cherubs scratched into the plaster when still wet.

Many of the frescos in the museum came from nearby churches, removed to expose earlier paintings beneath. Several are displayed with their *sinopia* alongside. These were the sketches roughed out in the plaster using red pigment (obtained from Sinope, on the Black Sea) to guide the artist when the finishing coat of plaster was added and the fresco painted.

The former boys' dormitory contains paintings commissioned for the orphanage, enriched by donations. The restrained Renaissance setting makes a suitably austere backdrop for an intimate collection of 15th-century chests and paintings.

Nearly all of the paintings are variations on the theme of the Madonna and Child. The most remarkable is the radiant *Adoration of the Magi* by Ghirlandaio, commissioned for the high altar of the church. The artist places himself in the work, and the rich Nativity scene in the foreground contrasts poignantly with the scenes of slaughter – the Massacre of the Innocents – in the background. Despite the gloom, the prevailing mood is of the tender care and consolation provided by the Madonna.

A stone's throw from the Ospedale, across Via della Colonna, lies one of the best collections of Etruscan art in Italy.

Museo Archeologico ❾

✉ Via della Colonna 38 ☎ 055-235 750 ☻ Tue–Fri 8.30am–7pm, Sat–Sun 8.30am–2pm, hours may change, telephone prior to your visit ☻ charge

The museum was badly hit by the 1966 flood, but a long period of restoration work is just about complete (the Etruscan tombs in the garden are still closed). School parties excepted, the museum is rarely crowded, and it is a pleasure to browse here peacefully – although the fact that Egyp-

ABOVE: the porticoed entrance to the Spedale degli Innocenti.
BELOW: San Marco architecture.

Recommended Restaurants, Cafés & Gelaterie on page 169

> *So Mrs Browning, every day, as she tossed off her Chianti and broke another orange off the branch, praised Italy and lamented poor, dull, damp, sullen, joyless, expensive, conventional England.*
>
> Virginia Woolf

tian treasures have been well restored while the indigenous art of ancient Florence and Tuscany has not is cause for some sadness.

Renovations have included the opening of a new foyer, extended exhibition space, restored Egyptian rooms and an impressive facelift to the second floor. However, staff shortages mean that the latter, which houses some of the museum's greatest features, can only be seen with a guide at appointed times during the day, usually every hour.

Etruscan tombs

The Etruscan tomb sculpture on the first floor seems, at first, a mass of hunting and battle scenes taken from the heroic myths of the Greeks. Little by little, though, one discovers the domestic scenes that were carved from real life rather than copied from Hellenic prototypes: banquet scenes, athletic dancers, coffins carved in the shape of Etruscan houses with columns and entrance gates, and an arch (exhibit 5539) that can be paralleled in many a 15th-century Florentine palace. Above the tombs, the reclining figures of the dead are obese and garlanded, a wine bowl in their hands, symbolising the eternal feasting and sensual pleasures of the afterlife.

Etruscan bronzes

The room devoted to bronze work (Room 14) shows another aspect of the Etruscan culture that the Florentine artists of the Renaissance later inherited: their skill in bronze casting. Here are delicate mirrors inscribed with erotic scenes, cooking pots, military equipment and harnesses, statues and jewellery.

Three of the most important pieces were excavated in the 16th century,

ABOVE LEFT: the Medici coat of arms on a fresco inside the Spedale.

Tree-Shaded Tombs

From Via della Colonna, Borgo Pinti leads north to Piazza Donatello. Here, marooned on an island in the middle of a major traffic intersection, is the **Cimitero degli Inglesi ⑩**, or English Cemetery (Piazzale Donatello 38; tel: 055-582 608; Mon 9am–noon, Tue–Fri 3–6pm, 5pm in winter; donation expected). Opened in 1827, this is the burial place of numerous distinguished Anglo-Florentines, including Elizabeth Barrett Browning, Arthur Hugh Clough, Walter Savage Landor, Frances Trollope (mother of Anthony and author in her own right) and the American preacher Theodore Parker. Sadly, traffic noise prevents this from being the restful spot it should be, despite the beauty of sheltering cypress trees. The library in the cemetery seeks books written by and about those buried here, and an emergency appeal is under way to restore the place to its former beauty.

KIDS

Dan Brown's *Da Vinci Code* has made Leonardo da Vinci more popular than ever before. And the Museo Leonardo da Vinci (Via dei Servi 66/68r, tel: 055-282 966; daily 10am–7pm; charge), which has interactive displays of his inventions, is also a hit with kids, who will enjoy dangling from the flying machines and manipulating the exhibits.

RIGHT: green balcony.
BELOW: Egyptian tablet depicting four scribes at work, *c.*1400 BC, Museo Archeologico.

when Florentine artists, aware of the brilliant work of their predecessors, went in search of the finest examples. The fantastical 5th-century BC Chimera, discovered at Arezzo in 1553, was entrusted to Benvenuto Cellini, who repaired its broken legs. The statue represents a mythical creature with a lion's body and three heads: lion, goat and snake *(see page 28)*.

The Arringatore (or Orator, *c.*1st century BC) was discovered in Trasimeno in 1566, and the statue of Minerva was found accidentally in Arezzo in 1541; Cosimo I once kept it in his office in the Palazzo Vecchio.

Egyptian treasures

The Egyptian collection resulted from the joint French-Italian expedition of 1828–9. It includes a chariot from a 14th-century BC tomb at Thebes, but equally compelling is the large quantity of organic materials that survived in the arid, oxygen-starved atmosphere of the ancient desert tombs: wooden furniture, ropes, baskets, cloth hats and purses, all looking as fresh as if they had been made only recently, and throw-

ing an illuminating light on the ordinary life of the ancient Egyptians.

Attic vases and ancient bronzes

The revamped second floor is dedicated to ancient Greek, Etruscan and Roman works of art. The attic pottery collection features the famous *Vaso François* (François Vase; Room 11), named after its discoverer, Alessandro François, and significant both for its size and detailed illustration.

In the central corridor is a series of Greek statues in marble; here, two outstanding figures representing Apollo (dated between 530 and 510 BC) demonstrate both the Hellenic origins of Etruscan art and the astounding similarities between the work of the Renaissance and the Etruscan sculptors, though separated by two millennia.

Access (with guide) is now available to the Medici Corridor, designed to allow Cosimo II's disabled sister, Princess Maria Maddalena, passage to the church of Santissima Annunziata away from the public gaze. Today the corridor displays numismatic and glyptic collections, with views into the church at the far end. ❑

BEST RESTAURANTS, CAFÉS AND *GELATERIE*

Restaurants

Prices for three-course dinner per person with a glass of wine:
€ = under €25
€€ = €25–40
€€€ = €40–60
€€€€ = more than €60

Accademia
Piazza San Marco 8r
C 055-217 343 L & D daily. €€ [p309, D3]
Close to the eponymous museum containing Michelangelo's *David*, this restaurant offers both a retreat from culture and a warm setting where pizzas and other food are washed down with the good house wine.

Pugi
Piazza San Marco 10
C 055-280 981 [p309, D3]
This place is famous among Florentines for their *schiacciate* (flat breads of various kinds). Buy focaccia or pizza by weight as a snack or lunch on the run.

Ristorante da Mimmo
Via San Gallo 57/59r
C 055-481 030 Closed Sun. €€ [p309, D2]
Set in a former theatre, with a changing menu of typical Tuscan cuisine, this place offers good food and wine at affordable prices.

Lo Skipper
Via degli Alfani 78r C 055-284 019 L & D Mon–Fri; D only Sat. €€ [p309, D3]
If you fancy something a little different, try this restaurant run by a nautical club. It offers good Italian food as well as changing dishes inspired by other culinary traditions, such as Mexican and Greek food. Hidden off the main tourist route.

Taverna del Bronzino
Via delle Ruote 27r C 055-495 220 L & D; closed Sun. €€€–€€€€ [p309, C2]
A variety of European cuisines served in an elegant restaurant with a vaulted ceiling and patio. Try the *ravioli alla senese* (ricotta-and-spinach-filled pasta parcels) or one of the less Italian but equally divine dishes.

Il Vegetariano
Via delle Ruote 30r C 055-475 030 D Tue–Sun, L Tue–Fri. € [p309, C2]
Il Vegetariano's use of the freshest vegetables in its dishes makes it the main contender for the city's best vegetarian eatery, although admittedly there are few in Florence between which to choose. The atmosphere here is informal and unassuming.

Cafés and Gelaterie

Caffèlatte
Via degli Alfani 39r.
Tel: 055-247 8878.
Open daily 8am–midnight. [p313, E1]
This cosy little café produces healthy home-made cakes, soups and other light snacks from the kitchen behind. Steaming milky lattes (appropriately, given its name) are served in huge, bowl-like mugs.

Gelateria Carabè
Via Ricasoli 60r.
Tel: 055-289 476.
Closed Mon in winter. [p309, D3]
Not to be missed if you are a fan of ice cream; Sicilian *gelato* made from ingredients shipped in from the island itself.

Nabucco
Via XXVII Aprile 28r.
Tel: 055-475 087.
Closed Sun. [p309, C2]
Serves a light lunch and brunch at the weekends. Also offers a nice wine list and an extensive buffet at *aperitivo* hour.

Robiglio
Via dei Servi 112 (other branches include Viale dei Mille). Tel: 055-212 784. Open Mon–Sat 8am–8pm. [p309, D3]
One of the chain of Robiglio cafés serving delicious pastries and chocolates as well as lunches. Try the squidgy choux buns.

ABOVE RIGHT: dairy delights at Caffèlatte.

THE ACCADEMIA

The world's first school of art, the gallery is now home to Michelangelo's most famous work, *David*

Michelangelo's *David* is the main attraction of the Galleria dell'Accademia, but the rest of the art is equally worthy of attention. The museum was originally part of the world's first art school, the Accademia delle Belle Arti, an institution established by Cosimo I de' Medici and of which Michelangelo was a founding academician. The current gallery was consolidated in the late 18th century by Grand Duke Leopoldo next to the art school housed in the same row of buildings.

The collection contains sculpture and early Renaissance religious art, and has been expanded to include a display of musical instruments. On entry, the Sala del Colosso shows the plaster cast of Giambologna's *Rape of the Sabine Women* (on display in the Loggia dei Lanzi – *see page 102*) and a collection of colourful religious art from the early Cinquecento (16th century). While the exit to the right of the entrance leads to the Museo degli Strumenti Musicali, the Accademia continues through the door to the left. The view of Michelangelo's

LEFT: a double bass made by Bartolomeo Castellani in 1792.

ABOVE: amongst the most notable pieces is Filippino Lippi's striking *Deposition from the Cross*, which was finished by Perugino on the former's death. Other highlights are *Christ as a Man of Sorrows* – a poignant fresco by Andrea del Sarto – and Fra Bartolomeo's *Prophets*.

David from the end of the corridor-shaped Galleria dei Prigionieri is stunning, the domed Tribuna di Michelangelo framing the statue.

Off to the left of the Tribuna di Michelangelo are three small rooms – the Sala del Duecento e Prima Trecento, the Sala dei Giotteschi and the Sala degli Orcagna. These all hold early Florentine works, including works by Taddi and Daddi. The *Tree of Life* by Buonaguida is one of the best-known and most impressive works in the small collection.

Stairs, adorned with Russian icons, lead to the first floor and four further rooms. The first two showcase decorative altar panels from the late 14th century. The following room is dedicated to Florentine painter Lorenzo Monaco, whose work expresses the bridge between Gothic and Renaissance art – the key to understanding the Florentine style.

The essentials

✉ *Via Ricasoli 60, www.polomuseale.firenze.it*

☎ *055-238 8612, for bookings 055-294 883*

🕐 *Tue–Sun 8.15am– 6.50pm*

💶 *admission charge includes entry to the Museo degli Strumenti Musicali*

ABOVE: the approach to the Tribuna is lined with sculptures by Michelangelo, including his *Slaves* (also known as *The Prisoners*), unfinished works which were intended for the tomb of Pope Julius II but became the property of the Medici family instead.

BELOW: Botticelli's delightful *Madonna and Child* is displayed in the Sale del Quattrocento Fiorentino, as is Paolo Uccello's masterpiece *Scenes of a Hermit Life.*

BELOW: front panel of a *cassone*, or wedding chest, painted by Lo Scheggia, depicting a wedding scene in front of the baptistery, *c.*1450.

DAVID

Standing at over 4 metres (13ft), Michelangelo's *David* is the most famous sculpture in Western art. It was sculpted between 1501 and 1504 as a symbolic commemoration of the start of republican Florence, through its depiction of the young boy who slew Goliath. Originally in front of the Palazzo Vecchio (a copy stands *in situ*), the statue was moved to the Accademia in 1873. The marble from which *David* was carved was famously rejected as faulty by other artists, but the then 29-year-old Michelangelo sought to embrace its faults and patches of discoloration. If the proportions seem imperfect (eg the large head in relation to the body), it is because the statue was originally commissioned for the facade of the Duomo, and so was designed to be seen from far below. Michelangelo's attention to minutiae is clear in the muscle contour of the legs and the veins in the arms, which can be admired from every angle thanks to the way the statue is displayed. The eyes are of particular interest for their heart-shaped pupils. Surrounding *David* in the main room are works by contemporaries, including di Tito and Allori. The Salone del Ottocento is cluttered with more modern and less attractive sculptures and busts, primarily by Lorenzo Bartolini – and the rooms known as the Sale del Quattrocento, which display 15th-century Florentine paintings, are sadly often closed.

Recommended Restaurants, Bars & Cafés on page 183

SANTA MARIA NOVELLA

A real "mixed bag" of attractions awaits visitors to the area west of the Duomo, but at its heart lies the church of Santa Maria Novella, with its magnificent collection of art

In the same colours as the Duomo and Santa Croce is the recently restored church of Santa Maria Novella.

The square in front of the church lies within the 14th-century city walls, but the city's population never grew to fill the space. It remained an undeveloped corner on the western edge of the city, used, from 1568 on, for annual chariot races: the obelisks supported on bronze turtles at either end of the square mark the turning points on the racetrack. In the 19th century the square was peaceful, its new hotels popular with foreign visitors. Henry James, Ralph Waldo Emerson and Longfellow, translator of Dante, all wrote in rooms looking down on the quiet piazza.

In contrast the modern piazza has long had a reputation as a seedy quarter with a mishmash of hotels and *pensiones*, and as a favourite haunt of pickpockets, touts and other undesirables. However, the square has recently seen a major overhaul with new paving and gardens, more police on the beat, a number of new upmarket hotels nearby and a facelift for the fine facade of Santa Maria Novella church. The new Alinari museum of photography, on the south side of the square, is an exciting new cultural addition to this up-and-coming area.

SANTA MARIA NOVELLA ❶

✉ Piazza Santa Maria Novella
📞 055-282 187 🕐 Mon–Thur 9am–5pm, Fri–Sun 1–5pm 💶 charge

The church of Santa Maria Novella is rewarding on the outside with its delicate white marble facade, although

Main attractions
SANTA MARIA NOVELLA
STAZIONE CENTRALE
OGNISSANTI
LE CASCINE
PIAZZA GOLDONI
PALAZZO RUCELLAI
MUSEO MARINO MARINI
PALAZZO CORSINI
SANTA TRINITÀ
PALAZZO BARTOLINI-SALIMBENI
SANTISSIMI APOSTOLI

LEFT: religious imagery on a street corner.
RIGHT: detail from *The Birth of St John the Baptist* from Ghirlandaio's fresco cycle in the Cappella Tornabuoni.

RIGHT: Thomas Aquinas in stained glass.
BELOW: Giotto's newly restored *Crucifix.*

more so on the inside. It is also one of Florence's great art churches.

Romanesque style

Building began in 1246, starting at the east end. The lower part of the facade, in typically Florentine Romanesque style, was added *c.*1360. Another 100 years passed before the upper part of the facade was finished; the inscription below the pediment dates it to 1470 and includes the name Ihanes Oricellarius, the Latinised form of Giovanni Rucellai, who commissioned the work from Battista Alberti.

Fear of plague

To the right of the church, the walled Old Cemetery with its cypress trees is lined with the tomb recesses of many a noble Florentine, and the lavishness of the church interior owes much to the wealth of these same families. Frightened into thoughts of eternity by the Black Death that devastated

the city in the 14th century, they donated lavish chapels and works of art in memory of their ancestors. It was here, in this church, that Boccaccio set the beginning of *The Decameron*, when a group of young noblemen and women meet and agree to shut themselves away to avoid contact with the disease, and entertain each other by telling stories.

The basic structure of the church is Gothic, but a toned-down version rather than the florid French style. Pointed arches and simple rib vaults

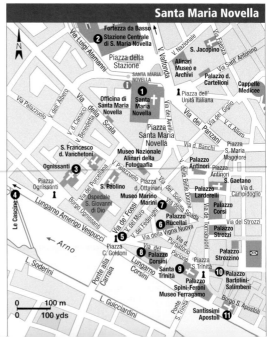

Recommended Restaurants, Bars & Cafés on page 183

are supported by widely spaced classical columns. The only architectural decoration comes from the alternate bands of white marble and soft grey *pietra serena*. Suspended from the ceiling, seemingly floating above the nave, is Giotto's *Crucifix* (1290).

The best of the monuments and frescoed chapels are at the east end. In the south transept (on the right) is the Cappella di Filippo Strozzi, with frescos by Filippino Lippi, son of Filippo Lippi and Lucrezia – the nun he seduced while painting the walls of the Carmelite convent in Prato. In style and subject matter, Filippino's work is nothing like that of his father, nor, indeed, that of any of his own contemporaries. His *St Philip*, standing in front of the Temple of Mars with the dragon he has just slain, is full of classical – rather than Christian – allusions, and his crowd-filled scenes and remarkable *trompe l'œil* architecture are brimming with energy.

Wooden crucifix

In the Cappella Gondi, to the left of the main altar, is a wooden crucifix by Brunelleschi, traditionally thought to have been carved to show Donatello how the Redeemer should be represented: Brunelleschi is said to have called Donatello's crucifix in Santa Croce "a mere peasant on the Cross". Brunelleschi's cross, his only sculpture to survive in wood, was carved sometime between 1410 and 1425.

In the north transept, the Cappella Strozzi di Mantova has frescos by Nardo di Cione, painted 1351–7. The *Inferno*, based on Dante's vision, is a maze of demons and tortured souls, while *Paradiso* is crowded with the saved, including portraits of Dante himself and the patrons, members of the Strozzi banking family, being led to heaven by an angel.

Last but not least, one of Santa Maria Novella's most famous frescos, Masaccio's *Trinity* (1428), is on the north aisle wall. This complex,

poignant masterpiece exemplifies the early Renaissance artist's pioneering work in perspective and portraiture. Look for Lorenzo Lanzi, Masaccio's patron, kneeling in the foreground of the painting, opposite his wife.

Museum and Cloisters

Ⓒ Mon–Thur 9am–5pm Ⓒ charge

The entrance to the Cloisters – with more great frescos, all restored since the 1966 flood – is tucked away to the left of the church facade. The first is the Chiostro Verde, or Green Cloister, so called after the frescos of Paolo Uccello, which are painted in a green pigment called *terra verde*.

Behind the main altar, the late 15th-century frescos by Ghirlandaio and his pupils (including Michelangelo) are among the most vibrant in Florence. The Life of the Virgin is set in the artist's own time, with details of everyday life and portraits of members of the Tornabuoni family, who commissioned the work. The fresh colours are almost gaudy, and the work was dismissed contemptuously by John Ruskin as verging on the vulgar.

ABOVE: turtles prop up the obelisks standing in front of the church.
BELOW: street fresco.

Stazione Santa Maria Novella may not be to everyone's taste, but it is regarded as a masterpiece of Functionalist style.

RIGHT: Madonna and Child on a wall inside the cloisters.
BELOW: the altar in the Cappellone degli Spagnoli.

Ironically, his major masterpiece, the *Universal Deluge* (*c.*1445), was severely damaged by the flood – although it is actually in better condition than most of the others.

On the north side of the cloister is the Cappellone degli Spagnoli (Spanish Chapel), built *c.*1350 as the chapter house and renamed in the 16th century when the entourage of Eleonora di Toledo (wife of Cosimo I) adopted it as their place of worship. The fresco cycle by the little-known Andrea di Buonaiuto (1365–7) – also called Andrea da Firenze – represents the teachings of St Thomas Aquinas; it includes a depiction of the Duomo, with a dome which did not then exist – nor did it for another 100 years.

AROUND THE SQUARE

Stazione Santa Maria Novella ❷

The church lies by the eponymous railway station (also called Stazione Centrale), the first building that most visitors to Florence see and the first building in Italy to be designed in the Functionalist style. Designed by Michelucci in 1935, the station is perhaps one of the finest modern buildings in Italy. Its clean, functional lines were remarkably avant-garde for the time, and the digital clock at the front is one of the earliest examples of its kind. In spite of this, its appearance was greeted by a joke at its unveiling: "I see the box the station came in, but where is the station?"

Museo Nazionale Alinari della Fotografia

✉ Piazza Santa Maria Novella 14a, www.alinarifondazione.it ☎ 055-216 310 ⏰ Thur–Tue 10am–7pm 💲 charge

On the south side of Piazza Santa Maria Novella, the **Alinari National Museum of Photography** now occupies a building which has been variously used over the centuries as a medieval hospital, a Dominican convent, a school for destitute girls and a prison. The Alinari Museum was founded in 1852 and once housed in Palazzo Ruccellai, the firm which supplied 19th-century Grand Tourists with prints, postcards and art books. It has one of the best photographic collections in Europe and still publishes handsome books whose outstanding black-and-white plates show Florence as it was in the time of George Eliot, the Brownings, Ruskin, E.M. Forster and Henry James.

After a major restoration of the building, the museum reopened in 2006. The first two rooms are devoted to temporary exhibitions. The rest charts over 160 years of photography, from its mid-19th century origins to cameras of the new millennium. Displays include daguerreotypes by the pioneers of the new invention, examples of the first photographic prints from paper negatives, camera obscuras and a collection of cameras ranging from the early rudimentary models to the sophisticated examples that became popular after the Kodak revolution.

From here, Via Valfonda leads north to the Viale and the **Fortezza da Basso**, built by Alessandro de' Medici in 1534 as a symbol of the family power. (Ironically, he was assassinated within its walls by his cousin, Lorenzaccio, in 1537.) After the 1966 flood, the fortress was used as a centre for the restoration of damaged works of art. An international exhibition centre, used to stage fashion shows and trade fairs, was built within the walls in 1978. The massive outer walls were smartened up in 1996 for the European summit held in Florence that year.

EN ROUTE TO OGNISSANTI

From Piazza Santa Maria Novella, there is a choice of routes to Ognissanti, of which Via de' Fossi has most to offer. It has the greatest concentration of art galleries in the city, some specialising in original paintings and others stacked with reproduction Davids, Venuses and female nudes, available in every size from mantelpiece ornaments to monumental.

Alternatively, Via della Scala followed by a left turn has the **Officina di Santa Maria Novella**, at No. 16 (tel: 055-436 8315; www.smnovella.it; Mon–Sat 9.30am–7.30pm, Sun

ABOVE: detail from the glazed terracotta lunette over the Ognissanti doorway. **BELOW:** inviting autumnal shop display.

Botticelli's St Augustine. Ognissanti *is the final resting place of the Renaissance artist, who lived locally. He is buried beneath a circular tomb slab in the south transept.*

10.30am–6.30pm); the descendants of the 16th-century Dominican friars who founded this pharmacy still make up herbal remedies to cure various ailments according to the old recipes. The shop is housed in a frescoed 13th-century chapel, and sells fragrant soaps and toilet waters.

Piazza Ognissanti is open to the river bank, and the hotel buildings on either side frame the view of the plain brick facade of the church of San Frediano on the opposite bank, and up to Bellosguardo on the hill beyond. Once upon a time the view would have been obscured by the many buildings that were erected across the river at this point, standing on wooden piles, to make use of the water in the processes of washing, fulling and dyeing cloth.

Ognissanti ❸

✉ Borgo Ognissanti 42 📞 055-239 8700 🕒 daily 9am–12.30pm, 4–7.30pm 🎟 free

The church of Ognissanti (All Saints) was itself built by an order of monks, the Umiliati, who supported themselves by wool-processing. It was completed in 1239 but later came under the patronage of the Vespucci family, merchants who specialised in importing silk from the Orient and whose most famous member, Amerigo, gave his name to the New World. The Vespucci built the adjoining hospital, and several of the family are buried in vaults beneath the great frescos they commissioned.

On the right side of the nave, Ghirlandaio's fresco of 1472 shows the Madonna della Misericordia, her arms reaching out in symbolic protection of the Vespucci family. Amerigo is depicted as a young boy; his head appears between the Madonna and the man in the dark cloak.

Further along the south aisle is Botticelli's *St Augustine*, companion piece to Ghirlandaio's *St Jerome* on the opposite wall, both painted in 1480 and based on the portrait of St Jerome by the Flemish artist Jan van Eyck, then in the collection of Lorenzo the Magnificent. It is thought that both works were commissioned by Giorgio Vespucci, Amerigo's learned tutor.

Le Cascine

From Borgo Ognissanti, a 15-minute walk west along the river bank (keeping to the north side) will take you to **Le Cascine ❹**, a pleasant park that runs along the embankment west of the city for 3km (2 miles). Cascina means "dairy farm", and that is what it was until it was acquired by Duke Alessandro de' Medici and laid out as a park by his successor, Cosimo I. A fountain in the park is dedicated to Shelley, who took a walk here on a particularly blustery day in 1819 before penning "Ode to the West Wind".

A large market is held here every Tuesday morning, and it is always crowded at weekends with families walking the dog, joggers and rollerbladers burning up the asphalt. At most times a place of innocent pleasure, it is also the haunt of transvestite prostitutes and is best avoided after dark.

In the sanctuary off the north transept, recently discovered frescos by father and son Taddeo and Agnolo Gaddi depict in brilliant colour and realistic detail the Crucifixion and Resurrection of Christ. A similar delight in the realistic portrayal of birds, flowers, fruit and trees enlivens a *Last Supper* of Ghirlandaio (1480) in the refectory of the next-door convent (Mon, Tue and Sat 9am–noon; free).

AROUND OGNISSANTI

At Borgo Ognissanti 26 is one of the few Art Nouveau buildings in Florence. It is an excellent example of the style, with exuberant bronze balconies, lamps and window boxes.

Back towards town, Borgo Ognissanti leads southeast to the **Piazza Goldoni** ❺, the busy meeting point of eight roads. The Via della Vigna Nuova leads past the **Palazzo Rucellai** ❻, halfway up on the left. This, one of the most ornate palaces in Florence, was built in 1446–51 for Giovanni Rucellai, humanist, author and intellectual, and one of the richest men in Europe. In style it blends medieval pairs of lancet windows with classical columns, pilasters and cornices.

Museo Marino Marini ❼

✉ Piazza San Pancrazio, www.museo
marinomarini.it 📞 055-219 432
🕐 Mon, Wed–Sat 10am–5pm,
closed Aug 🎫 charge

Off Via della Spada, behind Palazzo Rucellai, is the Museo Marino Marini, which is housed in the ancient church of San Pancrazio. The museum is dedicated to Marino Marini (1901–80); it contains some 180 of his sculptures, paintings and prints, with recurring themes of horses and riders, jugglers and female figures.

PUBLIC FASHION, PRIVATE ART

Via della Vigna Nuova emerges in **Via de' Tornabuoni**; these two are Florence's most upmarket shopping streets. The former is home to such names as Valentino, Versace and La Perla, while the latter is lined with palaces that house the showrooms of

ABOVE: Pucci, on Via de' Tornabuoni, is the quintessential Florentine fashion house.
BELOW: window-shopping on Via della Vigna Nuova.

Milan may be the fashion capital, but Florence has its fair share of home-grown designers of international repute. Nearly all have their outlets at the southern end of Via de' Tornabuoni, including the shoemaker Ferragamo.

BELOW:
reading by the river.

Pucci, Ferragamo, Armani, Gucci and Prada – names that evoke a world of style and craftsmanship that the Florentines believe is another legacy of the Renaissance.

The bridge near here is the **Ponte alla Carraia**, the easternmost of the four ancient bridges across the Arno. When it was constructed in 1220 it was called the Ponte Nuovo to distinguish it from the older Ponte Vecchio. What we see now is a modern reconstruction. All of Florence's bridges, except for the Ponte Vecchio, were blown up during the Nazi retreat from Florence in 1944 in an attempt to halt the advance of the Allies. Even so, it is a faithful reproduction of the graceful 14th-century bridge, perhaps designed by Giotto, which replaced the first timber one.

Palazzo Corsini ❽

✉ Via del Parione 11, www.palazzo corsini.it ☎ 055-218 994 ☺ gallery and palace by appointment only Mon–Fri (closed for restoration) ☺ charge

On the Lungarno Corsini, this is one of the city's largest palaces, built in

1650–1717 and unmistakable for its villa-like form, with two side wings and classical statues lined along the parapet. It holds an extensive private art collection with works by Raphael, Bellini, Signorelli and Pontormo.

Further along, the **Palazzo Gianfigliazzi** (built in 1459) was the former home of Louis Bonaparte, king of the Netherlands (he died in 1846).

SANTA TRINITÀ DISTRICT

The Palazzo Masetti overlooks the **Ponte Santa Trinità**, the most graceful of the four Arno bridges. Some of the original masonry was recovered from the river after 1944, and the quarries of the Boboli Gardens were reopened to enable the bridge to be rebuilt in the original material and to the original design commissioned by Cosimo I from Ammannati in 1567.

The statues of the *Four Seasons*, carved by Pietro Francavilla for the wedding of Cosimo II in 1593, were also dredged from the river bed and restored to their original position.

A left turn into the elegant shopping street of Via de' Tornabuoni leads to **Piazza Santa Trinità**. On the right, the battlemented and formidable **Palazzo Spini-Feroni** is one of the city's few remaining 13th-century palaces. It was once the home of the couturier Salvatore Ferragamo, and his boutique (usually full of Japanese tourists and the Florentine great and good) is now on the ground floor. Above the shop, the small but excellent **Museo Ferragamo** (Via de' Tornabuoni 2; tel: 055-336 0456; Mon–Fri 9am–1pm, 2–6pm by appointment, closed Aug; free) is a testament to the life and work of one of modern Florence's best-known figures. Some of the most spectacular shoes in the world are on display, as well as memories of his trade and travels.

Opposite the *palazzo* stands the plain but noble Baroque facade of Santa Trinità.

Santa Trinità ❾

✉ Piazza Santa Trinità 📞 055-216 912 🕒 daily 8am–noon, 4–6pm

💶 free

Sadly now peeling, the church's facade has capitals ornamented with cherubs and the Trinity carved in the pediment above the central door. This facade was added in 1593–4 by Buontalenti, but the inner face retains its almost complete 12th-century Romanesque form, indicating the appearance of the original late 11th-century church. The rest of the church, rebuilt in 1250–60, is a simplified form of Gothic, typical of Cistercian austerity.

The life of St Francis

The frescos of the **Sassetti Chapel**, in the choir of Santa Trinità, were painted by Ghirlandaio in 1483 and illustrate the life of St Francis. The scene above the altar, in which Pope Honorius presents St Francis with the Rule of the Franciscan order, is set in the Piazza della Signoria. Lorenzo the Magnificent and the patron, the wealthy merchant Francesco Sassetti, are depicted on the right.

The altarpiece itself is a delightful painting, also by Ghirlandaio (1485), the *Adoration of the Shepherds*. Joseph turns to watch the arrival of the Magi, clearly bewildered by the extraordinary events in which he has been caught up, but Mary remains serene and beautiful throughout.

Instead of a manger, the infant Christ lies in a Roman sarcophagus; this, along with the scene on the outside wall in which the Sibyl foretells

ABOVE:
Ghirlandaio's *Adoration of the Shepherds.*
BELOW:
Ponte Santa Trinità.

the birth of Christ to the Emperor Augustus, shows the Florentine preoccupation with establishing continuity between their own Christian civilisation and that of the classical world.

On the opposite side of the road to the church is the Roman column taken from the Baths of Caracalla in Rome and offered by Pius IV to Cosimo I in 1560. It is now surmounted by the figure of Justice. Behind it is one of the last great palaces to be built in the city.

Palazzo Bartolini-Salimbeni

Built in 1521, this is a curiously feminine building, with a tiny and endearing inner courtyard covered with sgraffito. Today it is considered a gracious work, especially the delicate shell-hood niches of the upper floor. Nevertheless, it was ridiculed by contemporary Florentines, who thought it over-decorated.

Behind and to the east of the palace is a warren of narrow alleys lined with medieval towers and palaces and, in the little **Piazza del Limbo**, one of the city's oldest churches.

The architect of the Palazzo Bartolini-Salimbeni, Baccio d'Agnolo, answered his critics by carving an inscription above the door in Latin which translates as "It is easier to criticise than to emulate".

RIGHT: taking the time to chat.
BELOW: the ornate Palazzo Bartolini-Salimbeni.

Santissimi Apostoli ⑪

✉ Piazza del Limbo 1 ☎ 055-290 642
🕐 daily 10am–noon, 4–7pm 💲 free

The inscription on the facade attributes the church's foundation to "Karolus Rex Romae" – otherwise known as Charlemagne – in AD 786, but the church is Romanesque in style and was most probably built in the 10th century.

The double arcade of dark-green marble columns and Corinthian capitals includes some salvaged from the Roman baths of Via delle Terme. ❑

BEST RESTAURANTS, BARS AND CAFÉS

Restaurants

Prices for three-course dinner per person with a glass of wine:
€ = under €25
€€ = €25–40
€€€ = €40–60
€€€€ = more than €60

Buca Lapi

Via del Trebbio 1r ☎ 055-213 768 ⊙ D only; closed Sun. €€€ [p312, B1]
In the cellar of the Palazzo Antinori, this charming restaurant is regarded as serving one of the best *bistecca alla fiorentina* (enormous and beautifully grilled). As expected, being in the basement of the *palazzo* of one of Tuscany's best wine producers, it has an excellent range of wines. Reservations essential.

La Carabaccia

Via Palazzuolo 190r ☎ 055-214 782 ⊙ Daily noon–3pm, 7–11pm. €€€ [p308, A3]
Set in a renovated old tavern, La Carabaccia offers a daily and seasonal menu using the freshest ingredients. Speciality of grilled meats cooked on coal-burning grills and traditional Tuscan recipes all served amongst the original features of a medieval Florentine room, supplemented by a stone cellar full of the best Tuscan wines, where they make their own basil liqueur.

Coco Lezzone

Via Parioncino 26r ☎ 055-287 178 ⊙ Closed Sun. €€€ [p312, B2]
Traditional food using the freshest ingredients in a classic, some say unatmospheric, setting. Peasant dishes of *ribollita* and *pappa ai pomodori* can be followed with *secondi* of roast pork or *bistecca alla fiorentina*.

Harry's Bar

Lungarno A. Vespucci 22r ☎ 055-239 6700 ⊙ L & D; closed Sun. €€€€ [p312, A2]
Modelled on the original in Venice made famous by Ernest Hemingway, Harry's is an American-style restaurant and bar. It is renowned more for its cocktails than its food, but the latter is often innovative, and fish figures largely on the menu.

Il Latini

Via dei Palchetti 6r ☎ 055-210 916 ⊙ Closed Mon. €€ [p312, A2]
Expect to queue to get into this sprawling, noisy eatery with communal tables. But the Tuscan food is good and filling and the ambience jovial.

J.K. Lounge

Piazza S. Maria Novella 7 ☎ 055-264 5282 ⊙ L & D daily. €€€€ [p312, B1]
A chic modern restaurant attached to boutique hotel J.K. Place; the ambience is modern but perhaps a little cold. The food, however, is good.

Trattoria Sostanza

Via del Porcellana 25r ☎ 055-212 619 ⊙ L & D Mon–Fri. €€ [p312, A2]
Also known as Il Troia, this is a relaxed restaurant with communal seating offering traditional Tuscan dishes including *tortellini in brodo* (tortellini in broth). Concessions are not made for tourists, and some Italian would be useful. However, this is a true Florentine dining experience: substantial and satisfying food.

BELOW: stunning creation at La Carabaccia.

Bars and Cafés

Caffè Amerini
Via della Vigna Nuova 63r. Tel: 055-284 941. [p312, B2]
Smart yet welcoming, this is a great place for light bites and drinks, and good to while away a bit of time.

Noir
Lungarno Corsini 12r. Tel: 055-210 752. [p312, B3]
One of a chain across Europe's more expensive locations, Noir is frequented by the beautiful and trendy of Florence. It offers elegant – if perhaps over-fashionable – dining and cocktails as well as sushi *aperitivi*.

Roses
Via del Parione 26r. Tel: 055-287 090.
Open Mon–Sat noon–1.30am. [p312, B2]
This small bar in a pleasant area close to the river is good for a drink or to eat sushi in the small restaurant.

Recommended Restaurants, Bars & Cafés on page 193

OLTRARNO WEST

The attractions of the "other" side of the Arno don't stop with the Palazzo Pitti – visitors who take the time to explore this part of Florence further will be pleasantly rewarded

Crossing south over any of the bridges that span the Arno, you'll arrive in the district of Oltrarno – meaning simply "beyond the Arno" – first enclosed by walls in the 14th century. Florentines persist in thinking of it as on the "wrong" side of the Arno, although it has gained currency as an up-and-coming area. It contains many ancient and luxurious palaces, as well as some of the city's poorest districts, and has a different, more relaxed atmosphere than the north side of the river.

The southern end of the Ponte Vecchio is actually the more picturesque, for here the Vasari Corridor *(see page 118)* makes several twists and turns, corbelled out on great stone brackets, to negotiate the 13th-century stone tower that guards this approach to the bridge. The corridor then sails over the **Via dei Bardi** and runs in front of **Santa Felicità**, forming the upper part of a portico that shelters the west front. On the opposite side of the busy little **Piazza Santa Felicità** is a charming fountain composed of a 16th-century bronze Bacchus and a late-Roman marble sarcophagus, brought together on this site in 1958.

LEFT: the Florentine art of making marbled paper is still alive in the Oltrarno workshops.
RIGHT: street painter near the Palazzo Pitti.

SANTA FELICITÀ ❶

✉ Piazza Santa Felicità 📞 055-213 018 🕑 Mon–Sat 9am–noon, 3–6pm, Sun 9am–1pm 💶 free

Santa Felicità stands on the site of a late-Roman church, thought to have been built in the 3rd or 4th century AD by Eastern merchants at a time when Christians were still liable to persecution. It was rebuilt during the 16th century, and again in 1736, making effective use of contrasting bands of grey and white stone. The

Main attractions
SANTA FELICITÀ
PALAZZO PITTI
GIARDINO DI BOBOLI
CASA GUIDI
MUSEO DI ZOOLOGIA "LA SPECOLA"
PALAZZO GUADAGNI
SANTO SPIRITO
SANTA MARIA DEL CARMINE AND CAPPELLA BRANCACCI
SAN FREDIANO
BELLOSGUARDO

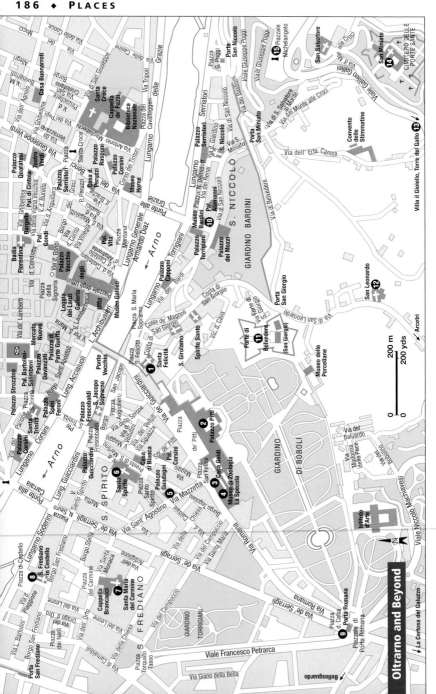

Oltrarno and Beyond

Recommended Restaurants, Bars & Cafés on page 193

frescos embellishing the Cappella Capponi (by Pontormo, 1525–8) include a remarkable *Annunciation*. The artist beautifully captures Mary as she climbs a staircase, one foot in the air, turning to hear the Archangel's scarcely credible message, with a look of genuine disbelief upon her face. Just as accomplished is the altarpiece, a *Deposition*, in which Pontormo succeeds in recreating, in oils, the vivid colours and translucence of fresco, and the deathly pallor of Christ's flesh.

AROUND THE PITTI

Via de' Guicciardini is named after the first historian of Italy, who was born in 1483 in the palace of the same name part-way down on the left. A slice of the fine garden and a relief of *Hercules and Cacus* can be glimpsed through the gate. Beyond lies the massive **Palazzo Pitti ❷** and the **Giardino di Boboli** *(see pages 194–9)*, the extensive gardens behind the Palazzo Pitti. The gardens are most usually accessed through the Palazzo Pitti, but can also be entered from Via Romana 39.

Casa Guidi ❸

✉ Piazza San Felice 8 📞 055-354 457 🕐 apartments: Apr–Nov Mon, Wed and Fri 3–6pm 💲 donation expected

On the first floor of the old Palazzo Guido is the residence where Robert and Elizabeth Barrett Browning lived from 1847, shortly after their secret marriage, until Elizabeth's death in 1861. Those with well-lined pockets can rent it through the Landmark Trust (www.landmarktrust.org.uk).

Beyond lies narrow Via Romana, a one-way street leading into town from Porta Romana and the southern suburbs. Along this road, a little way up on the left at No.17 is the Palazzo Torrigiani, which houses the zoology museum.

Museo di Zoologia "La Specola" ❹

✉ Via Romana 17 📞 055-228 8251 🕐 Thur–Tue 9am–1pm 💲 charge

This museum houses a vast collection of anatomical wax models, made

Pontormo's delicate Virgin in Santa Felicità church.

BELOW LEFT: the rising Boboli Garden provides sweeping views over the city.
BELOW: the gardens are dotted with sculptures of various eras and styles.

SHOP

For the ultimate in
Florentine style, make a
stop at historic Madova
(Via de' Guicciardini 1r;
tel: 055-239 6526;
www.madova.com)
near Palazzo Pitti, glove-
makers to the city's great
and good since 1919.

ABOVE RIGHT: a
Baroque *palazzo* with
sgraffito work on Via
Maggio. **BELOW:** book-
binder in his workshop
on Piazza Pitti.

between 1775 and 1814 by the artist
Susini and the physiologist Fontana.

The models were made for the serious purpose of teaching human and
animal anatomy. Provided that you
can overcome your squeamishness at
the site of apparently real human bodies laid out like meat on a butcher's
slab, there is much to be learnt, and
much to enjoy, in this unusual museum. The zoological section has an
enormous collection of stuffed or

pinned specimens of just about every
creature on earth or in the seas.

ANTIQUE SPLENDOUR ALONG VIA MAGGIO

Via Maggio, despite heavy traffic, is a
magnificent palace-lined street whose
many antiques shops are stuffed with
rich and expensive treasures – the
sheer quantity is an indication of the
past wealth of Florence and how
much furniture and art has survived.
At night, when the lights come on,
and before the shutters are drawn, it
is possible to glimpse richly frescoed
ceilings through the windows of
many an upper room – revealing the
splendour in which those Florentines
fortunate enough to have inherited
property pass their daily lives.

Immediately west of the Via Maggio, the scale and atmosphere changes
completely. The homes of the aristocracy give way to the homes of the
people in the districts of Santo Spirito
and San Frediano, adjacent parishes
that even have their own dialects and
were once the areas in which the
wool-dyers and leather workers
toiled at their noxious trades.

Recommended Restaurants, Bars & Cafés on page 193

The **Palazzo Guadagni** ❺ in Piazza Santo Spirito is one of the few palaces to be built this far west. The pillared upper loggia, open to the air, was an innovation when the palace was built, around 1505. Subsequently, many other palaces had an extra storey built in the same style, providing a retreat in which to enjoy the cool evening air above the noise of the city. The top floor now houses an old-fashioned *pensione*.

The piazza itself – also home to a large number of furniture restorers' workshops – is an attractive square, planted with trees, with an early morning market on weekdays and an antiques and flea market on the second Sunday of the month (8am–6pm). On the first Saturday and third Sunday of each month, the Fierucola (8am–6pm) is an eco-market, with organic food and natural remedies for sale.

SANTO SPIRITO ❻

✉ Piazza Santo Spirito   ☎ 055-210 030   ⏰ Apr–Oct Thur–Tue 8am–noon, 4–6pm, winter until 5pm   💶 free

The church of Santo Spirito was designed by Brunelleschi for the Augustinians and begun in 1436, but he never lived to see it finished. Over time, his plan was modified and compromised – not least by the 17th-century *baldachin* that dominates the eastward view of the nave and introduces a note of flamboyance into an otherwise measured classical composition. Mentally strip this away and you are left with a building that is

ABOVE: this masterpiece by Buontalenti on Via dello Sprone is probably the most famous fountain of Oltrarno.
BELOW: the facade of Santo Spirito.

*Il Torchio (Via de'
Bardi 17) makes
marbled paper to
a secret recipe in its
Oltrarno workshop.*

ABOVE RIGHT: bucolic
restaurant entrance.

secular in inspiration, modelled on
Roman civic architecture, and a
complete break with the Gothic style
that prevailed elsewhere in Europe.

A total of 40 chapels with side-
altars and paintings radiate from the
aisles and transepts. If Brunelleschi's
design had been executed in full, these
would have formed a ring of conical-
roofed apses around the exterior of
the church, clinging like a cluster of
limpets to the main structure. The one
artistic masterpiece, Filippino Lippi's
Madonna and Saints, painted around
1490, is now in the right transept, and
there are many other accomplished
16th-century paintings to enjoy.

Next door is the refectory housing
the **Cenacolo di Santo Spirito** (Piazza
Santo Spirito 29; tel: 055-287 043;
Apr–Oct Sat 9am–5pm, Nov–Mar
10.30am–1.30pm; charge), which
contains Orcagna's 14th-century
fresco *The Last Supper*. The fresco
was badly damaged in the 18th century, when doors were built into it so
that the building could be used a carriage depot, but the outer part can
still be seen. Above it is a more complete *Crucifixion*.

From here it is worth taking an
indirect route to the church of Santa
Maria del Carmine by way of Via
Sant' Agostino, left into the Via de'
Serragli and right into Via dell' Ardiglione. The last is the reason for the
detour, a simple, narrow street which
appears to have changed little since
Filippo Lippi was born here in 1406.
Scarcely wide enough to admit a car,
its buildings exclude the city noise,
and it does not take much imagination to think oneself back into the
15th century. Halfway down, an aer-
ial corridor links the two sides of the
street, and close to it is Lippi's birthplace, No. 30.

At the northern end, a left turn
into Via Santa Monaca leads to the
church of Santa Maria del Carmine.

SANTA MARIA DEL CARMINE ❼

✉ Piazza del Carmine 📞 055-238
2195 🕐 Mon, Wed–Sat 10am–5pm,
Sun 1–5pm Ⓖ charge (chapel)

The original church was destroyed
by fire in 1771, but by some miracle
the **Cappella Brancacci** (booking
required; tel: 055-238 2195; charge,
joint ticket with Palazzo Vecchio
available), with its frescos by Masaccio and Masolino, was unaffected
(see box).

Frescos in the Cappella Brancacci

The two artists who embellished the Chapel – Masaccio and Masolino
– had strikingly different styles. Masolino, a court painter, had a graceful, elegant touch, while Masaccio's was more realistic; it is the latter's
emotive depictions which leave a lasting impression. Masaccio lived for
only 27 years, and was just 24 when he began work on *The Life of St
Peter*, as a pupil of Masolino, in 1425. In 1427, Masaccio was put in sole
charge of the work, and the result has been called the first truly Renaissance painting. He developed the technique of chiaroscuro to highlight
the faces of Christ and the Apostles and, for the first time, applied the
principles of linear perspective, previously developed in architecture and
sculpture, to painting. However, these alone do not account for the extraordinary power of his work, or the influence it had on 15th-century artists.

Instead, it is the bold draughtsmanship and
the humanity expressed in the faces and
animation of the figures, such as Adam and
Eve in the powerful *Expulsion from Paradise*.
Masaccio's self-portrait is in a doorway to
the right of the enthroned St Peter.

The frescos' status as one of the city's unmissable sights has been enhanced by comprehensive restoration. The chapel is tiny and a maximum of 30 visitors are allowed entry for 15 minutes only. In high season it is wise to reserve weeks in advance.

SAN FREDIANO

Across the spacious Piazza del Carmine, spoilt by its use as a car park, lies **Borgo San Frediano**. This is the principal street of a district full of character, whose tough and hard-working inhabitants are celebrated in the novels of Vasco Pratolini, one of the city's best-known authors.

The district is no longer as rough or as squalid as it was earlier last century, when rag pickers made a living from sifting the nearby refuse dump, and tripe (for sale all over the city) was boiled in great cauldrons in back alleys. Cleaned up, it is now a neighbourhood of small shops selling everything from provocative underwear to fishing tackle.

The church of **San Frediano** ❽ looks unfinished because of its rough stone facade, but its fine dome unde-

niably adds a touch of glamour to this part of the city, and it looks over the Arno to the campanile of Ognissanti on the opposite bank.

At the western end of the Borgo is **Porta San Frediano**, built in 1324 and one of the best-preserved stretches of the 14th-century city walls.

BEAUTIFUL VIEW

One of the great joys of being in Florence is the proximity of the beautiful surrounding countryside. Other cities are ringed by sprawling suburbs, but in Florence such developments are thankfully limited to the north bank of the Arno, leaving the south side, Oltrarno and beyond, surprisingly rural. Natural landscapes, small farms and fine views are only 10 minutes' walk from the city centre.

Such is the case with **Bellosguardo**. Its name means "beautiful view", and that is exactly what attracts walkers up the steep paths to this hilltop village south of Florence, just above Porta Romana. The No. 13 bus goes as far as Piazza Torquato Tasso, and from here it takes no more than 20 minutes to walk up to the summit by

Oltrarno may be a bohemian neighbourhood but it still boasts beautiful religious imagery on many a street corner.

BELOW LEFT: having a chat in front of San Frediano.
BELOW: Borgo San Frediano facade.

way of Via San Francesco di Paolo and Via di Bellosguardo. You can stop at the viewpoint just before the Piazza di Bellosguardo.

A plaque in the piazza records the names of the many distinguished foreigners who have lived in the villas on this hillside, including Aldous Huxley, Nathaniel Hawthorne, the Brownings and D.H. Lawrence. At the very summit, offering the best views over Florence, is the **Villa dell' Ombrellino** – the home, at various times, of Galileo, the tenor Caruso, and Edward VII's mistress Alice Keppel and her daughter, Violet Trefusis (Vita Sackville-West's companion).

ABOVE: attractive villas cling to the hillsides above Florence.
BELOW: handmade books with marbled paper covers make tasteful souvenirs.

Back at the **Porta Romana** ❾, some 5km (3 miles) to the south (on the No. 37 bus route) lies the **Certosa del Galuzzo** (Via Buca di Certosa 2; tel: 055-204 9226; Tue–Sun, summer 9am–noon, 3–5pm, winter 9–11am, 3–4pm; donation expected). Sitting like a fortress above the busy arterial road that leads out of town towards Siena (the Via Senese), the imposing complex was founded in 1342 as a Carthusian monastery by Niccolò Acciaiuoli and is the third of six such monasteries to be built in Tuscany in the 14th century. Inhabited since 1958 by a small group of Cistercian monks, it is a spiritual place full of artistic interest.

The main entrance leads into a large rectangular courtyard and the church of **San Lorenzo**, said to be by Brunelleschi, who was also thought to be responsible for the graceful double-arched, lay brothers' cloister. Although the church itself is not very interesting, there are some imposing tombs in the crypt chapel.

Sixty-six majolica tondi by Giovanni della Robbia decorate the Chiostro Grande (Main Cloister), around which are the 12 monks' cells. Each of these has its own well, vegetable garden and study room; one is open to visitors.

The **Palazzo degli Studi** houses an art gallery which contains, most notably, a series of fine frescoed lunettes by Pontormo. ❏

BEST RESTAURANTS, BARS AND CAFÉS

Restaurants

Prices for three-course dinner per person with a glass of wine:
€ = under €25
€€ = €25–40
€€€ = €40–60
€€€€ = more than €60

Antico Ristoro di' Cambi
Via Sant' Onofrio 1r ☎ 055-217 134 ☺ Closed Sun. €
[p310, A1]
This restaurant fits perfectly into the heart of the bustling San Frediano area. Traditional in feel and fare, it offers excellent Tuscan cooking and no-nonsense service.

Borgo Antico
Piazza Santo Spirito 6r
☎ 055-210 437 ☺ L & D daily. €€ [p312, A4]
A cosy restaurant with a standard menu and an extensive range of daily specials. Try the ravioli for a rich, filling pasta dish, or one of the *secondi* from the specials menu.

Cavolo Nero
Via dell'Ardiglione 22
☎ 055-294 744 ☺ D
Mon–Sat. €€€ [p310, A2]
The "black cabbage" is an elegant place in which Mediterranean food is served. The place is well lit and not one which is on the main tourist trail, though it is well known from its rising popularity with guidebooks.

Napoleone
Piazza del Carmine 24
☎ 055-281 015 ☺ D only.
€€ [p310, A1]
A colourful trattoria-cum-pizzeria set in a quiet location across the river. Try the *spaghetti ai gamberi* (spaghetti with prawns).

Osteria del Cinghiale Bianco
Borgo San Jacopo 43r
☎ 055-215 706 ☺ D only Thur–Tue. €€ [p312, B4]
A restaurant styled to evoke medieval times in keeping with its location in a 14th-century tower. The pasta and any of the dishes using *cinghiale* (wild boar) are well worth trying.

Osteria Santo Spirito
Piazza Santo Spirito 16r
☎ 055-238 2383 ☺ L & D daily. €€–€€€ [p312, A4]
A hip hang-out with colourful decor and noisy music. The food is inventive, and fish figures largely. Make sure to try the *orecchiette* for a real pasta experience.

Quattro Leoni
Piazza della Passera, Via de' Vellutini 1r ☎ 055-218 562
☺ L & D daily. €€€
[p312, B4]
Founded in 1550, this restaurant is in a quiet square where diners can sit outside in the summer months. There

are new additions to the Tuscan menu on a daily basis.

Sant' Agostino 23
Via Sant' Agostino 23r
☎ 055-210 208 ☺ L & D Tue–Sun. €€ [p312, A4]

Trattoria between Santo Spirito and the Brancacci Chapel, combining Tuscan staples (osso bucco and *ribollita*) with simple international fare. The emphasis is on fresh ingredients.

BELOW: dim lighting at über-trendy bar Dolce Vita.

Bars and Cafés

Caffè degli Artigiani
Via dello Sprone 16r.
Tel: 055-291 882.
Open Mon–Sat 9am–11pm. [p312, B4]
Friendly café with lunch specials of sandwiches, *piadine* and pasta. In the evening, locals come for the aperitif buffet.

Caffè Pitti
Piazza de' Pitti 9.
Tel: 055-239 9863.
[p310, B2]
A swish venue opposite the Palazzo Pitti, which offers light lunches, dinners and snacks, as well as being an intimate evening venue.

Dolce Vita
Piazza del Carmine. Tel: 055-284 595. Open 8.30am–late, lunch noon–3pm. [p310, A1]
Trendy bar across the Arno frequented for the cocktails. Often overcrowded, the *aperitivo* can be a stressful experience. Live music Wed and Thur.

Hemingway Caffè
Piazza Piantellina 9r.
Tel: 055-284 781.
[p310, A1]
Hearty Sunday brunches and wonderful homemade cakes and chocolates.

PALAZZO PITTI

Former seat of the Medici, Palazzo Pitti is the largest and most lavish of Florentine palaces

The Pitti houses seven museums, and leads to the gardens that became a model for Italian landscaping. The massive Renaissance palace, built of large, rough-hewn stones, dominates the area to the south of the Ponte Vecchio. The rising gardens provide great views over the city. A visit to one or two museums combined with the gardens will take up at least half a day. Tickets can be purchased in the right wing of the palace, and entrance to all the museums is from the internal courtyard. The Appartamenti Reali and the Galleria Palatina (Royal Apartments/Palatine Gallery) combine luxurious rooms with spectacular works of art. A ticket to the Giardino di Boboli (Boboli Gardens) includes admission to the Museo degli Argenti, the Museo delle Porcellane and the Galleria del Costume (Silver/Porcelain Museum/Costume Gallery). These smaller museums are worthwhile for a second visit or if you have a specific interest. The Galleria d'Arte Moderna (Gallery of Modern Art) is accessed by another joint ticket with the Appartamenti Reali and the Galleria Palatina. The Museo delle Carrozze (Carriage Museum) is closed at present for restoration.

LEFT: Lippi's tondo of the Madonna and Child (Prometheus Room).

BELOW: at the end of the Medici reign in 1737, the *palazzo* became the home of the Lorraines, and its elongated cubic form was further extended by the wings which curve round to frame the square at its front. Work on the outside was paralleled by alteration to the interior decor, which exhibits the ostentatious tastes of the period of the Lorraines and the Savoys later on. There was a brief tenure by the Bourbons and Napoleon before the last ruling monarch, Vittorio Emmanuele III, transferred the house to the public.

The essentials

✉ *Piazza de' Pitti, www. polomuseale.firenze.it*
☎ 055-213 070
⊙ *check the website*
€ *charge; avoid queues by getting a fixed entry time-slot for a small fee, or by phoning in advance* (tel: 055-294 883)

BELOW: the Palazzo Pitti was commissioned in the 15th century by Luca Pitti, and was designed by Brunelleschi, although he never lived to see the final results. The Medici family took over ownership in 1549 when Eleonora di Toledo, wife of Cosimo I *(see her portrait by Bronzino, above)*, purchased the *palazzo* when the Pitti family ran into financial strife. She transferred her family from the Palazzo Vecchio to this more tranquil location, though still close to the political heart of the city. This link was strengthened by the Vasari Corridor, which directly connects the residence with Piazza della Signoria by way of the Uffizi and the Palazzo Vecchio. Under the Medici family work on the *palazzo* continued, substantially increasing both its size and grandeur. Ammannati was given total architectural control, and he constructed the inner courtyard and redesigned the outer facade, which was later further extended.

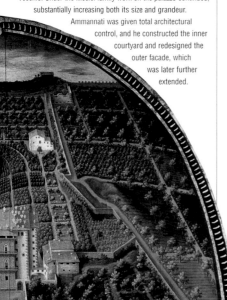

THE MOST SPLENDID APARTMENTS

As custom dictates, the most splendid apartments are on the piano nobile, overlooking the main piazza. The regal setting of these six rooms is matched by masterpieces on the walls by Raphael, Rubens and Titian. The Iliad Room (23) is one of the most sumptuous in the palace, with a frescoed neoclassical ceiling inspired by Homeric myths. The splendid Saturn Room (24) is weighted down in masterpieces with a 17th-century ceiling, depicting an Olympian scene in gilt and stuccowork and some of Raphael's finest works.

The adjoining Jupiter Room (25) has the grandeur befitting a Medici throne room and is decorated by Pietro da Cortona's frescos glorifying the young Prince Ferdinando. The ceiling is supported by a seething mass of nymphs, gods and entwined cherubs, while the far door is framed by masterpieces painted by Raphael and Giorgione. Raphael's *Portrait of a Lady* is a study of formal perfection, marked by the luminosity of the sitter's face and the virtuosity with which the portraitist captures the shimmering detail of her ruched sleeve and veil.

In the Mars Room (26) an array of Flemish and Italian masterpieces, set against vibrant red damask walls, include Rubens's martial masterpiece, *The Consequences of War* (1637), referring to the Thirty Years War that was wreaking havoc in his homeland. The vibrant colours,

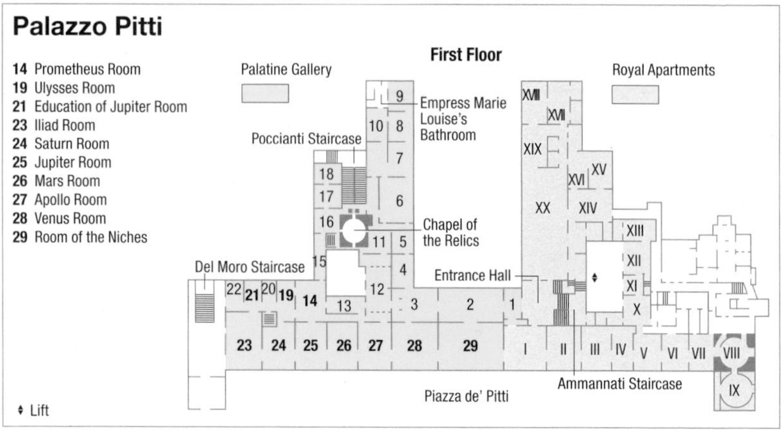
Palazzo Pitti
14 Prometheus Room
19 Ulysses Room
21 Education of Jupiter Room
23 Iliad Room
24 Saturn Room
25 Jupiter Room
26 Mars Room
27 Apollo Room
28 Venus Room
29 Room of the Niches
First Floor
Palatine Gallery
Royal Apartments
Empress Marie Louise's Bathroom
Poccianti Staircase
Chapel of the Relics
Del Moro Staircase
Entrance Hall
Ammannati Staircase
Piazza de' Pitti
Lift

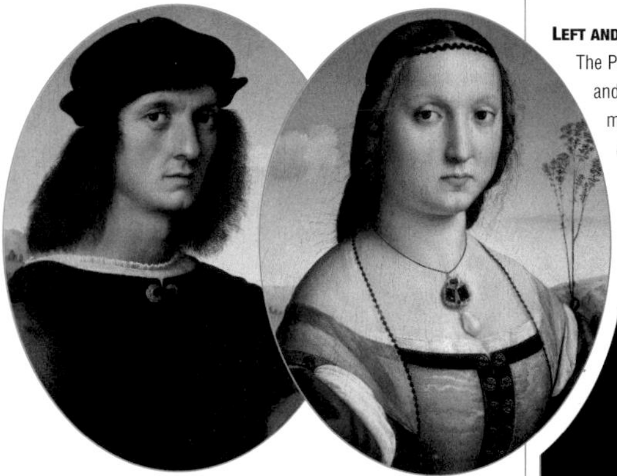

Left and Below: Raphael's Florentine lagacy is remarkable. The Palatine Gallery has the portraits of *Maddalena Doni* and *Agnolo Doni*, which were designed as a pair, much like Piero della Francesca's *Duke and Duchess of Urbino (see page 115)*. As the prototype of the Renaissance portrait, these works became the model for generations of painters. In his *Portrait of a Lady* (*below*, in the Jupiter Room), Raphael depicts a placid-looking pregnant woman.

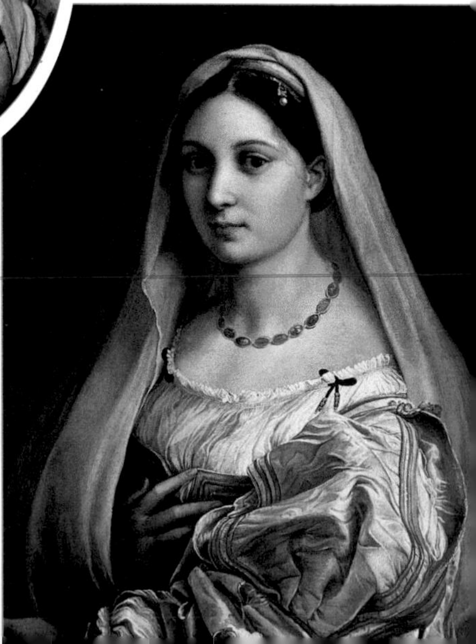

fluidity and narrative sweep also show how marked Rubens was by the Italian High Renaissance. The frescoed Apollo Room (27) is equally ornate and dotted with statuary. Framing the entrance doorway are masterpieces by Titian, whose ineffable technique and polished High Renaissance style are clear in his *Mary Magdalene*, a nude wreathed in the artist's trademark Titian hair.

The Venus Room (28) is named after Canova's *Venus Italica*, commissioned by Napoleon as a replacement for the *Venus de' Medici*, which he had spirited away to Paris. This masterpiece of neoclassical statuary, all sweet curves and coyness, is the companion piece to the *Venus de' Medici*, which has been returned to the Uffizi.

SILVER AND PORCELAIN

On the ground floor, the Museo degli Argenti is in the left-hand corner of the courtyard, whilst the Museo delle Porcellane is situated in the Boboli Garden *(both open daily 8.15am–4.30pm, longer hours in summer, closed 1st and last Mon of month; charge)*. The former contains much more than silver, ranging from antique vases much loved by Lorenzo the Magnificent to baubles encrusted with semi-precious stones and jewellery. The frescoed rooms alone make a visit worthwhile – in particular the Sala di San Giovanni, which formed part of the summer apartments. The frescos by the artist after whom the room is named depict the reign of Lorenzo de' Medici, portrayed as a great patron of the arts. The latter museum displays pottery as well as objets d'art.

The **Galleria d'Arte Moderna** *(Tue–Sun 8.15am–6.50pm, last admission 6.05pm; charge)* contains mainly Italian works from the neoclassical and Romantic movements, dating from the 18th century to the period after World War I (including this fine portrait of *The Artist's Daughter-in-Law* by Giovanni Fattori). The most notable feature of the second-floor collection is its paintings by the Macchiaioli, late-19th-century Italian Impressionists. Also situated on the second floor is the **Galleria del Costume** *(daily 8.15am–4.30pm, longer hours in summer, closed 1st and last Mon of month)*, whose 6,000-piece holding of clothing, theatrical costumes and accessories are supplemented by frequent special exhibitions.

ABOVE AND RIGHT:
one of the finest rooms is the Sala di Apollo (27), in which are are important works by Andrea del Sarto (including his *Lamentation of Christ*, 1522–3, *above*) and another master of the High Renaissance, Titian (notably his *The Interrupted Concert, c.*1510, *right*). The latter was described by art historian Bernard Berenson as "the most complete Renaissance artist; his range remains unsurpassed in Western art".

GIARDINO DI BOBOLI

The vast landscaped park provides the perfect antidote to city sightseeing

The gardens span four centuries and as many styles, from the Renaissance to Mannerism, Baroque and neoclassicism. At every turn, classical and Renaissance statues give way to whimsical Mannerist grottoes dotted with grotesque sculpture. The gardens (daily 8.15am–sunset, closed 1st and last Mon of the month; charge) were commissioned by Cosimo I and created by prolific figures of the day.

THE AMPHITHEATRE

The gateway to the gardens lies off Ammannati's grotesque courtyard, a Mannerist masterpiece, now the setting for summer concerts. The middle archway in the walls conceals a 17th-century grotto and pool, dominated by a statue of Moses, complete with a Roman torso. The gateway opens onto a terrace surmounted by a Baroque fountain encrusted with cupids. Beyond is the panoramic amphitheatre, intended as an arena for Medici entertainment; Cosimo II replaced the amphitheatre's trees with six-tiered stands adorned with classical statuary, and, in 1790, the Lorraine Grand Dukes added an obelisk of Ramses II in the centre.

RURAL VIEWS

A couple of Roman statues mark the path to the ornamental pool known as the *Bacino di Nettuno*. The path climbs past the towering statue of *Abundance*, begun by Giambologna in 1608. At the summit is the enchanting Giardino del Cavaliere rose garden, abutting the Porcelain Museum. Set on bastions designed by Michelangelo, the garden overlooks one of the loveliest rural views imaginable: beyond stretches a truly Tuscan scene of churches, cypresses, olive groves, ochre-coloured villas and grey-green hills.

THE GROTTOES, POOLS AND FOUNTAINS

Staying on the lower level, follow the avenue that hugs Via Romana back towards the Palazzo Pitti, passing the 18th-century rococo Lemon House, which still houses pots of rare citrus trees in winter. From here, continue along the lower avenue, ignoring tempting tunnels of greenery that lead back into the gardens. After passing the facade of the Palazzo Pitti, follow sporadic signs to the grottoes, passing a hanging camellia garden and neat parterres.

Even if closed, the Grotticina di Madama, the oldest architectural feature in the gardens, can be admired through its gates. A path leads to the Grotta Grande. One chamber houses replicas of Michelangelo's *Slaves*; the originals were moved to the Accademia in 1908. Supervised by Vasari in the 1550s, the folly was completed by Ammannati and Buontalenti. Take the side exit from the gardens, passing the pot-bellied *Bacco*, representing Cosimo I's favourite dwarf sitting astride a giant turtle *(below)*.

Follow the steep cypress avenue known as Il Viottolone, lined by Roman studies of Greek statues, which leads downhill to the most romantic part of the gardens. At the end lies the Vasca dell'Isola (Island Pool), conceived as a citrus grove and flower garden. There are carp and turtles in the pool, and an allegorical Ocean Fountain sculpted in granite by Giambologna. The central figure of Neptune is now in the Bargello, but the 17th-century statues of Perseus on horseback and Andromeda are original.

LEFT: the Bacino di Nettuno is named after the slimy statue of Neptune who brandishes his trident at threatening sea-monsters.

BELOW: the lovely pink facade of the Porcelain Museum.

ABOVE: because of the massive size of the palace, the enterprise ruined the Pitti family; however, the Medici completed the project according to Brunelleschi's plans, with the facade enlarged to its mammoth proportions in 1620.

OLTRARNO EAST

The eastern part of Oltrarno has many attractions, from the Forte Belvedere to the church of San Miniato, and there are stunning views over the city from Piazzale Michelangelo

Main attractions
MUSEO BARDINI
FORTE DI BELVEDERE
SAN LEONARDO CHURCH
TORRE DEL GALLO
SAN MINIATO CHURCH
PIAZZALE MICHELANGELO

From the Ponte Vecchio, the Via dei Bardi leads eastwards to the Piazza dei Mozzi, where you'll find the Museo Bardini (also known as the Galleria Corsi).

MUSEO BARDINI ⑩

✉ Piazza dei Mozzi 1 ☎ 055-234 2427 ◷ Sat–Mon 11am–5pm ◎ charge

Stefano Bardini (1836–1922), known as "the prince of art dealers", created his *palazzo* over the 13th-century church and monastery of San Gregorio in 1881. Fragments of ancient buildings were incorporated into the palace, and the rooms used to showcase Bardini's vast collection of art. He bequeathed the palace and its entire contents to Florence in 1923.

After 15 years of restoration the palace has reopened to the public, with the original decoration restored to its former glory. Ancient, medieval and Renaissance sculpture, altarpieces, glazed terracottas, furniture and armoury are displayed in spacious and finely decorated halls. Among the highlights are an enamelled terracotta altarpiece by Andrea della Robbia, a *Madonna* attributed to Donatello and *St Michael* by Antonio del Pollaiuolo.

Just south of the museum, at Via dei Bardi, lies one of the entrances to the **Giardino Bardini**, now open to the public after five years of restoration.

Originally an olive orchard belonging to the 13th-century Palazzo dei Mozzi, the present gardens were created by Stefano Bardini. Behind the Giardino di Boboli, the gardens rise up in terraces and feature statues and fountains, a neo-Baroque stairway and stunning views over Florence. The many horticultural delights include 60

LEFT: the magnificent San Miniato at night.
RIGHT: looking out over the city.

The fortress was built on the orders of Ferdinando I, beginning in 1590, to Buontalenti's design. It symbolises the Grand Duke's sense of insecurity, for though the structure was explained as part of the city's defences, there was only one means of access – a secret door entered from the Boboli Garden. Clearly it was intended for his own personal use in times of attack or rebellion.

BELOW: grand villas dot the hills around San Miniato.

species of hydrangea. The restored 17th-century **Villa Bardini** (daily 10am–4pm, closed 1st and last Mon of the month; charge) is home to two museums: one of 19th-century portraits by the Renaissance-influenced artist Pietro Annigoni, and another devoted to a rotating collection of extravagant creations by fashion-designer Roberto Capucci. (The gardens can also be accessed from the Giardino di Boboli.)

A good route up the hill that characterises this part of Oltrarno is via the Costa di San Giorgio, a narrow lane that begins at the church of **Santa Felicità** (just south of the Ponte Vecchio) and winds steeply upwards. After a short climb, the granite-flagged lane flattens out at the Porta San Giorgio. This is the city's oldest surviving gate, built in 1260. On the inner arch is a fresco by Bicci di Lorenzo, *Our Lady with St George and St Leonard* (1430). On the outer face is a copy of a 13th-century carving of St George in combat with the dragon (the original is in the Palazzo Vecchio).

FORTE DI BELVEDERE ⓫

✉ Via di San Leonardo ☎ 055-27681
🕐 currently closed to the public

To the right of the gate the sheer and massive walls of the Belvedere rise to a great height and cause you to wonder what lies behind. In fact, the interior is almost empty and used now for occasional exhibitions of contemporary art. Restored after a long period of neglect, the fort (when it has reopened) will offer fabulous views.

SCENTED ALLEYS

The fort marks the beginning of Via di San Leonardo, a cobbled rural lane that climbs between the walled gardens of scattered villas. Here and there a gate allows a view of the gardens behind, and the wisteria and roses grow so vigorously that they spill over the walls, their abundant and fragrant blossoms tumbling into the lane.

On the left is the church of **San Leonardo ⓬**, which contains a fine 13th-century pulpit. Both Tchaikovsky and Stravinsky lived in this

Recommended Restaurants, Bars & Cafés on page 207

lane. Florence was a favourite resort, before the 1917 Revolution, for Russians seeking an escape from the rigours of their own climate.

Cross Viale Galileo and continue along Via di San Leonardo, before taking the first left turn to follow Via Viviani. This road climbs steeply, with the promise of fine views ahead, until it levels out at the Piazza Volsanminiato in the village of Arcetri. Follow the Via del Pian de' Giullari until, after a few metres, the views suddenly open up.

To the right, the only signs of modernity are the receiver dishes of the **Astrophysical Observatory**. On the left is its ancient predecessor, the **Torre del Gallo** ⓭, which was once used for astronomical research, and much restored in the 19th century by Stefano Bardini (of Museo Bardini fame, *see page 201*); he used it as a repository for the larger architectural materials that he rescued from demolished buildings.

On the hillside below the tower is the 15th-century **Villa "La Gallina"**. This contains very fine frescos of nude dancers by Antonio del Pollaiuolo (*c.*1464–71), but is not normally open to the public.

CHOICE OF ROUTES

At the crossroads in the village of Pian de' Giullari there is a choice of routes. Via Santa Margherita leads to the early 14th-century village church and some far-reaching views up the Arno valley. Via San Matteo leads to the monastery of the same name. An inscription on the nearby house (No. 48) forbids the playing of football in the vicinity – a rule that local children joyfully flout.

The route back to Florence involves backtracking as far as Arcetri and taking the Via della Torre del Gallo downhill to the Piazza degli Unganelli. As the road descends, there are fine views of the city's distinctive cathedral glimpsed across olive groves, a reminder of just how small and rural a place Florence is.

ABOVE: the Ponte alle Grazie leads to the peaceful San Niccolò district, dominated by the imposing gateway Porta di San Niccolò, which has been restored (*c.*1340).

Galileo's Exile

To the right of the Villa "La Gallina", the hillside falls away steeply in a series of attractive terraced gardens, vineyards and orchards. Beyond is a typically Tuscan view of a series of low hills covered in sculptural groups of pencil-thin cypress trees, echoing the shape of medieval towers and church campaniles, rising above the red-tiled roofs of villas and simple village homes.

This is a view that Galileo enjoyed, by force, during the last years of his life. He lived at the **Villa il Gioiello** (Via del Pian de' Giullari 42) from 1631 until his death in 1642, virtually under house arrest, although he was permitted to continue his work and to receive a stream of distinguished admirers. Both the villa and the gardens are open very occasionally to the public. Ask at the tourist office.

North of the church is a small graveyard, dating back to 1839, full of 19th- and early-20th-century monuments. Family tombs are supplied with electricity to light the "everlasting lamps" of Etruscan form, and there are many highly accomplished figures and portraits in stone and bronze of former Florentine citizens.

BELOW: the city's 16th-century fortifications.

Only the occasional sounds of traffic, echoing up the Arno valley, disturb the peace – and even this is drowned out by the pleasing sound of church bells at midday or, if you are out on a Sunday, at regular intervals throughout the morning.

VILLAS OF THE GREAT

Cypress trees, like beautiful clusters of green pillars, tumble down the hillside. Many of the villas you will pass have marble plaques recording that they were once the home of philosophers, artists, poets and architects, so many has Florence produced over the centuries. Sunlight warms the scene, and, even in winter, lizards bask on the warm garden walls.

At the **Piazza degli Unganelli**, ignore the main road that bends to the left and look instead for the narrow Via di Giramonte, an unpaved track that leads off to the right between high walls. This cool and shady path follows the sheer walls of the city's 16th-century fortifications and eventually climbs up through trees and oleander bushes to the church of San Miniato.

SAN MINIATO ⑭

✉ Via dei Monte alle Croci ☎ 055-234 2731 ☉ Apr–Sept daily 8am–7pm, Oct–Mar Mon–Sat 8am–noon, 3–6pm, Sun 3–6pm ⓒ free ⏏ 12 & 13

This is arguably one of the most beautiful and least spoilt churches in Italy. St Minias was a merchant from the East (the son of the king of Armenia, according to one story) who settled in Florence but was executed around AD 250 during the anti-Christian purges of the Emperor Decius. A church was probably built on the site of his tomb soon after, but the present building was begun around 1018 and completed around 1207.

Roman origins

Like the cathedral's baptistery, the delicate geometrical marble inlay of the facade was much admired by Brunelleschi and his contemporaries, who believed it to be the work of the Romans. Certainly some of the columns of the nave and crypt, with their crisply carved Corinthian capitals, are reused Roman material.

Again, like the baptistery, the Calimala Guild was responsible for the maintenance of the church, and the guild's emblem – an eagle carrying a bale of wool – crowns the pediment. The interior has, remarkably, survived in its original state, except for the 19th-century repainting of the open timber roof and an attempt

to line the walls with marble, copying the walls with marble, copying the motifs of the facade. Frescos on the aisle walls include a large 14th-century *St Christopher* by an unknown artist. The nave floor has a delightful series of marble intarsia panels depicting lions, doves, signs of the zodiac and the date, 1207.

At the end of the nave, between the staircases that lead to the raised choir, is a tabernacle made to house a miraculous painted crucifix (now located in Santa Trinità) that is said to have spoken to Giovanni Gualberto, the 11th-century Florentine saint. The tabernacle is the collective work of Michelozzo, Agnolo Gaddi and Luca della Robbia, made around 1448.

On the left of the nave is the chapel of the cardinal of Portugal, who died, aged 25, on a visit to Florence in 1439. The very fine tomb is by Rossellino; the glazed terracotta ceiling, depicting the Cardinal Virtues, by Luca della Robbia; the *Annunciation* above the Bishop's throne by Baldovinetti; and the frescos by the brothers Antonio and Piero Pollaiuolo.

The highlight of the church is the raised choir and pulpit, all of marble and inset with intarsia panels depicting a riot of mythical beasts. The splendid mosaic in the apse, of 1297, shows Christ, the Virgin and St Minias in all their golden finery. The combined effect is distinctively Byzantine in feel.

The martyr's shrine

The choir was elevated in order to accommodate the 11th-century crypt below, in which the remains of St Minias were placed beneath the altar

Time a trip
Miniato to co
with the Gregoria
chant sung daily at
5.30pm by the monks.

LEFT: San Miniato is a good place to reflect. **BELOW:** the sweeping view over Florence from the hillside church.

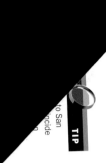

into the grand cascade of terraces and staircases laid out by the city architect, Giuseppe Poggi, in 1865–73.

PIAZZALE MICHELANGELO ⑮

These terraces descend the hillside to the broad Piazzale Michelangelo. This viewpoint is crowded with visitors at all times of the year, who come for the celebrated panorama over the red roofs of Florence to the green hills beyond. Despite the milling hordes and the sellers of tacky souvenirs, the sight is awe-inspiring, and never better than on a clear Sunday in spring at around 11.45am, when the bells of the city's churches all peal to call the faithful to midday Mass, and the surrounding peaks are sharply delineated against the pale-blue sky.

The best route back to the Ponte Vecchio is the steep descent, through acacia groves and past overgrown grottoes, along the Via di San Salvatore to **Porta San Niccolò**. Turn left along the Via di Belvedere to Porta San Miniato, now little more than a hole in the wall. A plaque opposite records that members of the Florentine Resistance were shot in August 1944 in a final vindictive act as the Nazis fled the city and the advance of the Allied troops.

From here there is a choice of routes, both of which have something to offer. Continue along the Via di Belvedere for a final taste of rural Florence. The tree-lined lane follows the high walls and bastions of the city's 14th-century defences, marking a sharp division between town and country. It climbs to the **Porta San Giorgio**, from where the Via della Costa San Giorgio leads directly back to the Ponte Vecchio. For a more direct route, take the Via di San Niccolò to the Via dei Bardi – lined with medieval buildings – to get back to the bustle of the city. ❑

Piazzale Michelangelo is decorated with reproductions of the artist's most famous works, including David of course.

visiting pilgrims. roof, with frescos ophets by Taddeo by a forest of pil- om diverse sources Roman – with ard for match and etry.

the church's ancient graveyard is the massive, but incomplete, campanile, built in 1523 to replace the original one that collapsed in 1499. This played a strategic role during the 1530 siege of Florence when the Medici, expelled in 1527, returned to take the city, backed by the army of the Emperor Charles V.

Under Michelangelo's direction, the tower was used as an artillery platform and wrapped in mattresses to absorb the impact of enemy cannon fire. Michelangelo also supervised the construction of temporary fortifications around the church; afterwards they were rebuilt in stone and made permanent. Later they were incorporated

BELOW: posing on Piazzale Michelangelo.

BEST RESTAURANTS, BARS AND CAFÉS

Restaurants

Prices for three-course dinner per person with a glass of wine:
€ = under €25
€€ = €25–40
€€€ = €40–60
€€€€ = more than €60

Antica Mescita
Via di San Niccolò 60r
📞 055-234 2836
🅒 Closed Sun. € [p311, D2]
Simple Italian food in a cheery, crowded atmosphere. Part of this *osteria* is set in a former chapel.

Bevovino
Via di San Niccolò 59r
📞 055-200 1709 🅒 L & D daily. € [p311, D2]
A moderately sized *enoteca*, offering daily first and second courses, carpaccio and bruschetta. Nice wine and cheese selections and friendly service. In the summer outdoor seating available.

Filipepe
Via di San Niccolò 39r
📞 055-200 1397
🅒 D daily. €€€ [p311, D3]
Filipepe is an elegant take on modern Mediterranean cuisine. Soft candle lighting, cove ceilings, and the bottles of wine lining the walls give each area a private, yet comfortable feel. Filipepe's menu offers a seasonal selection of typical ingredients frequently from the southern regions of Italy including different kinds of carpaccio, salads, soups and pastas.

Fuori Porta
Via dei Monte alle Croci 10r
📞 055-234 2483 🅒 L & D Mon–Sat. €€ [p311, D3]
An *enoteca/osteria* near Piazzale Michelangelo, renowned for its superb selection of wines. The food is rustic and plentiful.

Osteria Golden View
Via dei Bardi 58r 📞 055-214 502 🅒 L & D daily. €€–€€€ [p312, C4]
A modern place with live jazz. It overlooks the Arno and serves Tuscan and European dishes.

Rifrullo
Via di San Niccolò 55r
📞 055-234 2621 🅒 B, L & D daily. €€ [p311, D3]
This hip hang-out is a café by day, serving morning pastries and coffee, then tasty pasta for lunch. By night, it is a popular *aperitivo* locale, offering drinks and a plentiful buffet. Rifrullo also offers an evening menu and a garden for alfresco meals.

Bars and Cafés

Caffè la Torre
Lungarno Benvenuto Cellini 65r. Tel: 055-658 2326. Open daily for lunch, *aperitivo* and dinner. [p311, E2]
Famous for having one of the better aperitif buffets in the city. The funky interior makes this bar a fun drinks place. In nice weather, the outdoor patio is open for seating.

Negroni
Via dei Renai 17r.
Tel: 055-243 647.
[p311, D2]
This café by day, bar by night hosts a lively aperitif crowd. Try the famous Negroni drink, for which the bar is named.

Le Volpi e L'Uva
Piazza dei Rossi 1r.
Tel: 055-239 8132.
Open Mon–Sat 11am–9pm. [p312, C4]
An *enoteca* that offers an excellent selection of wine by the glass. A stone's throw from the Ponte Vecchio, yet it still feels tranquil.

ABOVE: a fine selection of grappa and an exquisite dessert at Osteria Golden View.

Recommended Restaurants on page 215

FIESOLE

Before there was Florence, there was Fiesole. Although now somewhat eclipsed by the city below, this once-powerful hilltop town of Etruscan origins is fascinating

Perched on a hilltop north of Florence, **Fiesole** is a small place of archaeological importance usually overrun by tourists admiring the views over Florence. Founded perhaps as early as the 8th century BC, Fiesole was colonised by the Romans in around 80 BC and later became the capital of Etruria. The growth of Florence overtook that of Fiesole, but it remained sufficiently important as a competitor to Florence in the 11th and 12th centuries for the two towns to be constantly at war with each other.

TOTAL DESTRUCTION

In 1125 Florentine troops stormed Fiesole and won what was, perhaps, the easiest victory in a long campaign to dominate the whole of Tuscany. Not content merely to subjugate Fiesole, the Florentines razed the village, sparing only the cathedral complex. With hindsight, this destruction had its benefits. Few buildings were erected in succeeding centuries, and important Roman and Etruscan remains were thus preserved relatively undisturbed beneath the soil.

Much of Fiesole is an archaeological zone, and, despite the snail's-pace progress typical of any process in Italy that involves bureaucracy, excavation has continued, and the results throw new light on the origins and achievements of the Etruscans.

The rejuvenation of Fiesole began in the 19th century. A handful of villas had been built in the 16th and 17th centuries, but the main impetus for growth came with the adoption of Fiesole by the Anglo-Florentine community. The Brownings praised

Main attractions
TEATRO ROMANO
MUSEO ARCHEOLOGICO
MUSEO BANDINI
CATTEDRALE DI SAN ROMOLO
SANT' ALESSANDRO CHURCH
SAN FRANCESCO FRIARY
VILLA MEDICI
SAN DOMENICO

LEFT: the steps of the Teatro Romano and, rising in the background, the Duomo's crenellated belltower.
RIGHT: enjoying the sunshine and the view from Sant' Alessandro.

TIP

Fiesole has an annual summer festival, Estate Fiesolana (www. estatefiesolana.it; mid-June–Aug). Music performances under the stars in the ancient Teatro Romano are not to be missed.

RIGHT: reading about the Roman theatre.

its beauty in their poetry, and here, unlike in Florence itself, there was space for the English to indulge their passion for gardening. Standing at nearly 295 metres (1,000ft) above sea level, Fiesole was considered more salubrious than the furnace of Florence (in fact the difference in temperature is marginal).

The best way to get up to Fiesole from Florence is by taking the No. 7 bus from Santa Maria Novella station, or to go on one of the sightseeing buses. Once past the Florentine suburbs, the bus climbs through semi-rural countryside where villas with trim gardens are dotted among orchards and olive groves. Psychologically, at least, the air feels fresher, and when the bus reaches **Piazza Mino ❶**, Fiesole's main square, there is an atmosphere of provincial Italy which seems miles from urbane Florence down below.

Everything you will want to see in Fiesole lies a short distance from Piazza Mino. Just north of the square is the reason why so many tourists flock to Fiesole: the Roman theatre. A little further afield, garden-lovers will enjoy a visit to **Villa Peyron** at Via Vincigliata 2, 2.5km (1½ miles) east of Fiesole (bus No. 45). The gardens only are open to the public and by appointment (tel: 055-264 321; daily 10am–1pm, 3–7pm, winter 10am–3.30pm; charge).

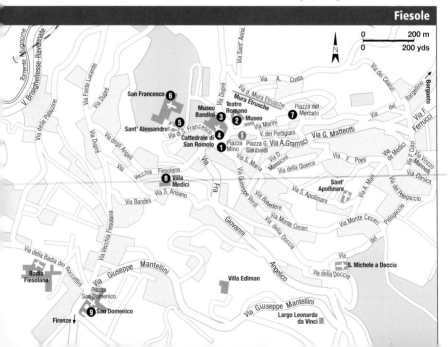

Fiesole

ARCHAEOLOGICAL TREASURES

Teatro Romano ❷

✉ Via dei Portigiani 1 📞 055-59477
🕒 summer daily 10am–7pm, winter
10am–5pm, closed Tue–Wed Nov–Mar
💶 combined charge covers
Archaeological Museum and
Bandini Museum

The amphitheatre is still used during the Estate Fiesolana, the summer arts festival. The larger blocks of stone represent original Roman seats, the smaller ones modern replacements.

The great and noble views from the amphitheatre are as dramatic as anything that takes place on the stage. The theatre, originally built at the end of the 1st century AD, was excavated out of the hillside, which drops steeply away, revealing the beautiful Tuscan landscape. To the left, the River Mugnone cuts a deep valley while, in the middle distance, an endless succession of hills and peaks stretches as far as the horizon, dotted with pretty villas and clusters of cypress trees.

Museo Archeologico

🕒 same hours as the Teatro Romano

Next to the theatre is one of the most important archaeological museums in Italy, erected in 1912–14. The building is an imaginative reconstruction of the 1st-century BC Roman temple, whose excavated remains are in the northwestern area of the theatre complex; parts of the original Roman frieze are incorporated into the pediment.

The exhibits on the ground floor consist principally of finds from local excavations and illustrate the historical development of the Florence region from the Bronze Age onwards. The upstairs gallery is used to display early medieval jewellery, coins and ceramics, as well as Etruscan treasures donated by Florentine families. The last room contains a very fine torso of Dionysus and early Roman funerary monuments. The important Costantini collection, consisting of beautiful antique vases from all over the ancient world (Greece, Magna Graecia and Etruria), is also displayed on the first floor.

*Bronze votive figures,
ceramics and pieces
of carved marble are
displayed on the
ground floor.*

BELOW LEFT: ancient
columns dot the site.
BELOW: the Teatro
Romano, with its
numbered seats, could
originally accommodate
up to 2,000 people.

The huge basilica of bare sandstone that is the cathedral is almost completely unadorned, except for four frescos.

An underground passage links the main body of the museum to what was once the Costantini collection and is now the bookshop. In this passage is a reconstruction of a Lombardic-era tomb; the skeleton of the deceased (a man aged about 50 who died *c.* AD 650) is surrounded by objects – including a beautiful blue-glass-wine goblet – placed there to accompany him to the next world.

Much of the rest of the site is overgrown and neglected, but below the museum, to the right of the theatre, there is a 1st-century AD bath complex with furnaces, hypocaust system and plunge baths. Next, a terrace follows a stretch of 3rd-century BC Etruscan town walls and leads to the ruins of the 1st-century BC Roman temple built on the foundations of an earlier Etruscan one.

Museo Bandini ❸

🕒 same hours as the Teatro Romano

RIGHT: Etruscan remains are scattered throughout the archaeological site.
BELOW: hilltop villas.

Opposite the theatre complex, on the right in Via Dupre, is the museum which contains the collection of Canon Angelo Bandini, an 18th-century historian and philologist, and features many fine Florentine and Tuscan Renaissance paintings, including works by Taddeo and Agnolo Gaddi, Nardo di Cione and Lorenzo Monaco. There is also furniture, various architectural fragments and a small but remarkable collection of Byzantine carved ivories.

The most striking work is a secular painting, an allegory of the *Triumph of Love, Chastity, Time and Piety*, painted on wooden panels and once forming part of a wedding chest *(cassone)* in which wealthy Florentine ladies traditionally stored their dowry of fine linen and clothing.

The cathedral occupies one end of Piazza Mino; the medieval town hall, which is currently closed off for works, the other. The latter's walls are covered in stemmae (stone-carved coats-of-arms) of Fiesole worthies.

CATTEDRALE DI SAN ROMOLO ❹

✉ Piazza Mino 📞 055-599 566
🕒 daily summer 7.30am–noon, 3–6pm, winter 7.30am–noon, 3–5pm
💰 free

The church looks rather uninviting from the outside owing to over-restoration in the 19th century, but the interior retains something of its

Recommended Restaurants on page 215

original Romanesque form and charm. Begun in 1028 and extended in the 14th century, the original nave columns survive (some with Roman capitals), leading to a raised choir above a crypt. The altarpiece by Bicci di Lorenzo (1440) and some 16th-century frescos are outstanding. The cathedral's jewel is the marble funerary monument to Bishop Leonardo Salutati, by Mino da Fiesole (1429–84), with a realistic portrait bust of the smiling bishop.

CITY VIEWS

The Via di San Francesco, west of the cathedral, climbs steeply to the little chapel of **San Iacopo** (Via di San Francesco 4a; tel: 055-59477; open by appointment only) and then on up, past gardens and viewpoints, to the church of **Sant' Alessandro** ❺, originally 6th-century and built on the site of earlier Roman and Etruscan temples. The *cipollino* marble columns of the nave are Roman, and there are breathtaking views over Florence from a nearby lookout point. The church is now used as an area for temporary exhibitions.

SAN FRANCESCO ❻

✉ Via di San Francesco 13 📞 055-59175 🕐 Mon–Sat 7am–noon, 3–7pm, off season 9am–noon, 3–5pm, Sun 3–5pm, Sun 3–6pm 🎟 free

Further up, on the summit, is the friary of San Francesco, unattractively restored in neo-Gothic style. However, it is packed with artistic treasures, including Jacopo del Sellaio's radiant *Adoration of the Magi* (late 15th century). A lavender-scented cloister to the left of the church leads to the Museo Missionario, a rambling

ABOVE: flowers over §the city walls.
BELOW: the fantastic lookout point near Sant' Alessandro.

The unfinished brick and stone facade of the Badia Fiesolana, which incorporates the lovely green and white Romanesque facade of an earlier and smaller church.

ABOVE RIGHT:
stained-glass window inside the Friary of San Francesco.
BELOW: the simple exterior of the church.
BELOW RIGHT: fresco representing St Francis.

junk shop of a museum packed with dusty and unlabelled Chinese ceramics of questionable aesthetic value, collected by Franciscan missionaries during the 19th century. More interesting is the fact that the museum is built right up an exposed section of the 3rd-century BC Etruscan city wall.

Back in the main square, you have to decide whether to have lunch in one of the town's overpriced – but picturesque – restaurants, or summon up the energy for further walks in the maze of lanes and footpaths leading east off the square.

ETRUSCAN WALLS

From the Teatro Romano, Via Marini leads to the **Piazza del Mercato ❼**, which overlooks the valley of the River Mugnone. A little further, on the left, the Via delle Mura Etrusche follows Fiesole's best-preserved stretch of Etruscan wall, composed of monolithic blocks of stone. From here, steep lanes lead back to the main road, Via Gramsci. The first fork left, Via del Bargellino, leads to an overgrown plot between two houses where two 3rd-

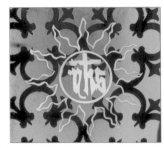

century BC Etruscan underground tombs have been preserved. A short distance further on, take the right turn for Borgunto to reach Via Adriano Mari, which joins Via Monte Ceceri to return to Piazza Mino in the centre of Fiesole.

THE STONES OF FLORENCE

To the east of the Etruscan walls rises the forested hill of Monte Ceceri. It was only planted so densely with trees in the early 20th century; previously, it was a barren outcrop dotted with quarries. From here the beautiful dove-grey *pietra serena* was used by Florentine Renaissance architects to embellish the city's churches.

GOING DOWNHILL

From the southwest corner of the main square, Via Vecchia Fiesolana descends to the **Villa Medici** ❽ *(see pages 216–17)*, one of the first Renaissance country villas, built by Michelozzo in 1458–61 for Cosimo de' Medici, and deliberately sited to make the best of the views.

Take any of the downhill paths from here to reach the hamlet of **San Domenico** ❾ after about 800 metres (½ mile). The church of San Domenico dates from 1406 and contains the restored *Madonna with Angels and Saints* (1430), an early work of Fra Angelico, who began his monastic life here before transferring to San Marco.

Directly opposite the church, the Via della Badia dei Roccettini descends to the Badia Fiesolana.

Badia Fiesolana

✉ Via Roccettini 9 ☏ 055-59155
🕑 Mon–Fri 9am–6pm, until 5pm off season, Sat 9am–noon 🎫 free

This monastery now houses the European University Institute, which was founded in 1976. The huge facade of

the Baroque church is built around another exquisite facade of inlaid marble. It is all that has survived of the original Fiesole cathedral, rebuilt around 1028 and again in the 15th century when Brunelleschi, it is thought, was responsible for the cruciform plan. The relatively isolated position of the Badia, with views south to Florence, west to the Mugnone valley and northeast to Fiesole, is superb.

The No. 7 bus can be caught in San Domenico for the return journey to the centre of Florence. ❏

ABOVE: the Villa Medici commands great views.

RESTAURANTS

Restaurants

Pizzeria Etrusca
Piazza Mino 2 ☏ 055-599 484 🕑 L & D; closed Tue off season. **€**
Set in the main piazza, this small pizzeria is a good place to grab a quick slice of pizza before heading back into Florence.

Pizzeria San Domenico
Piazza San Domenico 11
☏ 055-59182 🕑 L & D; closed Mon off season.
€–€€

This is a simple restaurant with a huge selection of pizzas and pastas and friendly service. If you don't fancy a blow-out on the carbohydrates, try one of the big salads followed by a *coppa della casa* (the house *dolce*) for dessert.

La Reggia degli Etruschi
Via di San Francesco 18
☏ 055-59385 🕑 L & D; closed Tue off season. **€€**

The patio of La Reggia degli Etruschi offers a wonderful view over the city of Florence spread out below. The food, if frankly not quite as breathtaking as the view, is nonetheless good, solid Italian fare.

● ● ● ● ● ● ● ● ● ● ● ●
Price includes dinner and a glass of wine.
€€€€ = *over €60*
€€€ = *€40–60*
€€ = *€25–40*
€ = *under €25*

RIGHT: *enoteche* are a good lunch option, with simple fare and great wines.

MEDICI VILLAS

All around Florence are country villas, most built for and owned by the Medicis

The style of these Renaissance Tuscan houses is representative of the peaceful period and ideal of gracious living that prevailed over Florence at the time. The villas are generally centred around an inner courtyard and feature porticoes and a loggia, but the centrepieces – often open even if the house is closed – are arguably the gardens. These reflect architectural rigour in their design and feature sculptures and fountains similar to those seen in the Boboli Garden *(see pages 198–9)*.

Many of the villas are now privately owned or have been transformed into American university campuses, thereby restricting what can be viewed and rendering the opening hours erratic. Most villas are accessible by a short bus ride out of Florence, although some companies organise trips by coach to combine visits.

BELOW: Villa Medici (Mon-Fri by appointment only; tel: 055-59164; charge) is easily accessible owing to its situation en route to Fiesole *(see page 215)*, although viewing must be arranged in advance. The Renaissance gardens are of great interest and the views superb.

ABOVE, an alternative destination is the Villa della Petraia (daily 8.15am–sunset, villa by guided tour only, every 45mins from 8.30am, closed 2nd and 3rd Mon of the month; free). This house was designed by Buontalenti for Ferdinando de' Medici and set on a sloping hill. Also attributed to Buontalenti, the Villa di Cerreto Guidi (daily 8.15am–7pm, closed 2nd and 3rd Mon of the month; includes admission to the Historical Hunting and Territorial Museum) was used as a fortified hunting lodge, a fact reflected in the small museum's collection of guns.

MEDICI GARDENS

Only the gardens of the Villa di Castello (daily 8.15am–sunset, closed 2nd and 3rd Mon of the month; secret garden viewable on request; free) can be seen. The original water effects are no longer evident, but grottoes and statuary abound. Other villas with attractive surroundings include the Villa Demidoff and Parco di Pratolino (*see right*; 10am–sunset Apr–Sept Thur–Sun, Mar and Oct Sun only; free) whose Mannerist gardens were restructured into the English Romantic style, and Villa Gamberaia (gardens: daily 9am–7pm, villa on request only) in the easily accessible, pretty village of Settignano. The latter now includes facilities for conferences, and dependencies of the house have been converted into pricey accommodation.

In the direction of Sesto Fiorentino is the Villa di Careggi (visits on request only) – historically the favoured retreat of the Medici family, which now houses hospital administration buildings. Villa La Pietra and Villa I Tatti have been converted into the Florentine campuses of New York University and Harvard University respectively but can be visited on request.

ABOVE: Villa (Medicea) Poggio a Caiano (daily 8.15am–sunset, villa by guided tour only, hourly from 8.30am, closed 2nd and 3rd Mon of the month; free) is often dubbed the perfect Tuscan villa. The facade, which was modelled on a Greek temple by Sangallo to satisfy the tastes of Lorenzo the Magnificent, is well preserved.

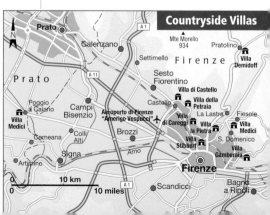

Recommended Restaurants, Bars, Cafés & Gelaterie on pages 234–5

SIENA

Siena's tumultuous history as arch-rival of Florence is written in the streets and squares, and resonates in the passionate souls of the Sienese. It is a magical Gothic city, full of pleasant surprises, but the glorious main square alone makes it worth a visit

From its striped marble cathedral to its tunnelled alleys, brilliant Campo and black-and-white city emblem, **Siena ❶** is a chiaroscuro city. In its surging towers it is truly Gothic. Where Florence is boldly horizontal, Siena is soaringly vertical; where Florence has large squares and masculine statues, Siena has hidden gardens and romantic wells. Florentine art is perspective and innovation, while Sienese art is sensitivity and conservatism. Siena is often considered the feminine foil to Florentine masculinity.

For such a feminine city, Siena has a decidedly warlike reputation, nourished by sieges, city-state rivalry and Palio battles. The pale theatricality in Sienese painting is not representative of the city or its inhabitants: the average Sienese is no ethereal Botticelli nymph, but dark, stocky and swarthy.

A BRIEF HISTORY

In keeping with Sienese mystique, the city's origins are shrouded in myths of wolves and martyred saints. According to legend, the city was founded by Senius, son of Remus, hence the she-wolf symbols in the city. St Ansano brought Christianity

to Roman Siena and, although he was promptly tossed into a vat of hot tar and beheaded, he has left a legacy of mysticism traced through St Catherine and St Bernardino to the present-day cult of the Madonna. The power of the Church came to an end when the populace rose up against the Ecclesiastical Council and established an independent republic in 1147. The 12th century was marked by rivalry in which the Florentine Guelfs usually triumphed over the Sienese Ghibellines.

Main attractions

IL CAMPO
PALAZZO PUBBLICO
TORRE DEL MANGIA
MUSEO CIVICO
THE DUOMO
MUSEO DELL'OPERA DEL DUOMO
BATTISTERO DI SAN GIOVANNI
PINACOTECA NAZIONALE
ORTO BOTANICO
SANTUARIO E CASA DI
  SANTA CATERINA
BASILICA DI SAN DOMENICO
FORTEZZA MEDICEA
BASILICA DI SAN FRANCESCO

PRECEDING PAGES: Siena's russet rooftops.
LEFT: Palio parade drummers.
RIGHT: the Campo from the Torre del Mangia.

The city is divided into three districts or terzi (thirds) – the Terzo di Città, Terzo di San Martino and Terzo di Camollia. But this is purely administrative: Siena's true identity is inextricably linked to the contrade, *the 17 medieval districts from which its social fabric is woven.*

Medieval Siena

In 1260 the battle of Montaperti routed the Florentines and won the Sienese 10 years of cultural supremacy which saw the foundation of the university and the charitable "fraternities". The Council of Twenty-Four – a form of power-sharing between nobles and the working class – was followed by the Council of Nine, an oligarchy of merchants which ruled until 1335. Modern historians judge the Nine self-seeking and profligate, but under their rule the finest works of art were either commissioned or completed, including the Campo, the Palazzo Pubblico and Duccio's *Maestà*.

The Renaissance

The ancient republic survived until 1529, when reconciliation between the Pope and the Emperor ended the Guelf–Ghibelline feud. The occupying Spanish demolished the city towers, symbols of freedom and fratricide, and used the masonry to build the present fortress. The final blow to the republic was the long siege of Siena by Emperor Charles V and Cosimo I in 1554. After the Sienese defeat, the city of Siena became absorbed into the

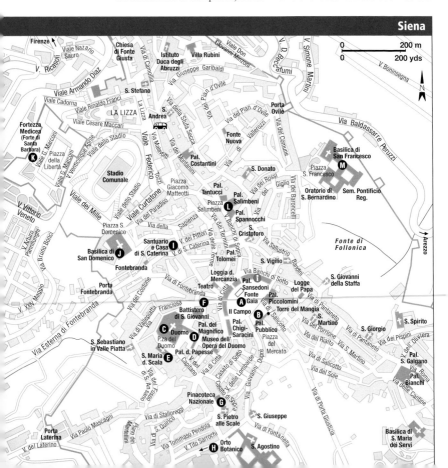

Siena

Recommended Restaurants, Bars, Cafés & Gelaterie on pages 234–5

Tuscan dukedom. As an untrusted member of the Tuscan Empire, impoverished Siena turned in on itself until the 20th century.

SIENA TODAY

Change is anathema to the city: traditional landowning, financial speculation, trade and tourism are more appealing than new technology or industry. Siena has made a virtue of conservatism; stringent medieval building regulations protect the fabric of the city; tourism is decidedly low-key; old family firms such as the Nannini cake shop – Siena's most famous café – do a roaring trade with locals (and also produced Gianna Nannini, one of Italy's best-known female singers). It is a city with the psychology of a village and the grandeur of a nation.

Il Campo ◐

All roads lead to Il Campo, the main central square, shaped like an amphitheatre – the Sienese say that it is shaped like the protecting cloak of the Virgin, who, with St Catherine of Siena, is the city's patron saint. From a pavement café on the curved side of the Campo you can note the division of the paved surface into nine segments, commemorating the rule of the

Council of Nine, which governed Siena from the mid-13th century to the early 14th, a period of stability and prosperity when most of the city's main public monuments were built.

The Campo is tipped with the Renaissance **Fonte Gaia** (Fountain of Joy). The marble carvings are copies of the original sculptures by Iacopo della Quercia, which are on display in Santa Maria della Scala *(see page 228)*. As legend has it, before the

ABOVE: from the top of the Torre del Mangia you get a great view of Siena's rust-coloured roofs.

Contrade Passions

Siena's cultural aloofness owes much to the *contrade*, the 17 city wards dating from the Middle Ages which continue to act as individual entities within the city. To outsiders, the only real significance of the *contrade* appears to be in connection with the Palio *(see pages 236–7)*, but their existence pervades all aspects of everyday life. Despite its public grandeur, much of Siena is resolutely working-class and attaches great weight to belonging to a community. Events such as baptisms and deaths are celebrated together, while the traditional Sienese will only marry within his or her *contrada*.

Plaques set into the wall testify to which *contrada* you are in (dolphin, caterpillar, goose and so on). Each neighbourhood has its own fountain and font, as well as a motto, symbol and colours. The latter are combined in a flag, seen hanging and draped around buildings for important *contrada* events, most notably a Palio triumph.

Local Flavour

Siena's food shops and markets are filled with gastronomic delights, and you will find many of the local specialities hard to resist

Siena's famously hearty cuisine has its roots with the Etruscans, who introduced the use of herbs. It evolved under the Romans and during the medieval era into a simple, frill-free cuisine, relying on prime, seasonal ingredients. Sienese meat and vegetables are plentiful and fresh, and the region's olive oil, which is of excellent quality, flavours many dishes. Thick soups are a staple, along with roasted meat, wild game in season, and pasta dishes.

Wild boar *(cinghiale)* meat is widely used for sausages and salami, left to cure for six months. The oak woods around Siena are home to the Cinta Senese pigs, a native breed raised in the wild and renowned for its wonderful, robust flavour. The breed fell out of favour with some, because of the meat's high fat content and the fact that the pigs take a long time to grow to maturity, but these are the very factors which contribute to their unctuous full-bodied flavour.

Also native to the area are the prestigious Chianina cattle, raised in the Val di Chiana; dating back to Etruscan times, these cattle are famous for their distinctive white skin and remarkable size.

ABOVE: *panforte* is a delicious Sienese speciality.
RIGHT: shopping for *cantuccini*.

Typical local dishes abound. On the menu of every rustic trattoria are *pici* (thick, irregular spaghetti-type pasta) and *panzanella* (a salad of dried bread soaked in water, basil, onion and tomato). *Ribollita* is a slow-cooked soup of bread, beans and vegetables. *Arista di maiale* – pork loin roasted with rosemary, garlic and wild fennel seeds – makes a hearty main course. *Fagioli all'Uccelletto* – beans flavoured with olive oil, garlic, tomatoes and sage, is a prime example of how the most humble dishes are made memorable thanks to the simplest of ingredients and centuries-old recipes.

Sweet-toothed visitors will be spoilt for choice: Sienese *pasticcerie* are crammed with a tempting assortment of traditional pastries. Good souvenirs are *panforte* (wedges of nuts, honey and candied fruit), *ricciarelli* (crumbly almond biscuits) and *cantuccini* (sweet, hard almond biscuits).

Via Banchi di Sopra, running off the northern side of the Campo, has a good selection of *pasticcerie*. An ever-reliable supplier of tasty sweets is **La Nueva Pasticceria di Iasevoli** (Piazzale Maestri del Lavoro; tel: 0577-41319; Tue–Sat 8am–12.45pm, 5–7.30pm, Sun 9am–12.30pm); Siena's traditional *cavallucci* (aniseed-spiced buns) are best sampled here. ❑

Recommended Restaurants, Bars, Cafés & Gelaterie on pages 234–5

the Madonna's life. Inside, in addition to council offices, is the Museo Civico *(see page 226).*

Torre del Mangia

✉ Piazza del Campo 📞 0577-226 230 🕐 daily Mar–mid-Oct 10am–7pm, mid-Oct–Feb 10am–4pm, last entry 45 mins before closing. Visits are limited to 30 people at a time, so be prepared to queue 🎫 charge

The distinctive, elegant Torre del Mangia, built between 1338 and 1348, towers over the Campo to a height of 87 metres (285ft); climb to the top to enjoy glorious views of the pink piazza and Siena's rooftops. The tower is named after the first bell-ringer, who was nicknamed

TIP

Siena has a baffling selection of combination tickets for its many sights which tends to change every year. Some tickets are valid for several days. To find the latest offers enquire at the tourist office on the Campo.

LEFT: Fonte Gaia.
BELOW: Torre del Mangia and the Palazzo Pubblico.

Fonte Gaia was built, workers unearthed an intact marble statue of Venus. When the Black Death struck in the mid-14th century, the citizens laid the blame on the statue; it was smashed to bits and its fragments buried in Florentine territory.

Beneath the fountain lies one of Siena's best-kept secrets – a labyrinth of medieval tunnels extending for 25km (15½ miles), constructed to channel water from the surrounding hills into the city. The undergound aqueduct has two main tunnels: one leads to the Fonte Gaia and the other to the Fonte Branda, the best-preserved of Siena's many fountains, northwest of here. The subterranean system (which featured in the Bond movie *Quantum of Solace*) is only rarely open to the public. Currently there is an eight-month waiting list to see it. To download an application form, go to www.ladianasiena.it.

Palazzo Pubblico ⓑ

On the south side of the square is the Palazzo Pubblico, the magnificent town hall with its crenellated facade and waving banners, surmounted by the tall and slender tower. The town hall, which has been the home of the city authorities since it was completed in 1310, is a Gothic masterpiece of rose-coloured brick and silver-grey travertine. Each ogival arch is crowned by the *balzana*, Siena's black-and-white emblem representing the mystery and purity of

Mangiaguadagni, the one who "eats all the profits". At the bottom of the tower, the **Cappella in Piazza** (Chapel in the Square) was erected in 1378 in thanksgiving for the end of the plague.

Round the back of the Palazzo Pubblico, Piazza del Mercato hosts an antiques market every third Sunday of the month.

Museo Civico

Once a year, in spring and summer, each of Siena's contrade *celebrates the feast day of its patron saint with solemn church services, raucous open-air dining and processions.*

RIGHT: the figure of Peace from the *Effects of Good Government,* by Lorenzetti (1338). **BELOW RIGHT:** ornate facade of the Duomo.

✉ Piazza del Campo 1; www.comune. siena.it/museocivico ☏ 0577-226 230 ⏰ daily mid-Mar–Oct 10am–7pm, Nov–mid-Mar 10am–5.30pm @ charge

The museum in the Palazzo Pubblico houses some of the city's greatest treasures. Siena's city council once met in the vast Sala del Mappamondo, although the huge world map that then graced the walls has disappeared. What remains are two frescos attributed to the medieval master Simone Martini: the majestic mounted figure of Guidoriccio da Fogliano and the *Maestà*. Martini's *Maestà*, a poetic evocation of the Madonna on a filigree throne, has a rich, tapestry-like quality. The muted

blues, reds and ivory add a gauzy softness. Martini echoes Giotto's conception of perspective, yet clothes his Madonna in diaphanous robes, concealing her spirituality in dazzling decoration.

Opposite is the iconic *Guidoriccio,* the diamond-spangled *condottiero* (mercenary) reproduced on calendars and *panforte* boxes. But in recent years, despite Sienese denials, doubts have been cast on the authenticity of the fresco. Art historians maintain

Sienese Festivals

The Palio horse race around Siena's Campo is the city's most famous celebration *(see pages 236–7),* but there is a wealth of other events to be enjoyed in the city, particularly in the summer months. A selection of the major festivals is below; see www.terresiena.it for up-to-date events information.

Accademia Musicale Chigiana (Via di Città 89; tel: 0577-22091; www.chigiana.it), a prestigious cultural organisation, puts on classical music events such as summer Settimane Musicali (music weeks).

Siena Film Festival (tel: 0577-222 999; www. sienafilmfestival.it) takes place in October and is gaining in importance.

Siena Jazz (Fortezza Medicea 10; tel: 0577-271 401; www. sienajazz.it) is a popular festival held in a variety of venues in Siena and nearby towns in July and August.

Recommended Restaurants, Bars, Cafés & Gelaterie on pages 234–5

that a smaller painting uncovered below the huge panel is Martini's original, and the *Guidoriccio* we see was executed long after the artist's death.

In the next room is a genuine civic masterpiece, Ambrogio Lorenzetti's *Effects of Good and Bad Government*, painted in 1338 as an idealised tribute to the Council of Nine. The narrative realism and vivid facial expressions give the allegory emotional resonance. A wise old man symbolises the common good, while a patchwork of neat fields, tame boar and busy hoers suggests order and prosperity. Bad Government is a desolate place, razed to the ground by a diabolical tyrant, the Sienese she-wolf at his feet.

The Duomo ⊙

✉ Piazza del Duomo; www.opera duomo.siena.it 📞 0577-283 048 🕒 June–Aug Mon–Sat 10.30am–8pm, Sun 1.30–6.30pm, Mar–May and Sept–Oct Mon–Sat 10.30am–7.30pm, Sun 1.30–5.30pm, Nov–Feb Mon–Sat 10.30am–6.30pm, Sun 1.30–5.30pm 💶 charge

Exiting the Campo, turn left and head up the hill via one of the winding streets to the Piazza del Duomo. Here is the cathedral, Siena's most controversial monument, either a symphony in black and white marble or a tasteless iced cake, depending on your point of view. It began in 1220 as a round-arched Romanesque church, but soon acquired a Gothic facade festooned with pinnacles. Bands of black, white and green marble were inlaid with pink stone and topped by Giovanni Pisano's naturalistic statues – the ones you see are copies; the originals are in the Museo dell'Opera del Duomo *(see page 228)*.

The cathedral interior is creativity run riot – oriental abstraction, Byzantine formality, Gothic flight and Romanesque austerity. A giddy chiaroscuro effect is created by the black and white walls reaching up to the starry blue vaults. The floor is even more inspiring: major Sienese craftsmen worked on the elaborate marble *pavimentazione* between 1372 and 1562. The finest are Matteo di Giovanni's pensive Sibyls and marble

The alternating black and white marble of the belltower, built around 1313, is a reference to the black and white of Siena's coat-of-arms.

BELOW: statue of Romulus, Remus and the she-wolf in front of the Duomo.

Interesting ceramics are found throughout Tuscany, and Siena is well known for its decorated glazed pottery.

BELOW: interior of the Duomo, showing inlaid marble floors.

mosaics by Beccafumi. In order to preserve the floors, many of the most interesting scenes are covered by hardboard for most of the year and only revealed to the public for two months at the start of autumn.

Nicola Pisano's octagonal marble **pulpit** is a Gothic masterpiece: built in 1226 and depicting scenes from the life of Christ, it is a dramatic and fluid progression from his solemn pulpit in Pisa Cathedral. Off the north aisle is the decorative **Libreria Piccolomini**, built in 1495 to house the personal papers and books of Pope Pius II. The glorious frescos by Pinturicchio (1509) show scenes from the life of the influential Renaissance Pope, a member of the noble Sienese Piccolomini family and founder of Pienza.

In 1339, a plan was laid down to expand the already impressive cathedral to create the biggest church in Christendom, with a nave measuring 50 metres (162ft) in length and 30 metres (97ft) in breadth. However, the city was struck by the Black Plague shortly afterwards, reducing the population from 100,000 to 30,000 in less than a year; the city was forced to abandon its ambitious plans for the cathedral.

Museo dell'Opera del Duomo ⓓ

✉ Piazza del Duomo 8; www.opera duomo.siena.it 📞 0577-283 048 ⏱ daily Mar–May and Sept–Nov 9.30am–7pm, June–Aug until 8pm, Nov–Feb 10am–5pm 💶 charge

In the unfinished eastern section is the cathedral's museum, famous for its collection of marble statues carved by Giovanni Pisano between 1285 and 1297 for the facade, and Duccio's great altarpiece of *The Virgin and Child Enthroned in Majesty*, known as the *Maestà*.

Siena's best-loved work is in the Sala il Duccio, a dramatically lit room which sets off to perfection one of the most important paintings in medieval art. The *Maestà* was completed in 1311 and escorted from the artist's workshop to the Duomo in a torchlit procession; the double-sided panel painting graced the High Altar until 1506. The biggest panel depicts the Madonna enthroned among saints and angels and, since the separation of the painting, facing scenes from the Passion. Although Byzantine Gothic in style, the *Maestà* is suffused with melancholy charm. The delicate gold and red colouring is matched by Duccio's grace of line, which influenced Sienese painting for the next two centuries. The Sienese believe that Giotto copied Duccio but sacrificed beauty to naturalism. The small panels do reveal some of Giotto's truthfulness and sense of perspective.

Santa Maria della Scala ⓔ

✉ Piazza del Duomo 2; www.santa mariadellascala.com 📞 0577-224 811 ⏱ daily 10.30am–6.30pm 💶 charge

Recommended Restaurants, Bars, Cafés & Gelaterie on pages 234–5

Opposite the Duomo is this former pilgrims' hospital, believed to have been founded in the 9th century; in its day it was one of the most important hospitals in the world; it has now been turned into a major arts centre and exhibition space. The building is above all a synthesis of the city and its history. Used as a practising hospital until 1995, its main ward, the Sala Pellegrinaio, is adorned with stunning frescos by Domenico di Bartolo depicting scenes of the history of the hospital, including 15th-century monks tending to the sick.

Much of this vast complex has been restored over recent years, and it has become a major arts and exhibition centre. The old hayloft or *fienile* now houses Jacopo della Quercia's original sculpted panels from the Fonte Gaia (Fountain of Joy) in Siena's Campo. On the same floor, the Oratorio di Santa Caterina della Notte, where St Catherine used to pray, is adorned with stuccos and paintings. Also incorporated into the complex are the Church of Santissima Annunziata and the Cappella del Sacro Chiodo with a fresco cycle by Vecchietta. The city's **Museo Archeologico** (www.archeologiatoscana. it), with its significant collection of Etruscan and Roman remains, is housed in the cavernous lower basement. Other rooms host temporary exhibitions.

A set of steps behind the Duomo leads to Piazza San Giovanni, a small square that is dominated by the baptistery.

ABOVE: street musician.
BELOW: snapshots of Siena: a deli, and the Duomo reflected in Ospedale di Santa Maria della Scala.

TIP

The Tourist Office organises guided walks (in English; Apr–Oct Mon–Fri 3pm), an excellent way of getting your bearings; book at their office on the Campo.

Battistero di San Giovanni F

✉ Piazza San Giovanni
🕐 Mar–May 9.30am–7pm, June–Aug 9.30am–8pm, Sept–Oct until 7pm, Nov–Feb 9am–1.30pm @ charge

Built between 1316 and 1325, the baptistery is distinguished by its tall Gothic facade adorned with human and animal busts. The interior, with walls and ceilings decorated in vibrant frescos by, among others, Lorenzo di

RIGHT: reflection in a church.
BELOW: strolling through Siena's narrow medieval streets.

Pietro (Vecchietta), is an outstanding example of 15th-century Sienese art. The extraordinary baptismal font, which was completed in 1431, features gilded bronze bas-reliefs by Jacopo della Quercia, Donatello and Lorenzo Ghiberti, the leading sculptors of the day.

Pinacoteca Nazionale G

✉ Via San Pietro 29 ☎ 0577-281 161 🕐 Tue–Sat 10am–5.15pm, Mon 8.30am–1.30pm, Sun 9am–1pm @ charge

To the south of the Campo is the Pinacoteca Nazionale, containing important works of art from the Siena School in the suitably Gothic Palazzo Buonsignori. It's particularly famous for its *fondi d'oro*: paintings with lavish, gilded backgrounds. The early rooms are full of Madonnas, apple-cheeked, pale, remote or warmly human. Matteo di Giovanni's stylised Madonnas shift to Lorenzetti's affectionate *Annunciation* and Ugolino di Neri's radiant *Madonna*. Neroccio di Bartolomeo's *Madonna* is as truthful as a Masaccio.

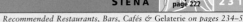

As a variant, the grisly deaths of obscure saints compete with a huge medieval crucifix with a naturalistic spurt of blood. The famous landscapes and surreal Persian city attributed to Lorenzetti were probably painted by Sassetta a century later. But his *Madonna dei Carmelitani* is a sweeping cavalcade of Sienese life.

Head back towards the Campo for a taste of something more modern.

Orto Botanico ❶

✉ Via Pier Andrea Mattioli 4
📞 0577-232 871 🕒 Mon–Fri 8.30am–12.30pm, 2.30–5.30pm, Sat 8am–12.30pm 🎟 free

For a breather and some rare outdoor space and greenery, head towards this small botanical garden owned by the university, just inside the city walls. In the summer months you can take a guided tour.

Santuario e Casa di Santa Caterina da Siena ❶

✉ Costa di Sant' Antonio
📞 0577-44177 🕒 daily 9am–12.30pm, 3–6pm 🎟 free

Slightly outside the historic centre is the sanctuary and home of Catherine Benincasa (1347–80), canonised in the 15th century by Pope Pius II and proclaimed Italy's patron saint in 1939 *(see box below)*. The house, garden and her father's dye-works now form the Sanctuary of St Catherine. The building has changed since Catherine's day, and is surrounded by cloisters and chapels, and decorated with paintings of events from her life.

ABOVE: the Renaissance facade of the Palazzo del Papese (or Palazzo Piccolomini; no public access), designed by Bernardo Rossellino, who was also the architect of the Palazzo Pubblico in the Campo.

Saint Catherine

Catherine Benincasa, beloved of the Sienese, was born on 5 March 1347. Allegedly the youngest of 24 daughters born to a dyer, Jacopo, and his wife, Lana, she started having divine visions and took the veil when she was eight. She lived a life of silent contemplation, joining a Dominican convent and rarely venturing out of her cell except to go to Mass. Following the catastrophic Black Death, which ravaged the city, Catherine took to the streets to support the suffering.

Not just a figure of kindness and mercy, Catherine was also a highly charismatic figure who attracted the support of scholars and religious leaders impressed by her zeal. At the end of the 14th century, the Church was divided, with the papacy forced to move to Avignon in France, and war and famine running rampant through many countries. Spurred on by her faith, Catherine strove for peace and justice. In 1377 she managed to persuade the Pope, against the will of the French cardinals, to come back to Rome and take on the task of reforming the Church. Shortly after seeing the Pope safely returned to his rightful place, Catherine died in Rome on 29 April 1380, aged just 33. Siena still proudly preserves the memory of this simple girl who grew into a mystic and an extraordinary politician.

SHOP

The city's lively general market (Wed 8am–1pm) stretches from the Fortezza Medicea to Piazza la Lizza; make sure to come early to be in with a chance of getting a bargain.

Basilica di San Domenico ❶

✉ Piazza San Domenico; www.basilica cateriniana.com ☎ 0577-286 848 ⏲ Mar–Oct 7am–6.30pm, Nov–Feb 9am–6pm ⊚ free

Nearby is a huge fortress-like church founded by the Dominicans in 1226. It is said that Catherine experienced many of her visions here, and in the Cappella Santa Caterina is a reliquary containing the saint's head. The chapel is decorated with frescos depicting events in the saint's life, the majority completed by Sodoma in the early 16th century. The view from outside the basilica across to the Duomo is spectacular.

Fortezza Medicea ❿

✉ Viale Maccari ☎ 0577-228 811 ⏲ Mon noon–8pm, Tue–Sat noon–1am; performances summer only ⊚ free

From the basilica it's a short walk to the Fortezza Medicea (also known as Fortezza di Santa Barbara), built by Cosimo I after his defeat of Siena in 1560. The red-brick fortress now

houses an open-air theatre, provides glorious views of the countryside from its public gardens and contains the **Enoteca Italiana**. This wine exhibition and shop offers visitors the chance to sample and buy from a wide range of Tuscan wines, and ask the experts about winemaking.

Bank of Siena

Via Banchi di Sopra, lined with fine medieval *palazzi*, is one of the three main arteries of the city centre, lined with enticing shops, boutiques and

RIGHT: church of Santa Maria di Provenzano.
BELOW: Basilica di San Domenico.

Recommended Restaurants, Bars, Cafés & Gelaterie on pages 234–5

galleries (the other two being Via Banchi di Sotto and Via di Città). It links the Campo with the splendid **Piazza Salimbeni** ① at its northern end. The grand *palazzi* flanking the square are the head office of the Monte dei Paschi di Siena, one of the oldest banks in the world. Founded in 1472 and still an important employer, it also ploughs a sizeable chunk of its profits back into the community and is known as "the city father".

Basilica di San Francesco ⓜ

✉ Piazza San Francesco ☎ 0577-289 081 ⓒ daily 7am–noon, 3.30–7pm ⓖ free

From the Piazza Salimbeni, Via dei Rossi leads east to the Basilica of St Francis. Now housing part of the university, the vast church exhibits fragments of frescos by Pietro Lorenzetti in the first chapel of the transept. Two lovely frescos by Lorenzetti's brother Ambrogio can be viewed in the third chapel. Next door, the 15th-century **Oratorio di San Bernardino** (tel: 0577-283 048; Mon–Sat mid-Mar–Oct 10.30am–

1.30pm, 3–5.30pm; charge), dedicated to Siena's great preacher and built on the site where he used to pray, contains frescos by Il Sodoma and Beccafumi on the first floor.

Here, as elsewhere, the city has many well-preserved walls and gateways. Siena's compactness makes these easy to reach, so you can wind through the narrow streets and stumble across hidden buildings and fountains on the way. ❑

It is like a bit of Venice, without the water. There are some curious old palazzi in the town, which is very ancient... it is very dreamy and fantastic, and most interesting.

Charles Dickens on Siena

LEFT: taking a break.
BELOW: Piazza Salimbeni.

BEST RESTAURANTS, BARS, CAFÉS AND *GELATERIE*

Restaurants

Prices for three-course dinner per person with a glass of wine:
€ = under €25
€€ = €25–40
€€€ = €40–60
€€€€ = more than €60

Al Mangia

Piazza del Campo 42
📞 0577-281 121 🕒 Daily.
€€€–€€€€
In a wonderful position on the Campo, this restaurant serves good, classic Tuscan cuisine, and is popular with tourists and locals alike. Outside tables in summer, and of course you pay a premium for the theatrical location, but it's worth it at least once.

Al Marsili

Via del Castoro 3 📞 0577-47154 🕒 Closed Mon in winter. €€–€€€
Elegant restaurant in an ancient building with wine cellars cut deep into the limestone. Sophisticated cuisine, including gnocchi in duck sauce and *faraona al Medici* (guinea fowl with prunes and pine nuts). Booking recommended, especially for the Sunday lunch slot.

Antica Trattoria Botteganova

Strada Chiantigiana 29
📞 0577-284 230 🕒 Closed Sun, period in Jan, early Aug. €€€–€€€€
This elegant restaurant serves some of the finest cuisine in Siena.

Specialities include local Tuscan delicacies, fish and divine desserts.

Certosa di Maggiano

Strada di Certosa 82
📞 0577-288 180 🕒 Daily.
€€€€
This converted Carthusian monastery, now a hotel, serves gourmet food in a magical setting: a cloistered courtyard overlooking Siena.

Da Guido

Vicolo del Pettinaio 7
📞 0577-280 042 🕒 Closed Wed and Jan. €€–€€€
Veritable Sienese institution, set in medieval premises and popular with visiting VIPs. Serves traditional Sienese cuisine.

Osteria del Castelvecchio

Via Castelvecchio 65
📞 0577-49586 🕒 Closed Tue. €€
Converted from ancient stables, this lovely informal *osteria* creates contemporary dishes with traditional flavours. There are reasonable choices for vegetarians and lots of good meat dishes, plus an interesting wine list.

Osteria Il Carroccio

Via Casato di Sotto 32
📞 0577-41165 🕒 Closed Wed and Feb. €€
Well-run, quaint and tiny trattoria serving simple local dishes not far from the Campo. Friendly and homely. Outdoor dining available.

Osteria La Chiacchiera

Costa di S. Antonio 4
☎ 0577-280 631 ⌚ Closed Tue. €
Small, rustic *osteria* offering typical Sienese fare (try the thick *pici*), on a steep street leading down to the Santuario e Casa di Santa Caterina.

Osteria La Taverna di San Giuseppe

Via G. Dupré 132 ☎ 0577-42286 ⌚ Closed Sun. €–€€
Delicious homely Tuscan fare in an atmospheric cavern with wooden furnishings. An *antipasto* is a must; delicious dishes using pecorino. Reservations recommended.

Osteria Le Logge

Via del Porrione 33 ☎ 0577-48013 ⌚ Closed Sun and Jan. €€€
Restaurant set in a 19th-century grocer's shop, with an authentic dark-wood and marble interior. On the menu you'll find duck and fennel, chicken and lemon, and such exotic dishes as stuffed guinea fowl *(faraona)*.

Pizzeria di Nonno Mede

Via Camporegio 21
☎ 0577-247 966. €
Serves a wide range of good pizzas and a great selection of desserts. Splendid view across to the Duomo, which is well lit in the evenings.

Trattoria Papei

Piazza del Mercato 6
☎ 0577-280 894 ⌚ Closed Mon (except public holidays) and end July. €€
Ideal place behind the Palazzo Pubblico for sampling genuine Sienese home cooking, like *pappardelle al sugo di cinghiale* (noodles in wild boar sauce) or *pici alla cardinale* (fat spaghetti in tomato sauce with hot peppers and chunks of pancetta). There's a variety of grilled meats, too.

Tre Cristi

Vicolo di Provenzano 1–7
☎ 0577-280 608 ⌚ Closed Sun. €€–€€€
Charming restaurant with a contemporary Mediterranean menu. Frescoed walls add to the atmosphere. Booking advised.

Bars, Cafés and Gelaterie

American Bar

Via di Città.
Tel: 0577-217 161.
A good refreshment stop between visiting the Duomo and the Pinacoteca.

Caffè del Corso

Banchi di Sopra 25.
Tel: 0577-226 656.
This café is chic by day and boisterous by night, when it offers cocktails and live music.

Enoteca Italiana

Fortezza Medicea, Piazza Libertà.
Tel: 0577-228 811.
Over 1,500 wines are on display in this Medici fortress. Taste them here or on the terraces.

Gelateria Caribia

Via Rinaldini 13.
Tel: 0577-280 823.
Located to the left of the Palazzo Pubblico, this *gelateria* serves creamy ice cream, granitas and sorbets.

Gelateria Costarella

Via di Littà 31/33.
Tel: 0577-288 076.
Ice creams and snacks with a tiny terrace overlooking the Campo.

Liberamente

Piazza del Campo.
Tel: 0577-274 733.
Friendly bar/*osteria* serving Prosecco, *aperitivi* and traditional Tuscan dishes.

Nannini

Banchi di Sopra 24.
Tel: 0577-236 009.
This is an obligatory coffee stop on the main shopping street; a Sienese institution.

The Tea Room

Via Porta Giustizia.
Tel: 0577-222 753.
Closed Mon. A cosy place for tea and cake, or a cocktail; live jazz.

LEFT: for the best view in town, sit at a restaurant terrace on the Campo.
ABOVE: the pleasure of eating out.

THE PASSION OF THE PALIO

In little more than a minute, the Campo is filled with unbearable happiness and irrational despair as centuries-old loyalties are put to the test

It is strange how a race that lasts just 90 seconds can require 12 months' planning, a lifetime's patience and the involvement of an entire city. But Siena's famous Palio (www.ilpalio.org) does just that, and has done since the 13th century, when an August Palio made its debut. At that time, the contest took the form of a bareback race the length of the city. The race run around Siena's main square, the Piazza del Campo, was introduced in the 17th century and takes place twice a year, on 2 July and 16 August. Held in times of war, famine and plague, the Palio stops for nothing. In the 1300s, criminals were released from jail to celebrate the festival. When the Fascists were gaining ground in 1919, Siena postponed council elections until after the Palio. In 1943, British soldiers in a Tunisian prisoner-of-war camp feared a riot when they banned Sienese prisoners from staging a Palio; Sienese fervour triumphed.

Although, as the Sienese say, *"Il Palio corre tutto l'anno"* ("The Palio runs all year"), the final preparations boil down to three days, during which there is the drawing by lots of the horse for each competing ward *(contrada)*, the choice of the jockeys and then the six trial races – the last of which is held on the morning of the Palio itself. Hundreds pack into the Campo for the race, others cluster around the TV set in the *contrada* square while some go to church to pray.

ABOVE: on the day of the Palio, the horses are taken to each *contrada* church for a blessing. The priest holds the horse's head and commands it, *"Vai e torni vincitore!"* ("Go and return victorious!").

LEFT: the words *"C'è terra in piazza"* ("There's earth in the Campo") are the signal to remove the colourful costumes from Siena's museums to feature in the great historical parade.

THE POWER OF THE *CONTRADE*

In Siena the *contrada* rules: ask a Sienese where he is from and he will say, "Ma sono della Lupa" ("But I'm from the She-Wolf contrada"). The first loyalty is to the city in the head, not to the city on the map.

Ten out of Siena's 17 *contrade* take part in each Palio: the seven who did not run in the previous race and three selected by lot. Each *contrada* appoints a captain and two lieutenants to run the campaign. In the Palio, the illegal becomes legal: bribery, kidnapping, plots and the doping of horses are all common.

Each of the *contrade* in the city has its own standard, many of which are displayed around the city during the Palio and play an important role in the ceremonial aspect of the event.

Flags, or standards, are a central theme of the Palio event. In fact, the Palio itself – the trophy of victory for which everyone is striving – is a standard: a silk flag emblazoned with the image of the Madonna and the coats of arms of the city, ironically referred to by the Sienese as the *cencio*, or rag. The *contrada* which wins the event retains possession of the Palio standard until the next race.

ABOVE: the ruthless race lurches around the Campo three times. If a riderless horse wins, the animal is almost deified: it is given the place of honour in the victory banquet and has its hooves painted gold.

LEFT: the costume parade, which is staged in the run-up to the main race, retraces Siena's centuries of struggle against Florence, from the glorious victory against its arch-rival in 1260 to the ghastly defeat in 1560.

BELOW: a highlight of the Palio pageantry is the spectacular display of the flag-wavers, famous throughout Italy for their elaborate manoeuvres of twirling and hurling the huge standards dozens of feet in the air.

EXCURSIONS

Temptingly close to Florence are such alluring destinations as Arezzo, San Gimignano, Lucca and Pisa, all of which can be reached easily by public transport

F lorence can be a claustrophobic city, and there may come a time when you need to escape. Fortunately it is well placed for all sorts of expeditions; to other major art centres (such as Siena, Lucca or Pisa), to smaller towns (such as Pistoia or Vinci), to the coast, or to the fabulous Chianti countryside for a gentle meander with stops for the odd wine-tasting and a lazy meal on a vine-clad terrace. The choice of destination will probably be dictated by means of transport; with a car, the possibilities are endless, but public transport would suggest Lucca, Arezzo, Siena or Pisa, all of which are well connected with Florence.

EN ROUTE TO AREZZO

Arezzo is 77km (48 miles) southeast of Florence. Heading south on the A1 autostrada, you come to **San Giovanni Valdarno ❷**, a lively centre with a surprising display of architectural and artistic wealth. Masaccio's *Virgin and Child* is housed in the church of Santa Maria, and Fra Angelico's *Annunciation* is preserved in the Renaissance monastery of Montecarlo just outside

the town. The village of **Castelfranco di Sopra**, 6km (4 miles) north, retains its military character, and many of the 14th-century buildings and streets have survived. The nearby villages of Loro Ciufenna and Cennina bear names derived from the Etruscan dialect, but a more medieval rusticity is evident in their alleyways and ruined castle fortresses.

The Arno basin was a lake in prehistoric times, and farmers still unearth remains and bones of longextinct animals. At **Montevarchi ❸**,

Main attractions

AREZZO
CHIANTI WINE TRAIL
IMPRUNETA
GREVE CHIANTI
PANZANO
CASTELLINA IN CHIANTI
RADDA IN CHIANTI
BADIA A COLTIBUONO
SAN GIMIGNANO
LEONARDO DA VINCI COUNTRY
SAN MINIATO
PRATO
PISTOIA
PISA

PRECEDING PAGES:
a golden Tuscan landscape.
LEFT: looking over San Gimignano.
RIGHT: a typical sight in summer in the countryside around Florence.

located 5km (3 miles) beyond San Giovanni, the **Accademia Valdarnese** (Via Poggio Bracciolini 36–40; tel: 055-981 227; Tue–Sat 9am–12.30pm, 4–6pm, Sun 10am–12.30pm; charge) is a great prehistory museum which holds an impressive collection of fossilised remains.

Arezzo ④

And so to Arezzo, one of Tuscany's wealthiest cities, best-known for its gold, art and antiques. Originally an Etruscan city, in 294 BC it became a rest station on the Via Cassia between Florence and Rome. The main Roman site is the amphitheatre, built in the 1st century BC; on the same site, the **Museo Archeologico** (Via Margaritone 10; tel: 0575-20882; daily 8.30am–7.30pm; charge) features some of the best examples anywhere of the red-glazed Coralline ware for which Arezzo has long been famous.

The "modern" city is dominated by the **Duomo** (Piazza del Duomo; tel:

0575-23991; daily 7am–12.30pm, 3–6.30pm; free), which has been described as one of the most perfect expressions of Gothic architecture in Italy – although the facade dates from 1914. Inside, there are clustered columns, pointed arches, 16th-century stained-glass windows by Guillaume de Marcillat and a fresco of St Mary Magdalene by Piero della Francesca.

The medieval **Piazza Grande** is dominated on one side by the Loggia di Vasari, built in 1573. But the most impressive building is the round

Florence Excursions

Romanesque apse of the 12th-century church of Santa Maria della Pieve, with its crumbling Pisan-Lucchese facade (on Corso Italia) and adjacent "campanile of a hundred holes".

Arezzo's artists and inventors

You can see Arezzo's greatest work of art in the otherwise dull church of **San Francesco** (tel: 0575-20630; daily 8.30am–noon, 2–6.30pm; free) in the piazza of the same name. Painted between 1452 and 1466, Piero della Francesco's fresco cycle *The Legend of the True Cross* (Apr–Oct Mon–Fri 9am–6.30pm, Sat 9am–5.30pm, Sun 1–5.30pm, Nov–Mar Mon–Fri 9am–5.30pm, Sat 9am–5pm, Sun 1–5pm; charge; booking recommended, tel: 0575-352 727, groups of 25, every 30 minutes) is a powerful and haunting series of paintings and one of the most significant reference points in the history of Italian painting.

The **Museo Statale d'Arte Medioevale e Moderna** (Via San Lorentino 8; tel: 0575-409 050; Tue–Sun 9am–6pm; charge) is situated diagonally opposite the Duomo in the 15th-century Palazzo Bruni. Its varied col-

lection includes excellent majolica, frescos and paintings.

The **Casa di Giorgio Vasari** (Via XX Settembre 55; tel: 0575-409 040; Mon, Wed–Sat 8.30am–7pm, Sun 8.30am–1pm; charge), built by Vasari himself in 1540 *(see page 107)*, is decorated with portraits of fellow artists and friends.

From there, walk up to the 13th-century church of **San Domenico** (Piazza di San Domenico; tel: 0575-23255; Mon–Sat 7am–1pm, 3.30–6pm, Sun 8am–1pm, 3.30–6pm;

ABOVE: Arezzo's Corso. **LEFT AND BELOW:** a jousting tournament (Giostra del Saracino) is held in Arezzo's Piazza Grande each June and September.

Chianti Wine Trail

A trip to Tuscany, home of the world-famous Chianti Classico and other fine Italian wines, is not complete without exploring some wine estates

What has become known as the Chianti area of Tuscany covers an enormous region, spanning seven different wine "zones". At its heart, in the hills between Florence and Siena, is Chianti Classico, while the remainder – the Colli Fiorentini, Colli Senesi, Colline Pisane, Colli Aretini, Rufina and Montalbano – spread out over central Tuscany.

The main centres in Chianti Classico are Greve, Panzano, Castellina, Gaiole, Fonterutoli and Radda – the official seat of the vintners' association known as the Consorzio del Gallo Nero. Scattered in and among these towns, many of them accessible off the picturesque route SS 222, are innumerable vineyards and estates. Most of the estates welcome visitors. The *Toscana and Chianti News* (online at www.toscanaechiantinews.com) lists estates open for wine-tasting and suggests enogastronomic itineraries. Estate owners are usually proud to show off their wines.

The Estates

Call the estate in advance to arrange a tasting *(degustazione)* combined with a tour. For general information, try www.florence wine.it and www.chianticlassico.com.

Badia a Coltibuono *(see page 247)*
Gaiole in Chianti; tel: 0577-74481; www. coltibuono.com
This wine estate markets itself as a "wine resort" – visitors can eat, sleep and take courses within the former abbey.

Castello di Brolio
Gaiole in Chianti; tel: 0577-7301; www. ricasoli.it
Baron Ricasoli, whose descendants now run the Castello di Brolio, first designated the grape mixes to be used in Chianti wine.

Castello di Fonterutoli
Castellina in Chianti; tel: 0577-73571; www.fonterutoli.it
Owned by the family since the 15th century, Fonterutoli's wines have won several awards. Guests can stay on the estate.

Castello di Gabbiano
Mecatale Val di Pesa; tel: 055-821 8059; www.gabbiano.com
Guests can stay in the castle and visit the winery.

Montevertine
Radda in Chianti; tel: 0577-738 009; www.montevertine.it
The Manetti family only founded this small estate in 1967, but its quality wines are already famous. Call for details on tastings.

Vignamaggio
Greve; tel: 055-854 661; www.vigna maggio.it
This is a wine estate and an *agriturismo* with rooms in a Renaissance villa. ❏

ABOVE: vineyards dominate the landscape.
LEFT: the Sangiovese grape.

free) to see a fine Gothic chapel, good frescos and a crucifix by Cimabue.

THROUGH CHIANTI COUNTRY

To take a drive through some of the most stunning countryside Tuscany has to offer, head south out of Florence from Porta Romana on the Via Senese and, when you get to the big roundabout where the Rome autostrada and Siena superstrada converge, take the road marked "Tavernuzze, Impruneta, Greve".

Impruneta ❺

This is a pleasant town noted for its production of terracotta (the tiles on Brunelleschi's dome were made here). It was an important early medieval sanctuary where a shrine was erected to house an image of the Virgin Mary, attributed to St Luke. This collegiate church was bombed during the war, but consequently restored, and now houses two beautiful chapels and some marvellous terracottas by della Robbia.

From Impruneta, take the Chiantigiana (SS 222). Just before Greve on the right, the tiny walled town of

Montefioralle has been beautifully restored, enclosing narrow streets and stone houses.

Greve in Chianti ❻

In the heart of Chianti, Greve is a bustling market town. The triangular, arcaded Piazza Matteotti is lined with shops selling wine and olive oil; Falorni (Piazza Matteotti 71; tel: 055-853 029; www.falorni.it; Mon–Sat 8am–1pm, 3.30–7.30pm, Sun 10am–1pm, 3.30–7pm), a butcher famous throughout the region, sells wonderful salami here.

Vignamaggio and into the hills

A detour off the Chiantigiana takes a circular route along a *strada bianca* (unpaved road) past wine villas and through fabulous countryside. Take a turning to the left just south of Greve signposted Vignamaggio. This mellow, pinkish-hued old villa was built by the Gherardini family; the subject of Leonardo da Vinci's famous *Mona Lisa* is said to have been born here, and it was used as the setting for Kenneth Branagh's film *Much Ado about Nothing* in 1992. A

A winemaker promotes his produce at the Chianti wine festival held in Greve every September.

BELOW: vineyards in the beautiful Chianti hills.

shop sells estate-produced wine and olive oil. Continue on this winding road into the hills, and you come first to **Casole** (where the trattoria serves good food with fabulous views) and then the hamlet of **Lamole**, before arriving back on the main road. Near **Panzano** ❼ (a partially walled town and an important agricultural centre

RIGHT: Brolio – a Chianti Classico of the highest calibre.
BELOW: cyclists in Greve.

set in glorious countryside), the **Pieve di San Leolino** (1km/⅔ mile to the south) is a Romanesque building with a pretty portico, and the nearby farm of Fattoria Montagliari (just north of Panzano at Via di Montagliari 29; tel: 055-852 014) sells its own wines, grappa, olive oil, honey and cheeses.

Castellina in Chianti ❽

Lying 15km (9 miles) further south is this delightful hilltop village whose ancient walls remain almost intact. The castle itself is now a fortified town hall hiding the small **Museo Archeologico del Chianti Senese** (Piazza del Comune; tel: 0577-742 090; www.museoarcheologicochianti. it; Thur–Tue 10am–1pm, 3.30–6.30pm; charge), surrounded by a warren of atmospheric backstreets. La Bottega del Vino (Via della Rocca 13; tel: 0577-741 110; www.enobottega. it) is a wine-tasting centre which also offers information on wine tours.

Radda in Chianti ❾

From Castellina you can either continue south and visit the **Enoteca di Fonterutoli** (see page 244), near the

ancient hamlet of the same name, to taste or buy some fabulous wines, or go straight to Radda in Chianti, 12km (8 miles) to the east. Here, towards the Monti di Chianti, the terrain becomes more rugged, with Radda perched high on a hill. The streets of this medieval town radiate out from the central piazza, where the **Palazzo Comunale** has a 15th-century fresco of the *Madonna with St John and St Christopher*. Just outside Radda are the medieval villages of **Ama** to the south and **Volpaia** to the north; both are home to excellent wine-producing estates.

Badia a Coltibuono ⑩

✉ near Gaiole in Chianti; www.badia-a-coltibuono.com ☎ 0577-74481 ⊙ guided tours May–Oct Mon–Fri 2–5pm; closed Aug ⊚ charge

Set among pine trees, oaks, chestnuts and vines is one of the most beautiful buildings in Chianti, the aptly named "Abbey of the Good Harvest". The abbey dates from the 12th century but was converted into a private villa in the 18th century. The estate *(see page 244)* now produces and sells excellent wine, olive oil and honey. The only drawback is that the abbey is on every tour itinerary, and so inundated by tour buses.

From Gaiole, a popular retreat from the heat of Florence, head south on the SS 484 to **Castello di Brolio** *(see page 244)*, which is set high in the hills with views that stretch to Siena and Monte Amiata. The castle's past spans Guelf–Ghibelline conflicts, sacking by the Sienese, and German occupation and Allied bombing during World War II.

San Gimignano ⑪

San Gimignano is a very popular excursion from Florence, and with good reason. Aim for an overnight stay if you can to see it when all the day-trippers have gone. From Poggi-

bonsi the approach is memorable as the famous towers come into view behind olives, cypresses and vines. Only 13 of the original 76 towers – the so-called *belle torri* (originally designed as keeps during the Guelf–Ghibelline feuds in the 12th and 13th centuries) – are left standing, but San Gimignano remains Italy's best-preserved medieval city.

Collegiata

The Romanesque **Collegiata** or **Duomo** (Piazza del Duomo; tel: 0577-940 316; Mar, Nov–Jan Mon–Sat 9.30am–4.40pm, Sun 12.30–4.40pm, Apr–Oct Mon–Fri 9.30am–7.10pm, Sat 9.30am–5pm, Sun 12.30–5pm; charge) no longer has the status of a cathedral because there is no bishop. The plain facade belies the gloriously lavish interior; vaulted ceilings painted with gold stars, similar in style to Siena's Duomo, and walls covered in fine frescos, mostly by Sienese artists. Look out for Bartolo di Fredi's vivid Old Testament scenes along the north aisle (Noah and his menagerie are delightful), and Barna di Siena's

WHERE

In 1716 a decree issued by the Grand Duke of Tuscany defined the boundaries of the Chianti area and established the laws governing the production and sale of wine. Today this region is in the world's oldest wine-producing league. The Chianti Classico area includes the communes of Barberino Val d'Elsa, Castellina, Greve, Gaiole, San Casciano and Tavernelle Val di Pesa.

BELOW: Chianti symbols are a popular decoration.

New Testament scenes covering the south wall. On the west wall are Benozzo Gozzoli's *Saint Sebastian* and Taddeo di Bartolo's gory *Last Judgement*. Off the south aisle lies the Santa Fina Chapel, with Ghirlandaio's flowery depiction of the local saint: legend has it that when she died in 1253, violets sprang up on her coffin and on the towers.

One of five circular towers dotted along San Gimignano's city walls.

Torre Grossa and Museo Civico

In the asymmetrical Piazza del Duomo lies the **Palazzo del Popolo** with its 54-metre (177ft) **Torre Grossa**, completed in *c*.1300, and the **Museo Civico** (tel: 0577-990 312; both daily Mar–Oct 9.30am–7pm, Nov–Feb 10am–5pm; charge, combined ticket, tower and museum). A climb up the 218 steps of the tower (it's the tallest in the city) will reward you with stunning views. The museum contains an excellent collection of Florentine and Sienese masters, including works of art by Gozzoli, Lippi, Taddeo di Bartolo and Giotto – plus the well-known domestic and profane scenes by Memmo di Filippuccio, an early 14th-century artist. The adjacent Piazza della Cis-

RIGHT: the countryside around San Gimignano.
BELOW: admiring the view, San Gimignano.

terna is a lovely triangular piazza with a 13th-century well and lined with medieval *palazzi*.

Monteriggioni

Back on the SR 2, just before you reach Siena, you get a good view of the tiny fortified town of Monteriggioni. Dating from 1219, this was once the northernmost bastion of Siena, and saw plenty of action during the wars with Florence. Now it perches peacefully on a little hill, its ancient walls broken by 14 towers. It is seen at its best first thing in the morning, when you can enjoy a coffee on the main square before the coach parties arrive.

LEONARDO COUNTRY

A gentle meander into the countryside due west of Florence takes in some lovely views, several small towns and Leonardo's birthplace at Vinci.

Head west of Florence along the SP 66 (in the direction of Pistoia), and turn south at **Poggio a Caiano**, site of an important Medici villa *(see page 217)*. The walled village of **Artimino** is the setting for a huge villa (Via Papa Giovanni XXIII; tel: 055-871 8124; Mon, Tue, Thur–Sat 9.30am–12.30pm, Sun 10am–noon, Wed by appointment, Nov–Jan by appointment Thur–Sat, Sun 10am–noon; charge) built by Bernardo Buontalenti as a hunting lodge for Ferdinando I in 1594 and curious for the number of tall chimneys stuck on the roof. It has been beautifully restored, and con-

verted into a distinguished hotel, complete with a restaurant specialising in dishes with Medici origins. Part of the villa is open to visitors, including a small Etruscan museum.

Vinci ⑫

A tortuous road leads through olive groves and vines from Artimino to Vinci, alleged birthplace of Leonardo. Here, the 13th-century castle of the Conti Guidi houses the **Museo Leonardiano** (tel: 0571-593 3251; www.museoleonardiano.it; Mar–Oct daily 9.30am–7pm, Nov–Feb 9.30am–6pm; charge), which contains a vast selection of mechanical models built to the exact measurements of Leonardo's drawings in the Codex Atlanticus notebooks. He is said to have been christened in the 14th-century Santa Croce church next door. In **Anchiano**, near his rustic birthplace, another museum features more prosaic mementos of his life.

Five km (3 miles) southwest of Vinci is the hill town of **Cerreto Guidi**. Once owned by the Guidi counts, it now produces a good Chianti Putto wine and boasts yet another Medici

villa, the **Villa di Cerreto Guidi** (Via dei Ponti Medicei 7; tel: 055-294 883; www.polomuseale.firenze.it; daily 8.15am–7pm, closed 2nd and 3rd Mon of month; free; *see page 216*), built in 1564 for Cosimo I as a hunting lodge. Now restored, it contains some fine portraits of the Medici family and a *Pietà* by Andrea della Robbia. Isabella, daughter of Cosimo I, is said to have been murdered here by her husband for her infidelities.

Another 8km (5 miles) southwest along a country lane will take you to **Fucecchio**, the ancient core of which is surrounded by more modern outskirts. A variety of its buildings,

ABOVE: Andrea del Sansovino's terracotta frieze at Poggio a Caiano. **BELOW:** dawn over the hills of San Gimignano.

San Miniato is famous for the highly prized white truffle. The Association of Trufflers of the San Miniato Hills issues a map showing where to find the aromatic tuber. Truffling season runs from mid-September to Christmas. On weekends in November a huge market and exhibition display the best of the season.

including Castruccio's Tower, are worth visiting. The town is also the birthplace of Puccini's rascally hero, Gianni Schicchi.

Bird haven

The **Palude di Fucecchio**, Italy's biggest inland swamp, covering 1,460 hectares (3,600 acres), offers much for the nature-lover. Some 50 species of migrating birds are protected here, and the same amount again nest in the area, including night herons, little egrets, squacco herons and, most recently, cattle egrets. The land is private property, but the Palude centre in **Castelmartini di Larciano** (tel: 0573-84540) organises guided tours.

RIGHT: flora at Padule di Fucecchio. **BELOW RIGHT:** San Miniato.

Empoli

From Fucecchio, take the back road to Empoli, a prosperous, modern market town with a small *centro storico* (historic centre) and a superb Romanesque church, the **Collegiata Sant'Andrea**. The green-and-white-striped facade is reminiscent of Florence's San Miniato, and the small **museum** (Piazza della Propositura 3; tel: 0571-76284; Tue–Sun 9am–noon, 4–7pm; charge) contains precious 13th- and 14th-century Florentine art.

Ceramics and Botticelli

Taking the SS 67 towards Florence, the last stop should be in **Montelupo Fiorentino**, famous for its history of terracotta and ceramic production. The new **Museo della Ceramica** (Piazza Vittorio Veneto 8–10; tel: 0571-51372; www.museomonte lupo.it; Tue–Sat 10am–6pm; charge) shows fine examples of both, going back centuries and charting the whole history of the ceramics of this small Tuscan town. An annual Festa Internazionale di Ceramica is held here in late June. There are plenty of shops in the town where you can buy

San Miniato

The ancient town of San Miniato, whose origins go back to Etruscan and Roman times, is set on the top of three hills and gazes out upon magnificent views. The nature and history of the town have always been closely linked to its geographical position, equidistant from the important cities that played a decisive historical role: Pisa, Florence, Lucca, Pistoia, Siena and Volterra. High on the hillside are the two towers of the **Rocca** (Apr–Sept daily 10am–7pm, Oct Tue–Sun 10am–6pm, Nov–Mar 10am–5pm), which was rebuilt in the 12th century by Frederick II. The oldest tower of the fortress, the Torre di Matilde, was converted into a belltower when the **Duomo** (daily 8am–12.30pm, 3–6.30pm) was added, with its Romanesque brick facade and later restructuring. The **Museo Diocesano d'Arte Sacra** (Apr–Sept Tue–Sun 10am–1pm, 3–6pm, Oct–Mar Sat–Sun 9am–noon, 2.30–5pm; charge), in the old sacristy of the Duomo, exhibits art and sculpture, including works by Lippi, Verrocchio and Tiepolo. Built by the Lombards in the 8th century, the magnificent church of **San Francesco** (same hours as the Duomo) is the oldest building in San Miniato.

The Pulpit of the Holy Girdle on Prato's Duomo.

modern ceramics. Don't leave without seeing the church of **San Giovanni Evangelista** (Via Baccio de Montelupo 37; tel: 0571-51048; daily 9am–8pm; free), with its beautiful painting of *Madonna and Saints* by Botticelli and his assistants.

Prato ⑱

Just 16km (10 miles) northwest of Florence, Prato is the third-largest city in Tuscany. It is a rich, industrial centre known for the manufacture of textiles. Examples can be seen in the **Museo del Tessuto** (Via Santa Chiara 24; tel: 0574-611 503; daily 10am–7pm, last entrance 6pm; charge, free on Sun). Numerous factory outlets sell fine fabrics, cashmere and designer clothes.

However, within Prato's modern outskirts lies a *centro storico* between medieval walls. The **Duomo** (Piazza del Duomo; tel: 0574-26234; Mon–Sat 7.30am–noon, 3.30–7pm, Sun 7am–noon, 1–7pm; free) is home to what is believed to be the girdle of the Virgin Mary (on public display on only five days per year). Inside, the Chapel of the Holy Girdle (on the left of the main entrance) is covered with frescos by Agnolo Gaddi illustrating the legends surrounding this most bizarre of holy relics; and built onto the facade of the church is the circular Pulpit of the Holy Girdle, designed by Donatello and Michelozzo. After a lengthy restoration, Filippo Lippi's rich and dramatic frescos in the apse,

depicting the lives of St John the Baptist and St Stephen, are once again on view (Mon–Sat 10am–5pm, Sun 3–5pm; charge).

The **Museo dell' Opera del Duomo** (Piazza del Duomo 49; tel: 0574-29339; Mon–Sat 10am–1pm, 3–6.30pm, Sun 10am–1pm; charge) in the cloister contains paintings, sculptures and reliefs by Donatello, Lippi and others.

The church of **Santa Maria delle Carceri** (Piazza delle Carceri; tel: 0574-27933; Wed–Mon 7am–noon, 4–7pm; free) lies behind the Castello dell' Imperatore. Begun in 1485, the church was built by Giuliano Sangallo in Brunelleschian style. The **Castle** (Piazza delle Carceri; tel: 0574-38207; Wed–Mon, Apr–Sept 9am–1pm, 4–7pm, Oct–Mar 9am–1pm; charge) was built by Frederick II Hohenstaufen in the first half of the 13th century; there are good views from its walls.

Head west through Piazza San Francesco to reach the mid 14th-century frescoed **Palazzo Datini** (Via Ser Lapo Mazzei 43; tel: 0574-21391; Mon–Fri 9am–12.30pm,

LEFT: Henry Moore sculpture in Prato's Piazza San Marco.
BELOW: a lone farmhouse and cypress trees – a classic Tuscan scene.

ABOVE: a della Robbia frieze on Pistoia's Ospedale del Ceppo.
BELOW: Piazza Anfiteatro, Lucca.
BELOW RIGHT: Pistoia's 12th-century Cathedral of San Zeno and campanile.

3–6pm, Sat 9am–12.30pm, Aug am only; free). This is the former home of Francesco Datini, founder of the city's riches in the wool trade and described as "The Merchant of Prato" in Iris Origo's book on life in medieval Prato.

On the outskirts is the **Centro per l'Arte Contemporanea Luigi Pecci** (Viale della Repubblica 277; tel: 0574-5317; www.centropecci.it; daily 10am–7pm, closed 3 weeks in Aug; free), a museum with temporary exhibitions of modern art.

Pistoia

Moving west along the autostrada, past the rows of *vivaie* (garden centres), brings you to the town of Pistoia. The fine medieval centre holds enough interest to satisfy the art-hungry, and the shops around Cavour, Cino, Vannucci and Orafi streets are as glamorous as those in Florence or Lucca. Most of the city's important buildings were constructed in the Middle Ages, when Pistoia flourished as a banking centre.

On the **Piazza del Duomo**, the **Cattedrale di San Zeno** (Piazza del Duomo; tel: 0573-25095; daily 8.30am–12.30pm, 3.30–7pm; free), with characteristic green and white stripes, dates originally from the 5th century, although it was rebuilt in Romanesque style some 700 years later. A blue-and-white Andrea della Robbia bas-relief decorates the porch, and inside are many medieval frescos, Renaissance paintings and, in the chapel of San Jacopo (charge), a silver altar.

The soaring campanile has three tiers of green-and-white Pisan arches, while opposite is Andrea Pisano's

14th-century octagonal **baptistery**. Within the Palazzo Comunale, the **Museo Civico** (tel: 0573-371 296; Apr–Sept Tue, Thur–Sat 10am–6pm, Wed 4–7pm, Sun 11am–6pm, Oct–Mar Tue, Thur–Sat 10am–5pm, Wed 3–6pm, Sun 11am–5pm; charge) in the same square houses an impressive art collection, including a rare 13th-century painting of *St Francis* and other 15th-century treasures. Pistoia has numerous minor churches which merit a visit for their important artworks and Pisano pulpits.

Lucca ⑮

The town of Lucca deserves as much time as possible; it is a delightful place, not least for its lack of mass tourism. It lies 55km (34 miles) due west of Florence along the A11 autostrada. In Roman times, it was the most important town in Tuscany, and this legacy can be seen today in the grid pattern of the streets, and, more obviously, in the elliptical **Piazza del Anfiteatro**, now lined with shops, bars and restaurants. Like Florence, Lucca's wealth was based on banking and, later, its silk industry. The **Torre Guinigi** (Via Sant' Andrea 41; tel: 0583-316846; daily Mar 9am–7pm, Apr–May and mid-Sept–Oct 9am–9pm, June–mid-Sept 9am–midnight, Nov–Feb 9.30am–6pm; charge), with oak trees sprouting from the top, was built by one of the wealthiest banking families; a tough climb leads to splendid views over the red rooftops, and is a good way to get your bearings.

Lucca's chief attraction is its particularly interesting and beautiful churches, many of which contain ornate organ cases. **San Michele**, built on the site of the old Roman forum, has one of the most spectacular Pisan Romanesque facades in Italy. The **Duomo di San Martino** (Piazza San Martino; tel: 0583-957 068; daily 9.30am–5.45pm in summer, 9.30am–4.45pm in winter; free), enhanced by

its crenellated tower, combines Romanesque and Gothic styles; three tiers of colonnades adorn the facade, while the arches are decorated with superb relief work. Inside the building, the sacristy contains the remarkable tomb of Ilaria del Carretto by Jacopo della Quercia, an outstanding and poignant effigy of Paolo Guinigi's young bride, complete with devoted dog at her feet.

Opera fans should visit Giacomo Puccini's birthplace in Via di Poggio 30, close to San Michele. Now a small museum, the **Casa di Puccini** (tel: 0583-584 0287; Mar–May and Oct–Dec Tue–Sun 10am–1pm, 3–6pm, June–Sept daily 10am–6pm; charge; currently closed) contains his piano and various personal effects along with letters, manuscripts and other memorabilia.

Pisa ⑯

Pisa, home to Italy's most famous landmark, lies 16km (10 miles) west of Lucca. The best place to begin a tour is at the **Campo dei Miracoli**, where the Leaning Tower, the Duomo and the baptistery soar above their

EAT

The offerings at Lucca's historic ice-cream parlour Gelateria Veneta (Chiasso Barletti 23; tel: 0583-493 727; daily 11am–midnight, shorter hours in winter) are out of this world.

BELOW: the rooftops of Lucca.

TIP

Leaning Tower: there are accompanied visits every 40 minutes; no children under 8 allowed. Tickets can be bought at the ticket office up to 15 days beforehand or online for a small fee.

ABOVE: detail from Lucca's San Martino.
BELOW: facade of San Michele, Lucca.

green lawns. The white marble facing of all three structures emphasises the exquisite harmony of this piazza.

The Duomo

One of the first monumental structures of the Middle Ages, the Duomo (Campo dei Miracoli; www.opapisa. it; tel: 050-560 547; daily Nov–Feb 10am–1pm, 2–5pm, Mar 10am–6pm, Oct 10am–7pm, Apr–Sept Mon–Sat 10am–8pm, Sun 1–8pm; charge) was built after a Pisan victory at Palermo in 1063. Buscheto, its architect, combined the ground-plan of an early Christian basilica with a transept – the first sacred building in the shape of a cross in Italy. Inside, due to the gen-

erous use of arches in the aisles, it resembles an enormous mosque. Buscheto was familiar with Islamic architecture, and the ornate marble intarsia decoration on the exterior also reflects Islamic influence; other features are typical of northern Italian Romanesque. This mix of styles makes it unique. Inside, the marble pulpit by Giovanni Pisano is a masterpiece of Gothic sculpture, depicting Old Testament prophets and New Testament Apostles.

The baptistery

Aligned with the cathedral is the baptistery (tel: 050-387 2210; daily Nov–Feb 10am–5pm, Mar 10am–6pm, Apr–Sept 8am–8pm, Oct 9am–7pm; charge). Begun in 1153 by Diotisalvi in the same style as the Duomo, the Gothic part (including the loggia) was supervised by Nicola Pisano and later his son Giovanni. Lack of funds meant that the cupola could only be added in the 14th century. In 1260 Nicola Pisano created the first ever free-standing pulpit for the baptistery, one of the most important Late Romanesque works of art in Italy.

The fascinating **Museo delle Sinopie** (same hours and telephone as the baptistery; charge) on the south side of the piazza has several earlier versions of the frescos discovered during restoration work.

Leaning Tower of Pisa

The Leaning Tower (Torre Pendente, Campo dei Miracoli; www.opapisa. it; 050 560 547; daily Nov, Feb 9.30am–5pm, Mar 9am–5.30pm, Oct 9am–7pm, Apr–Sept 8.30am–8pm, mid-June–mid-Sept until 11pm; charge) is one of the best-known structures in the world. Work began on the cathedral's campanile in 1173, but the belltower soon began to lean, due to the unstable subsoil, and work was abandoned. In 1275, Giovanni di Simone decided to continue building and

rectify the inclination as he went. But the tower continued to lean. It does lean to a frightening degree, but work to stabilise it has been a success. Only a few people at a time are allowed to climb the tower.

Museums

The highlight at the **Museo dell' Opera del Duomo** (same telephone and opening hours as the baptistery; charge), in the cathedral's 13th-century Chapter House, is the sculp-

ture collection; there are several fine 12th-century works, and masterpieces by Nicola and Giovanni Pisano. More magnificent works of sculpture and paintings, dating from the 12th to the 17th centuries, can be admired in the **Museo Nazionale di San Matteo** (Piazzetta San Matteo in Soarta, by the Arno; tel: 050-971 1395; Tue–Sat 9am–7pm, Sun 9am–1pm; charge).

In the town centre

In the Piazza dei Cavalieri in the heart of the student district is the vast **Palazzo della Carovana**, designed by Vasari, with coats-of-arms, and black-and-white sgraffito decoration. Next door is the church of **Santo Stefano dei Cavalieri**, also by Vasari. The interior contains several captured standards and sections of ships dating from Pisan naval victories against the Ottomans.

Pisa's only surviving brick *palazzo*, the Palazzo Agostini, is not only famous for its splendid 15th-century terracotta decoration; it also contains the Caffè dell'Ussero which was frequented by the revolutionaries during the Risorgimento.   ❏

In mid-June Pisa holds its Regatta di San Ranieri, where boat races and processions of decorated boats are held on the River Arno. The evening before the regatta, tens of thousands of candles and torches are placed on the buildings along the river – a stunning sight.

LEFT: close-up of the Leaning Tower. **BELOW:** Campo dei Miracoli.

INSIGHT GUIDES

FLORENCE
Travel Tips

TRANSPORT

GETTING THERE AND GETTING AROUND

F lorence is an easy city to get around, compact enough to explore on foot. The Piazza del Duomo became entirely pedestrianised in 2009, making sightseeing in the heart of the city a good deal more relaxing. Small electric buses skirt the centre or, if you want to go further afield, you can take one of the city's speedy orange buses. Most of the principal attractions lie north of the Arno around two main piazzas, Piazza del Duomo and Piazza della Signoria, and their connecting street, Via dei Calzaiuoli.

GETTING THERE

By Air

The two main airports that serve Tuscany are Pisa and Florence. Pisa's Galileo Galilei Airport handles an ever-growing number of scheduled services as well as charter flights. For most visitors, flights to Pisa are the better option, being more frequent and usually cheaper than flights to the smaller Peretola Airport (also known as Amerigo Vespucci), which lies 4km (2½ miles) northwest of Florence. Getting from Pisa to Florence takes over an hour, whether by train or by the Terravision coaches which link with budget airline flights and operate from the airport to Florence's Santa Maria Novella train station (www.terravision.it). Peretola is just a 15-minute bus or taxi ride away from the centre *(see Getting Around)*.

You could also consider taking the plane to Bologna or Bologna

Forli; budget airlines operate to both airports.

Finding a Fare

As a general rule, you will get the best deals on the internet, and from so-called "no frills" airlines, such as Ryanair (www.ryanair.co.uk) and easyJet (www.easyjet.co.uk). For the cheapest flights, book as far in advance as possible and be prepared to travel early in the morning or late at night.

Europe

British Airways (www.britishairways. com) operate regular scheduled flights from London to Pisa. These are heavily booked in summer, and advance reservations are essential. Ryanair flies from London Stansted to Pisa three times a day in summer, twice in winter, and charter flights are also available, chiefly through tour operators who specialise in "flight only" packages to Italy. Meridiana (www.meridiana.it) operates regular flights between London Gatwick

and Florence Peretola and a variety of domestic flights within Italy. Scheduled services fly from Florence to many major European destinations, and both Florence and Pisa are well served by Alitalia's internal flights to Milan, Rome, Sardinia and Sicily.

United States

Delta (www.delta.com) flies direct from New York JFK to Pisa from May to October. The alternative

AIRLINES

Alitalia: tel: 0871-424 1424; www.alitalia.com.
easyJet: tel: 0905-821 0905; www.easyjet.com.
Meridiana: Arena House, 66 Pentonville Road, London N1 9HS; tel: 0845-355 5588; www.meridiana.it.
Ryanair: tel: 0906-270 5656; www.ryanair.com.

is to fly direct to Milan or Rome; the excellent airport train linking Rome's Fiumicino Airport with Termini station (in central Rome) and frequent, fast trains to Florence make this a viable option for visitors from the US.

By Rail

The train journey from London to Florence via Paris takes between 15 and 18 hours – just over 2 hours from London (St Pancras) to Paris (Gare du Nord) on Eurostar, and another 13- to 16-hour journey from Paris (Gare de Bercy) on the overnight Palatino to Florence (Santa Maria Novella), depending on the time of day you leave and the connection times. If you enjoy rail travel, it's a pleasant journey, but it is not cheaper than flying.

For international rail information, including train times and reservations, call **Rail Europe** on 0844-848 4064 (www.raileurope.co.uk).

In addition to first and second class, there are some useful special tickets. InterRail passes are available to European citizens, either a Global Pass, valid in 30 European countries, or a One Country pass. Those under 26

BELOW: small is beautiful.

can purchase a discounted Youth Pass which is only valid on second-class travel. Passes allow unlimited travel, but supplements must be paid on the faster trains.

For more information on rail travel within Italy *see Getting Around, pages 260–1.*

By Road

For those travelling to Italy in their own vehicle, there are several routes to Florence. The best Channel crossing to opt for is the Channel Tunnel from Folkestone to Calais on Eurotunnel (tel: 0844-335 3535; www.eurotunnel.com) or use one of the Folkestone/Dover to Calais/Boulogne ferry crossings; you can also sail to Ostend from Dover.

The most direct way to drive is to head for Milan via northern France, Germany and Switzerland. The total journey from the Channel port to Florence on this route takes a minimum of 15 hours. The obvious alternative is to head for the south of France and cross into Italy at the north western border.

For detailed information on route-planning, mileage, petrol and toll fees, and general advice for motorists, visit the **AA** route-planning service at www.theaa.com

or the Michelin website at www.viamichelin.com.

By Coach

Given the low cost of flights to Tuscany, travelling to Florence by bus is not a popular option. A London to Rome service is operated by **National Express**. The coach departs from Victoria Coach Station and travels via Dover–Paris–Milan–Parma–Bologna–Florence (Via Santa Caterina da Siena) and on to Rome.

The journey as far as Florence takes about 27 hours. For details go to www.eurolines.co.uk, tel: 0871-781 8177.

Package Holidays

The **Italian State Tourist Office** (1 Princes Street, London W1B 2AY; tel: 020-7408 1254; www.italiantouristboard.co.uk) can supply free maps and brochures on a wide range of holidays and activities, as well as stays based in Florence, and produces a useful booklet with practical information on unusual travel itineraries.

Citalia also offers holidays covering the whole of Italy. Contact them at The Atrium, London Road, Crawley, West Sussex RH10 9SR; tel: 0871-200 2004; www.citalia.com. Package deals to Florence, especially weekend breaks, are reasonable.

The Italian Connection (The Chapel, East Sussex, TN34 3BS; tel: 01424-728 900; www.italian-connection.co.uk) is a small, specialist company which organises bespoke hotel and villa holidays. Themed holidays include cookery, sailing and family activities.

GETTING AROUND

On Arrival

The easiest way to get from **Pisa (Galileo Galilei) International Airport** (tel: 050-849 300; www.pisa-airport.com) to Florence is by

ABOVE: the most useful bus routes for tourists are Nos 12 and 13.

the coach service (www.terravision. eu), whose departures are timed to coincide with flights. The journey time is 75 minutes and the coaches arrive at Florence's main railway station, Santa Maria Novella.

The airport also has its own railway station, but there are only six direct trains a day to Florence. If there are no airport trains to coincide with your flight arrival it is worth taking a 5-minute shuttle to Pisa Central, where the connections to Florence are far more frequent. Journey time is 60–80 minutes. Train tickets (which are cheaper than the bus) can be bought in the main airport concourse.

Car hire is available from the airport, and so are taxis. A toll-free *superstrada* links Pisa Airport with Florence.

Peretola (Amerigo Vespucci) International Airport (www.aero porto.firenze.it) is situated in the northwestern suburbs of Florence (tel: 055-306 1630) and is connected every 30 minutes by the airport shuttle bus – Vola In Bus – to the Sita bus company depot not far from Santa Maria Novella railway station; the journey time is about 20 minutes, and taxis are available on the bus. A taxi into the centre of Florence will

cost around €20 and takes approximately 20 minutes.

By Air

Alitalia offers a range of internal flights from both Florence and Pisa airports. This is supplemented by Meridiana's domestic services, and which leave from Florence and are usually slightly cheaper.

By Train

The FS (*Ferrovie dello Stato*), the state-subsidised railway network, is excellent, and a cheap and convenient way of travelling between major cities in Tuscany.

The principal Rome–Milan line stops at Bologna, Florence and Arezzo, while the Rome–Genoa line serves Pisa, Livorno and Grosseto. However, the Florence–Siena route is faster by coach than by train.

Note that Florence has several train stations: **Santa Maria Novella** is the main station for

TRAIN INFORMATION

For train information 24 hours a day call 892021 or visit www.trenitalia.it.

the city, but some trains use **Rifredi** or **Campo di Marte**.

Categories of Trains

Eurocity (EC): these trains link major Italian cities with other European cities – in Germany and Switzerland, for instance.
Eurostar Italia (ES): these swish, high-speed trains have first- and second-class carriages, both with supplements on top of the ordinary rail fare.
Intercity (IC): this fast service links major Italian cities.
Interregionali (IR): these cheaper inter-regional trains link cities within different regions (for example Tuscany and Umbria) and stop reasonably frequently.
Regionali: these regional trains link towns within the same region (for example Tuscany) and stop at every station.

Tickets

Seat reservations are mandatory for journeys on the superior trains (Eurostar and Eurocity services), and tickets should be purchased in advance, especially around Easter and in the summer season. Tickets are not dated; you have to stamp (*convalidare*) your ticket before beginning the journey at one of the small machines at the head of the platforms. Failure to do so may result in a fine.

If you board a train without a ticket, one can be bought from a conductor, though there is a penalty payment of 20 percent extra. You can also pay the conductor directly if you wish to upgrade to first class or a couchette (should there be places available).

Expect long queues for tickets at major stations, but, for a small fee, tickets can also be purchased from many travel agents. There are automatic ticket machines at major stations, which also give timetable information. Payment can be made by either cash or credit card.

There are a wide variety of train tickets and special offers available, which vary constantly and with the season. Some of

the more stable are:
- **Group fares**: groups of at least 10 people can benefit from a 10–30 percent discount.
- **Youth fares**: students between 12 and 26 can buy a yearly *Carta Verde* (green card). This season ticket entitles them to a 10 percent discount on national trains and a 20 percent discount on international trips.
- **Children's fares**: children under four travel free; children aged between four and 12 are eligible for a 50 percent discount on all trains, but must pay the full price of the supplement for Intercity and Eurocity trains.
- **Family Groups**: groups of 3–5 of whom at least one is an adult and one is a child under 12 are entitled to discounts of 50 percent for children under 12, 20 percent for the others.
- **Pensioners' fares**: the over-60s can buy a *Carta Argento* (silver card). Valid for a year, this card entitles them to a 20 percent discount on all train tickets.

Railway Stations

The main railway stations in Italy are integrated with road and sea transport. They provide many additional services, including telecommunications, left luggage, food and drink outlets and tourist information.

In Florence, the train information office at Santa Maria Novella station is next to the waiting room. The train-reservation office is just inside the building (open daily from 6am–10pm), with the international reservations counter off to the side. There is a left-luggage counter near platform 16 where pieces of luggage are left at your own risk, though badly packed or awkwardly shaped packages might be damaged (€4 for the first 5 hours, 0.60 for the next 6 hours, 0.20 per hour thereafter).

Beneath the station lie shops and a small supermarket which supplement the bars and pharmacy in the main hall.

By Coach

Coaches are very comfortable and sometimes quicker, though usually more expensive, than trains for local journeys. In addition, numerous sightseeing tours are available in Florence. City Sightseeing Italy, Piazza Stazione 1; tel: 055-290 451; www.city-sightseeing.it offers two itineraries, one to Fiesole and one to Piazzale Michelangelo. The frequent service includes multilingual commentary, and the tickets are valid for 24 hours, allowing you to hop on and off but not within the city centre which is closed to traffic.

The main bus companies in Florence are **Lazzi** (Piazza Stazione 3r; tel: 055-363 041; www.lazzi.it) and **SITA** (Via Santa Caterina di Siena; tel: 055-214 721; www.sitabus.it) for travel in Tuscany and other parts of Italy.

Local Transport

Buses

Buses are now banned from the city centres but small electric buses *(bussini)* C1, C2 and D weave their way around the periphery and can drop you off near the main sights. However, by the time you have mastered the routes you could have got to your

destination on foot. The bus network is run by ATAF which also provides an efficient service out to suburbs such as Fiesole. Tickets can be bought from tobacconists *(tabacchi)*, news-stands, bars, and from ATAF offices or automatic ticket machines at main points throughout the city, including Santa Maria Novella station.

You can buy a variety of tickets. With the 100-minute ticket you can make as many journeys as you like; the *biglietto multiplo* consists of four single 100-minute tickets, and the 3-hour, 24-hour, 3-day, 5-day and 7-day tickets are self-explanatory. All tickets must be stamped in the appropriate machines on board the bus at the beginning of the first journey. Tickets bought on board are more expensive and only last 90 minutes.

For information and route maps go to the ATAF office at Piazza Stazione (open Mon–Sun 7am–8pm; freephone tel: 800-424 500; www.ataf.net); there are also bus maps at tourist offices.

The No. 7 bus takes you to Fiesole, the Nos 12 and 13 go to Piazzale Michelangelo.

Taxis

Cabs are white with yellow stripes, and are hired from ranks in the main piazzas and at the station. They seldom stop if you hail them in the street. Meters are provided, and fares should always be displayed. A tip of 10 percent is expected from tourists.

The Radio Taxi system is fast and efficient, and cabs will arrive within minutes (unless it is rush hour, when you may have to call back several times); tel: 055-4390, 055-4798 or 055-4242.

Tramvia

The controversial new tramline network now has one line open, from Santa Maria Novella to Scandicci in the southwest of the city. Two further lines are planned, from Peretola Airport to Piazza della Libertà, via the station, and from Careggi to Begno a Ripoli.

Walking and Cycling

The city is compact and easily covered on foot, and the centre is now fully pedestrianised. Where traffic is allowed, the main drawbacks are the narrow pavements frequently blocked by cars or motorbikes, and noisy traffic.

Cycling is becoming increasingly popular among Florentines, though no bike lanes cross the city centre, and cyclists need their wits about them to steer a course through the hordes of tourists around the Duomo.

Bicycles can be hired from Alinari (Via San Zanobi 38r; tel: 055-280 500; www.alinarirental.com) and Florence by Bike (Via San Zanobi 120r; tel: 055-488 992; www.florencebybike.it). Motorbikes or mopeds, useful for trips to the countryside, can also be hired from these companies.

Horse-drawn carriages, which have been banned from Piazza del Duomo but can be hired in Piazza della Signoria, are now solely used by affluent tourists. If you take one, be prepared to do some hard bargaining.

Travelling outside Florence

Tuscany is well served by motorways (though tolls are expensive). Siena, Arezzo, Pisa and the coast are all within easy reach. A good map to have is the Touring Club Italiano map of the region. However, if you do not have your own or a hired vehicle, public transport out of Florence is very efficient *(see above)*.

A wide network of bus services operates throughout Tuscany, and fares are reasonable. The main companies are Lazzi and SITA *(see "By Coach" above)*. The latter operates a rapid coach service to Siena, roughly every half an hour in season, which takes 75 minutes. Lazzi runs a good service to Lucca, and fast trains to Arezzo and Pisa depart regularly from the railway station.

ABOVE: getting about on a Segway.

Several companies organise coach excursions of the historic cities and Tuscan countryside. One operator is **CIT** (Piazza Stazione 51r; tel: 055-284 145).

Tourist information for towns and cities located outside the Provincia di Firenze (Province of Florence) is not available in the city. You should apply to the local branch of the APT, the tourist office. In smaller towns, the *comune*, or town hall, holds tourist information.

Driving

Florence has introduced a city-centre driving ban and cars must be left in car parks on the edge of the historic centre.

State highways in Tuscany include the SS1 Via Aurelia, which runs north–south, to the west of Pisa. The national motorways *(autostrade)* are the A11, the "Firenze–mare", and the A12, the "Sestri Levante–Livorno". Both of these are toll roads. The two *superstrade* (Florence–Siena and the new Florence–Pisa–Livorno or Fi–Pi–Li) are toll-free.

Car Hire

You can rent cars from major rental companies (Hertz, Avis, Europcar, etc.). Generally, booking from the UK is much cheaper than hiring on arrival. Even with four or five people sharing, hiring a car can be fairly expensive. Rates usually allow unlimited mileage and include breakdown service. Basic insurance is included, but additional cover is available at fixed rates. Watch out for hidden extras such as high insurance excesses, out-of-hours fees and second-driver charges. Most firms require a deposit equal to the estimated cost of the hire. They normally take and hold a credit card payment, which serves as the charge on return of the car.

In Florence, cars may be hired from the following outlets and also at Pisa and Florence airports. Most of the car-hire companies have offices on or near Borgo Ognissanti.
Avis, Borgo Ognissanti 128r; tel: 055-213 629; www.avis.com.
Europcar, Via Forlanini 2; tel: 055-422 1088.
Hertz, Via Maso Finiguerra 33r; tel: 055-282 260; www.hertz.com.
Maxirent, Borgo Ognissanti 133r; tel: 055-265 4207; www.maxirent.com.

Licences and Insurance

Drivers must have a full driving licence, the original vehicle registration document and a Motor Insurance Certificate. Make sure you have adequate insurance cover and the necessary documents to prove it. For real peace of mind you should also take out breakdown insurance, which offers compensation for the hire of replacement vehicles and transport home if you break down.

Rules of the Road

These generally follow the norm for Western Europe. Drive on the right, overtake on the left. Unless otherwise indicated, speed limits in Italy are 50kmh (30mph) in towns and built-up areas, 90kmh (55mph) on main roads and 130kmh (80mph) on motorways *(autostrade)*. At roundabouts the

TRANSPORT ◆ **263**

TRANSPORT

ACCOMMODATION

SHOPPING

ACTIVITIES

A – Z

LANGUAGE

traffic from the right has right of way. Seat belts are compulsory in the front and back, and children should be properly restrained. It is mandatory to switch on dipped headlights during the daytime outside built-up areas. A warning triangle and reflective jackets must be carried in case of breakdown.

Italian traffic police are authorised to impose on-the-spot fines for speeding and other traffic offenses, such as driving while intoxicated. The use of hand-held mobile telephones while driving is prohibited.

Parking: outside cities and towns, parking on the right-hand side of the road is allowed, except on motorways, at crossroads, on curves and near hilly ground not having full visibility.

Rush Hours

The busiest time in Florence is 8am–1pm. There is a lull in the afternoon until 3pm, and traffic is heavy again 4–8pm. On country roads and motorways, heavy traffic into the cities builds up in the mornings and again in the evenings around 7pm. In summer, roads to the coast on Saturday mornings are especially busy, and, on late Sunday afternoons, long queues can form on routes into the cities, with people returning from a day or weekend away.

Motorway Tolls

Charges for driving on motorways in Italy can be considerable. Within Tuscany, there is a charge on the A11 from Florence to Pisa of about €5 for cars; from Florence to Lucca, €4. For more information on tolls, charges and routes, as well as traffic, visit the Autostrade per l'Italia's website at www.autostrade.it.

Breakdowns and Accidents

In case of a breakdown, dial 116 from the nearest telephone box. Tell the operator where you are, the registration number and type

of car, and the nearest Automobile Club d'Italia (ACI) office will be informed for immediate assistance. They are very efficient.

On motorways, telephones are 2km/1¼ miles apart, with special buttons to call for the police and medical assistance. Both have to be contacted if an accident involves an injury.

If your car breaks down, or if you stop or block the road, you must try to move your vehicle right off the road. If this is impossible, you are required to warn other vehicles by placing a red triangular danger sign at least 50 metres (150ft) behind the vehicle. All vehicles must carry these signs, which can be hired from all ACI offices at the border for a deposit.

Petrol Stations

Some service stations close over the lunch period and on Saturday afternoons and Sundays, but there are plenty of 24-hour petrol stations with self-service dispensers accepting euro notes and major credit cards.

Parking

Parking is a major problem in Florence; the safest place is in one of the costly private underground car parks found all over

the city. Somewhat cheaper, but still equipped with surveillance cameras, are the city car parks (www.firenzeparcheggi.it). **Parcheggio Parterre**, Via Madonna delle Tosse 9 (near Piazza della Libertà; tel: 055-500 1994) and the **Parcheggio Piazza Stazione**, Via Alamanni 14 (under the railway station; tel: 055-230 2655) are both open 24 hours a day.

Street parking is almost impossible, as the historic centre is a limited traffic zone (ZTL). Ignore the warning signs and you will almost certainly incur a fine by post (and hired cars are no exception). If your hotel is within the restriction zone, telephone in advance so your hotel can inform the police of your licence number and obtain a temporary transit pass.

Public street parking is marked by blue stripes on the road, and these must be paid for by the hour. There are now some parking meters in the city. Do not leave your car on a space next to a *passo carrabile* or a *sosta vietato* sign or in a disabled space (marked in yellow). If your car gets towed away, contact the *vigili urbani* (the traffic police) at tel: 055-32831, or call the central car pound, tel: 055-328 3944, quoting your number plate.

BELOW: scooters are still the preferred mode of transport for the young.

ACCOMMODATION

SOME THINGS TO CONSIDER BEFORE YOU BOOK THE ROOM

As might be expected in a city which caters for millions of visitors every year, the quality and range of accommodation in Florence is extremely varied. You can choose between anything from a grand city *palazzo* (a historic family-run establishment) or a small *pensione*-style hotel, to numerous budget places that are either cheap and cheerful or rather dingy. Prices are higher than elsewhere in Tuscany, and hotels need to be booked well in advance, especially for the peak periods of Easter, Christmas and the summer.

Choosing a Hotel

Florence is well provided with accommodation, but there is a huge variation in what you get for your money; all hotels are star-rated from one to five, but the star-rating system refers to facilities rather than other qualities like atmosphere, comfort or location, so while it is useful up to a point, it shouldn't be the only factor taken into consideration.

Hotels are required by law to display official maximum room rates at reception and in each room. Prices for rooms can vary within the same hotel, so if you've been shown a room which is too expensive, ask to see another – those without bathrooms are always cheaper.

Some hotels with restaurants insist on a half- or full-board arrangement, particularly in the high season.

The APT website (www.firenze turismo.it) has listings of hotels in Florence and is worth using. Hotels can be booked at the **ITA**

office (*Informazioni Turistiche Alberghi*) at the train station (daily 8.30am–7pm) for a small fee. Alternatively you can find rooms on the free hotel booking service, tel: 066-991 000; www.hotelreservations.it. There is also a tourist information desk at Peretola Airport which is open from 8.30am–6.30pm daily.

The cheapest hotels in Florence tend to be situated around the Santa Maria Novella station area and the most expensive along the banks of the Arno. In the upper price bracket, the essential decision is between a historic, centrally located *palazzo* in the city or a beautifully appointed villa in the hills. One thing to look for, especially in the summer, is a hotel with a garden or terrace; it can make all the difference after a long, hot day's sightseeing to be able to sip an *aperitivo* in the open air, and even the more modest establishments often have some kind of outside space.

Visitors should also consider staying just outside the city, in one

of the many grand country villas, or opting for the increasingly popular *agriturismo* – farm-stay holidays, which are often self-catering. It is also possible to rent an apartment or villa, or arrange a private home stay (bed and breakfast is a relatively new concept in Italy; breakfast is not always provided).

Villas and Apartments

Prices vary enormously, depending on the season and the luxuriousness of the accommodation. In general, prices range from a simple four-person villa in the low season for about €500 per week to a magnificent secluded villa for about €2,000 in the high season. The following agency is one of the many that deal with rentals:
• **Milligan and Milligan**, Via Alfani 60, tel: 055-268 256; www.italy-rentals.com.
• Apartments are also listed with links on www.firenze.net.

Residences

Serviced apartments, or residences, are an attractive alternative to hotels, but often have to be taken for a minimum of one week. Again, prior booking (several months in advance for the summer season) is essential. One of the best has been converted from a historic palace: the **Residence Palazzo Ricasoli**, Via delle Mantellate 2; tel: 055-352 151; www.ricasoli.net. Also available on a daily basis.

Private Home Stays

This is a fairly new development in Florence, but is a good way of experiencing closer contact with the locals while paying modest prices. Private homes are carefully graded from simple to luxurious, with prices varying accordingly.

Contact **ABBA** *(Associazione Bed & Breakfast Affittacamere)* at Via P. Maestri 26, 50135 Florence; tel: 055-654 0860; www.abba-firenze.it.

Youth Hostels and Camping

A list of youth hostels is available from ENIT (Ente Nazionale Italiano per il Turismo or the Italian National Tourist Office), and places can be booked through them or through local Tuscan tourist offices. Florence only has a handful of hostels, some out of the centre. The most appealing is on the north edge of town, just below Fiesole: **Villa Camerata**, Viale Augusto Righi 2–4, 50137 Florence; tel: 055-601 451. **Hostel Archi Rossi**, Via Faenza 94r; tel: 055-290 804; www.hostelarchi rossi.com, is a converted hostel close to the station with excellent facilities. Further out towards the stadium is the **7 Santi Hostel**, Viale del Mille 11; tel: 055-504 8452.

The closest campsite to town is the **Camping-Michelangelo** at Viale Michelangelo 80 (tel: 055-681 1977), open all year round and very crowded in summer. The **Camping Panoramico in Fiesole** (tel: 055-599 069) is also open all year and has lovely views. There is also a campsite at the **Villa Camerata** *(see above)*. A free list of sites, with a map, published by **Federazione Italiana Campeggiatore** (www.federcampeggio.it) is available from Italian National Tourist Offices; alternatively visit www.camping.it for detailed information on Italian campsites.

Hotels

The selection of Florence hotels listed below are arranged corresponding to the areas in the Places section. The price indication refers to the cost of a standard double room, usually with breakfast. Note that many hotels in Florence lower these rates dramatically at less crowded times of the year, and it can sometimes pay to bargain a little. Websites offering last-minute deals can also give good offers if you are willing to be flexible: try www.laterooms.com, which also has a link to a sister site for apartments.

ACCOMMODATION LISTINGS

THE DUOMO

Bellettini
Via dei Conti 7
Tel: 055-213 561
[p312, C1]
www.hotelbellettini.com
Close to San Lorenzo market, a friendly hotel with rooms decorated in simple Florentine style. Good, generous breakfasts. €€

Brunelleschi
Piazza Santa Elisabetta 3
Tel: 055-273 70
[p312, C2]
www.hotelbrunelleschi.it
Comfortable four-star hotel located in a tiny central piazza and partly housed in a

church with a 6th-century tower. €€€€

Guelfo Bianco
Via Camillo Cavour 29
Tel: 055-288 330
[p309, C3]
www.ilguelfobianco.it
Comfortably furnished rooms in two adjacent 15th-century houses just north of the Duomo. €€

PIAZZA DELLA SIGNORIA

Alessandra
Borgo SS Apostoli 17
Tel: 055-283 438
[p312, B3]
www.hotelalessandra.com
A central *pensione* with
rooms ranging from the
quite grand to the more
ordinary without bath-
room. **€€**

Continentale
Vicolo dell'Oro 6r
Tel: 055-27262
[p312, C3]
www.lungarnohotels.com
Chic retro-style hotel
offering top-class
service and panoramic
terrace. **€€€€**

Fiorino
Via Osteria del Guanto 6
Tel: 055-210 579
[p313, D3]
www.hotelfiorino.it
A basic and unpreten-
tious hotel near the
Galleria degli Uffizi and
the river. **€€**

Hermitage
Vicolo Marzio 1
Piazza del Pesce
Tel: 055-287 216
[p312, C3]
www.hermitagehotel.com
A delightful hotel
directly above the Ponte
Vecchio, with a lovely
roof garden overlooking

the city. Some of the
(rather small) rooms
have wonderful river
views, although for
sleeping you may prefer
to stay in the quieter
ones at the back. **€€€**

Relais Uffizi
Chiasso de' Baroncelli 16
Tel: 055-267 6239
[p313, C3]
www.relaisuffizi.it
This tiny hotel is tucked
away behind the Galle-
ria degli Uffizi, with
spectacular views over
Piazza della Signoria
and the Palazzo Vec-
chio. **€€–€€€**

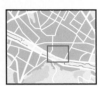

Torre Guelfa
Borgo SS Apostoli 8
Tel: 055-239 6338
[p312, C3]
www.hoteltorreguelfa.com
Part of this hotel
includes the tallest
privately owned tower in
Florence. Pretty furnish-
ings in bedrooms and
smart bathrooms. **€€**

SANTA CROCE AND THE NORTHEAST

Four Seasons
Borgo Pinti 99
Tel: 055-26261
[p309, E3]
www.fourseasons.com/florence
A sumptuous
Renaissance palace
which was home to five
centuries of Florentine

BELOW: attention to detail.

nobles before its
conversion to a hotel in
2008. Meticulously
restored, it boasts
beautiful frescos,
painted ceilings, art-
filled bedrooms in silks
and velvet, and sumptu-
ous marble bathrooms.

Slightly out of the centre,
it has an 11-acre (4.5-
hectare) garden and an
on-site spa. **€€€€**

Grand Hotel Cavour
Via del Proconsolo 3
Tel: 055-266 271
[p313, D2]
www.albergocavour.com
A modernised luxury
hotel in the historic
14th-century Palazzo
Strozzi-Ridolfi. It is in a
quiet location and has
fine views over the city
from the intimate roof
garden. **€€€**

J and J
Via di Mezzo 20
Tel: 055-26312
[p309, E4]
www.jandjhotel.net
Housed in a former
convent near Sant'
Ambrogio, this smart
and discreet hotel has
an interior designer's
touch throughout.
To add to the style,
breakfast is served in
the cloister in summer.
The rooms are very

comfortable; some of
them are enormous.
€€€

Liana
Via Alfieri 18
Tel: 055-245 303
[p309, E3]
www.hotelliana.com
A quiet, pleasant and
slightly faded hotel
some way north of the
centre in the former
British Embassy
building (the Consulate

PRICE CATEGORIES

Prices are per night for
a double room during
the high season.
€ = under €100
€€ = €100–150
€€€ = €150–300
€€€€ = over €300

is now in a *palazzo* overlooking the Arno). The
rooms range from the
clean
and simple to the quite
elegant "Count's
Room". Private car park-
ing is available. €€–€€€

Monna Lisa
Borgo Pinti 27
Tel: 055-247 9751
[p313, E1]
www.monnalisa.it
A small but in part
characterful hotel set
in a 14th-century
palazzo, furnished with
paintings and antiques.
The quieter rooms,

overlooking the delight-
ful courtyard garden,
are the best. It is best
to avoid the charmless
rooms in the new
extension. Private
parking is available. €€€

Hotel Plaza & Lucchesi
Lungarno della Zecca
Vecchia 38
Tel: 055-26236
[p313, E4]
www.plazalucchesi.it
A comfortable and
efficiently run hotel
overlooking the Arno,
some 10 minutes' walk
to the east of the Ponte
Vecchio. The rooms are

decent, and some of
them have lovely
views. €€€

Regency
Piazza Massimo d'Azeglio 3
Tel: 055-245 247
[p309, E3]
www.regency-hotel.com
This is a grand hotel in
a restored 19th-century
palazzo, with a highly
regarded restaurant
and an elegant garden
set between the two
wings. The rooms are
elegant and comfort-
able with good facili-
ties. Private parking is
available for guests.

PIAZZA DELLA REPUBBLICA

**Antica Torre di Via
Tornabuoni**
Via de' Tornabuoni 1
Tel: 055-265 8161
[p312, B3]
www.tornabuoni1.com
On the top floor of a
medieval tower over-
looking Piazza Santa
Trinità, with bird's-eye
views of the city. €€€

Hotel Davanzati
Via Porta Rossa 5
Tel: 055-286 666
[p312, C3]
www.hoteldavanzati.it
In a building dating back
to the 1400s, this hotel
has been tastefully
refurbished and is in a
great location. €€€

Firenze
Via del Corso/Piazza Donati 4
Tel: 055-214 203
[p313, D2]
www.hotelfirenze-fi.it
A reasonable hotel with
clean rooms whose main
advantage is its location.
All the rooms have pri-
vate bathrooms. €–€€

Helvetia & Bristol
Via dei Pescioni 2
Tel: 055-26651
[p312, B2]

www.royaldemeure.com
A small but grand hotel,
with antiques and paint-
ings. Sumptuous
rooms, a winter garden
and a gourmet restaur-
ant. €€€€

Hotel Savoy
Piazza della Repubblica 7
Tel: 055-27351
[p313, C2]
www.hotelsavoy.it

A luxury hotel on the
central piazza. Com-
fortable rooms with con-
temporary and elegant
Italian decor. €€€€

Tornabuoni Beacci
Via de' Tornabuoni 3
Tel: 055-212 645
[p312, B3]
www.tornabuonihotels.com
A lovely hotel, set in a
14th-century *palazzo*

in the city's most
prestigious shopping
street. Private parking
is available. €€€

BELOW: refined elegance at the Hotel Tornabuoni Beacci.

SAN LORENZO

ABOVE: Hotel Botticelli.

Hotel Botticelli
Via Taddea 8
Tel: 055-290 905
[p309, C3]
www.hotelbotticelliflorence.com
A recently renovated
hotel at the back of the
central market, this is
both comfortable and
appealing, with all mod
cons alongside original
architectural features
such as vaulted ceilings
and the odd fresco. **€€**

Casci
Via Cavour 13
Tel: 055-211 686
[p309, C3]
www.hotelcasciflorence.com
Situated north of the
San Lorenzo market
area, this frescoed Quat-
trocento *palazzo* is
family-run, with a wel-
coming atmosphere. All
of the bedrooms are
pleasantly decorated and
air-conditioned. **€–€€**
Centro
Via dei Ginori 17
Tel: 055-230 2901
[p309, C3]
www.hotelcentro.net
A historic place to stay,
situated near the Via
Cavour and the Palazzo
Medici-Riccardi. This
palazzo was once
Raphael's residence,
and has now been reno-
vated to provide spa-
cious, light rooms. **€€**
Hotel Collodi
Via Taddea 6
Tel: 055-291 317
[p309, C3]
www.relaishotel.com

A small, family-run
hotel just to the north of
San Lorenzo. It is nicely
furnished and has some
good offers on its rates
throughout the year.
€–€€
Residenza Johanna I
Via Bonifacio Lupi 14
Tel: 055-481 896
[p309, D1]
www.johanna.it
One of a set of great-
value-for-money resi-
dences across the city.
Set in a residential area
to the northwest of the
centre, the rooms are
comfortable and nicely
decorated, but there are
few hotel frills; not all
rooms have attached
baths. A do-it-yourself
breakfast kit is provided
in each room. **€–€€**

SAN MARCO

Andrea
Piazza Indipendenza 19
Tel: 055-483 890
[p308, C2]
www.andrea.hotelinfirenze.com
Situated on a monu-
mental square, this
imposing three-star
hotel has decent rooms
and a great view of the

Duomo. **€€**
Antica Dimora Johlea
Via San Gallo 80/76
Tel: 055-463 3292
[p309, D2]
www.johanna.it
Excellent-value place to
stay, part of a well-priced
set of residences, not
too far from the centre.
The two apartments
here are set in the pleasant area around the
church of San Marco.
They retain an authentic
Tuscan feel, have com-
fortable rooms and are
equipped with modern

conveniences. *(See also the Residenza Johanna 1 near San Lorenzo above.)* €–€€

Athenaeum
Via Cavour 88
Tel: 055-589 456
[p309, D3]
www.hotelathenaeum.com
One of Florence's newer hotels, converted from an art school to provide a comfortable and contemporary four-star base. Well designed, with warm tones and predominant use of leather and wood. Friendly, helpful staff, free WiFi throughout, cocktail bar and a leafy courtyard for alfresco meals in summer. The young chef at the Reflessi Restaurant produces creative Italian fare that's a cut above the average for the San Marco quarter. €€€

Loggiato dei Serviti
Piazza della Santissima Annunziata 3
Tel: 055-289 592
[p309, D3]
www.loggiatodeiservitihotel.it

A fabulous place to stay and part of the historic fabric of the city. San Gallo's gracious 16th-century *palazzo* is set on a lovely traffic-free piazza and looks out onto Brunelleschi's Ospedale degli Innocenti. Antiques adorn the vaulted interior, and the rooms are beautifully decorated. One of Florence's most refined small hotels. €€€

Morandi alla Crocetta
Via Laura 50
Tel: 055-234 4747
[p309, E3]
www.hotelmorandi.it
This is an informal and quiet hotel with only 10 rooms, housed in an ex-convent. The peaceful rooms are comfortable and furnished with a few antiques. Several rooms have their own private terraces. €€–€€€

Orto dei Medici
Via San Gallo 30
Tel: 055-483 427
[p309, D2]
www.ortodeimedici.it
This small yet imposing *palazzo* near San Marco has been recently refurnished. The public rooms have frescoed ceilings, rich in stucco work . Staff are friendly, and the breakfasts are plentiful. €€

BELOW: key fobs Italian-style.

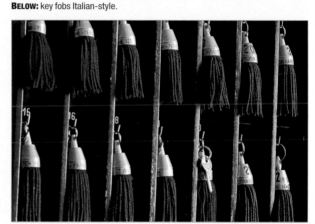

SANTA MARIA NOVELLA

Alba
Via della Scala 22/38r
Tel: 055-282 610
[p312, A1]
www.hotelalbafirenze.it
Comfort at reasonable prices. Cheerful, brisk and conveniently central. €€

Albion
Via Il Prato 22r
Tel: 055-214 171
[p308, A4]
www.hotelalbion.it
Set in a stylish neo-Gothic *palazzo*, the hotel is a showcase for modern art. Bicycles

are available for guests. €€–€€€

Aprile
Via della Scala 6
Tel: 055-216 237
[p312, A1]
www.hotelaprile.it
More appealing than most hotels near the station, this is an ex-Medici palace complete with frescos, a pleasant breakfast room and a garden. Rooms range from simple to quite grand, as do prices. €€

Hotel Baglioni
Piazza dell'Unità Italiana 6

Tel: 055-23580
[p312, B1]
www.hotelbaglioni.it
This classic hotel retains its air of discreet elegance while providing extremely comfortable rooms. The rooftop restaurant has fabulous views of the city skyline. Popular with the business community. €€€

Casa Howard
Via della Scala 18
Tel: 06-6992 4555
[p312, A1]
www.casahoward.com

PRICE CATEGORIES

Prices are per night for a double room during the high season.
€ = under €100
€€ = €100–150
€€€ = €150–300
€€€€ = over €300

Casa Howard is a very stylish guesthouse, offering upmarket accommodation in a fine old mansion; each of the 12 rooms is decorated in a striking individual style, with bold colours contrasting with antiques and old furniture. Great location too, next to the Officina di Santa Maria Novella, one of the oldest pharmacies in the world. €€€

Hotel Croce di Malta
Via della Scala 7
Tel: 055-261 870
[p312, A1]
www.crocedimalta.it
Conveniently located just off of Piazza Santa Maria Novella, near the station, the hotel offers 98 single and double rooms, and 15 exclusive suites. €€€

Goldoni
Borgo Ognissanti 8
Tel: 055-284 080
[p312, A2]
www.hotelgoldoni.com
A central hotel in a historic *palazzo* near the river, not far from the train station. €€

Grand
Piazza Ognissanti 1
Tel: 055-27161
[p308, A4]
www.starwoodhotels.com
Recently refurbished sister hotel to the Excelsior and just as luxurious in terms of *fin de siècle* grandeur (in a corresponding price bracket). €€€€

Grand Hotel Minerva
Piazza Santa Maria Novella 16
Tel: 055-27230
[pA1, 312]
www.grandhotelminerva.com

One of the few centrally located hotels with a pool, and what's more, it's a rooftop pool with views to die for. €€€€

Kraft
Via Solferino 2
Tel: 055-284 273
[p308, A3]
www.krafthotel.it
Ideally placed for music-lovers, this refurbished hotel is a stone's throw from the Teatro Comunale and also has a rooftop pool. €€€€

Kursaal & Ausonia
Via Nazionale 24
Tel: 055-496 547
[p308, C2]
www.kursonia.com
Welcoming and good-value hotel near the station which opened in 2007. Paola, who runs the hotel with her husband, is a qualified tour guide and will equip you with a personalised itinerary for the city. €€

Mario's
Via Faenza 89
Tel: 055-216 801
[p308, B3]
www.hotelmarios.com
Most of the hotels in

Via Faenza near the Mercato Centrale are scruffy, but Mario's is an exception. Decorated in rustic Tuscan style with comfortable bedrooms (the back is quieter) and a pretty breakfast room. €–€€

Montebello Splendid
Via Garibaldi 14
Tel: 055-27471
[p308, A3]
www.montebellosplendid.com
A traditional hotel in a residential area west of the centre, near the station. There is a conservatory restaurant and pleasant garden. Private parking. €€€–€€€€

Westin Excelsior
Piazza Ognissanti 3
Tel: 055-27151
[p312, A2]
www.starwood.com
Olde-worlde grandeur combined with modern conveniences in this former Florentine address of Napoleon's sister, Caroline; polished service, luxurious rooms and fine views of the Arno from the roof garden. Private parking. €€€€

BELOW: simple, elegant room at Aprile.

OLTRARNO WEST

Annalena
Via Romana 34
Tel: 055-222 402
[p310, A3]
www.hotelannalena.it
Excellent-value antique-furnished rooms in a gracious 15th-century convent, originally built as a refuge for widows of the Florentine nobility. Near the Giardino di Boboli, with views over a pretty garden.
€–€€

Boboli
Via Romana 63
Tel: 055-229 8645
[p310, A3]

www.hotelboboli.com
This simple but appealing two-star hotel has decent rooms and is conveniently situated for the Palazzo Pitti, Giardino di Boboli and the Oltrarno district. **€**

Classic Hotel
Viale Machiavelli 25
Tel: 055-229 351
[p310, A4]
www.classichotel.it
An attractive, pink-washed villa set in a shady garden on a tree-lined avenue just above the Porta Romana. **€€**

Lungarno
Borgo San Jacopo 14
Tel: 055-2726 4000
[p312, B4]
www.lungarnohotels.com
Smart, modern hotel popular for its superb position on the river and views of the Ponte Vecchio from the front rooms. Outstanding collection of modern art too. **€€€–€€€€**

Pitti Palace
Borgo San Jacopo 3
Tel: 055-239 8711
[p312, B4]
www.vivahotels.com
Small, traditional hotel

just south of the Ponte Vecchio, popular with English-speaking visitors, largely because the co-owner is American. Private parking. **€€**

La Scaletta
Via Guicciardini 13
Tel: 055-283 028
[p312, B4]
www.lascaletta.com
Near the Palazzo Pitti, this family-run *pensione* has an attractive roof garden. However, some rooms are rather dowdy. **€–€€**

Torre di Bellosguardo
Via Roti Michelozzi 2
Tel: 055-229 8145
[off map p310, A4]
www.torrebellosguardo.com
Set in the hills just above Porta Romana, this atmospheric, quiet and roomy hotel consists of a 14th-century tower attached to a 16th-century villa. It has frescoed reception rooms and highly individualistic and charmingly decorated bedrooms, with antiques and quirky details. Secluded swimming pool, delightful grounds with lily pond. **€€€**

Villa Belvedere
Via Benedetto Castelli 3
Tel: 055-222 501
[off map p310, A4]
www.villa-belvedere.com
Exceptionally friendly, modern hotel on the hill just above Porta Romana. Sunny rooms, gardens with a swimming pool and tennis court, and lovely views over Florence. **€€€**

Villa Cora
Viale Machiavelli 18
Tel: 055-271 840
[p310, B4]
www.villacora.it
This 19th-century villa on the avenue leading up to Piazzale Michelangelo is closed for renovation until autumn 2010. The lavish public rooms, extensive gardens, pool and fine views of the city will still be on offer on reopening. **€€€€**.

OLTRARNO EAST

Hotel Villa La Vedetta
Viale Michelangelo 78
Tel: 055-681 631
[off map p311, E3]

www.villalavedettahotel.com
Five-star luxury in a neo-Renaissance villa near Piazzale Michelangelo. From the pool is a panoramic view of the city, dominated by Brunelleschi's dome. Free shuttle service to the centre. **€€€€**

Silla
Via de' Renai 5
Tel: 055-234 2888
[p311, D2]

www.hotelsilla.it
An old-fashioned *pensione* to the south-east of the Ponte Vecchio looking over a leafy piazza onto the River Arno. It has a pleasant breakfast terrace. **€€**

Villa Liberty
Viale Michelangelo 40
Tel: 055-681 0581
[off map p311, E2]
http://liberty.hotelinfirenze.com
Situated in a chic

residential area of Florence, winding up towards Piazzale Michelangelo, this early-20th-century villa is homely and set in a lovely garden. **€€**

FIESOLE

Pensione Bencistà
Via Benedetto da Maiano 4
Tel: 055-59163
www.bencista.com
Set on the Florence road just south of Fiesole, this delightful 14th-century villa lives up to its name which means "stay well": one immedi-

ately feels at home here. The interior of the sprawling building is full of antiques and rustic furnishings. There are cosy reception rooms, fine hillside views, and in the warmer seasons breakfast is served alfresco on the lovely terrace.
€€–€€€
Il Salviatino
Via del Salviatino
Tel: 055-944 1111
www.salviatino.com
Following a €15 million restoration, this 15th-century villa in the Fiesole hills has opened as a 61-room luxury hotel and Europe's first Thai Devarana Spa. Individually designed rooms feature finest handmade linens, rich Florentine leathers and Renaissance art. The spa's "East meets West" treatments draw on both Thai healing therapies and Western disciplines. Restaurant, two swimming pools

and classic Italian garden. **€€€**
Villa Bonelli
Via Francesco Poeti 1
Tel: 055-59513
www.hotelvillabonelli.com
This friendly and welcoming family hotel lies on a steep but clearly signposted road 7km (4 miles) from the town centre. The restaurant offers good, solid Tuscan fare. **€–€€**
Villa San Michele
Via Doccia 4,
Tel: 055-567 8200
www.villasanmichele.com
Eight km (5 miles) from the centre of Florence, this hotel is one of the finest and most expensive in Tuscany. As befits a building supposedly designed by Michelangelo, this former monastery has harmonious lines and heavenly views, particularly from the loggia and restaurant. The antique-filled interior is beautifully tiled, and vast

grounds, a panoramic pool and piano bar complete the picture. There is also a successful cookery school on isite offering courses on Tuscan gastronomy. **€€€€**
Villa Ulivi
Via Bolognese 163
Tel: 055-400 777
www.villaulivi.com
West of Fiesole, this 15th-century Florentine villa, surrounded by a garden of roses and lavender, provides a relaxing retreat from the bustle of the city centre. Rooms are on a B&B basis, but the entire villa can also be rented. The centre of Florence, 3.5km (2 miles) away, can be reached by foot or bus. **€–€€**

OUTSIDE FLORENCE

Arezzo
Val di Colle
Località Bagnoro
Tel: 0575-365 167
www.valdicolle.it
A meticulously restored 14th-century house, 4km (2½ miles) from Arezzo. Antique furniture rubs shoulders with modern art. **€€**

Candeli
Villa La Massa
Via della Massa 24
Tel: 055-62611
www.villalamassa.it
Situated 7km (4 miles)

north of Florence, this cluster of beautifully converted 17th-century villas radiates elegance. In addition to a piano bar and riverside restaurant, there is a wellness centre, facilities for swimming and tennis and a free shuttle bus into the city centre. **€€€€**

Castellina in Chianti
Belvedere di San Leonino
Località San Leonino
Tel: 0577-740 887

www.hotelsanleonino.com
Imposing 15th-century country house with a swimming pool surounded by olive groves and vineyards. **€**

Gaiole in Chianti
Castello di Spaltenna
Tel: 0577-749 483
www.spaltenna.it
This former fortified monastery is now a luxurious hotel with an excellent restaurant. Supremely comfortable, individualistic rooms.
€€€€

Galluzzo
Relais Certosa
Via Colle Romole 2
Tel: 055-204 7171
www.bettojahotels.it
A former hunting lodge (once attached to the Carthusian monastery)

PRICE CATEGORIES

Prices are per night for a double room during the high season.
€ = under €100
€€ = €100–150
€€€ = €150–300
€€€€ = over €300

now turned into a welcoming residence, with pleasant, spacious grounds, swimming pool and tennis courts. €€€

Greve in Chianti

Villa Sangiovese
Piazza Bucciarelli 5, Panzano
Tel: 055-852 461
www.villasangiovese.it
A restored villa offering additional rooms in a converted traditional farmhouse. Noted for its restaurant and excellent local wines. Closed Jan–Feb. €€–€€€

Lucca

Piccolo Hotel Puccini
Via di Poggio 9
Tel: 0583-55421
www.hotelpuccini.com
A small, friendly hotel just round the corner from Puccini's house and crammed with mementoes of the maestro. Excellent value for money and helpful staff. €
Universo
Piazza del Giglio 1
Tel: 0583-493 678
www.universolucca.com
Large, slightly faded Victorian hotel where Ruskin always used to stay when in Lucca. Good fish restaurant. €€
Villa Lucia
Vorno
Tel: 01252-790 222
www.vedicsparesorts.com
Exclusive American-owned spa resort in the village of Vorno near Lucca. Guests stay in a sumptuous Renaissance villa, and eat around a communal table, house-party style. The state-of-the-art Vedic spa offers a calming "Mind Body and Soul Retreat", and comes with massage rooms, hammam and cooling ice cascade.

Fitness is gently encouraged with a gym, pilates and walks in the surrounding hills. €€€

Mercatale Val di Pesa

Salvadonica
Via Grevigiana 82
Tel: 055-821 8039
www.salvadonica.com
This feudal estate has been sensitively converted into a rural hotel. Tiled floors, beamed ceilings and a setting amidst olive groves add to the charm. Tennis court and a pool. €€–€€€

Pistoia

Il Convento
Via San Quirico 33
Tel: 0573-452 651
www.ilconventohotel.com
Tranquil and comfortable hotel, once a Franciscan monastery. Has a lovely garden, pool, restaurant and even a chapel. Five km (3 miles) from town. €€

San Gimignano

L'Antico Pozzo
Via San Matteo 87

Tel: 0577-942 014
www.anticopozzo.com
Old townhouse, carefully restored and simply but tastefully furnished. Reservations essential. €€

Siena

Antica Torre
Via Fiera Vecchia 7
Tel: 0577-222 255
www.anticatorresiene.it
A tiny, atmospheric hotel, essentially a conversion of a 17th-century tower. Early booking is advised. €€
Palazzo Ravizza
Pian dei Mantellini 34
Tel: 0577-280 462
www.palazzoravizza.it
Recently refurbished townhouse with lovely gardens and a good restaurant. Well-chosen antiques and fabrics in the bedrooms, and welcoming public rooms. €€

Trespiano

Villa Le Rondini
Via Bolognese Vecchia 224
Tel: 055-400 081
www.villalerondini.it

Situated 6km (4 miles) to the northeast of the city, this secluded villa is notable for its wonderful setting; from the pool, set in an olive grove, there are lovely views down over the city. The pool and restaurant are open to non-residents. A bus links the hotel with the centre of town. €€€

Vicchio

Villa Campestri
Via di Campestri 19/22
Tel: 055-849 0107
www.villacampestri.com
An imposing Renaissance villa in a wonderful, rural setting in the Mugello area some 35km (25 miles) north of Florence. Impressive public rooms, excellent food and a relaxed atmosphere. Bedrooms in the main villa are quite grand; those in the annexe less so. With a swimming pool; horse riding and olive oil-tasting courses available for booking. €€–€€€

SHOPPING

WHAT TO BUY AND WHERE

Florence is probably the best city in Tuscany for shopping. The Florentines have been producing exquisite goods for centuries, from gilded furniture and gorgeous leather goods to silver jewellery and marbled paper. Despite tourism, consumerism and high labour costs, you can still find high standards of craftsmanship in many spheres, and prices are fairly reasonable for the quality on offer. As well as all the shops, there are markets and market stalls dotted around the centre. It is worth shopping around and bargaining, for which a little Italian will go a long way.

WHERE TO SHOP

There are a number of small artisan shops as well as boutiques, chain stores and designer shops in Florence. For standard purchases, department stores and supermarkets are just as good and offer cheaper prices (included in listings below). Markets are also a feature of Italian life, where real bargains can be had. Apart from the permanent open-air markets in the city, many neighbourhoods have a weekly market where, if you are lucky, bargains can be found.

The Oltrarno neighbourhood south of the river is the traditional home of craft workshops. Guided tours of studios and workshops take place at 3pm Monday and Thursday from the Pitti Palace from mid-September to the last week of July.

Tobacconist's shops (*tabacchi*) are licensed to sell postage stamps, *schede* (telephone cards), salt and candles, besides cigarettes and tobacco. *Farmacie* (pharmacies) abound, and take it in turns to open at night. They sell a range of items, including baby food.

WHAT TO BUY

Antiques

There are two main areas for antiques shops: Via Maggio and the surrounding streets in the Oltrarno, and Borgo Ognissanti, west of the centre. Look out for old picture frames, antique jewellery, ceramics and statues, paintings and furniture; however, you are unlikely to find a bargain.

Books

After Dark
Via de' Ginori 47r
Tel: 055-294 203
English-language bookstore with a good supply of magazines.

Edison
Piazza della Repubblica 27
Tel: 055-213 110
www.libreriaedison.it
A large bookshop with an extensive range of language resources and guidebooks. Café on the first floor which hosts regular talks as well as internet points. Open daily until midnight.

La Feltrinelli International
Via Camillo Cavour 12r
Tel: 055-219 524
www.lafeltrinelli.it
The most comprehensive bookshop in Florence, with a range of foreign-language books.

The Paperback Exchange
Via delle Oche 4r
Tel: 055-293 460
www.papex.it
Close to the Duomo, this shop stocks just about every English-language book ever written on Florence still in print, and many that are no longer published. You can also trade books in here, and

choose from its vast stock of quality second-hand English and American paperbacks.

Seeber-Melbookstore
Via Cerretani 16r
Tel: 055-287 339
www.melbookstore.it
A range of books and music as well as a café.

Ceramics

La Botteghina del Ceramista
Via Guelfa 5r
Tel: 055-287 367
www.labotteghinadelceramista.it
Hand-painted ceramics – mostly from Deruta and Montelupo – in intricate designs and bright, jewel colours, including many by the renowned Franco Mari.

Sbigoli Terrecotte
Via Sant'Egidio 4r
Tel: 055-247 9713
www.sbigoliterrecotte.it
Has a good choice of beautiful hand-painted Tuscan ceramics, both traditional and contemporary designs.

Clothes

Florence is a high-spot for fashion, and the centre is full of top designer boutiques. The most elegant streets are Via de' Tornabuoni and Via della Vigna Nuova, where Versace, Valentino Armani, YSL, Prada, Gucci and all the other big names in fashion have their outlets; the shop windows are an attraction in themselves. Via dei Calzaiuoli and Via Roma also contain expensive shops, whilst along Via del Corso and the streets leading from the Duomo to the railway station are some cheaper options. Below is a selection of the best of both.

Designer Shops

Giorgio Armani
Via della Vigna Nuova 51r
Tel: 055-219 041
Clean, tailored lines are the Armani trademark.

Emporio Armani
Piazza Strozzi 14–16r
Tel: 055-284 315

For more affordable Armani, although quality is not always guaranteed.

Brioni
Via dei Rondivelli 7r
Tel: 055-267 0539
Classic style; exquisitely made clothes for men and women. Brioni has dressed James Bond in his latest films.

Ferragamo
Palazzo Spini-Feroni
Via de' Tornabuoni 4r–14r
Tel: 055-292 123
This famous Florentine shoemaker has now branched out into accessories and clothes.

Gucci
Via de' Tornabuoni 73r
Tel: 055-266 4011; www.gucci.it
This international Florentine firm has developed a tighter, more sophisticated range in recent years; but the belts and handbags are still their trademark.

Prada
Via de' Tornabuoni 67r
Tel: 055-283 439
One of the biggest names in fashion today; highly desirable, sophisticated designs.

Pucci
Via de' Pucci 6
Tel: 055-265 8087
Kaleidoscopic prints are the hallmark of Emilio Pucci.

Raspini
Via Roma 25–29r
Tel: 055-213 077
www.raspini.com
A chic fashion empire, where the young Giorgio Armani started out.

Valentino
Via dei Tosinghi 52r
Tel: 055-293 142
Valentino, a favourite of Jacqueline Kennedy, has been in Florence since 1962.

Versace
Via de' Tornabuoni 13r
Tel: 055-239 6167
One of the world's leading international fashion houses.

Other

Echo
Via dell'Oriuolo 37r
Tel: 055-238 1149
An interesting selection of women's clothing arranged by colour.

Department Stores

Coin
Via dei Calzaiuoli 56r
Tel: 055-280 531
This department store has a good selection of women's and

BELOW: lingerie at La Perla.

men's fashions, as well as accessories and shoes.

Limoni
Via dei Panzani 31r
Tel: 055-265 8929
The best shop in Florence for a range of cosmetics and make-up.

La Rinascente
Piazza della Repubblica 1
Tel: 055-219 113
Cosmetics, household items, clothes, shoes and accessories are sold in this upmarket store, which has a rooftop café.

Fabrics

Antico Setificio
Via L. Bartolini 4
Tel: 055-213 861
This wonderful shop specialises in fabrics produced along traditional lines, above all silk, which is still woven on 18th-century looms. For the best service, telephone in advance for an appointment.

Casa dei Tessuti
Via de' Pecori 20–24
Tel: 055-217 385
Fine silks, linens and woollens.

Food and Wine

Alessi
Via delle Oche 27r
Tel: 055-214 966

A popular *enoteca* selling a huge selection of cakes, biscuits and chocolates, as well as a wide range of wines and liqueurs. Regular free wine-tastings.

La Bottega dell'Olio
Piazza del Limbo 2r
Tel: 055-267 0468
Shelves of Tuscan olive oil and all things related, like olive-wood salad bowls, soaps and gifts.

Dolceforte
Via della Scala 21
Tel: 055-219 116
www.dolceforte.it
The best chocolate, plus novelty treats like chocolate Davids and Duomos (replaced in the hot summer months by jams, preserves and delicious sweets).

Pegna
Via dello Studio 8
Tel: 055-282 701
www.pegna.it
If you're planning lunch on the hoof, try this well-stocked deli, selling cheeses, charcuterie and all manner of edible goodies.

Gifts and Paper

Marbled paper is very closely associated with Florence, and many of the designs echo ancient themes or Medici crests.

Giulio Giannini e Figlio
Piazza Pitti 37r

Tel: 055-212 621
Founded in 1865, this is the city's longest-established marbled-paper shop.

Il Papiro
Via Cavour 49r
Tel: 055-215 262
Piazza del Duomo 24r
Tel: 055-281 628
www.ilpapirofirenze.it
Many marbled-paper designs are on display here.

Signum
Various branches around town, including Borgo de' Greci 40r and Via de' Benci 29r
www.signumfirenze.it
These shops sell postcards, pens, paper and jigsaws, all of high quality.

Il Torchio
Via dei Bardi 17
Tel: 055-234 2862
Cheaper than some of the other shops, and with interesting designs. You also see the artisans at work here. They sell to Liberty, where prices are sky-high.

Gloves

Madova
Via Guicciaroini 1r
Tel: 055-239 6526
www.madova.com
Every kind of glove imaginable, all of them beautifully made in the factory round the corner.
See also under Leather.

Jewellery

The Ponte Vecchio is the best place to see Florentine jewellery. The setting is atmospheric, but

BELOW: shopping for ties in La Rinascente department store.

not typical of the craftsmen's working conditions. Most gold jewellery is made in Arezzo now.

Angela Caputi
Via Santo Spirito 58r
Tel: 055-212 972
www.angelacaputi.com
Bucking Florentine tradition, well-known designer Angela Caputi creates bold, brightly coloured contemporary costume jewellery, predominantly in plastic and other synthetic materials.

Brandimarte
Via Bartolini 18r
Tel: 055-23041
Handcrafted silver goods and jewellery in a large store. This is where Florentine *signore* go to buy wedding presents. Good prices.

Gatto Bianco
Borgo SS Apostoli 12r
Tel: 055-282 989
Contemporary designs in gold and silver.

Torrini
Piazza del Duomo 10r
Tel: 055-230 2401
Torrini has been producing fine jewellery for over six centuries. Wide choice of both traditional and innovative pieces, with an emphasis on gold.

ABOVE: marbled paper from Il Torchio.

Leather

Leather goods are the best buy in the city. Quality ranges from the beautifully tooled creations of local artisans to shoddy goods aimed at undiscerning tourists. For top-of-the-range quality (and prices), you should start with the designer boutiques in the Via de' Tornabuoni or shops in streets around the Piazza della Repubblica.

Il Bisonte
Via del Parione 31/33r
Tel: 055-215 722
Long-established, internationally famous name producing chunky bags, luggage and other leather goods at high prices.

Furla
Via della Vigna Nuova 47r
Tel: 055-282 779
Bags and accessories in contemporary designs.

Madova
Via de' Guicardini 1r
Tel: 055-239 6526
The Donnini family have been producing leather gloves since 1919. Their shop has a gorgeous selection in all colours with linings of silk, wool and cashmere.

Raspini
Via Roma 25r
Tel: 055-213 077
Sells superb leather bags and coats as well as fashions.

For more down-to-earth prices, head for the San Lorenzo market northwest of the Duomo. The straw market also sells bags and accessories, and the Santa Croce area is the place to go to find leather shops.

The Santa Croce leather school (Scuola del Cuoio, Via San Giuseppe 5/r, or through Santa Croce Church, www.leatherschool. com) inside the monastery of Santa Croce, is a popular place for visitors to watch skilled Florentine leather-workers and to purchase their creations.

Markets

The best market is the 19th-century covered food market, Mercato Centrale. For full details, *see page 59*.

Pharmacy

Officina Profumo Farmaceutica di Santa Maria Novella
Via della Scala 16
Tel: 055-216 276; www.smnovella.it

In a frescoed chapel, this fascinating shop was founded by monks in the 16th century. It sells herbal remedies, but more tempting is the range of beautifully packaged perfumes, shampoos, lotions and room scents.

Shoes

Baldinini
Via della Vigna Nuova 32r
Tel: 055-213 014
www.baldinini.it
A chic boutique selling women's and men's shoes and accessories. Designer Gimmi Baldinini is famous for his slender and sensual heels.

Calvani
Via degli Speziali 7r
Tel: 055-265 4043
A good range of shoes both in terms of type and price, with some quirky designs.

Cresti
Via Roma 14r
Tel: 055-214 150
You will find beautifully crafted shoes on sale here, at much lower prices than at Ferragamo.

Ferragamo
Via de' Tornabuoni 4r–14r
Tel: 055-292 123
Italy's most prestigious shoe-maker, providing hand-tooled shoes and beautifully crafted ready-to-wear collections.

For those wishing to spend a bit less, the roads leading from the Duomo to Santa Maria Novella station have a good range of slightly cheaper shoe shops.

ACTIVITIES

THE ARTS, FESTIVALS, NIGHTLIFE, SPORT AND OUTDOOR ACTIVITIES

There's plenty to keep you entertained in Florence; after a day spent absorbing so much art and history, you can unwind in one of the many bars or catch an opera, ballet or concert at the city's much-loved Teatro del Maggio Musicale Fiorentino. Between May and September cloisters and piazzas host classical concerts, bars and restaurants move their tables onto pavements and terraces, and outdoor cinemas screen movies. The big student population means that nightlife is lively.

THE ARTS

Art and Architecture

Florence is a treasure-trove of architectural history, with churches and civil buildings dating from the Romanesque through the Gothic to the Renaissance periods. Tuscany as a whole abounds with examples of all these styles, but Florence is the most important centre.

Renaissance art is, of course, what Florence is most famous for. The most outstanding collections are in the Uffizi gallery, the Palatine Gallery in the Palazzo Pitti, the Bargello and the Accademia, but there are countless museums with fine examples of the period.

Works of art from the late Renaissance and Mannerist periods, the Baroque, the neoclassical and Romantic and, to a lesser degree, the 20th century are exhibited at most galleries and museums.

Museums and Galleries

Details of important museums and art galleries, together with opening hours and entrance fees, are included in the *Places* section of this book. Note, however, that museum opening hours are notoriously unreliable, and strikes, union meetings and "staff shortages" frequently result in the closure of all or part of a museum without notice. Opening hours also change with the season. Information on many of the museums can be found at www. polomuseale.firenze.it and www. firenzemusei.it.

Special Tickets

To avoid queuing at the Uffizi, it is well worth booking in advance, which you can do by phoning the gallery directly, tel: 055-294 883 (Mon–Fri 8.30am–6.30pm, Sat 8.30am–12.30pm).

There is a small booking-service fee per person, but the ability to collect your tickets at

the museum and walk straight in, instead of standing in line for an hour or two (or sometimes even three), is well worth it. Note that many museums and galleries hosting temporary exhibitions will charge you several euros on top of the normal entrance fee even if you do not intend to visit the exhibition. At the time of writing there were no special museum cumulative tickets available, though plans are in the pipeline to introduce a tourist card for state museums. Serious sightseers could consider becoming a member of the Amici degli Uffizi (Friends of the Uffizi) which entitles you to free entry to all state museums. Membership is €60 and the card is valid for a year.

Visitors from the EU, and other countries with reciprocal arrangements, who are under 18 and over 60 years of age, are

ACTIVITIES ♦ 279

TRANSPORT

ACCOMMODATION

SHOPPING

ACTIVITIES

A – Z

LANGUAGE

entitled to free entrance into state museums. Be sure to carry identification to take advantage of this. There are no discounts for students.

Firenze Spettacolo, available from news-stands, is a monthly events magazine and covers exhibitions and museums. A section of it is in English.

Florence Concierge Information, free of charge from hotels, gives up-to-date opening hours of museums, galleries and churches, and there are weekly entertainment listings in the weekend edition of the Italian-language *La Repubblica* newspaper.

Entrance fees for museums and galleries range from €2.50–12, with the Uffizi, the Accademia and the Palatine Gallery among the most expensive. State museums (such as the Uffizi) are closed on Mondays, while other museums' closing days vary.

Every year, Florence offers a free museum week *(La Settimana dei Beni Culturali)*, when

BELOW: the Museo Casa di Dante is not far from the Duomo.

ABOVE: buskers at work.

all the state museums offer free admission to visitors. Look out for this in December or May.

Music, Opera and Dance

To keep up to date with events, buy *Firenze Spettacolo*, the monthly listings magazine (although it is in Italian, the listings themselves are quite straightforward; see also www.firenzespettacolo.it). Alternatively, check the entertainment pages of *La Nazione*, the regional newspaper, or the Firenze section of *La Repubblica*. If you read Italian well, then get *Toscana Qui*.

The **Maggio Musicale** music festival, held from the end of April to the end of June, is a big event, with top names in opera, music and ballet (Jonathan Miller and Zubin Mehta have long been associated with the festival) performing in the Teatro Comunale, Corso Italia 16, which these days prefers to style itself the Teatro del Maggio Musicale Fiorentino. This will be home to the festival until 2012, when it will move to the new Auditorium Parco della Musica in the Porta al Prato area. Information can be found and tickets

can be booked online at www.maggiofiorentino.com, or in person at the box office, tel: 055-277 9350, Tue–Fri 10am–4.30pm or contact the call centre, tel: 055-277 9350.

The **Estate Fiesolana** (www.estatefiesolana.it) – Fiesole's summer festival of concerts, opera, ballet and theatre – is held in the town's Roman amphitheatre, but has somewhat diminished in importance over the past years.

Outside this festival, many concerts are held throughout the summer in cloisters, piazzas, churches or even in the Boboli Garden. These are of varying standard, but the settings are often highly evocative. More information can be gathered from tourist offices.

The opera and ballet season at the **Teatro Comunale** (Corso Italia 16, 50123 Florence; tel: 055-210 804) opens around the middle of September and runs through to Christmas. International performers and scenographers appear regularly, particularly in operatic productions.

The principal venue for quality chamber-music concerts in Florence is the **Teatro della Pergola** (Via della Pergola

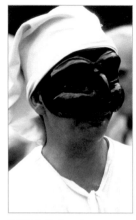

ABOVE: festival reveller.

12–32, 50100 Florence; tel: 055-22641; www.teatrodellaper gola.com), which is a superb example of a 17th-century theatre (inaugurated in 1656). These concerts, featuring world-famous chamber groups and singers, are generally held at weekends.

Tickets can be booked from

the call centre with a credit card, tel: 800-907 080, Mon–Fri 10am–5pm, or by calling the box office on 055-210 804.

The **Teatro Verdi** (Via Ghibellina 99r, 50122 Florence; tel: 055-212 320; www.teatroverdifirenze. it) is also the venue for a wider range of entertainment, from light opera and ballet to jazz and rock concerts, while the Orchestra Regionale Toscana's lively concert series runs from December to May.

The **Fiesole Music School** in San Domenico also organises a series of concerts (tel: 055-597 851; www.scuolamusica.fiesole.fi.it).

To find out what rock, jazz and Latin American music is on offer, check in the latest issue of the *Firenze Spettacolo* listings magazine.

MaggioDanza is the resident ballet company at the Teatro Comunale, and they perform throughout the year; the most interesting productions are likely to be between September and December or during the *Maggio Musicale* festival from April until June.

The **Florence Dance Festival**, held in late June/early July and again in December, features both well-known international and national names along with up-and-coming dancers and choreographers (tel: 055-289 276; www. florencedance.org for information).

There are also numerous smaller dance events during the year; for information about these and other visiting companies see the Dance section in *Firenze Spettacolo*.

Theatre

Florence is home to numerous theatres and theatre companies, ranging from the classical season at Teatro della Pergola to contemporary and fringe productions at some tiny venues. To find out what plays are on, buy *La Repubblica* newspaper or look in the appropriate section of *Firenze Spettacolo*; most productions are in Italian.

The main theatre is the state-subsidised **Teatro della Pergola** *(see above)* – some of the best-known Italian actors and

BELOW: street performers.

directors appear regularly here.

The **Teatro Metastasio** in Prato (some 30km/19 miles west of Florence) is another place to see high-quality drama productions (tel: 057-460 8501; www.metastasio.net).

Cinema

Almost all films are dubbed into Italian, but there are a few cinemas that occasionally show original versions, screenings by organisations such as the British Institute *(see below)* and the odd film festival or special season which will use subtitles rather than dubbing. The main cinema for foreigners is the **Odeon** (Piazza Strozzi; tel: 055-214 068), which shows recent films in English on Mondays, Tuesdays and Thursdays and is packed with foreign students and expatriates.

During the summer a number of films are shown in the open air – details of where and when can be sought from the tourist offices.

Specialist Holidays

Art Courses

Università Internazionale dell'Arte (Villa Il Ventaglio, Via delle Forbici 24/26, 50134 Florence; tel: 055-570 216; www.uiafirenze.com) offers various art-appreciation courses, which include specialisation in museum collections, conservation and restoration, and graphic design.
Istituto d'Arte di Firenze (Piazzale di Porta Romana 9, 50125 Florence; tel: 055-220 521; www.isa.firenze.it) offers courses in drawing, interior design, photography, painting, fashion and costume.
British Institute (Piazza Strozzi 2, 50123 Florence; tel: 055-267 781; www.britishinstitute.it) conducts art and language courses. This is the centre with the best reputation for such courses in Florence. It also has an excellent English and Italian library at

ABOVE: the architecture inspires artists of all talents.

Palazzo Lanfredini (Lungarno Guicciardini 9; tel: 055-2677 8270), of which one can have temporary membership.
Istituto per l'Arte e Il Restauro (Palazzo Spinelli, Via Maggio 13, 50125 Florence; tel: 055-282 951; www.spinelli.it) This art-restoration school has a reputation for being the best in Italy, and offers restoration courses in Italian.

Art Tours

Prospect Music and Art Tours (79 William Street, Herne Bay, Kent CT6 5NR; tel: 01227-743 307; www.prospecttours.com) is a specialised upmarket company which runs sophisticated art tours to Florence.

Cookery Courses

Scuola di Arte Culinaria "Cordonbleu" (Via di Mezzo 55r, 50121 Florence; tel: 055-234 5468; www.cordonbleu-it.com) offers Italian cookery courses in English, French and Italian.
Judy Witts Francini (www.divina cucina.com). At the other end of the scale, Judy Witts offers personalised, informal courses which can last for anything from a single day up to a week and

include a shopping trip to the nearby central market.

Fashion Institutes

Centro Moda, Via Faenza 111, 50123 Florence; tel: 055-36931; www.pittimmagine.com
Polimoda, Via Pisana 77, 50143 Florence; tel: 055-739 961; www.polimoda.com

Language Courses

There are numerous language schools in Florence. The reputable ones are run by Florence University or are organised by long-established centres, such as the British Institute *(see above)*. The following are some others worth looking into:
Centro di Cultura per Stranieri, Università degli Studi di Firenze, Via Francesco Valori 9, 10132 Florence; tel: 055-503 2703; www.ccs.unifi.it
Koinè Center, Via de' Pandolfini 27, 50122 Florence; tel: 055-213 881; www.koinecenter.com
Machiavelli, Piazza Santo Spirito 4, 50125 Florence; tel: 055-239 6966; www.centromachiavelli.it
Scuola Leonardo da Vinci, Via Bufalini 3, 50122 Florence; tel: 055-261 181; www.scuola leonardo.com

ABOVE: medieval revival on the Ponte Vecchio.

FESTIVALS

Like most Italian cities, Florence has numerous events and festivals – religious, cultural or commercial – throughout the year. The following are the main events held in or near the city:

Easter Day: *Scoppio del Carro*, the Explosion of the Cart (actually fireworks on a float). An ancient ritual accompanied by processions of musicians and flag-throwers in Renaissance costume, who start at the Porta a Prato and end at a packed-out Piazza del Duomo.

Ascension Day: *Festa del Grillo*, Festival of the Crickets, in Parco delle Cascine. Children used to bring or buy cricket in cages, but the insects have now been replaced by toy versions. There's also a large general market.

End of April: *Flower Show* in the Parterre, near Piazza della Libertà – a riot of colour and heady scents.

May and June: *Maggio Musicale Fiorentino* festival of opera, ballet, concerts and recitals. It closes with two free concerts held in the Piazza della Signoria.

Sunday in mid-June, Arezzo: *Giostra del Saracino* – the Saracen's Joust. Another ancient pageant accompanied by colourful processions.

16–17 June, Pisa: *Luminaria di San Ranieri* – a spectacular event, with thousands of candles lit on the buildings along the Arno. Boat race on the second day.

24 June: *San Giovanni* – Florence's patron saint's day and

BELOW: *contrada* drummer.

a public holiday in the city. The *calcio in costume* football game is played in Piazza Santa Croce; other matches are also played around this time.

June–August, Fiesole: Estate Fiesolina – dance, music and theatre in Fiesole's open-air Roman theatre.

Last Sunday in June, Pisa: *Il Gioco del Ponte* – a kind of medieval tug-of-war played out on the Ponte di Mezzo.

2 July, Siena: the first of the *Palio* horse races takes place in Siena *(see pages 236–7)*. The second is on 16 August.

July: *Florence Dance Festival* – a three-week festival of dance in outdoor venues in Florence.

25 July, Pistoia: *Giostra del Orso* – Joust of the Bear in Piazza del Duomo. A mock battle is staged between a wooden bear and 12 knights in costume.

Late July–mid-August, Torre del Lago: *Puccini Opera Festival* – the shores of Lake Massaciuccoli provide an evocative setting for a series of Puccini operas.

NIGHTLIFE

The Scene

Italians enjoy going out, and Florence has a good number of bars, often with live music. The pre-prandial *aperitivo* has become a way of life. The price of the drink may seem steep but often a whole buffet is included in the price, providing a cheap alternative to having dinner in a restaurant. Nightclubs are not as popular and tend to be located out of town, although in the summer more open up to cater for the tourists and foreign students. There are also a number of English, Irish and Scottish pubs in the city – these often show sport on Sky. To keep up with the ever-changing scene, buy *Firenze Spettacolo* or pick up a free copy of *Vivi Firenze* (www.vivifirenze.it).

ABOVE: relaxing in style.

Bars and Live Music

Some of these Florence bars are closed on Mondays.

Astor
Piazza del Duomo 20r; tel: 055-284 305
Cocktail bar with dance floor; largely frequented by Americans.

Be Bop
Via dei Servi 76r
Cocktail bar with live music: country, blues and jazz.

Il Caffè
Piazza Pitti 9r; tel: 055-239 9863
Chic and refined: a cosy spot to chat to friends, during the day or evening.

Caffè Cibrèo
Via del Verrocchio 5r; tel: 055-234 5853
Annexe to the famous restaurant, this beautiful and intimate wood-panelled bar is ideal for anything from a morning coffee to a late-night *digestivo*. Great snacks which come from the Cibrèo kitchen. Closed Sundays and Mondays.

Caffèdeco
Piazza della Libertà 46r; tel: 055-571 135
This stylish, Art Deco-style bar is popular with jazz-lovers.

Caruso Jazz Café
Via Lambertesca 14–16r; tel:
055-670 207; www.carusojazzcafe.com
Relaxed café with art exhibitions and live music Wednesday to Friday. Closed Sundays.

Dolce Vita
Piazza del Carmine; tel: 055-284 595; www.dolcevitaflorence.com
Fashionable bar in the bohemian Oltrarno quarter.

Hemingway
Piazza Piattellina 9r; tel: 055-284 781; www.hemingway.fi.it
Beautifully decorated café where you can have a drink and a snack, or sample the superb chocolates. Comfy chairs and books to browse.

Jazz Club
Via Nuova dei Caccini 3; tel: 055-247 9700; www.jazzclub firenze.com
Relaxed basement bar with live music daily. Small fee to become a member. Closed Sunday and Monday.

Moyo
Via dei Benci 23r; tel: 055-247 9738; www.moyo.it
Swanky cocktail bar in the Santa Croce area with outside seating and delicious cocktails.

Nova Bar
Via dei Martelli 14r
Pleasant bar during the day, turns into a noisy cocktail bar with dance floor in the evening.

Piccolo Caffè
Borgo Santa Croce 23r; tel: 055-200 1057
This small café is primarily a gay men's bar, but is a friendly place which provides welcome relief from unwanted attention for women as well.

Il Rifrullo
Via San Niccolò 55r; tel: 055-234 2621
The long bar groans with munchies during cocktail hour, and there is an open fire in the back room. The expert bar-man mixes great cocktails. Open daily.

Tabasco
Piazza Santa Cecilia 3; tel: 055-213 000
Men only; this was the first gay bar in Italy.

I Visacci
Borgo Albizi 80r; tel: 055-200 1956
Art café with friendly staff, relaxed music and a good selection of wines and cocktails.

Zoe
Via dei Renai 13r; tel: 055-243 111
Popular spot for summer cocktails, along with aperitif buffet and DJ music.

BELOW: cocktails at the Dolce Vita.

ABOVE: rollerblading, Cascine park.

Nightclubs

Central Park
Via Fosso Macinante 1,
Parco delle Cascine; tel: 055-
353 505
One of the trendiest discos in
Florence. Open Tuesday to
Saturday.
Dolce Zucchero
Via Pandolfini 36–38r; tel: 055-
247 7894
One of the few discos in the city
centre, it operates a drinks card
whereby you pay on exit.
Maracanà
Via Faenza 4;
tel: 055-210 298
A lively Latino club playing mostly
salsa and samba. Closed
Mondays.
Space Electronic
Via Palazzuolo 37;
tel: 055-293 082;
www.spaceelectronic.net
Lasers and videos are the
hallmarks of the largest disco in
Florence. This is the usual hang-
out of foreign teenagers and
would-be Latin lovers.
Twice
Via Giuseppe Verdi 57r;
tel: 055-247 6356;
www.twiceclub.com
So called because it transforms
at 11pm from a wine bar (with
Tuscan buffet) into a lively disco.

YAB
Via Sassetti 5r; tel: 055-215
160; www.yab.it
Fashionable glassy club-disco
open from June to September,
with themed nights. Monday's
hip-hop night is hugely popular.

SPORT

Participant Sports

Below are a selection of the
numerous sports and health
clubs in Florence; for fuller listings visit the tourist office on
arrival or purchase *Firenze
Spettacolo*.

Gyms

Klab
Tel: 055-718 4300; www.klab.it
A chain of three fitness centres
in Florence, which also run a
number of classes.
Palestra Ricciardi
Borgo Pinti 75; tel: 055-247

BELOW: rowing along the Arno.

8444; www.palestraricciardi.it
A central gym where staff speak
good English as well as some
French and Spanish.
Tropos
Via Orcagna 20a; tel: 055-678
381; www.troposfirenze.it
A luxurious, and pricey, fitness
and beauty centre with gym and
swimming pool.

Tennis

Tennis is popular in Italy. If you
wish to play a game, try these
clubs:
Circolo Carraia
Via Monti alle Croci, Florence;
tel: 055-234 6353
Circolo del Tennis
Parco delle Cascine; tel: 055-
332 651; www.ctfirenze.org

Swimming

Many luxury hotels outside the
centre of Florence have swimming pools which may allow
guests for a small fee. There are
also public pools in towns –
although these have erratic open-

ing hours and can be by subscription only. The following swimming pools are in Florence:

Piscina Comunale Bellariva
Lungarno Aldo Moro 6; tel: 055-677 521
Open-air during the summer.

Piscina Costoli
Viale Paoli, Campo di Marte; tel: 055-623 6027
This is in the north of the city and has a clean outdoor pool in the summer.

Piscina Le Pavoniere
Via Catena 2; tel: 055-367 506
Set in the Parco delle Cascine and only open in summer, this is one of the city's most appealing pools.

Horse Riding

For further information about horseback holidays, contact the **Federazione Italiana Sport Equestri** (www.fise.it).

For riding near Florence, try: **Centro Ippico I Noccioli**, Via dei Noccioli 3, Bagno a Ripoli; tel: 055-643 407; www.inoccioli.it or **Centro Ippico La Marinella**, Via di Macia 21, Calenzano; tel: 055-887 8066; www.maneggiola marinella.it.

For horse-riding centres in other parts of Tuscany, contact the **Centro Ippico Toscano**, tel: 055-315 621; www.centroippico toscano.it.

Spectator Sports

The main spectator sport in Tuscany is football. Florentines are football fanatics and passionate supporters of the local team "La Fiorentina". They play regularly at the **Stadio Artemio Franchi** (tel: 055-503 0190), and the season runs on Sundays from August to May, with games in the afternoon or the evening.

Next to the stadium is the athletics arena, which also hosts a number of events during the year. The Firenze Marathon takes place annually – www.firenze marathon.it.

OUTDOOR ACTIVITIES

If you feel like getting out of the city, Tuscany is a perfect destination for holidays involving hiking, cycling or some other outdoor activity. In recent years, a number of specialist tour operators have started offering cycling and hiking tours of Tuscany. Some include a house-party element, attempting to combine people of similar backgrounds and tastes. Others mix the outdoor side with more leisurely pursuits, such as painting, cookery or history of art courses (suitable for those with less energetic partners). The tours range greatly in terms of accommodation (from classic villas to simple farms). Nonetheless, the quality (and price) is usually well above that offered by a two-star hotel.

These holidays tend to be all-inclusive, except for optional excursions. Some packages involve staying in different accommodation along the route; in this case, the company generally transports your luggage for you from hotel to hotel.

A fairly expensive but highly recommended UK company which arranges walks and other outdoor tours in Tuscany is **The Alternative Travel Group Limited**, 274 Banbury Road,

Oxford OX2 7GH; tel: 01865-315 678; www.atg-oxford.co.uk. Its walking holidays are designed for anyone – not just serious walkers – and all transport and hotel accommodation is arranged.

Two other companies worth contacting are **Explore Worldwide** (Nelson House, 55 Victoria Road, Farnborough, Hants GU14 7PA; tel: 0845-013 1537; www.explore. co.uk) and **Inn Travel** (Whitehall Grange, Nr Castle Howard, York, YO60 7GU; tel: 01653-617 001; www.inntravel.co.uk).

For a full list of reputable companies specialising in adventure, nature, walking and cycling tours, contact your national ENIT (Italian Tourist Board) office.

The **Italian Alpine Club** (CAI), the principal walking organisation in Italy, is also worth contacting. The branch in Florence can be contacted at Via del Mezzetta 2, 50135 Florence; tel: 338-201 2726; www.caitoscana.it.

BELOW: jogging on the Lungarno.

A–Z

AN ALPHABETICAL SUMMARY OF PRACTICAL INFORMATION

A ddresses

If the letter "r" appears after numbers in an address, it refers to *rosso* (red) and denotes a business address; Florentine addresses operate a dual numbering system, with "red" numbers usually denoting businesses and blue or black numbers usually denoting residential addresses.

Admission Charges

Museum and gallery charges range from €3 to €12, plus €3–6 extra if you book tickets in advance. However, if you visit when a temporary exhibition is on, the cost goes up by several euros – even if you only want to see the main collection. Currently there are no multiple-sight or transport cards on offer. Entrance to churches or small church museums is €2.50–3.

Admission to state-run museums is free for EU members under 18 and over 65, and half price for 18–25s. Presentation of a passport or driving licence is required.

B udgeting for Your Trip

Beer: €1.50–4; glass of house wine €2–4 (waiter service will often cost twice as much as drinking at the bar).
Main course at a budget restaurant: cheap: €7–12, moderate:

€12–18, expensive: €18–30.
Twin or double room with bath and breakfast: cheap: under €110, moderate: €110–250, de luxe: €250–450.
Taxi from Florence's Amerigo

Vespucci airport to the centre of town: €20
Single bus ticket: €1.20

Children

At first sight, Tuscany does not appear an immediate choice for kids, but there are some museums and other sights which hold a certain amount of appeal. Teenagers may well be interested in a study holiday focusing on crafts, sports, cooking or languages. Most importantly, finding a place to eat with the kids in tow is never a problem in Italy. Florence is full of ice-cream parlours and child-friendly restaurants.

In Florence

The newly expanded Egyptian collection at the Archaeological Museum (see page 166) is full of mummies. The Galileo Museum (see page 110) contains working experiments of the great astronomer. The Anthropological Museum (see page 122) is crammed with curiosities including Peruvian mummies, Indian shadow puppets and Eskimo anoraks made from whaleskins. For children with a gruesome fascination for the human body, La Specola (in the Museo di Zoologia, see page 187) exhibits realistic anatomical waxworks of body parts.

The Boboli Garden and Le Cascine are Florence's two main parks, whilst one of the few children's playgrounds is to be found in Piazza dell'Azeglio. Further ideas can be found at www.firenze turismo.it (click on "Themes").

Canadian Island (Via Gioberti 15; tel: 055-677 567; www.canadian island.it) is an English-speaking company which runs summer camps, courses and day centres for children in Tuscany. The Ludoteca Centrale (Via Fibbiai 2; tel: 055-247 8386) is a fun children's centre with books, games and audiovisual equipment.

Outside Florence

Outside Florence are a number of parks and the coast, which offer

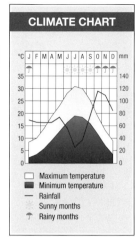

CLIMATE CHART

°C J F M A M J J A S O N D mm

35 — 140
30 — 120
25 — 100
20 — 80
15 — 60
10 — 40
5 — 20
0 — 0

☐ Maximum temperature
■ Minimum temperature
— Rainfall
☂ Sunny months
☂ Rainy months

possibilities for children. The resorts of Viareggio and Elba are well set up for children, and most coastal cities have permanent funfairs.

The Maremma is a good place for wildlife-spotting, whilst the Parco di Pinocchio at Collodi near Pisa (tel: 0572-429 342; www.pinocchio.it) is an obvious choice for children.

There is a compact but interesting zoo open daily at Pistoia: Pistoia Zoo, Via Pieve a Celle 160a; tel: 0573-911 219; www.zoodipistoia.it.

Climate

The climate in Florence can be extreme. Its position, lying in a bowl surrounded by hills, accounts for the high degree of humidity that is often a feature of the weather in midsummer. The heat and humidity are generally at their most intense between mid-July and mid-August, when temperatures frequently climb into the 30s Celsius (high 90s Fahrenheit). Winters can be very cold and damp, but there are a good number of cold, crisp and sunny days, and visiting the city at this time of year, without the crowds, can be very pleasant.

The city seems to get more and more crowded each year, the peak periods being around Easter time and from June to the end of August. The only relatively tourist-free months are November to February. The best months to visit are May, September and early October, when the temperatures are pleasantly warm but not too hot for sightseeing.

Clothing

Casual wear is acceptable in all but the grandest hotel dining rooms and restaurants. Clothing should be as light as possible for summer, but take a light jacket or sweater for the evenings, which

can be surprisingly cool. If you go in spring or autumn, it's worth taking a light raincoat or umbrella. In winter (Nov–Mar), the temperature frequently drops to freezing or below, and warm clothing is essential for the outdoors. A pair of comfortable shoes is invaluable for sightseeing and walking the cobbled streets. Shorts and bare shoulders are frowned upon and frequently forbidden in churches.

Crime and Safety

Petty crime is a major problem in Florence, particularly pickpocketing and the snatching of handbags and jewellery in the street and on buses. Always carry valuables securely, either in a money belt or handbag which can be worn strapped across the body. One popular scam is for someone to approach you to distract your attention while someone else steals your purse or wallet.

Cars are also vulnerable, so avoid leaving personal belongings out of view, and always lock the doors and boot. Car radios are a common target, so take your radio with you if you have one of the detachable types; most Italians do.

Make sure you report any thefts to the police, since you will need evidence of the crime in the form of a police report to claim insurance.

Customs and Duty-Free

It is no longer possible to buy duty-free or tax-free goods on journeys within the EU. VAT and duty are included in the purchase price. Shops at ports and airport terminals will sell goods duty- and tax-paid to those travelling within the EU; they may choose not to pass on price increases.

Disabled Travellers

Despite difficult cobbled streets and poor wheelchair access to tourist attractions and hotels, many people with disabilities visit Florence and Tuscany every year. However, unaccompanied visitors will usually experience some difficulty, so it is best to travel with a companion.

Conditions and disability awareness are improving slowly in Italy in general, although the situation is certainly not ideal, and access is not always easy. More museums now have lifts, ramps and adapted toilets, newer trains and buses are accessible (although wheelchair-users may need help when boarding), and recent laws require restaurants, bars and hotels to provide the relevant facilities. These laws, however, do not always cover access to those facilities. This sometimes results in the absurdity of a new wheelchair-accessible room

being located on the fourth or fifth floor of a hotel with a lift that is too narrow to admit a wheelchair.

For details of which sights and museums are accessible and to what degree, contact the Florence Tourist Office (see page 92). Its website has detailed information on getting around, where to stay and what to see. For drivers with disabilities, there are plenty of reserved parking places in Florence, and these are free.

In the United Kingdom, you can obtain further information from **RADAR** (12 City Forum, 250 City Road, London EC1V 8AF; tel: 020-7250 3222; www.radar.org.uk). In the United States, contact **SATH** (347 Fifth Avenue, Suite 605, NY 10016; tel: 212-447 7284; www.sath.org).

Embassies & Consulates

Australian Embassy: Via Antonio Bosio 5, 00161 Rome; tel: 06-852 721
UK Embassy: Via XX Settembre 80a, 00187 Rome; tel: 06-4220 0001
UK Consulate: Lungarno Corsini 2, 50123 Florence; tel: 055-284 133
US Embassy: Via Vittorio Veneto 121, 00187 Rome; tel: 06-46741
US Consulate: Lungarno A. Vespucci 38, 50123 Florence; tel: 055-266 951

Emergencies

Police (Carabinieri): 112
Police (Polizia): 113
Fire Brigade (Vigili del Fuoco): 115
Medical Aid/Ambulance (Misericordia): 118
Police HQ (Questura, to report theft, including vehicles): Via Zara 2; tel: 055-49771
Police: Via Pietrapiana 50; tel: 055-203 911. Help with reporting theft, lost property or any other police problems; interpreters available.
Railway Police: tel: 055-212 296

TRANSPORT

ELECTRICITY

Italy uses 220v and two-pin plugs – adaptors can be purchased from airports or department stores in the city.

Tourist Medical Service (24-hour fee-paying home visits, with English- or French-speaking doctors): Via Lorenzo il Magnifico 59; tel: 055-475 411
Associazione Volontari Ospedalieri: Via Carducci 8; tel: 055-234 4567; www.avofirenze.it. This group of volunteers will translate (free) for foreign patients.
Lost Property Office: Via Circondaria 19; tel: 055-328 3942
Automobile Club d'Italia *(Soccorso ACI)*: 803 116
24-hour breakdown: 116

Etiquette

Italians are an expressive people: they are very friendly but will have no qualms about showing you their displeasure should you do something to offend them. Being polite and trying to speak a little Italian goes a long way. Both men and women greet each other with a kiss on each cheek.

G ay & Lesbian Travellers

Florentines are tolerant of gays and lesbians and there are several gay bars in the city. ARCI-gay, the national gay rights organisation, has a branch in Florence at Via di Mezzo 39r, tel: 055-0123 121; www.arcigayfirenze.it. For an excellent guide to gay life and tourism in Italy, visit www.gayfriendlyitaly.com.

H ealth and Medical Care

Insurance

EU residents are entitled to the same medical treatment as an Italian citizen. Visitors will need to complete an EHIC form (see www.ehic.org.uk for information) before they go. This covers medical treatment and medicines,

although it is still necessary to pay prescription charges and a percentage of the costs for medicines. Note that the EHIC does not give any cover for trip cancellations, nor does it provide repatriation in case of illness. For this, you will need to take out private insurance. US citizens are advised to take out private health insurance. Canadian citizens are also covered by a reciprocal arrangement between the Italian and Canadian governments.

If you are covered by a reciprocal scheme and need to visit a doctor while in Italy, take the EHIC form (if an EU resident) or proof of citizenship and residence (eg passport) to the local health office (Unità Sanitaria Locale), which will direct you to a doctor covered by the state system and supply the necessary paperwork.

Medical Services

Pharmacies: the staff in chemist's shops *(farmacie)* are usually very knowledgeable about common illnesses and sell far more medicines without prescription than their colleagues in other Western countries (even so, most drugs still require a prescription).

Every *farmacia* has a list of the local pharmacies which are open at night and on Sundays. Chemist's shops which are open

24 hours *(farmacie aperte 24 ore su 24)* in Florence are:
Farmacia Comunale, in Florence station; tel: 055-216 761.
Farmacia Molteni, Via dei Calzaiuoli 7r; tel: 055-289 490.
Farmacia all'Insegna del Moro, Piazza San Giovanni 20r; tel: 055-211 343.

For English-speaking doctors and information on other health services go to the "Info" section of www.firenzeturismo.it.

There is an **accident and emergency department** in the city centre at Ospedale Santa Maria Nuova, Piazza Santa Maria Nuova 1; tel: 055-27581.

Other emergency numbers are listed above.

I nternet and Email

Internet services are good in Florence, with wireless having been brought to the city. The Florence WiFi initiative provides free one-hour internet access in 12 city squares and parks. Many hotels offer access, and there are a huge number of internet cafés which are open until late.
Internet Train
A number of points, including Via Porta Rossa 38r, Via de' Benci 36r, Railway station, Via dell' Oriuolo 40r; www.internettrain.it.

This company offers internet access from its terminals or personal laptops, as well as a number of other services including

ACCOMMODATION

SHOPPING

ACTIVITIES

A – Z

LANGUAGE

phonecards and mobile telephone rental.

For useful addresses, see under Websites on page 293.

Left Luggage

The left luggage office at Florence's main railway station, Santa Maria Novella, is open from 6am–11.50pm. One piece of luggage costs €4 for the first six hours, 60 cents for each additional hour up to 12 hours, 20 cents per hour thereafter.

Lost Property

There is a lost property office at Santa Maria Novella station, at platform 16.

Media

Print

La Stampa, *Il Corriere della Sera* and *La Repubblica* are national papers with local sections, whilst the gossipy *La Nazione* is the region's paper favoured by most Florentines for its coverage of local news. A wide variety of foreign press is available. English-language freebies include the monthly *Florence Concierge Information*, packed with practical information, including listings, and *The Florentine* newspaper,

published every other week with excellent articles on Florence.

Firenze Spettacolo is the most informative monthly listings magazine on nightlife, clubs, bars, restaurants and the live arts in Florence. It is available from all news-stands.

Television and Radio

The Italian state TV network, the RAI, broadcasts three channels, which compete with various independent channels. There are also a vast number of radio stations, including many regional ones. Many hotels have cable connections which offer world news in English including Sky and BBC.

Money

Italy's monetary unit is the euro (€), which is divided into 100 cents. Banknotes are issued in denominations of 5, 10, 20, 50, 100, 200 and 500 euros. Coins are denominated in 1 and 2 euros, and 1, 2, 5, 10, 20 and 50 cents.

Travellers' Cheques

Dollar, sterling or euro travellers' cheques (preferably issued by a major bank or well-known company such as Thomas Cook or American Express) can be used to obtain cash in any commercial bank and in exchange for goods and ser-

vices in shops and hotels. Expect to pay a commission charge.

Credit Cards

Most major credit cards, including Visa and MasterCard, are accepted in hotels, restaurants and shops, for air and train tickets, and for cash in any bank and some cash dispensers.

Direct Money Transfers

Western Union has a number of agents for direct money transfers. A central one is Changepoint, Via dei Calzaiuoli 3r; tel: 055-288 107.

Banks, Exchange Bureaux and ATMs

Normal banking hours are Mon–Fri 8.30am–1.30pm and at varied times between 2.30–4pm. Changing money in a bank can be time-consuming, but the rates are generally better than in exchange offices. Exchange rates are displayed outside banks and exchange offices and are also printed in daily newspapers.

Exchange rates obviously fluctuate according to world markets; check www.xe.com for the current rate. There is one rate for buying euros and one for selling.

Major banks have several branches in the city, as well as ATMs *(Bancomats)* dotted around. A high concentration of banks, including some foreign companies, is to the west of Piazza della Repubblica, around Via de' Tornabuoni.

Exchange offices *(negozi di cambio)* are to be found all over Florence. The offices at the airports and main railway station are open late in the evening and at weekends.

Tipping

Some restaurants in Florence still levy a *coperto* of around €2–4 – a cover and bread charge, and often a 10 percent service charge is added to the bill. It's customary to leave a little extra if the service has been good, and some small change if you are in a

bar. Taxi drivers will appreciate it if you round up the fare (between 5 and 10 percent).

O pening Hours

Opening hours of museums and art galleries vary hugely and some change their hours from season to season. Hours are generally 8.15/9am–4.30pm or, in the case of some of the main sights, 6.50pm. Closing day is usually Monday, and some sights have restricted opening hours at weekends, especially Sundays. Consult www.firenzemusei.it and www.polo museale.firenze.it for latest openings

of some of the main museums.
For shopping opening hours see page 275.
Banking hours are normally Monday to Friday 8.30am–1.30pm and 2.30–4pm, but currency exchange offices have longer opening hours. Offices usually open from 8am–1pm and from 2–4pm, though many now stay open all day.
On Italian national holidays, all shops and offices are closed.

P ostal Services

The main **post office** in Florence is in Via Pellicceria 3 (near Piazza della Repubblica; www.poste.it), and it is open Monday–Friday 8.15am–7pm, Saturday 8.15am–12.30pm. It offers a full range of postal and telegraph services. There is also a postal courier service which provides a quick and efficient way to send letters and parcels worldwide in 24/48 hours.
There are local post offices in each area of the city, and these are generally open from Monday–Friday 8.15am–1.30pm and until 12.30pm on Saturday.
Stamps are sold at post offices and tobacconist's shops *(tabacchi)*. There are yellow or red postboxes (usually set into the wall) on most main streets, at post offices and at railway stations.

PUBLIC HOLIDAYS

The dates of the national holidays are:
1 January *Capodanno* (New Year's Day)
Easter *Pasqua*
Easter Monday *Pasquetta*
25 April *Anniversario della Liberazione* (Liberation Day)
1 May *Festa del Lavoro* (Labour Day)
24 June *San Giovanni* (St John the Baptist – Florence's patron saint)
15 August *Ferragosti* (Assumption of the Blessed Virgin Mary)
1 November *Tutti Santi* (All Saints' Day)
8 December *Immacolata Concezione* (Immaculate Conception)
25 December *Natale*
26 December *Santo Stefano* (Boxing Day)

R eligious Services

Florence is full of Catholic churches, and Mass is celebrated in Italian at varying times. The **Duomo** holds a Mass in English every Saturday at 5pm. Services are held in English at the **American Episcopal Church of St James**, Via B. Rucellai 9 (tel: 055-294 417) and the **Anglican Church of St Mark**, Via Maggio 16 (tel: 055-294 764). The **Synagogue** is at Via L.C. Farini 4 (tel: 055-245 252). The **Islamic Community Centre** at Borgo Allegri 64 (tel: 055-263 9639) has a place of worship.
Anyone who attempts to enter a church in shorts or with bare shoulders will be ejected.

S moking

A ban on smoking in enclosed public places was brought into force in January 2005 and, owing to the hefty penalties with which owners are threatened, it is the most obeyed law in Italy.

Strikes

Italy has active trade unions, and strikes are frequent, causing disruptions to transport and other services. Strikes are usually publicised in advance on posters or in newspapers.

Student Travellers

State-run museums are free for EU citizens under 18 and half-price for those aged between 18–25 years (passport or driver's licencse required). An ISIC (International Student Identity Card) or IYTC (International Youth Travel Card) can be useful for discounts on shops and entertainment, and occasionally for accommodation and eating out. For details go to www.isic.org.

Telecommunications

Italy has fewer and fewer telephone kiosks, but almost every bar has a public phone. Not all of them can be used for long-distance calls, but you can make international calls from any phone kiosk, nearly all of which take **telephone cards** *(schede telefoniche)*, which can be purchased from tobacconists *(tabacchi –* look out for the black-and-white

TIME ZONE

Italy works on GMT + 1 and switches to DST – daylight saving time, GMT + 2 – at the same time as the rest of Europe.

"T" sign), newspaper stands and internet cafés, and some also take credit cards. International phonecards are particularly good value for long-distance calls. They also work for local calls, and can be used from your hotel-room phone. A number of call centres have opened up in Florence, and these are often more convenient and offer better rates.

To make calls within Italy, first use the three- or four-number city codes (including the initial zero), even if you are calling locally. When calling Italy from outside the country, you should retain the initial zero of the local city code. Directories are easy to understand and give comprehensive information – www.paginegialle.it is Italy's Yellow Pages online.

EU mobiles can be used in Italy, but check compatibility before you leave. Charges for using a UK-based mobile to make and receive calls and texts

BELOW: demonstration on Piazza della Signoria.

abroad are high. If you are in Italy for some time, it's worth purchasing an Italian "pay as you go" SIM card for the length of your stay.

International Calls

To telephone Florence from overseas: dial the number for an international call in the country you are calling from (usually 00); dial Italy's country code (39), then the area code for Florence with the initial zero (055), and the number of the person you are contacting.
To telephone/fax overseas from Florence: dial the overseas connection number (00) followed by the country code (eg UK: 44, US: 1), then the area code, without the initial zero, and then the contact number.

Toilets

Public toilets are few and far between and not always clean and well maintained. All bars have facilities, and so visitors are best off purchasing a coffee and making use of these. Otherwise, La Rinascente in Piazza della Repubblica has clean toilets on the top floor.

Tourist Offices

The headquarters of the tourist board, the APT (**Azienda per il Turismo**; www.firenzeturismo.it) is at Via Manzoni 16 (tel: 055-23320), but this is a long way from the city centre. The most central office of the

APT is Via Cavour 1r; tel: 055-290 832/ 833. It is open 8.30am–6.30pm Mon–Sat and until 1.30pm Sun. Other offices are at:
• Borgo Santa Croce 29r; tel: 055-234 0444. Open Mon–Sat 9am–7pm and Sun 9am–2pm.
• Piazza Stazione; tel: 055-212 245. Open Mon–Sat 8.30am–7pm and Sun 8.30am–2pm.

In Fiesole the office is at Via Portigiani 3–5; tel: 055-596 1256.

U seful Addresses

United Kingdom

Artstur: 59 Knightsbridge, London SW1X 7RA; tel: 020-7235 6650. Italian cultural institution with art lectures, opera courses and cultural tours to Italy for small groups.
Italian Embassy: 14 Three Kings Yard, London W1Y 2EH; tel: 020-7312 2200.
Italian Consulate: 38 Eaton Place, London SWIX 8AN; tel: 020-7235 9371.
Italian Cultural Institute: 39 Belgrave Square, London SWIX 8NX; tel: 020-7235 1461; www.icilondon.esteri.it. Advice on culture, events, language and art courses in London and Italy.
Italian Chamber of Commerce: 1 Princes Street, London W1B 2AY; tel: 020-7495 8191; www.italchamind.eu.
Italian Government Tourist Board (ENIT): 1 Princes Street, London W1B 2AY; tel: 020-7408 1254; www.italiantouristboard.co.uk.

North America

Italian Government Tourist Board: www.enit.it
175 Bloor Street East, Suite 907, South Tower, Toronto, M4W 3R8, Canada; tel: 416-925 4882.
630 Fifth Avenue, Suite 1565, New York, NY 10111; tel: 212-245 5618.
12400 Wilshire Bvd, Suite 550, Los Angeles, CA 90025; tel: 310-820 1898.
500 N. Michigan Avenue, Chicago, Suite 506, Illinois, IL 60611; tel: 312-644 0996.

Visas and Passports

Subjects from EU countries require either a passport or a Visitor's Identification Card to enter Italy. A visa is not required.

Holders of passports from most other countries do not require visas for stays of less than three months, except for nationals of Eastern European countries, who need to obtain visas from the Italian Embassy in their own country.

ABOVE: on the steps of San Miniato church.

Police Registration

A person may stay in Italy for three months as a tourist, but police registration is required within three days of entering Italy. If staying at a hotel, the management will attend to the formality. Although this regulation seems to be rarely observed, it is advisable that you carry a set of passport photos in case you need them for registration.

You are legally obliged to carry a form of identification (passport, driving licence, etc.) with you at all times. This rule is often flouted, but bear in mind that it would be unwise to call the police or attempt to report a problem (eg theft) unless you are carrying ID.

ebsites

Websites are given throughout the book in the relevant sections. Some of the more important are:
General Information: www.enit.it
Tourist information plus hotels and restaurants: www.firenze turismo.it
Tourist Information for Tuscany: www.turismo.toscana.it
Museums: www.firenzemusei.it and www.polomuseale.firenze.it
Events: www.firenzespettacolo.it

Women Travellers

The difficulties encountered by women travelling in Italy are overstated. However, women do, especially if they are young and blonde, have to put up with male attention. Ignoring whistles and questions is the best way to get rid of unwanted attention. The less you look like a tourist, the fewer problems you will have.

WEIGHTS AND MEASURES

The metric system is used for weights and measures. Italians refer to 100 grams as *un etto*; 200 grams are therefore *due etti* and so on.

LANGUAGE

UNDERSTANDING ITALIAN

Language Tips

In Tuscany, the Italian language is supplemented by regional dialects. In large cities and tourist centres you'll find many people who speak English, French or German. In fact, due to the massive emigration over the past 100 years, do not be surprised if you are addressed in a New York, Melbourne or Bavarian accent: the speaker may have spent some time working abroad.

It is worth buying a good phrase book or dictionary, but the following will help you get started. Since this glossary is aimed at non-linguists, we have opted for the simplest options rather than the most elegant Italian.

Pronunciation and Grammar Tips

Italian speakers claim that pronunciation is straightforward: you pronounce it as it is written. This is approximately true, but there are a couple of important rules for English-speakers to bear in mind: *c* before *e* or *i* is pronounced "ch", eg *ciao, mi dispiace, la coincidenza. Ch* before *i* or *e* is pronounced as "k", eg *la chiesa.* Likewise, *sci* or *sce* are pronounced as in "sheep" or "shed" respectively. *Gn* in Italian is rather like the sound in "onion", while *gl* is softened to resemble the sound in "bullion".

Nouns are either masculine (*il*, plural *i*) or feminine (*la*, plural *le*). Plurals of nouns are most often formed by changing an *o* to an *i*

and an *a* to an *e*, eg *il panino, i panini; la chiesa, le chiese.*

Words are stressed on the penultimate syllable unless an accent indicates otherwise.

Like many languages, Italian has formal and informal words for "You". In the singular, *Tu* is informal while *Lei* is more polite. Confusingly, in some parts of Italy or in some circumstances, you will also hear *Voi* used as a singular polite form. (In general, *Voi* is reserved for "You" plural.) For visitors, it is simplest and most respectful to use the polite form unless invited to do otherwise.

There is, of course, rather more to the language than that, but you can get a surprisingly long way towards making friends with a few phrases.

Basic Communication
Yes *Sì*
No *No*
Thank you *Grazie*
Yes please *Sì grazie*
Many thanks *Mille grazie/tante grazie/molte grazie*
You're welcome *Prego*
All right/OK/That's fine *Va bene*
Please *Per favore* or *per cortesia*
Excuse me (to get attention) *Scusi* (singular), *Scusate* (plural)

Excuse me (to get through a crowd) *Permesso*
Excuse me (to attract attention, for example of a waiter) *Scusi!*
Excuse me (sorry) *Mi scusi*
Wait a minute! *Aspetta!*
Could you help me? (formal) *Potrebbe aiutarmi?*
Certainly *Ma, certo*
Can I help you? (formal) *Posso aiutarLa?*
Can you help me? *Può aiutarmi, per cortesia?*

I need... *Ho bisogno di...*
Can you show me...? *Può indicarmi...?*
I'm lost *Mi sono perso*
I'm sorry *Mi dispiace*
I don't know *Non lo so*
I don't understand *Non ho capito*
Do you speak English/French/ German? *Parla inglese/ francese/tedesco?*
Could you speak more slowly, please? *Può parlare piu lenta-mente, per favore?*

Could you repeat that please?
Può ripetere, per favore?
slowly/quietly *piano*
here/there *qui/là*
What? *Quale/come?*
When/why/where?
Quando/perchè/dove?
Where is the lavatory? *Dov'è il bagno?*
open *aperto*
closed *chiuso*
pull *tirare*
push *spingere*

Days and Dates

morning/afternoon/evening *la mattina/il pomeriggio/la sera*
yesterday/today/tomorrow *ieri/oggi/domani*
the day after tomorrow *dopodomani*
now/early/late *adesso/presto/ritardo*
a minute *un minuto*
an hour *un'ora*
half an hour *un mezz'ora*
a day *un giorno*
a week *una settimana*
Monday *lunedì*
Tuesday *martedì*
Wednesday *mercoledì*
Thursday *giovedì*
Friday *venerdì*
Saturday *sabato*
Sunday *domenica*
first *il primo/la prima*
second *il secondo/la seconda*
third *il terzo/la terza*

Numbers

1	*uno*
2	*due*
3	*tre*
4	*quattro*
5	*cinque*
6	*sei*
7	*sette*
8	*otto*
9	*nove*
10	*dieci*
11	*undici*
12	*dodici*
13	*tredici*
14	*quattordici*
15	*quindici*
16	*sedici*
17	*diciassette*
18	*diciotto*

19	*diciannove*
20	*venti*
21	*ventuno*
30	*trenta*
40	*quaranta*
50	*cinquanta*
60	*sessanta*
70	*settanta*
80	*ottanta*
90	*novanta*
100	*cento*
200	*duecento*
500	*cinquecento*
1,000	*mille*
2,000	*duemila*
5,000	*cinquemila*

Greetings

Hello (Good day) *Buon giorno*
Good afternoon/evening *Buona sera*
Good night *Buona notte*
Goodbye *Arrivederci*
Hello/hi/goodbye (familiar) *Ciao*
Mr/Mrs/Miss *Signor/Signora/Signorina*
Pleased to meet you (formal) *Piacere di conoscerLa*
I am English/American *Sono inglese/americano*
Irish/Scottish/Welsh *irlandese/scozzese/gallese*
Canadian/Australian *canadese/australiano*
Do you speak English? *Parla inglese?*
I'm here on holiday *Sono qui in vacanze*
Is it your first trip to Florence? *E il suo primo viaggio a Firenze?*
Do you like it here? (formal) *Si trova bene qui?*
How are you? (formal/informal) *Come sta/come stai?*
See you later *A più tardi*

Emergencies

Help! *Aiuto!*
Stop! *Fermate!*
I've had an accident *Ho avuto un incidente*
Watch out! *Attenzione!*
Call a doctor *Per favore, chiama un medico*
Call an ambulance *Chiama un'ambulanza*
Call the police *Chiama la*

Polizia/i Carabinieri
Call the fire brigade *Chiama i pompieri*
Where is the telephone? *Dov'è il telefono?*
Where is the nearest hospital? *Dov'è l'ospedale più vicino?*
I would like to report a theft *Voglio denunciare un furto*
Thank you very much for your help *Grazie dell'aiuto*

In the Hotel

Do you have any vacant rooms? *Avete camere libere?*
I have a reservation *Ho fatto una prenotazione*
I'd like... *Vorrei...*
a room with twin beds *una camera a due letti*
a single/double room (with a double bed) *una camera singola/doppia (con letto matrimoniale)*
a room with a bath/shower *una camera con bagno/doccia*
for one night *per una notte*
for two nights *per due notti*
We have one with a double bed *Ne abbiamo una matrimoniale*
Could you show me another room please? *Potrebbe mostrarmi un'altra camera?*
How much is it? *Quanto costa?*
on the first floor *al primo piano*
Is breakfast included? *E compresa la prima colazione?*
Is everything included? *E tutto compreso?*
half/full board *mezza pensione/pensione completa*
It's expensive *E caro*
Do you have a room with a balcony/view of the sea? *C'è una camera con balcone/con una vista del mare?*
a room overlooking the park/the street/the back *una camera con vista sul parco/che da sulla strada/sul retro*
Is it a quiet room? *E una stanza tranquilla?*
The room is too hot/cold/noisy/small *La camera è troppo calda/fredda/rumorosa/piccola*
Can I see the room? *Posso vedere la camera?*
What time does the hotel close? *A che ora chiude l'albergo?*

I'll take it La prendo
big/small grande/piccola
What time is breakfast? A che ora è la prima colazione?
Please give me a call at… Mi può chiamare alle…
Come in! Avanti!
Can I have the bill, please? Posso avere il conto, per favore?
Can you call me a taxi please? Può chiamarmi un tassì, per favore?
dining room la sala da pranzo
key la chiave
lift l'ascensore
towel l'asciugamano
toilet paper la carta igienica
pull/push tirare/spingere

Eating Out

Bar Snacks and Drinks
I'd like… Vorrei…
coffee un caffè (espresso: small, strong and black)
    un cappuccino (with hot, frothy milk)
    un caffelatte (like café au lait in France)
    un caffè lungo (weak, served in a tall glass)
    un corretto (laced with alcohol, probably brandy or grappa)
tea un tè
lemon tea un tè al limone
herbal tea una tisana
hot chocolate una cioccolata calda
orange/lemon juice (bottled) un succo d'arancia/di limone
fresh orange/lemon juice una spremuta di arancia/di limone
orangeade un'aranciata
water (mineral) acqua (minerale)
fizzy/still mineral water acqua minerale gasata/naturale
a glass of mineral water un bicchiere di minerale
with/without ice con/senza ghiaccio
red/white wine vino rosso/bianco
beer (draught) una birra (alla spina)
a bitter (Vermouth, etc.) un amaro
milk latte
a (half-) litre un (mezzo) litro
bottle una bottiglia

ice cream un gelato
pastry una pasta
sandwich un tramezzino
roll un panino
Anything else? Desidera qualcos'altro?
Cheers Salute
Let me pay Offro io
That's very kind of you Grazie, molto gentile

Bar Notices
Prezzo a tavola/in terrazza Price at a table/terrace (often double what you pay standing at the bar)
Si paga alla cassa Pay at the cash desk
Si prende lo scontrino alla cassa Pay at the cash desk, then take the receipt (lo scontrino) to the bar to be served – a common procedure
Signori/Uomini Gentlemen (lavatories)
Signore/Donne Ladies (lavatories)

In a Restaurant
I'd like to book a table Vorrei riservare una tavola
Have you got a table for…? Avete una tavola per…?
I have a reservation Ho fatto una prenotazione
lunch/supper il pranzo/la cena
We do not want a full meal Non desideriamo un pasto completo
Could we have another table? Potremmo spostarci?
I'm a vegetarian Sono vegetariano/a
Is there a vegetarian dish? C'è un piatto vegetariano?
May we have the menu? Un menu, per favore
wine list la lista dei vini
What would you like? Che cosa prende?
What would you recommend? Che cosa ci raccomanda?
home-made fatto in casa
What would you like as a main course/dessert? Che cosa prende di secondo/di dolce?
What would you like to drink? Che cosa desidera da bere?
a carafe of red/white wine una caraffa di vino rosso/bianco

fixed-price menu il menu a prezzo fisso
the dish of the day il piatto del giorno
VAT (sales tax) IVA
cover charge il coperto/pane e coperto
That's enough; no more, thanks Basta (così)
The bill, please Il conto, per favore
Is service included? Il servizio è incluso?
Where is the lavatory? Dov'è il bagno?
Keep the change Va bene così
I've enjoyed the meal Mi è piaciuto molto

Menu Decoder

Antipasti (hors d'oeuvres)
antipasto misto mixed hors d'oeuvres (including cold cuts, possibly cheeses and roasted vegetables – ask, however)
buffet freddo cold buffet (often excellent)
caponata mixed aubergine, olives and tomatoes
insalata caprese tomato and mozzarella salad
insalata di mare seafood salad
insalata mista/verde mixed/green salad
melanzane alla parmigiana fried or baked aubergine (with parmesan cheese and tomato)
mortadella/salame salami
pancetta bacon
peperonata grilled peppers (drenched in olive oil)

Primi (first courses)
il brodetto fish soup
il brodo consommé
i crespolini savoury pancakes
gli gnocchi dumplings made from potato or semolina
la minestra soup
il minestrone vegetable soup
pasta e fagioli pasta and bean soup
il prosciutto (cotto/crudo) ham (cooked/cured)
i suppli rice croquettes
i tartufi truffles
la zuppa soup

Secondi (main courses)

La Carne (Meat)
arrosto roast meat
al ferro grilled without oil
al forno baked
alla griglia grilled
stufato braised, stewed
ben cotto well done (steak, etc.)
al puntino medium (steak, etc.)
al sangue rare (steak, etc.)
l'agnello lamb
il bresaolo dried salted beef
la bistecca steak
il capriolo/cervo venison
il carpaccio lean beef fillet
il cinghiale wild boar
il controfiletto sirloin steak
le cotolette cutlets
il fagiano pheasant
il fegato liver
il fileto fillet
il maiale pork
il manzo beef
l'ossobuco shin of veal
il pollo chicken
le polpette meatballs
il polpettone meat loaf
la porchetta roast suckling pig
la salsiccia sausage
il saltimbocca (alla romana) veal escalopes with ham
le scaloppine escalopes
lo stufato stew
il sugo sauce
la trippa tripe
il vitello veal

Frutti di Mare (Seafood)
Beware the word *surgelati*, meaning frozen.
affumicato smoked
alle brace charcoal-grilled
alla griglia grilled
fritto fried
ripieno stuffed
al vapore steamed
le acciughe anchovies
l'anguilla eel
l'aragosto lobster
i bianchetti whitebait
il branzino sea bass
i calamaretti baby squid
i calamari squid
la carpa carp
i crostacei shellfish
le cozze mussels
il fritto misto mixed fried fish

i gamberetti shrimps
i gamberi prawns
il granchio crab
il merluzzo cod
le molecche soft-shelled crabs
le ostriche oysters
il pesce fish
il pesce spada swordfish
il polipo octopus
il risotto di mare seafood risotto
le sarde sardines
la sogliola sole
le seppie cuttlefish
il tonno tuna
la triglia red mullet
la trota trout
le vongole clams

I Legumi/La Verdura (Vegetables)
a scelta of your choice
i contorni accompaniments
ripieno stuffed
gli asparagi asparagus
la bietola similar to spinach
i carciofini artichoke hearts
il carciofo artichoke
le carote carrots
il cavolo cabbage
la cicoria chicory
la cipolla onion
i funghi mushrooms
i fagioli beans
i fagiolini French (green) beans
le fave broad beans
il finocchio fennel
l'indivia endive/chicory
l'insalata mista mixed salad
l'insalata verde green salad
la melanzana aubergine
le patate potatoes
le patatine fritte chips
i peperoni peppers
i piselli peas
i pomodori tomatoes
le primizie spring vegetables
il radicchio red, slightly bitter lettuce
i ravanelli radishes
la rucola rocket
gli spinaci spinach
la verdura green vegetables
la zucca pumpkin/squash
gli zucchini courgettes

I Dolci (Desserts)
al carrello from the trolley
un semifreddo semi-frozen

dessert (many types)
la bavarese mousse
la cassata Sicilian ice cream with candied peel
le fritelle fritters
un gelato (di lampone/limone) (raspberry/lemon) ice cream
una granita water ice
una macedonia di frutta fruit salad
il tartufo (nero) (chocolate) ice-cream dessert
il tiramisù cold, creamy rum-and-coffee dessert
la torta cake/tart
lo zabaglione sweet dessert of eggs and Marsala wine
lo zuccotto ice-cream liqueur
la zuppa inglese trifle

La Frutta (Fruit)
l'albicocca apricot
l'arancia orange
le ciliege cherries
il cocomero watermelon
i fichi figs
le fragole strawberries
i frutti di bosco berries
i lamponi raspberries
la mela apple
il melone melon
la pera pear
la pesca peach
il pompelmo grapefruit
le uve grapes

Basic foods
l'aceto vinegar
l'aglio garlic
il burro butter
la focaccia bread made with olive oil and herbs
il formaggio cheese
la frittata omelette
la grana/il parmigiano parmesan cheese
i grissini bread sticks
la marmellata jam
l'olio oil
il pane bread
il pane integrale wholemeal bread
il pepe pepper
il riso rice
il sale salt
la senape mustard
le uova eggs
lo zucchero sugar

FURTHER READING

General

Italy, Tuscany and Florence have inspired a huge number of books of all genres – below is just a small selection. Italian Touring Club regional guides and maps are available from **Stanfords**, 12–14 Long Acre, Covent Garden, London WC2E 9LP; tel: 020-7836 1321; and online at www.stanfords.co.uk.

Other Insight Guides include our regional guides to Tuscany and Northern Italy, while Berlitz publishes guides to Florence, and Tuscany and Umbria.

Art and Architecture

Much has been written on the art and architecture of Florence. A good reading list would include: Giorgio Vasari, *Lives of the Most Excellent Painters, Sculptors and Architects* (1568 and later editions); Benvenuto Cellini, *Autobiography* (1562 and later editions); C. Avery, *Florentine Renaissance Sculpture* (J. Murray, 1970); M. Baxandall, *Painting and Experience in Fifteenth-Century Florence* (Oxford, 1972); J. Beck, *Italian Renaissance Painting* (Konemann, 1999); A. Blunt, *Artistic Theory in Italy 1450–1600* (Oxford, 1940, and later editions); J. Burckhardt, *The Civilisation of the Renaissance in Italy* (Phaidon, 1944, and later editions); S. Greedberg, *Painting in Italy 1500–1600* (Yale, 1993); J. White, *Art and Architecture in Italy 1250–1400* (Yale, 1993); and R. Wittkower, *Art and Architecture in Italy 1600–1750* (Yale, 1982).
The Architecture of the Italian Renaissance. Peter Murray (Schocken, 1997). Originally published in 1967, this volume by a professor of Birkbeck College, London, remains the classic guide to art and architecture of the Renaissance period.
Autobiography. Benvenuto Cellini (Penguin Classics, 1999). The troubled life of the Florentine artist gives an insight into life in the Renaissance period.
Brunelleschi's Dome: The Story of a Great Cathedral in Florence. Ross King (Pimlico, 2005). This book charts one of the greatest architectural feats ever to have been accomplished – the dome of Santa Maria del Fiore cathedral – and its creator.
Florence: The City & Its Architecture. Richard Goy (Phaidon, 2002). Organised thematically as opposed to chronologically, this is a modern account of the history, culture, politics and art of Florence. Includes drawings and photographs.
The Florentine Renaissance. Vincent Cronin (Pimlico, 1992). A comprehensive guide to the years of the Renaissance and its intellectual output.
Italian Architecture from Michelangelo to Borromini. Antony Hopkins (Thames & Hudson, 2002). Tracking the artistic period from the High Renaissance through Mannerism to Baroque, this helps explain the background to much of Florence's artistic patrimony.
The Italian Painters of the Renaissance. Bernard Berenson (Phaidon, 1968). Hard to find, the essays in this book provide a good guide to a number of important figures in Italian art, including Caravaggio and Giotto.
Lives of the Artists: Volumes 1 and 2. Giorgio Vasari (Oxford World's Classics, 1998). An account of the lives of many important figures in Florentine art by the figure renowned for the corridor linking the Palazzo Vecchio to Palazzo Pitti via the Uffizi.
Villas of Tuscany. Carlo Cresti & Massimo Listri (I.B. Tauris and Co., 2003). Writing and photographs about Tuscan houses, including the Medici villas around Florence, designed by masters such as Buontalenti.

Culture and History

The City of Florence: Historical Vistas and Personal Sightings. R.W.B. Lewis (Henry Holt and Co., 1996). A personal view on Florence and its legacy – the perfect travel companion.
The Civilisation of the Renaissance in Italy. Jacob Burckhardt (Penguin, 1990). Published in 1860, this was a defining work in the study of the Italian Renaissance. It remains an illuminating account of the myriad developments of the era.
Dark Water: Art, Disaster and Redemption in Florence. Robert

Clark (Anchor, 2009). Gripping description of the floods which ravaged Florence in 1966 – and the aftermath.

Florence: The Biography of a City. Christopher Hibbert (Penguin, 1994). This book weaves together the history and culture of Florence, with photographs and illustrations to make the narrative come to life.

Italians. David Willey (BBC Publications, 1984). Although now slightly out of date, this provides a colourful portrait of the Italian people.

The Italians. Luigi Barzini (Penguin, 1991). Originally published in the sixties, this is still worthwhile reading for the frankness of Barzini's portrait of his fellow countrymen.

Medici Money: Banking, Metaphysics and Art in 15th century Florence. Tim Parks (Enterprise 2005). Fascinating account of the rise and fall of the Medici bank, and thus of the famous dynasty.

The Oxford Illustrated History of Italy. George Holmes (Oxford, 2001). An extensive, though concise, insight into Italy's colourful past for those who want a deeper understanding of the country as a whole.

The Rise and Fall of the House of Medici. Christopher Hibbert (Penguin, 1979). By an author who has written extensively on Florence, this book provides a witty insight into the dynasty which ruled Florence and is responsible for gathering much of the art to be found there today.

Tuscany and Its Wines. Hugh Johnson and Andy Katz (Chronicle Books, 2005). Providing a guide to the best wines in the region, with stunning pictures by photographer Andy Katz.

Literature

A Room with a View. E.M. Forster (Penguin Classics, 2000). Classic novel and social study of the English holidaying in Florence.
The Da Vinci Code. Dan Brown (Corgi, 2004). This best-selling thriller is based in Western

history and includes interesting titbits relevant to Italy and Florence.

D.H. Lawrence and Italy. D.H. Lawrence (Penguin, 1997). Three books based on Lawrence's journals during his travels in Italy which make an interesting travel companion.

The Enchantress of Florence. Salmon Rushdie (Vintage, 2009). A rich blend of history, folly and fantasy where East (Mogul India) meets West (Renaissance Florence).

Florence Explored. Rupert Scott. (New Amsterdam Books, 1990). A great little book, which is presented through a series of walks around the city.

Italian Hours. Henry James. (Penguin Classics, 1995). Essays on 19th-century travel in Italy by another classic author.

Love and War in the Apennines. Eric Newby (Hodder & Stoughton, 1971). A story of the escape of a

FEEDBACK

We do our best to ensure the information in our books is as accurate and up-to-date as possible. The books are updated on a regular basis, using local contacts. However, some mistakes and omissions are inevitable, and we are reliant on our readers to put us in the picture.

We welcome your feedback on any details related to your experiences using the book "on the road". Maybe we recommended a hotel you liked, or you found a new attraction. We will acknowledge all contributions, and we'll offer an Insight Guide to the best letters received.

Please write to us at:
Insight Guides
PO Box 7910
London SE1 1WE
United Kingdom
Or send email to:
insight@apaguide.co.uk

British prisoner of war in Italy during World War II.

Pictures from Italy. Charles Dickens (Penguin Classics, 1998). A travelogue of Dickens's tour of Italy, which he took during a break from writing.

The Prince. Niccolò Machiavelli (Oxford World's Classics, 2005). Translation by Peter Bondanella of Machiavelli's classic treatise on power in the Renaissance.

The Stones of Florence. Mary McCarthy (Penguin, 2000). An accessible introduction to art history and Florence.

A Traveller's Companion to Florence. Harold Acton and Edward Chaney Eds (Interlink, 2002). A guide to Florence based on letters, memoirs etc. from renowned Florentine personalities.

War in the Val d'Orcia. Iris Origo (HarperCollins, 2002). A true story of civilian life in Tuscany during World War II.

Films

The following English-language films are set in or around Florence and show the area in its full glory:
A Room with a View (1985, directed by James Ivory) An acclaimed adaptation of the novel by E.M. Forster starring Maggie Smith, Helena Bonham-Carter and Simon Callow.

Tea with Mussolini (1999, directed by Franco Zefferelli) Starring Judi Dench and Maggie Smith, the film charts the life of a boy left in the care of a millionairess and three eccentric British women in Florence during the Fascist occupation of Italy.

Under the Tuscan Sun (2003, directed by Audrey Wells) The story of a woman in search of a new life in Tuscany.

Italian cinema has also produced some classic films (Cinema Paradiso, La Dolce Vita, La Vita è Bella), actors and actresses (Sophia Loren, Monica Bellucci) and directors (Franco Zefferelli, Federico Fellini). The most famous films can be found subtitled.

ART AND PHOTO CREDITS

All photography Britta Jaschinski/ Apa except the following:

Alamy 220
Alinari Picture Library 38T & B
Art Archive 29T, 30TR, 31B, 32B, 34T, 43BL, 44CR, 60, 64TL, 68, 89T, 107BL, 126BL, 127B, 226TR
akg-images 12TL, 28BL, 61, 64TR, 66TL & TR, 69B, 70T & B, 71TL & TR, 138T, 161T
Bridgeman Art Library 9TR, 10CT, 10TR, 28TR, 30TL, 30B, 31T, 33T, 36TR, 37T, 43TR & TL, 45CL, 63TL, 63BR, 67TL, 67B, 69T, 91B, 95B, 140T, 141T, 168B, 173, 178T
Chris Coe 156T, 164T
Esteve Cohen 104T
Corbis 8R, 13BR, 35TR, 35B, 39B, 40TR, 43CR, 106T, 110B
Jerry Dennis/Apa 8TR, 9CR, 12TR, 12B, 37B, 62T, 77B, 80, 86, 91TR, 96TL, 126T, 126BR, 129T, 131T, 142BR, 153B, 164C, 175T, 190B, 278, 279BL, 280T
4Corners 108T
Guglielmo Galvin & George Taylor/Apa 250C
Getty Images 36B, 40B, 41, 45T, 45B, 131B
Frances Gransden/Apa 27, 32TR
Albano Guatti 35TL, 127T, 153T, 223B, 245B
Herbert Hartmann 72TR, 144B, 154B, 165B
Hemis 228B
John Heseltine 130TL
Hans Höfer 26

Mary Evans Picture Library 35TL, 44TL, 111C
Anna Mockford & Nick Bonnetti/ Apa 1, 7all, 8BR, 9TL, 10BL, 11BR, 14/15, 16/17, 46/47, 49, 54TL, 55, 62B, 63TL, 87, 88TL, 88CR, 92C, 93T, 98, 99, 101T & B, 102B, 104B, 105T & B, 106B, 108B, 121, 124T, 125all, 136, 144T, 147B, 148, 149, 155T, 160BL, 165TR, 174BL, 174CR, 177T, 180T & B, 181B, 189T, 192T, 200, 201, 215T, 221, 225TL, 238/239, 240, 241, 242, 243T & B, 244T & B, 245T, 246B, 247, 248all, 249T & B, 250B, 251all, 252all, 253all, 254all, 255B & CL, 280B, 282B
National Portrait Gallery 167B
PA Photos 40TL
Pisa Tourist Office 255TR
Andrea Pistolesi 139T, 163T
Rex Features 76/77, 124B
Robert Harding Picture Library 120
Alessandra Santarelli/Apa 51T, 52CR, 52B, 53, 155B, 169T, 207TR & TL
Scala 112T
Topfoto 39T
Werner Forman Archive 28TL

PHOTO FEATURES

Pages 56–9: all images by Britta Jaschinski/Apa except Alessandra Santarelli 59CB
Pages 74–5: Mary Evans Picture Library 74TL; Getty Images 74BL; Corbis 74CR, 74BR; Rex Features 74/75T, 75TR; Kobal 75BL

Pages 114–19: akg-images 114B, 115B, 116TL, 116BL, 117TR; Art Archive 114/115T, 115CT & TR; Bridgeman Art Library 114BR, 115CL, 117CR; Corbis 116CR; 4Corners 118/119T; Anna Mockford & Nick Bonetti/Apa 118B; Scala 118TL, 119BL & BR
Pages 126–127: akg-images 127BL; Art Archive 126CL, 127TR; Bridgeman Art Library 126/127T; Corbis 127BR; Jerry Dennis/Apa 126BR
Pages 170–71: akg-images 170CL; Bridgeman Art Library 171CL, 171B; Corbis 170TR, 171T, 171C
Pages 194–7: akg-images 194TL, 196BR, 197CL, 197BR; Art Archive 194/195B 197TR, 195TL; Bridgeman Art Library 195TR 196CL; Anna Mockford & Nick Bonetti/Apa 194CR
Pages 198–9: Jerry Dennis/Apa 199CR, 199BL; Anna Mockford & Nick Bonetti/Apa 198TL
Pages 216–17: all images by Anna Mockford & Nick Bonetti/Apa
Pages 236–7: Alamy 237BL & BR; 4Corners 236BL; Foto 236CR; Getty Images 236/237T; Hemis 237TR

Map Production: original cartography Berndtson and Berndtson, updated by Phoenix Mapping and Apa cartography department

©2011 Apa Publications GmbH & Co. Verlag KG, Singapore Branch

Production: Tynan Dean, Linton Donaldson, Rebeka Ellam, Mary Pickles

FLORENCE STREET ATLAS

The key map shows the area of Florence covered by the atlas
section. An index of street names and places of interest
shown on the maps can be found on the following pages.
For each entry there is a page number and grid reference.

Map Legend

Autostrada with Junction	Airport	Autostrada	Bus Station
Autostrada (under construction)	Church (ruins)	Dual Carriageway	Tourist Information
Dual Carriageway	Monastery	Main Roads	Post Office
Main Road	Castle (ruins)		Cathedral/Church
Secondary Road	Archaeological Site	Minor Roads	Mosque
Minor Road	Cave		Synagogue
Track	Place of Interest	Footpath	Statue/Monument
International Boundary	Mansion/Stately Home	Railway	Tower
State Boundary	Viewpoint	Pedestrian Area	Lighthouse
National Park/Reserve	Beach	Important Building	Tramvia
Ferry Route		Park	

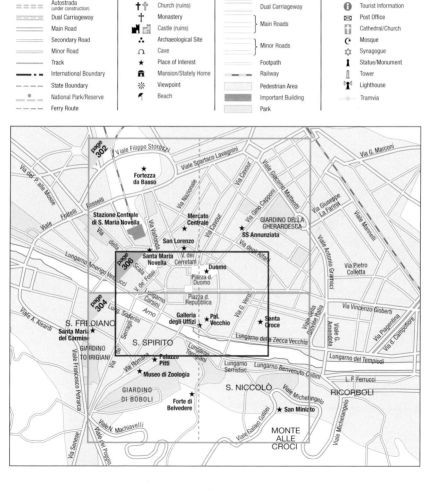

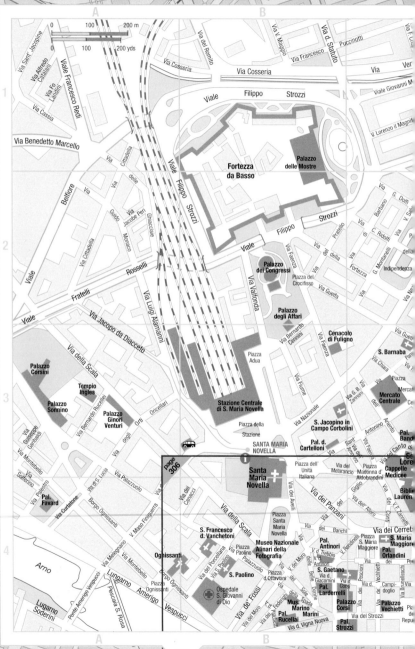

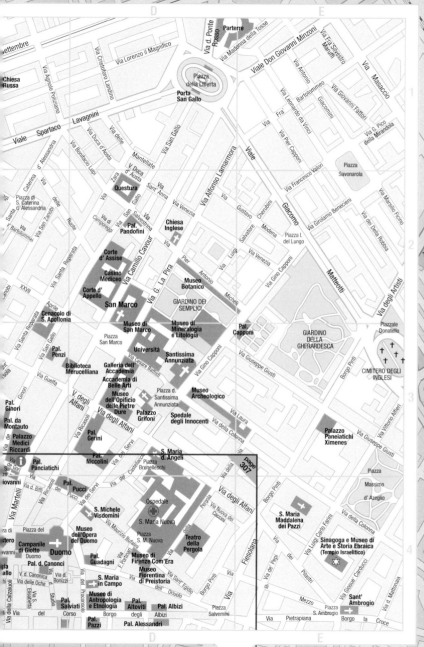

Parterre

Via d. Ponte Rosso

Via Lorenzo il Magnifico

Via Cristoforo Landino

Viale Don Giovanni Minzoni

Via Madonna della Tosse

Via Fra' Silvestro Maruffi

Via Antonio

Via Giovanni Fattori

Via Masaccio

Chiesa Russa

Via Agnolo Poliziano

Piazza della Libertà

Porta San Gallo

Via Bartolommeo

Via Leonardo da Vinci

Giacomini

Via G. Pico della Mirandola

Viale Spartaco Lavagnini

Via delle

Via Duca d'Aosta

Via San Gallo

Via Pier Cappони

Via Francesco Valori

Via Girolamo Benecieni

Via Marsilio Ficino

Via d' Alessandria

Via Bonifacio Lupi

Mantellate

Via Duca d'Aosta

Via Sant' Anna

Via Alfonso Lamarmora

Viale

Via Della Robbia

Piazza di S. Caterina d' Alessandria

Santa

F. Bartolommei

Via Sant Zanobi

Via delle

Ruote

Via di Camporeggi

Via San Gallo

Salvestrina

Questura

Pal. Pandofini

Chiesa Inglese

Via Venezia

Gustavo

Cherubini

Salvatore

Modena

Piazza I. del Lungo

Via degli Artisti

igi

XXVII

Via Santa Reparata

Via San Zanobi

Corte d' Assise

Via Camillo Cavour

Via G. La Pira

Pier

Antonio

Via Luigi

Via Venezia

Via Gino Capponi

Matteotti

Casino Mediceo

Museo Botanico

Michell

Cenacolo di S. Apollonia

Corte d' Appello

San Marco

GIARDINO DEI SEMPLICI

GIARDINO DELLA GHERARDESCA

Piazzale Donatello

Via Santa Reparata

Aprile

Via San Gallo

Pal. Penzi

Piazza San Marco

Museo di San Marco

Museo di Mineralogia e Litologia

Pal. Capponi

CIMITERO DEGLI INGLESI

Via degli Alfani

Via Guelfa

Biblioteca Merucelliana

Galleria dell' Accademia

Università

Via Cesare Battisti

Santissima Annunziata

Via Gino Capponi

Via Giuseppe Giusti

Borgo Pinti

Via Vittorio Alfieri

Pal. Ginori

V. degli Alfani

Accademia di Belle Arti

Museo dell'Opificio delle Pietre Dure

Piazza d. Santissima Annunziata

Museo Archeologico

Via Giuseppe Giusti

Pal. da Montauto

Via Ricasoli

Palazzo Grifoni

Spedale degli Innocenti

Via della Colonna

Via Laura

Palazzo Paneiatichi Ximenes

Piazza Massimo d' Azeglio

Palazzo Medici Riccardi

Pal. Gerini

Pal. Niccolini

Via dei Servi

S. Maria d. Angeli

page 307

Via degli Alfani

Borgo Pinti

S. Maria Maddalena dei Pazzi

Via Martelli

Pal. Panciatichi

Via Ricasoli

Piazza Brunelleschi

Via della

Via Nuova dei Caccini

Via Luigi Carlo Farini

Via della Colonna

Via de Gori

iovanni

Pal. Pucci

Via de' Pucci

Via dei Servi

Ospedale

Pergola

Piazza

Sinagoga e Museo di Arte e Storia Ebraica (Tempio Israelitico)

Via de' Biffi

S. Michele Visdomini

Via Maurizio Bufalini

S. Maria Nuova

Fiesolana

Via de' Pepi

Via de' Pilastri

ta di

Museo dell'Opera del Duomo

Piazza S.M. Nuova

Teatro della Pergola

stero

Campanile di Giotto

Duomo

Pal. Guadagni

Museo di Firenze Com'Era

Via Sant' Egidio

Borgo Pinti

Sant' Ambrogio

Via della Matтonaia

Pal. d. Canonici

S. Maria in Campo

Museo Fiorentina di Preistoria

dell' Oriuolo

Piazza Salvemini

Piazza S. Ambrogio

V. d. Canonica

Via delle Oche

Via d. Bonizzi

Museo di Antropologia e Etnologia

Pal. Altoviti

Pal. Albizi

Mezzo

Via della Calzaiuoli

Studio

Via Elisabetta

Pal. Salviati

Borgo

degli

Albizi

Via Pietrapiana

Borgo

la

Croce

della

del

Corso

Pal. Pazzi

Pal. Alessandri

A B

Via L. Bartolini
Via Sant'Onofrio
Via d. Tiratoio
Via del Piaggione
Piazza del Tiratoio
Via d.

Piazza di
Cestello

Lugarno Soderini

Piazza
C. Goldoni

Via della Vigna Nuova
Via d. Purgatorio
Via d. Tornabuoni

Pal.
Giaconi

Pal.
Strozzi

V. degli
Anselmi

Pal.
Strozzino

Pal.
Altovita

Pal. Pellicceria
Part
Gue

Pal.
Davanzati

Borgo San Frediano
Via dei
Cardatori

Via d. Serragli
Via di Cestello

San Frediano
in Cestello

Palazzo
Corsini

del

Lungarno

Via
Porta

delle
terme

1

Piazza
dei
Nerli

Via del Drago d'Oro
Via del Lione

Borgo San Frediano

Via N. Sauro
Ponte alla Carraia

Corsini

S. Trinità

Pal.
Spini
Ferroni

Borgo

Santissimi
Apostoli

Lungarno

Via del

C. Corso
Sant'Apostoli

Acciaioli

Lung

Via dell'Orto
Via dei Tessitori
Via della

Borgo Stella

Lungarno Guicciardini

Pte S. Trinità

Ponte
Vecchio

Piazza
Piattellina

Piazza
del Carmine

Borgo Stella

Chiesa
Scozzese

Palazzo
Guicciardini

Piazza
Frescobaldi

Pal.
Frescobaldi

S. Jacopo
Soprarno

Corridoio Vasariano
Via Lambertesca

V. dei Bardi

Santa
Monaca

Via Santa Monaca

S. SPIRITO

Santo Spirito

Borgo

San Jacopo

V. dei Marsigliani

Piazza S.
Felicità

Cappella
Brancacci

Via dell'Ardiglione

Via Maffia

Via S. Agostino

Santo
Spirito

V. d'Presto di S. Martino

V. Mazzo

Pal. R.
Firidolfi

Via dei Velluti

V. di Toscanella

Santa
Felicità

Santa Maria
del Carmine

Pal.
Rosselli
Casa
di Bianca

Via del
Michelozzi

V. Sguazza

Pal.
Ridolfi

Via Toscanella

Via de' Guicciardini

Costa

2

Via della Chiesa
S. FREDIANO

Via Maffia

Piazza
Santo
Spirito

Via Mazzetta

V. del Presto
Fretti

Pal.
Corsini

V. del Maggio

Pal.
Guadagni

Palazzo
Guicciardini

S.
Girola

Via del Campuccio

Via dei

Via d'Chiesa

Via delle Caldaie

Piazza
de' Pitti

Grotta di
Buontalenti

Si

Viale

GIARDINO
TORRIGIANI

Via del

Via delle Caldaie

S.
Felice

Piazza
San Felice

Palazzo Pitti
(Galleria Palatina)

Sp

Vic

Borgo Tegolaio

Santa
Maria

Via Romana

Museo Zoologia
(La Specola)

Palazzina della
Meridiana

Ampitheatre

Forte
di Belve

Via Serumido
Via Mori

Via del Ronco

Fontana di
Nettuno

(San Gior

3

Francesco

Via de' Serragli

Via Romana

GIARDINO DI

BOBOLI

Abundance

GIARDINO DEL
CAVALIERE

Museo delle
Porcellane

Petrarca

Fontana
dell
Oceano

Viottolone

Via del Bobolino

Piazza
della Calza

Porta Romana

Piazzale
di
Porta Romana

Via Madonna della Pace

Via del Macherno

Via del Bobolino

Viale Niccolò Machiavelli

Instituto
d'Arte

Via del Belvedere

Via del Bobolino

Villa il
Gioiello

4

Via Sense

Via Cantagalli

Viale del Poggio

Via Farinata degli Uberti

Via Michele di Lando

Via Dante da Castiglione

BOBOLINO

Viale Niccolò Machiavelli

Grand Hotel
Villa Cora

A B

page
306

303

Calzaiuoli

Via del Presto

Orsanmichele

Via dei Magazzini
Via Dante Alighieri
Via dei Cimatori
Via della Condotta

Pal. Pazzi

Badia Fiorentina

Bargello

Via Ghibellina

Pal. Uguccioni
Pal. Gondi
Via d. Gondi

S. Firenze

Piazza della Signoria

Loggia dei Lanzi

Palazzo Vecchio

Via d. Ninna

Uffizi

degli Uffizi

Via di Castello

Via dei Neri

Museo Galileo

Pal. Vita

Loggia d. Grano

Piazza d. Giudici

Borsa

Pal. Bardi Serzelli

Lungarno G. Armando Diaz

Palazzo Mannelli

Palazzo Capponi

Torrigiani

Ponte alle Grazie

Lungarno delle Grazie

Pal. Alberti

Lungarno delle Grazie

Arno

Costa Scarpuccia

S. Lucia d. Magnoli

Lungarno

Palazzo Torrigiani

Museo Bardini

Palazzo Alamanni

Costa di San Giorgio

Palazzo dei Mozzi

S. NICCOLÒ

Via di San Niccolò

Via di Giardino Serristori

San Niccolò

GIARDINO BARDINI

Via di Belvedere

Porta San Miniato

Via di Belvedere

Via di Belvedere

Giorgio

Pal. Pazzi

Pal. Alessandri

Casino Borghese

Via dei Pandolfini

Via Ghibellina

Pal. di Cintoia

Pal. Quaratesi

S. Nicolò

Teatro Verdi

Via Ghibellina

S. Simone

V. d. Burella

Casa Buonarroti

Via delle Pinzochere

V. d. Vanzetta

Pal. Serristori

Piazza Santa Croce

Casa dell' Antella

Borgo Santa Croce

Casa d. Peruzzi

Via dei Benci

Pal. Vita

Pal. Corsini

Museo Horne

Corso dei Tintori

Pal. Rasponi

Santa Croce

Cappella de' Pazzi

Museo dell'Opera di Santa Croce

Biblioteca Nazionale

Piazza dei Cavalleggeri

Via Tripoli

Lungarno delle Zecca Vecchia

Via del Macci

Piazza dei Ciompi

Piazza dei Martiri del Popolo

Via dell' Ulivo

Via dei Macci

Borgo Allegri

Mercato di Sant' Ambrogio

Ghiberti

Carceri S. Verdiana

Via dell' Agnolo

Carceri della Murate

Via Ghibellina

Via dei Conciatori

Via delle Casine

Via Pietro Thouar

Via delle Casine

Via dei Malcontenti

Via Tripoli

Piazza Piave

Lungarno delle Zecca Vecchia

page 307

Pescaia S. Niccolò

Lungarno Benvenuto Cellini

Piazza N. Demidoff

Via dei Renai

Pal. Serristori

Serristori

Via di Olmo

Piazza Giuseppe Poggi

Porta San Niccolò

Via dei Bastioni

Viale Giuseppe Poggi

Viale Giuseppe Poggi

Piazzale Michelangelo

Viale Michelangelo

San Salvatore

Bellavista

Viuzzo d. Corti

Via di San Miniato al Monte

MONTE ALLE CROCI

Convento delle Stimmatine

Via dell' Erta Canina

Via d. Salvatore al Monte

Viale Galileo

Viale Galileo

San Leonardo

San Miniato

CIMITERO DELLE PORTE SANTE

V. Giramontino

Villa Franchi

Passo all' Erta

Via Giramontino

| | 100 | 200 m |
| 0 | 100 | 200 yds |

302

A   B

1

Santa Maria Novella

Piazza dell' Unità Italiana

Via del Melarancio

Piazza Madonna d. Aldobrandini

San Lore

Bibliote Laurenzi

Via dei Panzani

Via del Giglio

Via dell'Alloro

Via de' Conti

V.E. Zannetti

Via dei Avelli

Via della Scala

Piazza Santa Maria Novella

Via dei Banchi

Via dei Cerretani

S. Francesco d. Vanchetoni

Museo Nazionale Alinari della Fotografia

Piazza Paolino

Via del Moro

Piazza S. Maria Maggiore

S. Maria Maggiore

Pa

Ognissanti

Via del Porcellana

Via S. Paolino

Piazzuolo

V. d. Trebbio

V. d. Antinori

Palazzo Antinori

Palazzo Orlandini

dell'Arcivesco

Piazza Ognissanti

S. Paolino

Piazza d. Ottaviani

Belle Donne

V. d. Giacomini

S. Gaetano

Via d. Corsi

Via d. Pecori

2

Lungarno Amerigo Vespucci

Borgo Ognissanti

Ospedale S. Giovanni di Dio

Via de' Fossi

Via del Moro

Via della Sole

Via della Spada

Mus. Marino Marini

Palazzo Larderrelli

Palazzo Corsi

Campidoglio

Piazza della Republic

Via d. Federighi

V. d. Palchetti

Palazzo Rucellai

Palazzo Vechietti

Via della Vigna Nuova

Via del Strozzi

Piazza C. Goldoni

Via d. Purgatorio

Palazzo Giaconi

Palazzo Strozzi

Via d. Anselmi

Palazzo Strozzino

Post e Telegrafi

Via del Parione

Parione

Palazzo Altovita

Lungarno Corsini

Palazzo Corsini

Ponte alla Carraia

Lungarno

Porta

Via d. Terme

Palazzo Bartolini-Salimbeni

Palazzo Davanzati

3

Lugarno Soderini

Piazza N. Sauro

Lungarno Guicciardini

Chiesa Scozzese

Via dei Leoni

S. Trinità

Piazza S. Trinità

Palazzo Spini Ferroni

Lungarno Acciaioli

Palazzo di Parte Guelfa

Via Por S.

V. rt. Bombarda

C. d. Comune

Santi Apostoli

Santissimi Apostoli

Arno

Via de' Serragli

Via Maffia

Palazzo Guicciardini

Via Santo Spirito

Piazza Frescobaldi

Palazzo Frescobaldi

Ponte Vecchio

Lungar

Corridoio Vasariano

Via d. Coverelli

S. Jacopo Soprarno

4

S. SPIRITO

Santo Spirito

Via del Prato di S. Martino

Palazzo R. Firidolfi

V. Maggio

Via dello Sprone

Via Toscanella

San Jacopo

Borgo

V. dei Ramaglianti

V. dei Bardi

Piazza S. Maria Soprarno

Palazzo Rodolfi

V. d. Vellutini

Casa di Bianca

Via S. Squazza

Via dei Velluti

Piazza S. Felicita

Santa Felicità

Costa

di

Via Sant'Agostino

Piazza Santo Spirito

Via dei Michelozzi

Palazzo Ridolfi

Via Toscanella

Via de' Guicciardini

Velluti

S. Giorgio

Borgo Tegolaio

Sdr. de' Pitti

Palazzo Corsini

Palazzo Guicciardini

Santa Girolamo

Via Maggio

Palazzo Guadagni

A   B

304

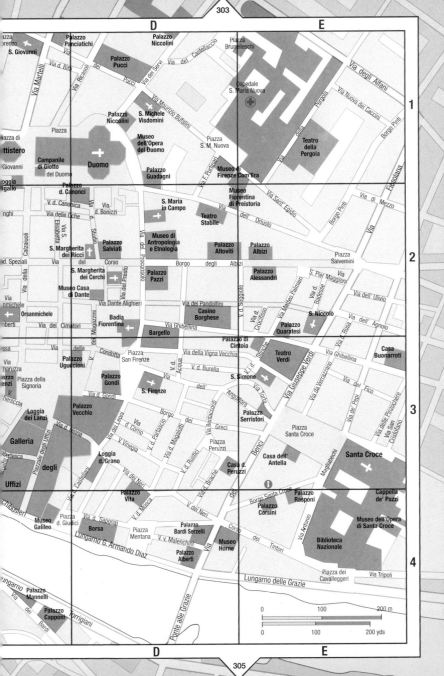

303

S. Giovanni
Palazzo Panciatichi
Palazzo Niccolini
Piazza Brunelleschi
Via degli Alfani

Via Martelli
Via di Birri
Palazzo Pucci
Via de' Servi
Via del Castellaccio
Via Nuova dei Caccini
Borgo Pinti

Via Ricasoli
Via de' Pucci
Ospedale S. Maria Nuova

Via Maurizio Bufalini
Via della Pergola
Fiesolana

Piazza
Palazzo Niccolini
S. Michele Visdomini
Museo dell'Opera del Duomo
Piazza S. M. Nuova
Teatro della Pergola

Campanile di Giotto
del Duomo
Duomo
Palazzo Guadagni
Via F. Portinari
Museo di Firenze Com'Era

Loggia
gallo
Palazzo d. Canonci
Museo Fiorentina di Preistoria
Via Sant' Egidio
Via di Mezzo

V. d. Canonica
Via d. Bonizzi
S. Maria in Campo
dell' Oriuolo
Borgo Pinti
Via

nghi
Via delle Oche
Teatro Stabile

Calzaiuoli
Via S. Elisabetta
Museo di Antropologia e Etnologia
Palazzo Altoviti
Palazzo Albizi
Piazza Salvemini

d. Speziali
S. Margherita dei Ricci
Palazzo Salviati
Via dello Studio
Via del Corso
Borgo degli Albizi
S. Pier Maggiore
Via

Via della
S. Margherita dei Cerchi
Palazzo Pazzi
Palazzo Alessandri
Via d. Badesse
Via dell' Ulivio

Via nmichele
Museo Casa di Dante
Via del Presto
Via Dante Alighieri
Via dei Pandolfini
Via Matteo Palmieri
Via d. Saggione
S. Niccolò
Via dell' Agnolo

Orsanmichele
Via Magazzini
Casino Borghese
Via Ghibellina
Via d. Crocifisso
Palazzo Quaratesi
Via M. Rosa

lberti
Via dei Cimatori
Badia Fiorentina
Bargello
Palazzo di Cintoia

ssa
Via della
Condotta
Palazzo Uguccioni
Piazza San Firenze
Via della Vigna Vecchia
V. d. Acqua
V. d. Burella
Teatro Verdi
Via Ghibellina
Casa Buonarroti

Via maruzza
Palazzo Gondi
Via d. Gondi
Via dell'
S. Simone
Via Torta
Via Giuseppe Verdi
Via da Verrazzano
Via de' Pepi
Via della Prandchiere

lazzo enzi
Piazza della Signoria
S. Firenze
Via dell' Anguillara
Palazzo Serristori
Piazza Santa Croce
Via San Cristoforo

hereccia
Palazzo Vecchio
Via de' Leoni
Via del Corno
Borgo dei Greci
Via de' Benci

Loggia dei Lanzi
Via d. Ninna
V. d. Parlascio
V. d. Rustici
Piazza Peruzzi
Casa dell' Antella
Santa Croce

Galleria
V. Vinegia
Via de' Neri
Via Bentaccordi
Magliabechi

bertesca
degli
Loggia d. Grano
Casa d. Peruzzi
Cappella de' Pazzi

Uffizi
Piazzale degli Uffizi
Palazzo Vita
Via d. Castellani
Via de' Neri
Borgo Santa Croce
Palazzo Rasponi
Museo dell'Opera di Santa Croce

chibusteri
Museo Galileo
Piazza d. Giudici
Borsa
Via d. Saponai
V. d. Mosca
Piazza Mentana
V. v. Malenchini
Palazzo Bardi Serzelli
Corso
dei
Tintori
Palazzo Corsini
Via Antonio
Biblioteca Nazionale
Via Tripoli

Lungarno G. Armando Diaz
Palazzo Alberti
Museo Horne
Piazza dei Cavalleggeri

ungarno
Palazzo Mannelli
Ponte alle Grazie
Lungarno delle Grazie

Palazzo Capponi
Torrigiani
Via de' Bardi

0   100   200 m
0   100   200 yds

305

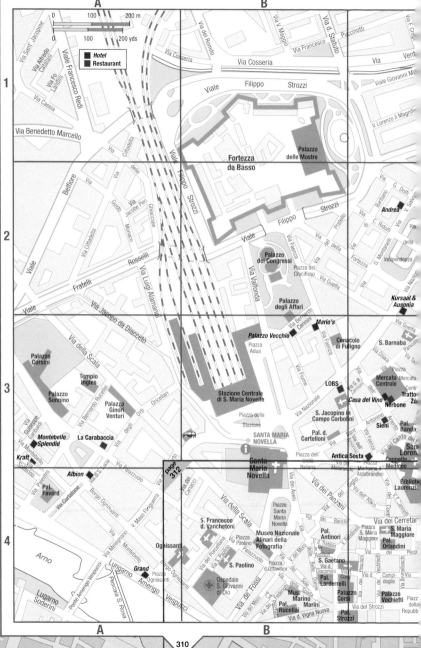

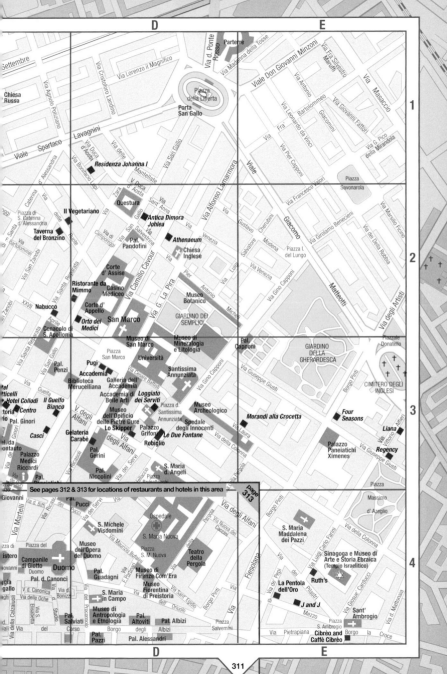

A

Via Bartolini
Via di Tiratoio
Via Sant'Onofrio
Via d' Pignone
Via d'Tiratoio
Antico Ristoro di' Cambi
Piazza del Tiratoio
Piazza di Cestello
Borgo San Frediano
Via del Lardatori
Via del Castello
San Frediano in Cestello

Lungarno Soderini

B

Piazza C. Goldoni
Via della Vigna Nuova
Pal. Giaconi
Pal. Strozzi
Via d. Anselmi
Via d' Purgatorio
Pal. Strozzino
Via d. Tornabuoni
Palazzo Corsini
Pal. Altovita
Via d. Pellicceria
Porta
Pal. Davanzati
Borgo della Parione
S. Trinita
Lungarno Corsini
Pal. Spini Ferroni
Pte S. Trinita
Santissimi Apostoli
C.d. Parte Guelf
Terme

1

Via del Leone
Borgo San Frediano
Borgo Stella
Via di Drago d' Dino
Napoleone
Hemingway Caffè
Piazza Piattellina
Via Santa Monaca
Dolce Vita
Santa Monaca
Piazza del Carmine
Piazza dei Nerli
Via dei tessitori
Via dell' Orto
Via del Campidoglio

Piazza N. Sauro
Ponte alla Carraia
Lungarno Guicciardini
Chiesa Scozzese
Via Maria
Palazzo Guicciardini
Santo Spirito
Piazza Frescobaldi
Pal. Frescobaldi
Lungarno Acciaioli
Ponte Vecchio
Borgo
S. Jacopo Soprarno
San Jacopo
Corridoio Vasariano

Cappella Brancacci
Santa Maria del Carmine
Cavolo Nero
Via dell' Ardiglione
Via Santa Monaca

S. SPIRITO
Via Sant'Agostino
Via Maria
Via S. Agostino
Via del Presto di S. Martino
Santo Spirito
Piazza Santo Spirito
Pal. R. Firidolfi
Pal. Rosselli
Casa di Bianca
Via Mazzetta
Via dei Michelozzi
Pal. Ridolfi
V. di Velluti
V. Sguazza
Via de' Guicciardini
Santa Felicità
V. dei Bardi
Piazza S. Felicità
S. Girolam

2

Via del Campuccio
Via del Campuccio
Via del Leone
Santa Maria
S. FREDIANO
Piazza Torquato Tasso
Via della Chiesa
Via de' Serragli
Via dell'Orto Chiesa
GIARDINO TORRIGIANI
Via delle Caldaie
Via delle Caldaie
Via del Presto
Via del Campuccio

Pal. Guadagni
Piazza dei Pitti
Pal. Corsini
Via del Presto
Caffè Pitti
de' Pitti
S. Felice
Piazza San Felice
Museo Zoologia (La Specola)
Palazzo Pitti (Galleria Palatina)
Palazzina della Meridiana
Grotta di Buontalenti
Via de' Guicciardini
Palazzo Guicciardini
S. Spi Sa

3

Via Francesco
Via Petrarca
Via de' Serragli
Via Romana
Via Mori
Via Serumido
Annalena
Via Romana
Boboli
Via del Ronco
Fontana dell'Oceano
Piazza della Calza
Porta Romana

GIARDINO DI BOBOLI
Viottolone
Fontana di Nettuno
Ampitheatre
Abundance
GIARDINO DEL CAVALIERE
Museo delle Porcellane
Forte di Belvedere
(San Giorg

4

Piazzale di Porta Romana
Via Senese
Viale Niccolò Machiavelli
Viale del Poggio
Via Cantagalli
Via Farinata degli Uberti
Classic Hotel
Via Michele di Lando
Via Dante da Castiglione
Torre di Bellosguardo, Villa Belvedere
BOBOLINO

Istituto d'Arte
Via Madonna della Pace
Via de' Machiavelli
Via del Bobolino
Via del Bobolino
Viale Niccolò Machiavelli
Grand Hotel Villa Cora
Villa il Gioiello

A

B

page 312

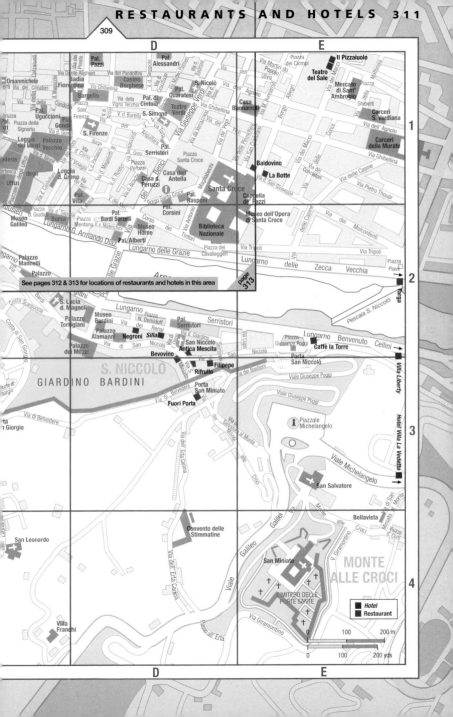

309

Pal. dei Presto
Calzaiuoli
V. d. Pandolfini
Pal. Pazzi
Pal. Alessandri
Piazza dei Ciompi
Il Pizzaiuolo
Via Dante Alighieri
Badia Fiorentina
Pal. di Cintoia
Casino Borghese
Via de Pandolfini
S. Nicolò
Via Martiri del Popolo
Teatro del Sale
Via del Mercato
Orsanmichele
erti   Via dei Cimatori
Via M Mezzanini
Bargello
Via della Vigna Vecchia
Pal. Quaratesi
S. Ambrogio
Mercato di Sant' Ambrogio
Condotta
Pal. Uguccioni
Piazza San Firenze
Via d. Burella
S. Simone
Teatro Verdi
Casa Buonarroti
Via Ghibellina
Ghiberti
Carceri S. Verdiana
Via delle Casine
Piazza della Signoria
Pal. Gondi
S. Firenze
Borgo
Angiolina
Via Ghibellina
Borgo Pinti
Carceri della Murate
Loggia dei Lanzi
Palazzo Vecchio
Via d. Gondi
Via de' Corno
Pal. Serristori
Piazza Santa Croce
Baldovino
Via delle Casine
Via della Ghibellina
lleria
Via de Neri
Via d. Vinegia
Via d. Saponai
Loggia d. Grano
Pal. Vita
Casa d. Peruzzi
Piazza Peruzzi
Borgo dei Greci
Casa dell' Antella
Pal. Rasponi
Santa Croce
La Botte
Via San Giuseppe
Via Pietro Thouar
rtesa   degli
Uffizi
i   Galileo
Museo Galileo
Borsa
Piazza d. Giudici
Pal. Corsini
Cappella de' Pazzi
Via d' Calimaruzza
Bardi Serzelli
Piazza Mentana
V. r. Malenchini
Pal. Alberti
Corso dei Tintori
Museo Horne
Museo dell' Opera di Santa Croce
Via dei Malcontenti
Lungarno G. Armando Diaz
Lungarno delle Grazie
Biblioteca Nazionale
Piazza dei Cavalleggeri
Via Tripoli
Via Tripoli
Palazzo Mannelli
Arno
Lungarno
delle
Zecca
Vecchia
Piazza Piave
Palazzo

See pages 312 & 313 for locations of restaurants and hotels in this area

page 313

Targa

Costa Scarpuccia
Bardi
S. Lucia d. Magnoli
Lungarno
Piazza N. Demidoff
Pal. Serristori
Serristori
Pescaia S. Niccolò

Museo Bardini
Via dei Renai
Palazzo Torrigiani

Palazzo Alamanni
Negroni
Sillaba
Via San Niccolò
Pal. Serristori
Via d. Giardino
Piazza Giuseppe Poggi
Lungarno   Benvenuto   Cellini
Caffè la Torre

Villa Liberty

Palazzo dei Mozzi
Bevovino
Antica Mescita
San Niccolò
Niccolò
Porta San Niccolò

S. NICCOLÒ
Filipepe
Rifrullo
Via dei Bastioni

GIARDINO BARDINI
Porta San Miniato
Fuori Porta
Viale Giuseppe Poggi

orfe di iorgio
Via di Belvedere
Viale Giuseppe Poggi
Hotel Villa La Vedetta

n Giorgio
Costa di San Giorgio
Via dell' Erta Canina
Piazzale Michelangelo

Viale Michelangelo
Via di San Salvatore al Monte

San Salvatore

Convento delle Stimmatine
Galileo
Bellavista
Viuzzo d. Corti

San Leonardo
Via dell' Erta Canina
Viale
Galileo
San Miniato
V. Giramontino
MONTE ALLE CROCI

Villa Franchi
Viale
CIMITERO DELLE PORTE SANTE

| | Hotel |
| | Restaurant |

Via Giramontino
0   100   200 m
0   100   200 yds

Passo all' Erta

D   E

A **B**

Hotel
Restaurant

Alba

Santa
Maria
Novella

Piazza dell'
Unità Italiana

Via del
Melarancio

Piazza
Madonna d'
Aldobrandini

San Loren

Hotel Baglioni

Bellettini

Biblioteca
Laurenzia

Nan

1

Aprile
Grand Hotel
Minerva

Casa Howard

Piazza
Santa
Maria
Novella

Via dei Panzani

Via del
Giglio

Via dell' Alloro

Via dei Cerretani

Scudi

Nuvoli

Pala
dell'Arcivescov

S. Francesco
d. Vanchetoni

Museo Nazionale
Alinari della
Fotografia

Via dei Banchi

Piazza
S. Maria
Maggiore

S. Maria
Maggiore

Palazzo
Orlandini

Ognissanti

Trattoria
Sostana

Piazza
Paolino

Joko Lounge

V. d. Trebbio

Buca Lapi

Palazzo
Antinori

Pecori

S. Paolino

Piazza
Ognissanti

Westin
Excelsior

Ospedale
S. Giovanni
di Dio

Piazza
d. Ottaviani

Il Latini

Mus.
Marino
Marini

S. Gaetano

Via d. Corsi

Palazzo
Larderelli

Campidoglio

Paszkowski

Gi

Harry's
Bar

Goldoni

Palazzo
Rucellai

Palazzo
Corsi

Helvetia
& Bristol

Palazzo
Vechietti

L'Inco

2

Lungarno Amerigo Vespucci

Piazza
C. Goldoni

Via della Vigna Nuova

Palazzo
Strozzi

Via d. Anselmi

Piazza
della
Repubblica

Caffè
Amerini

Coco
Lezzone

Palazzo
Giaconi

Palazzo
Altovita

Palazzo
Strozzino

Post e
Telegrafi

Giubbe Rosse

Palazzo
Corsini

Roses

Tornabuoni
Beacci

Caffè della
Posta

Antica Torre di
Via Tornabuoni

S. Trinità

Piazza
S. Trinita

Palazzo
Bartolini-
Salimbeni

Porta

Hotel Davanzati
Palazzo
Davanzati

Noir

Oliviero

Palazzo
di
Parte
Guelfa

3

Lugarno Soderini

Lungarno Guicciardini

Palazzo
Spini
Ferroni

Alessandra

Lungarno
Acciaioli

Arno

Santissimi
Apostoli

Torre Guelfa

Continentale

Chiesa
Scozzese

Beccofino

Palazzo
Guicciardini

Piazza
Frescobaldi

Palazzo
Frescobaldi

Pte S. Trinita

Ponte
Vecchio

Hermitage

Buc
dell'O

Via de' Serragli

Piazza
N. Sauro

S. Jacopo
Soprarno

Lungarno

S. SPIRITO

Osteria del Cinghiale Bianco

Palazzo
R. Firidolfi

Pitti Palace

Corridoio Vasariano

Osteria
Golden View

4

Santo
Spirito

Palazzo
Rosselli

Caffè degli Artigiani

Piazza S.
Felicita

V. dei Bardi

Piazza
S. Maria
Soprarno

Osteria
Santo
Spirito

Casa
di Bianca

Quattro
Leoni

Le Volpi e L'Uva

Sant
Agostino
23

Piazza
Santo
Spirito

Palazzo
Ridolfi

La Scaletta

Santa
Felicità

Borgo
Antico

Palazzo
Corsini

Santa
Girolamo

Palazzo
Guadagni

A **B**

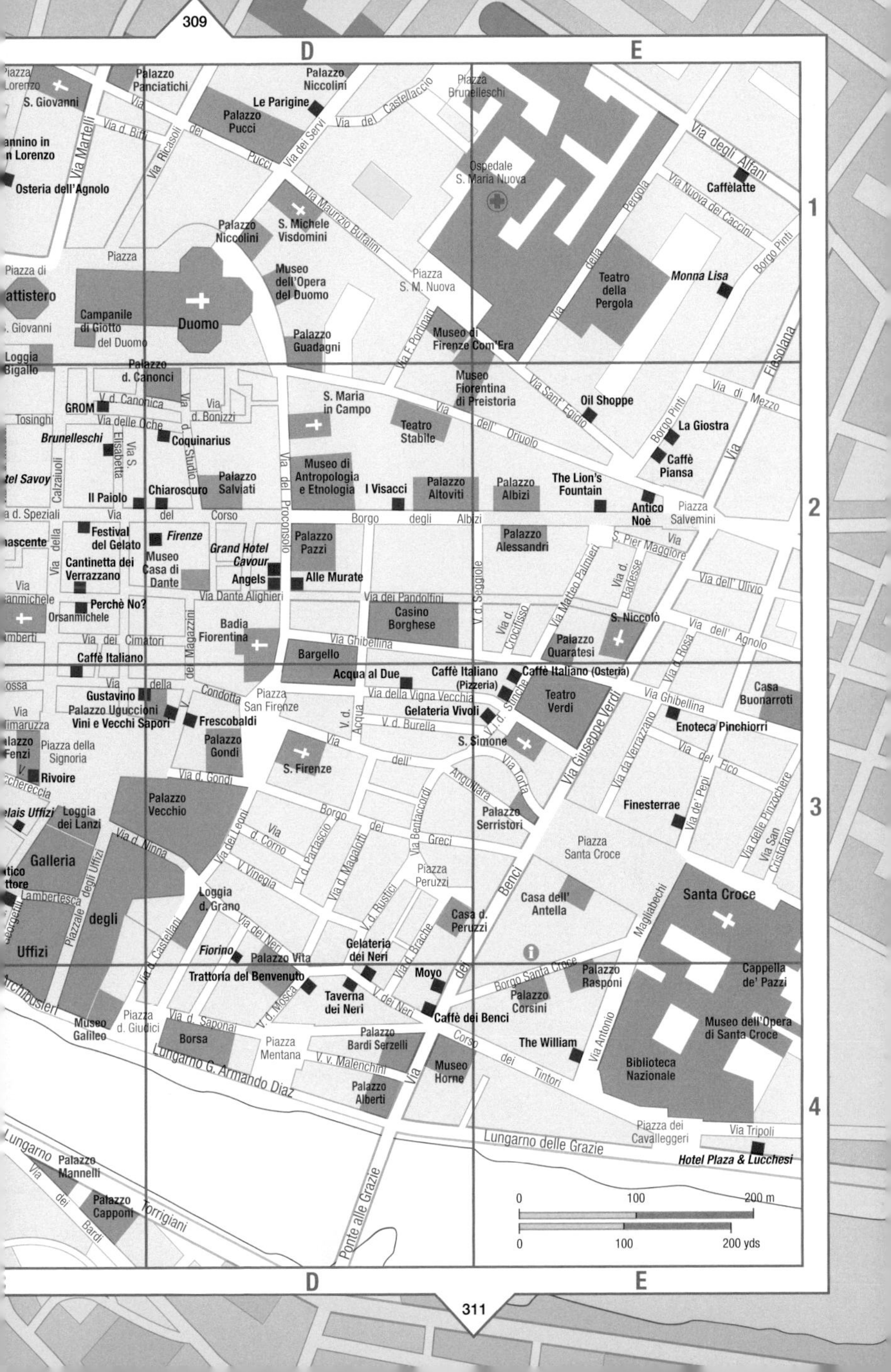
309
D
E
1
2
3
4
311
Palazzo Panciatichi
Palazzo Niccolini
Le Parigine
Palazzo Pucci
Piazza Brunelleschi
Via del Castellaccio
S. Giovanni
Via d. Biffi
Via Ricasoli
Via dei Pucci
Via dei Servi
Via Martelli
Osteria dell'Agnolo
Ospedale S. Maria Nuova
Via degli Alfani
Caffèlatte
Via Nuova dei Caccini
Via Maurizio Bufalini
Palazzo Niccolini
S. Michele Visdomini
Piazza
Piazza di
Museo dell'Opera del Duomo
Piazza S. M. Nuova
Via della Pergola
Teatro della Pergola
Monna Lisa
Borgo Pinti
Campanile di Giotto
Duomo
Palazzo Guadagni
Via F. Portinari
Museo di Firenze Com'Era
Via Fiesolana
Loggia Bigallo
Palazzo d. Canonci
Museo Fiorentina di Preistoria
Via Sant' Egidio
Oil Shoppe
Via di Mezzo
GROM
V. d. Canonica
Via d. Bonizzi
S. Maria in Campo
Teatro Stabile
Via dell' Oriuolo
La Giostra
Tosinghi
Via delle Oche
Brunelleschi
Coquinarius
Via S. Elisabetta
Via d. Studio
Caffè Piansa
Museo di Antropologia e Etnologia
Via del Proconsolo
Palazzo Salviati
Palazzo Altoviti
Palazzo Albizi
The Lion's Fountain
Calzaiuoli
Il Paiolo
Chiaroscuro
I Visacci
Antico Noè
Piazza Salvemini
Via del Corso
Borgo degli Albizi
Festival del Gelato
Firenze
Palazzo Pazzi
Palazzo Alessandri
Via S. Pier Maggiore
Grand Hotel Cavour
Via della
Cantinetta dei Verrazzano
Museo Casa di Dante
Angels
Alle Murate
Via Matteo Palmieri
Via d. Badesse
Via dell' Ulivio
Via Dante Alighieri
Via dei Pandolfini
V. d. Seggiole
Perchè No?
Orsanmichele
Badia Fiorentina
Casino Borghese
Via d. Crocifisso
S. Niccolò
Via dell' Agnolo
Via dei Cimatori
Via Ghibellina
Palazzo Quaratesi
Via dei Magazzini
Caffè Italiano
Bargello
Acqua al Due
Caffè Italiano (Pizzeria)
Caffè Italiano (Osteria)
Via d. Rosa
Casa Buonarroti
Gustavino
Via della Condotta
Piazza San Firenze
Via della Vigna Vecchia
Teatro Verdi
Via Ghibellina
Palazzo Uguccioni
Vini e Vecchi Sapori
Frescobaldi
V. d. Acqua
Gelateria Vivoli
V. d. Burella
Via delle Stinche
Via Giuseppe Verdi
Enoteca Pinchiorri
Piazza della Signoria
Palazzo Gondi
Via dell'
S. Simone
Via da Verrazzano
Via del Fico
Rivoire
S. Firenze
Via Torta
Via d. Gondi
Anguillara
Palazzo Vecchio
Finesterrae
Via de' Pepi
Loggia dei Lanzi
Borgo dei Greci
Palazzo Serristori
Via delle Pinzochere
Via d. Ninna
Via dei Leoni
Via d. Corno
Via d. Partascio
Via d. Magalotti
Via Bentaccordi
Piazza Santa Croce
Via San Cristofano
Galleria degli Uffizi
V. Vinegia
Piazza Peruzzi
Via de' Benci
Lambertesca
Piazzale degli Uffizi
Loggia d. Grano
V. d. Rustici
Casa dell' Antella
Santa Croce
Casa d. Peruzzi
Via d. Castellani
Via dei Neri
Gelateria dei Neri
Via d. Bruche
Magliabechi
Fiorino
Palazzo Vita
Trattoria del Benvenuto
Moyo
Borgo Santa Croce
Palazzo Rasponi
Cappella de' Pazzi
Taverna dei Neri
V. dei Neri
Palazzo Corsini
Archibusieri
Museo Galileo
Piazza d. Giudici
Via d. Saponai
V. d. Mosca
Caffè dei Benci
Museo dell'Opera di Santa Croce
Borsa
Piazza Mentana
Palazzo Bardi Serzelli
Corso dei Tintori
The William
Via Antonio
Lungarno G. Armando Diaz
V. v. Malenchini
Museo Horne
Biblioteca Nazionale
Palazzo Alberti
Piazza dei Cavalleggeri
Via Tripoli
Lungarno delle Grazie
Hotel Plaza & Lucchesi
Lungarno
Palazzo Mannelli
Via dei Bardi
Palazzo Capponi
Torrigiani
Ponte alle Grazie
0
100
200 m
0
100
200 yds

STREET INDEX

PLACES OF INTEREST

GENERAL INDEX